Open Road—Your Family Travel Pros!

Valerie Gwinner

"Our family is similar to the authors: Franco-American, two kids (also boys) and a love of Paris. We thought we knew everything there was to know about Paris with kids, but this book taught us a wealth of new material, revealing an entire "new" city. If it could teach these old Paris hands a thing or two, just think what families new to Paris will learn. This book has a great mix of facts, fun, frivolity and fascination scattered throughout its pages, and is all you really need for a well-rounded trip to the City of Light. Buy it, pack it, and go!" – *Amazon.com*

Open Road Publishing

We offer travel guides to American and foreign locales. Our books tell it like it is, often with an opinionated edge, and our experienced authors always give you all the information you need to have the trip of a lifetime. Write for your free catalog of all our titles.

Open Road Publishing
P.O. Box 284, Cold Spring Harbor, NY 11724
E-mail: jopenroad@aol.com • Web: www.openroadguides.com

2nd Edition

*To my parents, for giving me the love of Paris,
and to Britt, Jeremy, and Addison for sharing it with me*

ISBN 1-59360-062-3
Library of Congress Control No. 2005938443

Acknowledgments

For their tips and moral support. my sincere thanks go to Kevin Reese and Mary Hall Surface, Brian and Deborah Howes, Mark Haskell and Elise Stork, Susan Campbell and Mark Pugliese, Charlie and Sue Calhoun, Victoria and Dale Pedrick, Karen Kuhlke and Suman Beros, Pam Roos, Zack Sorensen, Pernette Lezine, Camille and Fernand Beaucour – and to my mother, Anta Montet White.

Table of Contents

Part 2: Planning Your Trip   261

Maps

Paris with Kids

1. INTRODUCTION

You're going to **Paris**? And taking the kids!!?

We heard this over and over when we first took our kids to Paris. For many people, a trip to Paris conjures images of beauty and romance, not strollers and diaper bags. It is a place for misty sunsets over the Seine, couples kissing under the chestnut trees, and lazy hours on café terraces.

Yes, Paris is all those things. However, what many people don't realize is that Paris is also the capital of one of the most kid-friendly nations in the world. France has prenatal care, parental leave, and child care policies that are the envy of most other industrialized countries. The country's national education budget surpasses its budget for national defense. Very simply, children are a priority in France – and it shows. It shows in the quality and creativity of the local playgrounds. It shows in the fact that every major museum and monument in Paris caters to children with special activities and workshops. It shows in the care that goes into products that are designed for children, whether it's books, clothing, or toys.

Even French food, a source of great national pride, caters to kids. Children in France are not just small people – they are gourmets-in-training. Thus you have cooking classes for kids at the Ritz Hotel, special children's menus in major restaurants, and jars of baby food at your local grocery store that feature choices such as sole meunière and canard à l'orange.

The truth about Paris is that it offers a seemingly unlimited supply of activities and wonders for visitors of all ages – and many opportunities for reconciling the interests of adults and children. Admire Nôtre Dame Cathedral and have your kids hunt for their favorite gargoyles. Search for the Secret of the Sorcerer's Stone together through the historic Marais neighborhood. Enjoy the serene beauty of the Luxembourg gardens as your children play with miniature sailboats in the central fountain. Take the stairs down the Eiffel Tower and check out the view from the inside of the structure. Run a rat through a maze at the Palais de la Découverte science museum. Look for the Phantom's traces on a tour of the Paris Opera house. Go to the horse races in the Bois de Boulogne. Admire Monet's Water Lilies like the storybook character Linnea. View some of Paris' greatest buildings, bridges, and monuments from a *bâteau mouche* tour boat. Enjoy scoops of Berthillon ice cream on the Ile Saint Louis. Go on a candlelit tour of the Vaux le Vicomte Palace. Have lunch in a café under the chestnut trees of the Tuileries Park. See a magic show at the *Musée de la Magie*. Take a family bike ride along the canals of the Versailles Palace gardens. Discover the underground labyrinth of Paris' Catacombs. Explore the Paris Sewers.

These are just some of the adventures that await you in Paris. Many more are described in the pages of this book. You'll also find kid-friendly strategies for visiting museums and monuments. There are recommendations for family-friendly hotels and restaurants, as well as tips on where to enjoy a light meal or snack. Also included are countless historical facts, legends, and anecdotes to bring the stories of Paris to life for kids and adults.

So what are you waiting for? Isn't it time you discovered Paris, with kids?

Paris with Kids

2. OVERVIEW

See It As a Great Adventure

Let's face it. For many people, the idea of bringing kids along on a trip can be quite intimidating. However, with a little preparation, you'll find that traveling with kids can be a great adventure. First of all, discovering a new place and culture with your children can be highly rewarding and supply family memories that last a lifetime. It's a chance to connect with each other without the distractions of home. It's also an opportunity to try new things that you might be embarrassed to do at home. For example, my first and only archery experience took place during a Medieval Festival in a French Château. The boys talked me into it, and they were more than pleased when I managed to hit the bull's eye in front of a cheering crowd. If that's not reason enough to pack up the family bags, here are a few more:

• Children bring new perspectives to your travels. They see the world from a different angle. Kids point out details we might miss, such as how the Coca Cola tastes different, the sidewalks are wider, or that there are more mopeds and motorcycles than at home.

• Kids take you places you might otherwise skip, but secretly enjoy: for example, to the top floor of the Eiffel Tower, onto that old-fashioned carrousel, or into the Museum of Magic.

• Traveling with kids helps break down cultural barriers. It gives you something in common with other parents and brings out the kid-lovers in people who don't have children of their own

• Finally, traveling with children reminds us that it's okay to slow down. Enjoy the city at a human pace. Take an afternoon nap. Have a leisurely café au lait while the kids quietly play in the hotel room. Spend some time watching the world go by from a park bench or café terrace. After all, you're on vacation.

Involve Your Kids

Children will be much more enthusiastic about traveling to Paris if you give them a role in the planning process – remember it's their trip, too. Even small kids can feel like they are part of the action if you include them in some background research. One of the best methods with young children is to introduce them to Paris ahead of time with books and videos that feature the city. It gives them a taste of what is ahead and things to look forward to. With small children, you can bring along the Madeleine books by Ludwig Bemelmans or *Eloise in Paris* by Kay Thompson and see how many places they recognize from the illustrations. In this guidebook we also highlight visits based on the story *Linnea in Monet's Garden* by Christina Bjork and Lena Anderson, the book/film of *The Red Balloon* by Albert Lamorisse, and the character Nicolas Flamel from the first Harry Potter volume.

If your children are older, encourage them to help plan your itinerary. You don't have to build your entire trip around their ideas, but you can give them a chance to pick their top choices. Cater to their interests. For example:

• Is your daughter a fashion slave? Take her to a (free) fashion show at the Galeries Lafayette Department Store. Follow up with lunch on the rooftop café where there is a magnificent view of the city.

Parent Tip

Need any good gift ideas for traveling kids? Here are some suggestions:
• Kid-friendly cameras
• Walky-talkies
• Binoculars (great for gargoyle hunting)
• Travel diaries
• Photo albums or scrap books
• Books on tape or on CD
• Cassette or CD walkmen
• I-pods
• Easy-to-pack art supplies
• Travel-size toys, games, or activity books
• Fanny packs, small day-packs, or small roller-board suitcases

• Is your child a budding scientist? Spend a morning in the *Cité des Sciences* at La Villette. Take a break in the park's wonderful playgrounds, then embark on a canal boat tour for a unique ride through the locks.

• Does someone in your group love horses? Plan a day trip to Chantilly with its magnificent live horse demonstrations and museum. Have an afternoon snack in the gardens of the Chantilly Palace. Give everyone a treat by ordering desserts smothered in Crème Chantilly (whipped cream).

• Do your kids play soccer? Tour the Paris team's Stade de France sports stadium in the nearby suburb of Saint Denis. While there, drop in to see the magnificent Saint Denis Cathedral with its tombs of all the French kings.

Balance Everyone's Desires

The secret to a successful family trip is to find ways to have something for everyone. If you build your whole trip around your children's desires, you will come home exhausted and frustrated. Similarly you can't expect a child to love Paris if he or she is made to sit through too many two-hour meals, wait for you to try on clothes in one store after another, or visit endless museums at a crawling pace. Paris is dotted with wonderful parks and playgrounds; pastry shops; and fun boutiques that spark kids' imaginations. It's easy to intersperse these with visits to museums, monuments, or other sights. Kids also love riding on a double-decker bus, taking a boat tour, or enjoying views from high places, so build these into your sightseeing plans.

Don't forget to incorporate your own tastes and interests, too. Children like to mimic and model adults, and it is surprising how often they will rise to the occasion when taken on a grownup outing. For example, my husband and I love to poke through flea markets and antique shops. After years of dragging our boys along with us, they have never broken anything. What's more, they have become excellent flea market treasure hunters, themselves.

Make Museums Fun

Few of us, kids or adults, can bear dragging ourselves through every room of a museum at a snail's pace. However, that doesn't mean museums can't be fun. Here are a few ideas:

• Go on a treasure hunt. You can let your kids choose some favorite post cards at the gift shop before your tour, and have them search for the objects they represent during the visit. You can also pick favorite themes, such as animals, dancers, or depictions of children, and hunt for these as you explore the museum.

• Pick up the free kids' booklets offered in most Parisian museums. They feature games and explanations. Although they are in French, kids can still enjoy the pictures, mazes, and other activities.

• Give your kids a lesson in navigation by handing them a copy of the museum's map (distributed for free at the entrance) and following their lead.

• Rent audioguides (available in English versions in many museums for a small fee) for your kids. They appeal to kids' natural love of gadgets and let them enjoy a private tour at their own pace.

• Cater to kids' interests. Paris has wonderful museums specializing in dolls, magic, science, fashion, ships, models, weapons and armor, animals, history, giant crystals, and more.

• Play "pick your favorite." Encourage your kids to choose which paintings, pieces of furniture, or objects they would put in their room if they could. Which armor would they wear if they were a knight? Which Greek god would they want to be? Which room would they want to sleep in if this was their mansion?

• Go for gore. Really! Kids are fascinated by tales of guillotines, monsters, martyrs, stranded sailors, and the like. You will find plenty of examples of these in paintings and historical objects in many Paris museums.

• Play a pretend round of Clue or other imaginary game. When visiting a museum that is housed in a mansion or palace (as many are), have your kids imagine in which room a crime would be committed, against whom, and with what weapon. Or have kids invent their own game based on favorite TV characters, video games, or collectors' cards.

• Surf online before you go. The major Parisian museums have websites that your kids can browse to pick out what they'd like to see.

• Take a break during your visit. Most Parisian museums have lovely cafés where you can refuel and rest weary feet.

• Divide and conquer. If part of your group just can't bear the idea of another museum, split up. Let one adult have a few hours of culture while the rest of the group goes on a boat tour, plays in a park, or does some shopping.

The Demography & Geography of Paris

More than 2 million people live in the city of Paris. That's down from nearly 3 million in the 1920s. Over time, many people have moved to the suburbs, and a surprising number of large apartments in the center of Paris are empty. If you add the surrounding suburbs, the total population for the Paris Metropolitan area is over 10 million people. In spite of its population decline, Paris is still more densely populated than any other city in the developed world. For example, there are about twice as many people per square mile in Paris than in Tokyo, three times more than in London, and 2.5 times more than in New York.

Paris is divided into 20 city districts known as *arrondissements*. The first arrondissement is located in the center of the city, near Les Halles, and the numbers radiate out following the pattern of a snail shell. The 1st, 2nd,

3rd, and 4th arrondissements are on the Right Bank of the Seine River. The 5th, 6th, and 7th are on the Left Bank. The 8th, 9th, 10th, 11th, and 12th form a second tier of districts on the Right Bank. The 13th, 14th, and 15th make up a second tier on the Left Bank. Finally, the 16th, 17th, 18th, 19th, and 20th, constitute a third tier of arrondissements on the Right Bank. Mailing addresses for Paris will start with the number 75 for Paris. The last two digits of the postal code indicate the arrondissement. Thus 75005 indicates an address in the 5th arrondissement and 75016 is in the 16th arrondissement.

Here are some of the sights you'll find in each arrondissement:

1st: Les Halles, Louvre, Place Vendome, Tuileries

2nd: Opéra Garnier, Place des Victoires, Galerie Vivienne, Passage des Panoramas

3rd: Marais, including Pompidou Center, Musée Carnavalet, Musée Picasso, Musée des Arts et Metiers, Nicholas Flamel's House

4th: Nôtre Dame and Ile de la Cité, Ile Saint Louis, Marais, including Jewish neighborhood and Place des Vôsges

5th: Latin Quarter, including Boulevard Saint Michel, Sorbonne, Cluny Museum, Rue Mouffetard, Jardin des Plantes, Natural History Museums, Paris Mosque, Arènes de Lutèce (Roman Arena)

6th: Saint Germain neighborhood, Luxembourg Gardens, Saint Sulpice

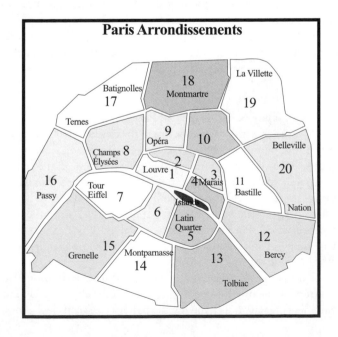

Paris Arrondissements

7th: Invalides, Musée Rodin, Musée d'Orsay, Eiffel Tower

8th: Arc de Triomphe, Champs Elysées, Grand Palais, Palais de la Découverte, Parc Monceau, Place de la Concorde, Gare Saint Lazare, Rue du Faubourg Saint Honoré Luxury Shops.

9th: Grands Magazins (Haussman Department Stores), Passage Jouffroy, Passage Véro Dôdat

10th: Gard du Nord, Gare de l'Est, Canal Saint Martin

11th: Bastille neighborhood

12th: Saint Antoine neighborhood, Viaduct des Arts, Promenade Plantée, Gare de Lyon, Bercy neighborhood and gardens, Bois de Vincennes

13th: Les Gobelins, Butte aux Cailles, Chinatown, Gare d'Austerlitz

14th: Montparnasse neighborhood, Gare Montparnasse, Catacombs, Parc Montsouris, Rue d'Alésia discount clothing stores

15th: Parc André Citroën, Parc Georges Brassens, Aquaboulevard (Water Park)

16th: Trocadéro, Maritime Museum, Musée de l'Homme; Musée des Plans Reliefs; Musée d'Art Moderne, Balzac's House, Passy Cemetary, Musée de la Mode et du Costume, Musée Marmottan, Bois de Boulogne, Jardin d'Acclimatation

17th: Residential

18th: Montmartre neighborhood, Porte de Clingancourt Flea Market

19th: Parc de La Villette, Cité des Sciences (Science Museum), Parc des Buttes Chaumont

20th: Belleville neighborhood, Père Lachaise Cemetery

3. THE ISLANDS

Ile de la Cité

The **Point Zero**, from which all distances to Paris are measured is located on the Ile de la Cité, which is only fitting since this City Island is where it all started. The Ile de la Cité, originally a cluster of smaller islands, was the spot where the first inhabitants of Paris settled in about 250 BC. When the Romans took over in 50 BC, they expanded the city (then known as Lutetia) across the Seine River to the south. The Roman Forum, Baths, Arena, and Amphitheater were all built in the area now known as the Latin Quarter. However, the Ile de la Cité remained the political, judicial, and religious center of the city. It housed both the Temple of Jupiter, in honor of the most important of the Roman gods, and the Roman Governor's Palace that included the law courts and government offices.

During the medieval period, the Temple of Jupiter was replaced with a small Christian church and later with the great Nôtre Dame Cathedral. The Roman Governor's Palace was rebuilt as a Royal Palace. One wing of the palace, known as the Concièrgerie, was later turned into a prison. This is where Queen Marie Antoinette was held before she was guillotined. Another wing of the former royal palace is now the city's Palace of Justice, which houses the law courts. The city's central police station is across the street. It has been made famous by the Inspector Maigret detective stories. Thus through thousands of years of wars and political changes, the Ile de la Cité has remained the city's legal and religious core.

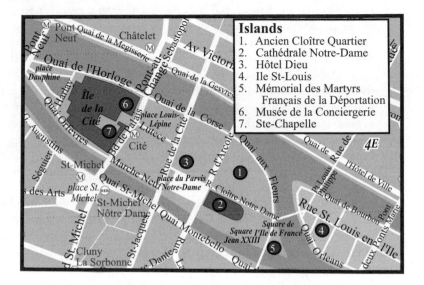

NÔTRE DAME CATHEDRAL, *Place du Parvis de Nôtre Dame , on Ile de la Cité (Metro: Cité or Saint Michel-Nôtre Dame). Open daily, 8 am-6 pm. Entrance is free. The Tower visit is open daily 9 am to 7:30 pm (Apr-Sep) and 10 am to 5 pm (Oct-Mar). Sat and Sun evenings the towers close after dark. Adults: €7; Kids: free.*

Parent's Note: lines to visit the tower can be long and slow during the summer tourist season. Try to arrive early when the tower first opens or later in the evening when the crowds are thinner.

Nôtre Dame Cathedral is truly the city's great lady, where some of Paris' most joyful or solemn moments have been celebrated. It was here that Napoleon crowned himself Emperor and that funeral services were held for Victor Hugo, Marechal Foch, and Charles de Gaulle. Nôtre Dame was also the sight of joyous masses to celebrate the ends of both World Wars.

Work on Nôtre Dame began in 1163 and took nearly 200 years to complete. The cathedral was built in the Gothic style, recognizable for its high walls, peaked arches, flamboyant decorations, and stained glass windows that seem to reach to the sky. Another telltale sign of a Gothic cathedral is the presence of flying buttresses on the sides, those elegant arcs that help carry the weight of the stone roof and walls. If you've brought your binoculars encourage your kids to check out the gargoyles and statues that decorate the cathedral. But beware that if it doesn't gurgle, it isn't really a gargoyle! True gargoyles are actually part of the roof's drainage system. They collect water from the gutters and spew it out away from the building to protect the walls and windows from water damage. Thus a real gargoyle contains a pipe or channel, and spits out water when it rains. Those other monstrous sculptures, often depicted as gargoyles in movies and comics, are just decorative statues known as grotesques. Both serve a common purpose: to warn passers-by of the scary fate that awaits them if they lead a sinful life.

One of the best ways to enjoy the outside of the cathedral is to climb the 386 steps to the top of the **north tower**. This tower tour offers one of the best views of the city, from its most central location. It also gives you a chance to get a close up view of the statues and gargoyles that decorate the cathedral, as well as its magnificent support arches. In the south tower you can see the cathedral's giant bell, Emmanuel. There used to be 8 smaller bells in the north tower. Each was tuned to a different note of the musical scale, but they were destroyed during the French Revolution.

The first church bell to ring as a symbol of the end of World War I was the main bell of Nôtre Dame. It also rang to announce the Liberation of Paris during World War II. This enormous bell hangs in the southern tower. It is named Emmanuel (all French church bells have names) and weighs 13 tons. The clapper alone weighs half a ton. It takes 8 men to ring the bell by hand. Legend has it that the metal for the bell came from jewelry donated by wealthy Parisian women and melted down. This is supposed to explain why the bell has such a sweet tone. It rings a perfect F sharp. The Emmanuel bell is only rung for big events or holidays like Christmas and Easter.

If you look directly at Nôtre Dame from the front, you can see three entrances. The left doorway is dedicated to Mary, the mother of Jesus. The middle one represents the last judgment. The doorway on the right is dedicated to Saint Anne, the mother of Mary. Notice all the statues and sculptures. Did you know that, originally, they were all painted in bright colors, even the gargoyles? Besides being decorations, these works served a practical function. In medieval times, most people were illiterate, but they did know the stories of the bible. They could thus "read" the illustrations and moral lessons depicted in the church's statues, carvings, and stained glass windows.

Ile de la Cité Highlights

• Find the Point Zero
• Hunt for gargoyles at Nôtre Dame Cathedral
• Go underground into the Crypte Archeologique
• Visit Marie Antoinette's cell and other prison cells at the Concièrgerie
• See the spectacular stained windows at the Sainte Chapelle
• Visit the Sunday Bird Market on the Place Louis Lepine
• Take a boat ride on a Bâteau Mouche
• See the Pont Neuf and Place Dauphine
• Spend a moment of contemplation at the Deportation Memorial

Twenty-eight statues of biblical kings originally decorated the cathedral's doorways. They were torn down during the French Revolution and replaced with copies in the 1850s. The revolutionaries thought the statues represented the French kings, so they chopped off all their heads. These stone heads were lost for nearly 200 years, until they were found unexpectedly by workers excavating a new building site in 1977. Today they are on display at the Cluny Museum.

During the French Revolution, many of the statues were damaged and the treasure was plundered, because of the close ties between the Church and the Crown. The cathedral was turned into a Temple of Reason. The Opera ballet performed in this Temple, with dancers jumping over broken statues and religious items. By the early 1800s, Nôtre Dame was in a sorry state. When the famous French author Victor Hugo wrote his book *The Hunchback of Nôtre Dame*, it helped rekindle interest in the cathedral and generate money for its restoration.

Inside Nôtre Dame there are spectacular stained glass windows, particularly the three round rose windows. The largest of these, above the front entrance, depicts Mary and the Infant Jesus flanked by two angels. The north rose window in the transept dates from the 13th century. It depicts the Virgin Mary surrounded by figures from the Old Testament. The south window, dating from the 14th century, depicts Christ surrounded by angels and saints. If you walk around the choir (the U-shaped area behind the alter), you can see 14th century wooden sculptures representing stories from the life of Jesus. Notice the organ. Built in 1730, it has nearly 8,000 pipes and 5 keyboards. There are free organ concerts on Sundays at 5:30 pm.

The cathedral can seat 6,000 people. It fills up for major holidays, funerals, or big events. Entrance is only restricted for national events or for Christmas Eve services, when only members of the parish and special dignitaries are invited.

Before we leave this magnificent cathedral, here's one more item of interest: more than 12 million people visit Nôtre Dame each year. But some of its most regular

Fun Fact

What's in a name? The Goths had nothing to do with the invention of Gothic architecture. In fact, these Germanic tribes were long gone by the time Gothic architecture was invented. Moreover, the term Gothic architecture was not even applied to this building style until after it had gone out of fashion. It was the Renaissance architects of the 15th century who coined the term Gothic. They used it as an insult to describe an architectural style that they considered too wild and barbaric, preferring the symmetry and forms of classical Greek and Roman buildings.

Fun Fact

The small side street of **Rue de la Colombe** (Dove Street) on Ile de la Cité gets its name from a legendary pair of doves who nested in the window of a house by the river. One day the Seine flooded, destroying the house. The male dove escaped, but his mate was trapped in the rubble. The male is said to have carried food and water (in a hollow stick) to the trapped female dove for days until the rubble could be cleared. A sculpture above the door at #4 honors their story.

visitors are not people, they are birds known as kestrels or sparrow hawks. Usually 5-6 pairs of these birds nest in high perches above the gargoyles each year. Bird watchers gather behind the cathedral every June to watch the birds feed their newly-hatched chicks.

PARVIS DE NÔTRE DAME. The large esplanade in front of Nôtre Dame is known as the **Parvis**. If you look carefully on the pavement in front of the main entrance, you will find the brass marker that indicates the **Point Zero**. Here you can really say that you are in the center of Paris. It is the point from which all distances to the city are measured.

Notice the statue of a man on a horse on the Parvis (toward the right as you face the cathedral)? It depicts Charlemagne, a great French king of the Carolingian dynasty. Charlemagne was a highly successful leader. He was crowned Holy Roman Emperor in the year 800 and ruled over an area that stretched across France, Germany, Switzerland, Holland, Belgium, and most of Italy. He instituted a policy of toleration of Jews throughout his kingdom. Charlemagne had five wives, and encouraged trade, literature, and education even though he himself never learned to read or write. This statue is one of the few traces of Charlemagne in Paris, since he moved his capital to Aachen, Germany, where he is buried. Although he is depicted here as tall and slender, the real Charlemagne is said to have been short and squat.

For most of the cathedral's history, the Parvis was only half of its current size. It went back to the point where you can just see the head of Mary's statue above the central doorway. The rest was filled with narrow streets and crowded buildings, torn down during Baron Haussman's urban renewal projects in the 1850s. The outlines of some old streets and buildings are marked on the Parvis pavement.

Although it was far smaller than today, the Parvis was no less busy. It was filled with street performers and vendors. There were jugglers, dancers, and clowns. There were dancing bears and other live animals. There were also theatrical performances called Mystères that depicted stories from the Bible and lives of the saints.

The Parvis pavement also covers a wealth of Paris history that you can discover in the **CRYPTE ARCHEOLOGIQUE.** *Place du Parvis de Nôtre Dame (Metro: Cité) Open daily, 9:30am-6pm (Apr-Sep), 10am-4:30pm (Oct-Mar). Adults: €3.30; Kids: free.*

This is an interesting tour for any budding archeologist or explorer. The visit takes place underground, past ruins spanning 16 centuries. The area is dimly lit, and children can turn on special spot lights to investigate sections more closely. There are vestiges of Gallo-Roman walls, an ancient Roman heating system, medieval fortress walls, 15th century cellars, and the foundations of an 18th century hospital for abandoned children. There are models that explain how archways or columns were erected, the inner workings of Roman plumbing, and other engineering feats that can capture a child's creative imagination.

Behind Nôtre Dame Cathedral is a small park called the **Square Jean XXIII.** Here you can find plenty of shade, benches, and room for children to run. There are also water fountains to quench your thirst or clean off sticky fingers.

Cross the small street to the eastern-most tip of the island and you can spend a moment of quiet contemplation at the **MEMORIAL TO THE DEPORTATION.** *Open daily 10am-12pm, 2pm-7pm (closes at 5 pm Oct-Mar). Adults and Kids: Free.*

Touching in its simplicity, this memorial begins with a narrow staircase that takes you to a triangular courtyard. From there you enter a small chamber lit with hundreds of thousands of lights. These represent the men, women, and children of France deported to Nazi prison and concentration camps during World War II. Their names are inscribed on the walls. An eternal flame lights a tomb to the unknown deportee.

SAINTE CHAPELLE. *4, Boulevard du Palais. Metro: Cité. Open daily, 9:30am-6:30pm (Apr-Sep), 9:30am-5pm (Oct-Mar). Ticket sales stop 1/2 hour before closing time. Adults: €6.50; Kids under 18: free if accompanied by an adult. You can purchase a combined ticket for both the Sainte Chapelle and Concièrgerie. Adults: €10.40; Kids under 18: free. Guided visits (in French) are offered at 11am and 3pm. Special kids' visits (in French) on Wed at 2:30pm. A free description of the stained glass windows is available in English.*

Parent Tip: If you think that you will only be able to drag your child to one church in Paris, the Sainte Chapelle is the one to see. The first view of the stained glass windows will surprise even the most reluctant visitor, especially on a sunny day.

The Sainte Chapelle (Holy Chapel) was built in the 13th century by France's most zealously religious king, Louis IX (also known as Saint Louis). He built this chapel within the walls of his royal palace to house two holy relics he had bought from the Emperor of Constantinople: a piece of Christ's crown of thorns and piece of the cross. Saint Louis hired the same architect who had designed the plans for Nôtre Dame Cathedral and the Basilica of Saint Denis. Like them it was built in the Gothic style. However, unlike those cathedrals that took hundreds of years to complete, the Sainte Chapelle was finished in only seven years.

The Sainte Chapelle actually contains both an upper and a lower chapel. The lower chapel is more somber. Its low ceiling is beautifully decorated with golden fleur-de-lys on a royal blue background. It looks like a star filled sky. The walls are also painted, as were those in most churches. Look on the floor. There are large engraved slabs of stone that cover tombs from the 14th and 15th centuries. Some children will enjoy their almost comic-book quality.

A small, spiral staircase leads to the upper chapel. This was the part reserved for the royal family, high officers, and the holy relics. Unlike the lower chapel, the ceiling of this one seems to reach to the sky. The stained glass windows are spectacular. They are 15 meters (nearly 50 feet) high, and most contain their original 13th century glass. Indeed, they are the oldest stained glass windows in Paris. The windows depict stories from the old testament and from the life of Jesus. The chronology progresses from left to right, and from bottom to top in each window. The last window shows King Saint Louis receiving the holy relics.

Fun Fact

• Near the fourth window from the left in the upper chapel, there is a secret entrance. The king could use this door to sneak in and out unobserved.

• An old French expression describes a good wine has having "all the colors of the Sainte Chapelle"

CONCIÈRGERIE. *1, Quai de l'Horloge. Metro: Cité. Open daily, 9:30am-6:30pm (Apr-Sep), 10am-5pm (Oct-Mar). Adults: €7.50; Kids under 18: free if accompanied by an adult. You can purchase a combined ticket for both the Sainte Chapelle and Concièrgerie. Adults: €10.42; Kids under 18: free.*

During the Roman Occupation of Paris, this was the site of the Palace of Caesar which held government offices, law courts, and lodgings for the Roman Governor. During the medieval period, the buildings were converted into a royal palace. King Philippe Auguste, who built a fortified wall around Paris, lived there, as did his grandson, Saint Louis, builder of the Sainte Chapelle. During the 14th century, King Francois I left this palace to live in the Louvre. The southern portion of the buildings were converted to the Palais de Justice (Law Courts), and the northern ones became a prison. The prison was known as the Concièrgerie, because it was where the Concièrge lived. He was the man who collected rents from the shopkeepers on the ground floor of the building, and from the prisoners in the upper levels.

Poor prisoners were put in cells called **paillasses** that were dirty, crowded, and lined with hay. Those who could afford it payed rent for better prison cells. These offered the possibility of furniture and more privacy.

The Concièrgerie is especially famous for the many prisoners who were held there after the French Revolution. During the Reign of Terror from 1794 to 1795, the revolutionary tribunal condemned nearly 3,000 people to their deaths. Most of them spent at least some time in the Concièrgerie.

You can visit the Concièrgerie and tour the guard room, kitchen, and prison cells. Some of the cells have been rebuilt as they would have looked during the Revolution, complete with wax figures depicting guards and prisoners. The visit begins with the guard room with its four large fireplaces. The pillars are decorated with sculptures of animals and people. One depicts the ill-fated medieval lovers, Héloise and Abélard. Notice the giant slab of dark marble on one wall. This used to be a table top used for royal feasts. When the palace became a prison, this was the room where trials were held and prisoners condemned. The kitchen is up a small stairway. It has several huge fireplaces for cooking food for as many as 3,000 people. The windows were originally just above the level of the river, so that supplies could be easily delivered by boat.

Fun Fact

Pierre Abélard was a brilliant scholar and teacher, born in 1079. He was also very handsome – a fact that did not escape the notice of his beautiful and equally brilliant pupil, Héloise. Though she was 22 years his junior, they fell in love, secretly married, and had a child. Héloise's furious guardian hired thugs to attack and castrate Abélard.

They spent the rest of their lives living separately in religious communities. Their touching love letters and other writings survive to this day. Héloise and Abélard were finally reunited in death, and share a common tomb in Paris' Père Lachaise Cemetery.

The next part of the visit takes you to the prisoners' galleries on the lower floor. Here, there were separate sections reserved for men and women. You can see the courtyard with its fountain where the female prisoners washed their laundry. There was a gate through which the women could speak to the male prisoners. You can also see the special cell reserved for Queen Marie- Antoinette (Note: this is a re-creation of her cell which was later turned into a chapel). Upstairs you can visit other prison cells, including those reserved for the poor and the more upscale ones for people who had access to money or political influence.

Famous Concièrgerie prisoners include::

• **Ravaillac**, a Catholic monk and religious extremist who murdered King Henri IV. He was executed.

• **Damiens**, who struck and lightly injured king Louis XV in 1757. He was tortured and executed.

• **Marquise de Brinvilliers**, who poisoned her father, brothers, and sister. She escaped but was ultimately caught, condemned, and beheaded.

• **Cartouche**, a popular, Robin Hood-like leader of a band of thieves. He died on the rack.

• **Jeanne de Valois**, a noblewoman who wrote false letters to persuade the Cardinal of Rohan to buy a diamond necklace for Queen Marie-Antoinette, which she kept for herself. She escaped from prison but later died in poverty in London.

• **Charlotte Corday**, who assassinated Jean-Paul Marat in his bathtub for being one of the leaders of the Terror. His death is depicted in a famous painting by David. She was guillotined.

• **Marie Antoinette**, married to King Louis XVI, born in Austria, and hated by her subjects. Her hair is said to have turned white overnight after her arrest by the revolutionaries. She was spared while they tried to negotiate a peace deal with warring Austria. It failed, and she was condemned to death. A faithful servant tried to help her escape. She was betrayed and transferred to a more secure cell. She was guillotined in 1793.

• **Danton and Robespierre**, revolutionary leaders who sent many others to the guillotine, only to be later executed themselves for their excesses.

During the day, prisoners who had already been condemned to death by guillotine were allowed to wander around in the prison. Each evening, there would be an announcement declaring who would die the next day. Then a bell would ring and all the prisoners would return to their cells. Those who were condemned to die were sent to the Salle de la Toilette where they were searched and their valuables removed. Their collars were cut off, their hair was cut, and their neck was shaven to leave a clear target for the guillotine's blade

A small museum on the upper floor features artifacts from the history of the prison and some of its more well-known residents.

As you leave the Concièrgerie, notice the beautiful CLOCKTOWER on the corner of the Quai de l'Horloge and Boulevard du Palais. It has an interesting history. During medieval times, most people could not afford a watch or clock, so they relied on church bells to tell them the time. The bell towers rang each hour from matines (dawn) to complines (dusk). The problem was that the churches relied on sundials to set the time of their bells, and sometimes the time at one church would be off from the time at another one. In 1370, King Charles V tried to resolve this problem by declaring that all the churches would ring the hours according to the time set by the royal palace. This clock was set on the tower of what was then the royal palace to show the official time. It was completed in 1371 and has never stopped working.

The face of the clock is set against a blue background filled with star-like fleurs de lys, symbol of French Royalty. The original bell that rang the hours was removed by the revolutionaries, who associated it with royal events. It was replaced in 1793 with a new bell made of silver. There are two statues on either side of the clock. They represent Law and Justice and date from the 16th century.

Fun Fact

The fleur de lys, also spelled fleur de lis, is the symbol of French royalty. It is a stylized depiction of three lys (lily flowers). According to some interpretations, the three flowers represent the holy trinity: father, son, and holy ghost. The lily is also a symbol of purity, candor, and virtue. One legend has it that the fleur de lys became a royal symbol when the 5th century King Clovis came across a patch of water lilies indicating where he could safely cross a river on the way into a battle. He is said to have plucked one of the lilies, placed it in his helmet, and created a royal symbol. Whatever its origins the fleur de lys began to decorate the royal arms in the 12th century and from then on remained the emblem of the French monarchy.

PLACE LOUIS LEPINE. *Metro: Cité.*

There is a lovely flower market here Monday through Saturday. Then on Sundays, it is transformed into a lively pet market that features all sorts of colorful birds, as well as Guinea pigs, rabbits, and other small animals that will delight kids.

The imposing building you see on the east side of the Place Lepine is the Hôtel Dieu, Paris' oldest hospital. This hospital was originally built in the 7th century to treat the poor. The title means, House of God, because for centuries it was primarily nuns and monks who took care of the sick and the poor. Although the hospital was expanded over the years, there were times during plague epidemics when patients had to sleep three to a bed.

To the west of the Palais de Justice complex is a pretty triangular-shaped square called the **Place Dauphine**. It was built during the reign of King Henri IV in honor of his son (the Dauphin is the title of the king's heir).

PONT NEUF. *On the western edge of the Ile de la Cité. Metro: Pont Neuf.*

Although its name means New Bridge, this is actually the oldest bridge in Paris. It was built from 1578 to 1604 and was the first bridge in Paris to be made of stone. If you look at the Pont Neuf from below, you can see that it is decorated with hundreds of grimacing faces. According to legend, the artist designed these faces as caricatures of famous men of the day. Although it was the first bridge to have no permanent buildings, the Pont Neuf attracted many street vendors and was the sight of a large, annual fair. The first bouquinistes (those book stalls you see lining the river) set up shop on the Pont Neuf. After the French Revolution, these stalls were filled with books looted from the mansions of fleeing aristocrats.

The Pont Neuf has often been celebrated in art, film, and music. In 1985, the modern artist, Christo, wrapped the entire bridge up in cloth for two weeks. In 1995, the clothing designer Kenzo covered the Pont Neuf with flowers.

BATEAUX VEDETTES DU PONT NEUF (TOUR BOATS) *Square du Vert Galant. Down the steps on the Pont Neuf, behind the equestrian statue of King Henri IV. Boats leave every 30-45 minutes, 10am-10pm. Adults: €10. Kids: €5. Kids under age 4: free.*

If you are jet-lagged, foot-sore, or just want a change of pace, this one-hour boat tour is a great way to see some of Paris' major sights and monuments. Kids enjoy the ride, and you'll see Nôtre Dame, the Eiffel Tower, and other attractions from a unique perspective. Tour guide explanations are in both English and French.

PONT NÔTRE DAME. *Connects Ile de la Cité to Hotel de Ville.*

This was one of Paris' first two bridges, and was originally called the Grand Pont. During the Middle Ages it was renamed Pont Nôtre Dame. At the time it was made of wood and covered with 60 houses, along with armor shops and book sellers. In the 17th century, the bridge was renovated and elaborately decorated for the arrival of Marie-Therese of Austria on her way to marry King Louis XIV. It was renamed the Pont de la Raison (Bridge of Reason) during the Revolution. It then became known as the Pont du Diable (Devil's Bridge) in the late 1800s and early 1900s because it was the scene of so many boating accidents. The bridge was rebuilt in 1919 with only one arch, so that boats could more easily navigate through it.

PONT AUX DOUBLE. *Connects Ile de la the Cité and the Left bank.*

This bridge was built in 1634 as an annex for the Hotel-Dieu Hospital. It was covered with a two-story building that housed the sick. People quickly figured out that it was faster to cross through the building than to fight the traffic jams on the nearby Petit-Pont. The hospital started charging a toll. Some sources claim that the name of the bridge comes from the fact that the charge was double denier (what we might call a two-cent piece). Others say that it comes from the fact that people on horseback had to pay twice as much as people on foot. In either case, the toll was abolished after the Revolution. The bridge collapsed once in 1709 and was rebuilt exactly as it had been. In 1883, the old bridge was taken down and replaced with the current one built of iron and cement.

PONT AU CHANGE. *Connects Ile de la Cité and Châtelet.*

This bridge gets its name from the fact that in 1141 King Louis VII ordered that all the money changers of Paris set up shop on this bridge. It went through several name changes, including Pont aux Colombes (Doves' Bridge), Pont aux Meuniers (Millers' Bridge), and Pont aux Oiseaux (Birds' Bridge) and eventually resumed its original name.

Ile Saint Louis

This small island in the middle of the Seine River is one of the fanciest neighborhoods in Paris. However, it wasn't always such a splendid spot. In the 17th century, the area was swampy and uninhabited. There were actually two separate islands. One was called the Ile Nôtre Dame, named for the cathedral. The other was called the Ile aux Vaches (Cow Island) – hardly a romantic beginning. In the 1660s, a building developer named Jean Christophe Marie got permission from King Louis XIII to drain and connect the islands. He then built elegant mansions that were bought up by wealthy financiers and magistrates. The island was named for King Louis IX, also known as Saint Louis.

If you walk along the outer streets of the island, you can enjoy nice views of the river and city. On warm, summer days, you'll probably see plenty of sunbathers on the walkways along the river. Be advised that topless women

Ile Saint Louis Highlights

- Have some **Berthillon** ice cream!
- Stand on the pedestrian **Pont Saint Louis** bridge and watch the boats pass underneath

and men in thongs are not uncommon. You can also walk through the main street of the island, which is filled with interesting little shops and restaurants.

GLACES BERTHILLON. *#31, Rue Saint Louis en l'Ile. Metro: Pont Marie.*

A treat not to be missed! Although there is one official shop for this ice cream, there are also Berthillon vendors all over the island. You can generally tell where they are by the line of people waiting patiently for some of the city's best ice cream and sorbets.

PONT SAINT LOUIS. *Connects the Ile Saint Louis and Ile de la Cité.*

This lovely pedestrian bridge is a nice place from which to watch the boat traffic go by on the Seine. It is the seventh bridge to have been built on this site. The first, built in 1630, collapsed in 1634 under the weight of a procession. The next version, built in 1656, was destroyed a year later in a flood. Another version, built in 1862, was the city's first iron bridge, but it was destroyed in 1939 by a gas explosion from a nearby gas pipe. From 1941 to 1968 there was just a temporary footbridge. The current bridge dates from 1970.

PONT MARIE. *Connects Ile Saint Louis and Right Bank.*

This bridge was built in the 1600s and named for the man who developed many of the buildings on the Ile Saint Louis. The bridge originally sloped upwards in the center and was covered with fifty 3-story houses. The houses made the bridge so top heavy that 20 of them came tumbling down during a flood in 1658. In 1859, the bridge was rebuilt and its design was flattened so that traffic could move across more easily.

Fun Fact

Did you know that Saint Louis, Missouri is named for the same king as this island? Originally called **Louis IX**, this French king was made a saint in honor of his extreme religious fervor. Legend has it that he would recite 50 Hail Mary prayers each night, genuflecting each time. He would attend mass twice each morning, wear a hair shirt, and invite beggars to join him for dinner. He received his subjects under an old oak tree to resolve their disputes. He built many churches, set up a hospital for blind knights, and founded the Sorbonne Univeristy. Louis IX led two Crusades to the Holy Land, and died of the plague in the process near the gates of Tunis, Tunisia. Only his heart and bones were returned to France, because the disease was so contagious. He was declared a saint in 1297.

4. LATIN QUARTER

The history of this neighborhood is seeped in its Latin roots. These roots stretch back through medieval days when great scholars and students walked its narrow streets speaking Latin. They reach back even further to the 1st century BC, when the Romans occupied Paris and built a great city in this area south of the Ile de la Cité. Today, the Quartier Latin still bustles with students and scholars. However, its rich assortment of museums, parks, markets, and shops also make it an ideal spot from which to discover some of the kid-friendly sides of Paris.

Roman Occupation of Paris

In the year 52 BC, Julius Caesar's Roman army defeated the Gauls (inhabitants of France) and captured their main city, **Lutetia** (today's Paris). When the Gauls saw that they were losing the battle, they set their city on fire so as to leave nothing for their enemies. The Romans rebuilt Lutetia, transforming it into a great Roman city, which served as a base for conquests further north. They constructed a forum, numerous aqueducts and public bath houses, an amphitheater, and an arena. They created a grid of paved roads. They built a Governor's Palace and judicial buildings. The Romans also erected many temples to their gods, including ones to Jupiter, Juno, Minerva, Mercury, Apollo, Bacchus, Hercules, Mars, Venus, Vulcan, and Ceres.

Several of the Latin Quarter's main avenues still follow the trace of old Roman roads, including the Boulevard Saint Michel, Rue des Écoles, and Rue Monge. Many Roman vestiges were either reused subsequently to build

Latin Quarter Highlights

- Have a mock gladiator battle in the Roman Arena (Arènes de Lutèce)
- Find the unicorns in the Cluny Museum
- Look for plaques to fallen heroes by the Place Saint Michel
- Play like princes and princesses in the Luxembourg Gardens
- Try some mint tea at the Paris Mosque
- Hunt for extinct and endangered animals at the Jardin des Plantes
- Shop for wild strawberries at the Rue Mouffetard Market
- Buy a book at Shakespeare and Company
- Find a 400-year-old tree that's still alive!

defensive walls and buildings, or they remain buried under modern Paris. However, you can still travel back in time to a gladiator battle in the Roman Arena or imagine a steam room in the old Roman Bath house.

ARENES DE LUTECE. *Entrances from the Rue des Arènes, Rue de Navarre, and through a passageway in the Rue Monge (Metro: Place Monge or Jussieu). Open daily, 8am-sunset. Entrance is free.*

The Arènes de Lutèce were built by the Romans in the 1st century BC. They featured entertainment such as gladiator matches, chariot races, Christians thrown to the lions, and even naval battles. There were also mime and dance performances. Dramatic plays were performed at the Roman Theater, now gone, that was located near the Cluny Roman Baths (see below).

The arena was built right into the side of a hill. There were 35 rows of seats that could hold as many as 17,000 spectators. It was used until the 3rd century A.D., at which time Paris was repeatedly invaded by Vikings, Goths, and Huns, and the Roman Empire began to crumble. The arena was abandoned, and many of the stones were used to build defensive walls and towers to protect the city.

For hundreds of years the Arènes de Lutèce were forgotten under rubble and new constructions. Then in 1869, workers widening the Rue Monge came upon some of the ruins of the old arena. At the time, the city was more interested in modernization than historical preservation, so a bus depot was built on top of them. In 1883, more of the ruins were discovered on the southern side of the arena. This time there was a great public outcry to save the site, including a letter to the President of the City Council from Victor Hugo (author of *Les Misérables* and *The Hunchback of Notre Dame*). The ruins of the arena were preserved and restored, although some parts remain buried under the Rue Monge and Rue de Navarre.

Today, people play much tamer games in the Arènes de Lutèce than those of the Roman period. It is a favorite spot for a round of boules, friendly soccer match, and children's games. There is a pretty little playground, just down the hill from the arena in the park.

THERMES DE CLUNY. *Located in the same building as the Musée National du Moyen Age (described below), 6, Place Paul Painlevé, just off the Boulevard Saint Michel. Metro: Cluny-La Sorbonne or Saint Michel. Open 9:15am-5:45pm (last entry tickets sold at 5:15). Closed Tues. Adults: €5.5; Kids: free. Free to everyone on the first Sunday of each month.*

These Roman Baths were built in the 2nd and 3rd centuries AD. They included at least a dozen different rooms on two floors, including steam rooms, warm baths, and cool pools. There were also gymnasiums and rooms reserved for conversation. They were richly decorated with marble and bronze statues, painted murals, and elaborate mosaic floor tiles. There was a sophisticated water system that provided steam and filled the pools.

The Roman baths were free to the public. However, people didn't just go to the baths to get clean. They also went to socialize, conduct business, exercise, and visit the library. Special pools were reserved for women. Men often took part in wrestling matches or calisthenics before going into the bathing rooms. Businessmen would meet in the baths or in the surrounding gardens. There were masseuses and hairdressers. There were food and drink vendors and other boutiques. All in all, it was a very lively place.

As you visit the museum, you can still see the large **Frigidarium** (cold room) that had a pool with cool water, much like a modern swimming pool. The room has a high ceiling supported by beams and arches. At the base of the arches you can make out decorations representing the hulls of ships. They were originally decorated with mermaids and tritons (male mermaids) and filled with goods and weapons. Archeologists disagree about what the ship hulls stand for, but they may be a tribute to the importance of shipping in early Lutetia. The Tepidarium (warm room) and Caldarium (hot steam room) were to the west of the Frigidarium. They are now part of the outside gardens along the Boulevard St. Michel.

With the barbarian invasions of Paris in the middle of the 3rd century AD, the

Fun Fact

The Roman Occupation of Lutetia began to collapse in the 3rd century AD. The Gauls reclaimed their city and built fortified walls to protect themselves. They renamed it Paris after their Celtic ancestors, the Parisii, who had originally settled the city.

In the 5th century, Paris was invaded by the Franks. Their leader, **Childeric**, captured the city and became the first of France's Merovingian Kings. His son, **Clovis**, made Paris his capital. It is from these Frankish invaders that France gets its name and its language.

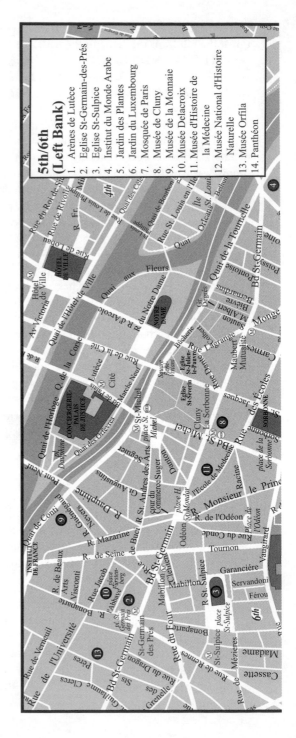

5th/6th (Left Bank)

1. Arènes de Lutèce
2. Eglise St-Germain-des-Prés
3. Eglise St-Sulpice
4. Institut du Monde Arabe
5. Jardin des Plantes
6. Jardin du Luxembourg
7. Mosquée de Paris
8. Musée de Cluny
9. Musée de la Monnaie
10. Musée Delacroix
11. Musée d'Histoire de la Médecine
12. Musée National d'Histoire Naturelle
13. Musée Orfila
14. Panthéon

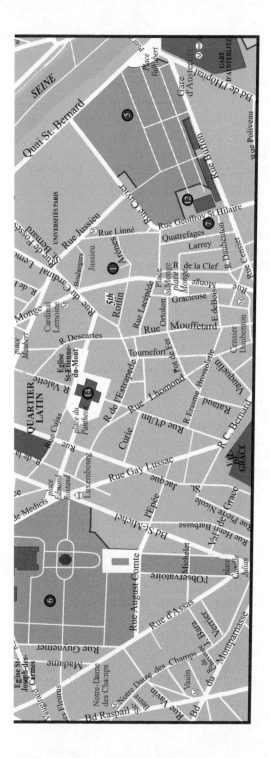

inhabitants of Paris fled to the fortified part of the city on the island of Ile de la Cité. The Thermes de Cluny were abandoned and fell into ruin. Some of the stones from the building were reused to build fortification walls.

Sainte Geneviève Saves Paris

The patron saint of Paris is **Sainte Geneviève**, to whom people pray when the city is in trouble. Geneviève was young shepherdess, born in 422 in a village west of Paris. She was extremely pious, had religious visions, and is said to have started performing miracles at age 9 when she cured a blind girl by sprinkling water in her eyes. She saved villagers from illness and Parisians from starving. However, Geneviève's most famous moment came in the year 451 when Paris was threatened by the Huns. Lead by Attilla the Hun, these invaders had crossed through Germany into eastern France, killing and pillaging all the way. Word came that Attila was approaching Paris. The Parisians panicked and began to flee, but Geneviève gave them the courage to stay, convinced by a dream that their city would be spared. In the end, the Huns never reached Paris. They were defeated, and Geneviève was credited with having saved the city.

Geneviève could not save Paris from the Franks, however, who took over the city in 464. She ultimately befriended their king, Clovis and his wife, Clothilde, and persuaded them to become Christians. When Geneviève died in 512 at the age of 90, she was buried next to Clovis. Today her remains are in the Eglise Saint Etienne du Mont, which sits atop the Montagne Sainte Geneviève in the Latin Quarter.

There is a statue of Sainte Geneviève on the Pont de la Tournelle (A bridge behind Notre Dame Cathedral, connecting the Ile Saint Louis and Left Bank). She is looking east, ready to face down Attilla the Hun.

EGLISE SAINT ETIENNE DU MONT. *Place Sainte Geneviève. Metro: Cardinal Lemoine. Open 10am-12pm, 4pm-7pm. Closed Mon.*

Although the original church here was built in the 6th century, this one was constructed from 1492 to 1626. It combines both Gothic elements, such as the fine stained-glass windows, and Renaissance features, such as the symmetrical facade. Children will be more interested in the story behind the name of the church, the intricate jubé, and the fact that Geneviève's relics are still preserved inside. The church is named for Saint Stephen, who was stoned to death by an angry mob in 34 AD for preaching the teachings of Christ. He is the first Christian martyr, and you can see a statue of him, with a pile of rocks, by the church's entrance. The other statue depicts Sainte Geneviève. Inside, notice the spectacular set of balconies and double spiral stairs, known as a *jubé*, or rood screen. These are carved in stone but look as delicate as lace. Rood screens were designed to separate the area reserved for the clergy from the more public part of the church, called the nave. Although they used to be common in churches, this is the only rood screen left in Paris.

It dates from 1541. On the right, beyond the rood screen is a shrine with Geneviève's relics. Pilgrims still come and ask her for favors, or leave plaques of thanks for her miracles.

The Medieval Latin Quarter

In the 1100s, Paris became one of Europe's most important centers of learning. Many important scholars and students congregated in the neighborhood around the **Montagne Sainte Geneviève.**

Students came from all over Europe. There were so many of them that there was a serious student housing crunch. In the 1200s, many "colleges" began to form. These started out as places for students to live and study together, often under the direction of resident "masters." One of these was founded in 1253, by Robert Sorbon, a priest at Nôtre Dame Cathedral and confessor to King Saint Louis. It was built to house students, professors, and a library. It would soon become one of the most famous and powerful universities in the world, the Sorbonne.

SORBONNE. *Rue Victor Cousin. Metro: Cluny-La Sorbonne. Open weekdays 9am-4:30 pm.*

Note: Although the Sorbonne is not really a place for tourists, children are awed by the sight of a school so much bigger than their own. Especially if your studies ever took you to Paris, don't be afraid to give your children a quick peek into the grand hallways or amphitheaters. Maybe they'll be back some day for their Junior Year Abroad.

Only boys could attend college in medieval days, and some started at the Sorbonne as early as age 14. Initiation to the college was similar to those in today's fraternities, and it could be cruel or dangerous. Classes were taught in Latin. Students studied literature, grammar, debate, arithmetic, geometry, astronomy, and music. After about 6 years they could study theology (the study of religion and the origins of God), arts, law, or medicine. They also took part in physical exercises, such as swimming in the Seine, wrestling, high jumping, and javelin throwing. Although the locals often looked on the students as thieves and troublemakers, the university became the central point of activity in the Latin Quarter.

Throughout its long history, the Sorbonne has maintained its reputation as a top rate university. But there have been dark periods as well. In the early 1300s, the powerful theology department sided with the king, Philippe le Bel, to condemn the Order of Templar Knights. As a result the Templars were massacred throughout France. When Joan of Arc was caught by the Burgundians and sold to the English as a prisoner in 1431, the heads of the Sorbonne joined the English in condemning her. In the 16th century, the leaders of the Sorbonne joined the fight against the French Huguenots (Protestants), and in the 18th century were fiery critics of the modern ideas of the Enlightenment thinkers, such as Descartes and Rousseau. With the French Revolution, the Sorbonne was closed due to its connection with the Catholic Church. It was re-opened under Napoleon I as part of his widespread education reforms. He severed its ties with the Church, and French became the official language of instruction.

In May 1968, the Sorbonne and other Paris university campuses exploded with student protests against the outdated rules, courses, and style of the university. Students built barricades, took over university buildings, and fought with police troops. Workers all over the country, unhappy with their lack of power and rights, joined the movement and went on strike. The strikes paralyzed the country for two months. In the end the government and university made some concessions. The Paris university system was split up to include more liberal campuses and ideas. Today the Sorbonne is one of 18 campuses in the University of Paris system.

CLUNY -MUSÉE NATIONAL DU MOYEN AGE, *in the same building as the Thermes de Cluny at 6, Place Paul Painleve, off Boulevard Saint Michel. Metro: Cluny-La Sorbonne or Saint Michel. Open 9:15am-5:45pm. Closed Tues. Closed Tues. Adults: €5.50; Kids: free. Free to everyone on the first Sunday of each month. Access to the Medieval Garden along the Boulevard Saint Germain is free.*

The Cluny museum is a charming place to visit, and parents are surprised at how much their children enjoy it. The museum is not terribly big, but offers interesting glimpses at both Roman and medieval life. The visit takes you through beautiful examples of stained glass, gold work, jewelry, fabric, ivory carvings, and illuminated books. It takes you into the old Frigidarium of the Roman Baths building (see above). There are the 21 stone heads that were knocked off the statues of the biblical kings of Notre Dame Cathedral during the French Revolution. There is the tombstone from the grave of Nicholas Flamel (discoverer of the Sorcerer's Stone). The most famous exhibit, and the one that really excites young children, is near the end of the museum visit. It features the Dame à la Licorne (Woman with a Unicorn) tapestries. There are six of them, and they are magnificent. Children delight in looking at the magical unicorn, and searching out all the different animals in each scene.

Fun Fact

The **Dame à la Licorne** tapestries represent each of the five senses: taste, touch, smell, hearing, and sight. Can you find them? And what about the sixth tapestry? This one is called, "My Only Desire," and no one can agree on its true meaning. Maybe you have a theory.

The courtyard in front of the museum features a 15th century well, and a facade decorated with gargoyles and other Gothic decorations. Downhill from the museum is a nice medieval Garden that features medicinal and decorative plants of the period.

BOULEVARD SAINT MICHEL NEIGHBORHOOD. *Metro: Saint Michel.*

The Boulevard Saint Michel is one of the major thoroughfares of the Latin Quarter, and has been since Roman times when it was lined with Roman Baths, a Theater, and a Forum. Today, the boulevard bustles with college students and tourists. It is lined with lively cafés, fast-food places, discount clothing stores, shoe stores, pedestrian streets, and the big Gibert bookstores that have been around for over 100 years.

PLACE SAINT MICHEL. *Located at the lower end of the Boulevard Saint Michel, by the Seine. Metro: Saint Michel.*

The statue in the Place Saint Michel depicts the biblical battle between Michael, an archangel who remained loyal to god, and Lucifer a former archangel who wanted to take over heaven. Michael defeated Lucifer, who was kicked out of heaven with his followers. They set up their own kingdom in Hell, with Lucifer as their leader. Lucifer became the symbol of evil (devil) and is often depicted in art as a snake, dragon, or monster.

In 1945, during the Liberation of Paris, the Place Saint Michel was the scene of real battles between members of the French Resistance and troops of the German Occupying force. There are plaques commemorating fallen heroes on the Place and along the Boulevard. A plaque by the fountain also presents the words of a famous radio speech by Charles de Gaulle given after the German invasion of Paris in 1940. In it he calls on his countrymen to resist the German Occupation. Today, the Place Saint Michel is a favorite hangout for young people and foot-sore tourists.

QUARTIER DE LA HUCHETTE. *Side streets to the east of the Place Saint Michel.*

This neighborhood of cobbled pedestrian streets is filled with tourist shops and restaurants. The streets date back to Roman times, including the tiny Rue du Chat Qui Pêche, which is the smallest street in the city. If your party includes a high schooler who is studying French, he or she may enjoy seeing Ionesco's The Bald Soprano, which has been playing at the little Théâtre de la Huchette since the play was written in the 1950s. The nearby Caveau de la Huchette has also been around for 50 years, offering jazz performances since the days of the Paris beatniks.

If you cross the Rue Saint Jacques, you can admire the old medieval houses in the rue Galande.

EGLISE SAINT SEVERIN, *1, Rue des Prêtres Saint Severin, Metro: Saint Michel.*

This church dates from the 13th-15th centuries. Built in a crowded section of the city, it has an unusually squat shape. Inside there are very pretty double rows of columns supporting the gothic arches. The modern painter Robert Delaunay created a series of paintings of these arches (three of them are in American museums in Minneapolis, Philadelphia, and New York). Outside, the church's garden has a funny series of archways and peaked roofs. These were once part of a 15th century cemetery. Wealthy people bought burial spots under the arches, while regular folk were buried in the open section. By the 17th century, Paris was so crowded that the living took over spaces that had been reserved for the dead. People established shops and apartments in the arcades.

EGLISE SAINT JULIEN LE PAUVRE, *Rue Saint Julien le Pauvre. Metro: Maubert Mutualité or Saint Michel.*

This church is named for a bishop who was so generous to others he was always poor himself (le Pauvre). It was built on the site of an early 6th century church that had been destroyed by Viking invaders. The church dates from the 12th-13th centuries and was built in the Romanesque style. Gothic touches were added later. Saint Julien le Pauvre was an important church in the 12th century. The Sorbonne held university meetings here. It was also a stop for pilgrims on their way to Saint Jacques de Compostelle in Spain.

What's the difference between an Romanesque and a Gothic church? Romanesque architecture is named for the fact that it imitates the rounded arches of classical Roman buildings. Romanesque churches were built in the 11th-12th centuries and pre-date the Gothic period of architecture. They feature thick walls, small windows, and arches that are rounded, not peaked like those of the later Gothic period.

SQUARE VIVIANI. *Between Eglise Saint Julien le Pauvre and the Seine. Metro: Maubert Mutualité or Saint Michel*

If you've ever read the book, *Linnea in Monet's Garden*, you might recognize this lovely little park. It is just across the Seine River from Notre Dame Cathedral and across the street the Hôtel Esmeralda, featured in Linnea's story. It was once the garden for the Eglise Saint Julien le Pauvre.

It also holds Paris' second oldest tree. Planted in 1681, the tree is a False Acacia, so old and gnarled that it leans on a stone crutch for support. The square offers a great view of Nôtre Dame Cathedral. It is also a good place to take a break or enjoy a snack. Right around the corner to your left as you face the river is the famous English-language bookshop, Shakespeare and Company.

SHAKESPEARE AND COMPANY. *37, Rue de la Bûcherie, across the river from Nôtre Dame Cathedral (Metro: Saint Michel). Open daily. Note: This store does not accept any credit cards.*

Filled with expatriate Brits and Americans, this is one of the English-language bookshops of Paris where you can stock up on new and used books, for kids or adults. It has an interesting history that actually involves two bookshops:

The original Shakespeare and Company was located at 12, Rue de l'Odéon and run by a woman named Sylvia Beach. It was here that writers such as Ernest Hemingway, F. Scott Fitzgerald, James Joyce, and Gertrude Stein crossed paths. It was both an English-language bookshop and a lending library. During the German occupation of Paris in World War II, Beach refused to sell her last copy of James Joyce's *Finnegan's Wake* to a German officer. He threatened to confiscate all her books. She was forced to close the shop, and it never re-opened. During the Liberation of Paris, Ernest Hemingway, a war correspondent who was among the first Allied troops to enter the city, made a point of dropping by Sylvia Beach's place to officially liberate it.

In 1951, George Whitman opened up his English bookshop, called Le Mistral, in a little street across the Seine from Nôtre Dame Cathedral. He also had a lending library on the second floor, and his shop became a meeting place for a new generation of English-language poets and writers. These included Americans, such as Alan Ginsberg, William Burroughs, Henry Miller, and James Baldwin. Whitman installed cots in the library where struggling young writers could spend the night for free provided they read a book a day, worked an hour in the shop, and left a short autobiography and photo. They still do. When Sylvia Beach died in 1962, Whitman renamed his shop Shakespeare and Company to honor her. The shop extends a warm welcome to all book lovers, whether they are starving writers or not.

LUXEMBOURG GARDENS. *Located between the Boulevard Saint Michel, Rue de Vaugirard, and Rue d'Assas. Metro: Luxembourg or Nôtre Dame des Champs. Open sunrise to sunset. Entrance is free.*

The Luxembourg Palace and Gardens were built in the 17th century by Queen Marie de Médicis after the assassination of her husband King Henri IV. She bought the property from a Duke of Luxembourg, which is where it gets its name. The queen had the palace built to look like one in Florence, Italy where she had spent her childhood. However, Marie de

Médicis did not get to enjoy her new palace for long. Her son, Louis XIII, banished her from France, and she was forced to live the rest of her life in Germany.

The palace served as a royal residence until the French Revolution when it was used as a prison. During the German Occupation of Paris in World War II, the palace was taken over as central headquarters for the German Luftwäffe (Air Force). Today it houses the French Senate.

In front of the palace is the **central fountain** of the Luxembourg Gardens. On weekends and holiday afternoons it is dotted with miniature sailboats that you can rent by the hour from a little stand. This is one of our boys' all-time favorite activities in Paris. It also provides great photo opportunities. Keep an eye on small children, however. The edges of the fountain slope downward toward the water.

Parent Tip: Note to junior sailing enthusiasts: You can purchase your own wooden sailboat to float in the fountain at a toy stored located just one and a half blocks from the main entrance to the Luxembourg Gardens. The store is called **Le Ciel est a Tout le Monde** (10, Rue Gay Lussac, 75005; Metro: Luxembourg) also has wonderful kites, wooden toys, and models.

The central fountain is a favorite hangout for students and other Parisians relaxing in the green metal chairs that fill the park. It is a lovely spot to rest your feet and soak in the sun on a nice day. As you sit there, notice the statues of the queens of France looking benevolently down at you from the surrounding terraces. Up the steps on the eastern side of the park there is a bandstand that offers free concerts in the summer, when the nearby outdoor café is also open.

Just east of the palace is the pretty, shady Médicis Fountain. Filled with goldfish, it presents an interesting optical illusion. Since the edges of the pool are on an incline, it looks like the water is slanted even though it is flat. The statue that adorns the fountain depicts a scene from the Greek myth of Acis and Galathea.

Fun (but Gory!) Fact

In Greek mythology, Galatea was a water nymph. Acis was a fawn. They fell in love and became engaged. But the giant, one-eyed Cyclops, Polyphemus, wanted Galatea for himself. When he found the two lovers kissing in a cave, he threw a huge stone at Acis and crushed him. Galatea escaped into the water. Acis was turned into a river god. Polyphemus later had his eye poked out by Odysseus.

The western side of the park has public tennis courts, a place reserved for playing *boules*, chess tables, a puppet theater, a wooden merry-go-round, and old-fashioned two-person swings. This is also where you will find the Luxembourg's amazing **playground**. Although there is a small fee to enter, it is well worth it. (It's the only place I know of where kids pay more than adults.) If you have small children you will want to go in with them. If they are a little older and more independent, you can do what many Parisian parents and nannies do: watch them from the metal chairs around the perimeter of the playground. The small building in the playground has a restroom and snack bar.

In the summer months there are also pony rides and little race cars for rent on the western side of the park. There is a beekeeping school (near the rue d'Assas entrance) with classes twice a week. You can buy the honey each October in the garden's **Orangerie**, which doubles as a small museum featuring temporary art exhibits. If you wander through the shady paths on the western side of the park, you may come across a small replica of the Statue of Liberty. It was one of the models for the big one in New York harbor.

On the southeastern side of the park are the garden's greenhouses (not open to the public). There is also an orchard that is nearly 200 years old. The apples and pears from these trees are reserved for members of the Senate.

On the north side of the Luxembourg Gardens at #36 Rue de Vaugirard under the arcades, there is an inscription in the wall designating the official length a one meter. It is on a building that used to be the Agency for Weights and Measures and harkens back to the time (1795) when France adopted its first standardized system of measures: the metric system. The length of the meter, which was the baseline of the system, was calculated to be the equivalent of one-ten-millionth of the distance of the arc of the earth from the North Pole to the Equator. To help people get used to using meters, meter-stick measures such as this one were inscribed on the walls of buildings throughout the city.

FRENCH SENATE. *15, Rue de Vaugirard, in the Luxembourg Palace. Metro: Odeon. Free public visits are organized on the first Sun of each month at 10:00am. Visitors are allowed to watch the Senate when it is in session, but you are not allowed to tour the building at that time.*

France has a parliamentary democracy. The President heads the executive branch of the government. There is a bicameral legislative branch, composed of the National Assembly and the Senate. There are 321 Senators who serve 9 years terms. They are not directly elected by the general public, but rather by locally elected representatives. Members of the Senate share similar legislative duties with the members of the National Assembly. To be adopted, any new law must be reviewed and voted on by both the Senate and

National Assembly. In the event of a disagreement between the two houses, the decision of the National Assembly prevails.

The inside of the Senate is palatial, which is not surprising since they meet in a former palace. If you don't have a chance to visit the interior but do have a child who is taking French at school you may want to visit the Senate bookshop. It is located at 20, Rue de Vaugirard. Here you can obtain a free kids' guide to the Senate. It features excellent photos and explanations (in French). Take a copy home to your favorite French teacher.

PANTHEON, *Place du Panthéon. Metro: Luxembourg or Cardinal Lemoine. Open 9:30am-6:30pm (summer); 10am-6pm (winter). Adults: €7; Kids under 18: free.*

Although there is not much to offer children inside the Pantheon, its history is interesting. The Pantheon was originally designed as a church, built by King Louis XV in 1759 in thanks for his recovery from a serious illness. It was to be dedicated to Saint Geneviève. The church was designed by an architect named Jacques Soufflot in the shape of a Greek cross. However, it was not finished when the French Revolution broke out in 1789. In their anti-clerical fervor, the revolutionaries transformed the church into a burial place for important men.

Through successive French governments, the Pantheon's role switched between religious and secular several times, and is now the final resting place for Victor Hugo, Jacques Soufflot (the building's designer), Jean-Jacques Rousseau (philosopher), Emile Zola (writer), Jean Jaurés (political leader), Louis Braille (who invented Braille writing), Jean Moulin (leader of the French Resistance), and Pierre and Marie Curie (who discovered Radium and studied radioactivity). Paintings inside the Pantheon depict the life of Sainte Geneviève, death of Saint Denis, story of Joan of Arc, and crowning of Charlemagne.

Behind the Pantheon, you can take the Rue Clovis to the Rue Descartes. Notice half a block further down the Rue Clovis is a remnant of the 12th century defensive wall that used to protect Paris from invaders, such as the English King Richard the Lionheart. If you take the Rue Descartes to the Place de la Contrescarpe, you will enter the Mouffetard neighborhood, famous for its ancient market street, shops, and restaurants.

RUE MOUFFETARD, *between Place de la Contrescarpe and Avenue des Gobelins. Metro: Place Monge or Censier Daubenton.*

This charming street has been paved with stones ever since Roman times when it led all the way to Italy. The road used to go along the Bièvre River, which now runs underground as part of the Paris sewer system. For centuries, the Mouffetard area was dotted with farms and vineyards. In the 12th century, wealthy Parisians built their country villas around here. Over time the Rue Mouffetard was lined with narrow houses (many of which are still there), shops, tanneries, cloth dyers, and an open-air market.

The Mouffetard neighborhood (familiarly known as **La Mouf**) has been home to many famous residents. Medieval author, Rabelais, used to get drunk in a tavern called the Pomme de Pin (Pine Cone) on the Place de la Contrescarpe. Age of Enlightenment thinker Denis Diderot lived at #3, Rue de l'Estrapade, and René Descartes lived at #14, Rue Rollin. Sculptor Auguste Rodin was born at #3, Rue de l'Arbalète. Ernest Hemingway lived around the corner at #74 Rue du Cardinal-Lemoine and at #39, Rue Descartes. He described the neighborhood in his books, *The Snows of Kilimanjaro* and *A Moveable Feast.*

At #60, Rue Mouffetard, there is a small fountain called the Fontaine du Pot de Fer that dates back to Roman times. It was later connected to an aqueduct used by Queen Marie de Médicis to bring water to her Luxembourg Gardens and Palace.

The house at # 53, Rue Mouffetard is famous for its hidden treasure. On May 24, 1938, workers tearing down an old house found gold coins in the walls, stamped with the likeness of King Louis XV. There were 3,351 coins in all. They had been left there by a man named Louis Nivelle, who had been Louis XV's secretary. Nivelle disappeared mysteriously in 1757, but left a will that was found with the coins. In the will, Nivelle bequeathed the treasure to his daughter, who died in 1810. The discovery of the coins led to a 15-year legal battle between Nivelle's heirs and the people who uncovered the treasure. In the end, the gold was split between Nivelle's 84 descendants. However, they had to pay fees to the genealogists and the construction crew, as well as a big inheritance tax to the City of Paris.

RUE MOUFFETARD STREET MARKET. *Metro: Censier Daubenton or Place Monge. Open Daily except Mondays, 8am-1pm, 4pm-7pm. Closed Sunday afternoon and Monday.*

This market has been here for hundreds of years. Notice some of the old shop signs on the buildings. It is famous for its wide variety of fresh produce, meats, cheeses, and ethnic boutiques. Check out the wonderful bakeries and delicatessens with their specialties from France, Greece, Italy, and Asia. On weekends, French shoppers come in from the suburbs to enjoy the colors and tastes this market offers.

EGLISE SAINT MEDARD. *Square Saint Médard at the bottom of the Rue Mouffetard. Open daily 8am-12pm, 2:30pm-7:30pm.*

This church is mainly famous for the story of the **Convulsionnaires**, people who used to experience hysterical religious convulsions in the church's small cemetery. It all started in the early 1700s with a man named François Paris. He gave up his family's inheritance to dedicate his life to prayer and helping the poor. He lived a humble life and when he died was buried in the Saint Médard cemetery. In 1727, the Jansenists, a religious group being persecuted by the more powerful Jesuits, began to honor François Paris as a Saint. They claimed to experience miracles at his tomb.

Some of his young female followers began to go into wild, religious fits in the cemetery. They would do things such as cry like animals, perform acrobatic stunts, and roll on the ground.

Within two years, some 800 people had experienced these convulsions. It was both a way to celebrate their faith and to stand up to their Jesuit persecutors. They became known as the Convulsionnaires de Saint Médard. After trying to stomp out this movement by force, the government finally closed the cemetery in 1732. The Convulsionnaires continued to meet and experience their fits in private homes until 1762 when persecutions of the Jansenists ended.

Parent Tip: Now that you've loaded up with food from the Rue Mouffetard, it's time to feed the budding scientist in every child with a visit to the nearby **Jardin des Plantes.** Here, children can run, have a picnic, ride a merry-go-round of extinct and endangered animals, get lost in a labyrinth, visit the zoo, and enjoy the wonderful **Natural History Museums.**

JARDIN DES PLANTES *(Botanical Gardens), Located between the Rue Cuvier, Rue Geoffroy Saint Hilaire, Rue Buffon, and Seine River. Metro: Jussieu or Gare d'Austerlitz. Open sunrise to sunset. Museums open daily except Tues, 10am-6pm (Thurs. until 10pm). Greenhouses open daily 1pm-5pm. Menagerie open daily 9am-5pm (summers until 6pm). Entrance to the park is free, though you do have to pay to enter the zoo, greenhouses, and museums.*

This park is a kid's haven. It contains a zoo, playground, labyrinth, and merry-go-round featuring extinct or endangered animals. There are huge greenhouses and botanical gardens. There is a paleontology museum, featuring skeletons of current and extinct animals; a gallery of evolution filled with real (stuffed) animals; a mineralogy museum with giant crystals; and a botanical museum.

The Jardin des Plantes began as a place where the royal botanists grew medicinal plants for the family of King Louis XIII. It was expanded during the reign of Louis XIV to accommodate plants brought back from expeditions to the New World and other foreign parts. The king's chief doctor headed the gardens. He oversaw the building of two greenhouses, including the Grande Serre (Large Greenhouse) that was designed to house France's first coffee tree. A 600-seat lecture hall was also added to promote the teaching of natural sciences and pharmacy.

Over time, many rare trees and plants were added to the park's collection. Some are still there today, including the oldest tree in Paris, planted in 1635. It is a False Acacia tree, and a twin to the one in the Square Viviani featured in *Linnea in Monet's Garden.* It is located in the Allée des Becquerels, near the Minerology Museum. The gardens also house a 150-year-old Ginkgo tree and a 250-year-old Chinese Sophora.

The park's **Labyrinth,** near the Rue Geoffroy Saint Hilaire side of the park, was built in 1640 on an artificial hill that had served as a trash pile. In the middle of the Labyrinth is a magnificent tree, a Cedar of Lebanon. This tree was secretly carried to Paris from London by botanist, Bernard de Jussieu in 1734. Along the route, the flower pot that held the small sapling broke. Legend has it that Jussieu carried the plant in his hat for most of the trip, catching a head cold as a result. The more reliable version of the story says that the pot broke only a few blocks from the park. Either way, the tree was safely delivered thanks to the botanist's hat.

MENAGERIE (ZOO). *Northwest corner of the Jardin des Plantes. Open daily except Tues. 9am-6pm (summer); 9am-5pm (winter). Closed Tues. Adults: €6; Kids ages 5-16: €3; Kids under 5: free.*

The Menagerie was created in 1793. It is the oldest public zoo in the world. Its first residents were animals that had been part of the royal menagerie at Versailles and were brought here after the French Revolution. They were joined by other animals that were confiscated from carnivals and street performers. More animals were added in 1795, including France's first live elephants, stolen from a Dutch zoo after a successful French military campaign. The first giraffe arrived in 1826. It was a gift from the King of Egypt. The giraffe went by boat to Marseilles, then traveled slowly up to Paris to give people a chance to see it. It was such a hit that giraffe decorations on combs, umbrellas, and other items became all the rage.

In 1870, the Prussians laid siege to the city of Paris, ultimately forcing ruler Napoleon III to surrender. During the siege, the people of Paris were cut off from their food supplies and had to eat anything they could find. Even the zoo animals were killed, and their meat was sold to local restaurants.

Today, the zoo is home to some 800 animals. There are many large mammals, reptiles, and birds. There is also a "microzoo," where you can look at tiny creatures through a microscope.

GALERIE DE PALEONTOLOGIE. *Northeastern edge of the park (near the Seine entrance). Open daily except Tues, 10am-5pm (weekdays); 10am-6pm (weekends). Closed Tues. Adults: €5; Kids ages 5-18: €3. Kids under 5: free.*

Note: This museum is slated to be renovated, so catch it while you can.

This museum holds an impressive array of animal skeletons, including an entire blue whale. The upper floor features magnificent dinosaur skeletons and fossils. The building itself was first opened in 1898 and with its intricate ironwork decorations is well worth a visit.

GRANDE GALERIE DE L'EVOLUTION. *Southeastern side of the park, by Rue Geoffroy Saint Hilaire and Paris Mosque. Open daily except Tues, 10am-6pm (until 10pm Thurs). Adults: €7; Kids 4-18: €5; Kids under 4: free.*

This spectacular building was recently renovated after being closed for decades. It features a long caravan of large mammals as you first walk in. The lower level has marine animals on exhibit. Birds are represented in flight along the upper floors. There is a fascinating room upstairs (level 2) featuring animals that are extinct or endangered. The top level has a rhinoceros that belonged to the royal menagerie of Louis XIV. It is the oldest animal in the museum.

GALERIE DE MINEROLOGIE. *Undergoing renovation.*

This is an interesting visit for anyone who really digs rocks and crystals. It features the world's greatest collection of giant crystals. There are jewels from the reigns of Louis XIII and Louis XIV. There are also meteorites from outer space. Unfortunately, this museum is in dire need of updating and is arranged like a dusty, private collection. It is not air conditioned, which can make it hard to tolerate if the weather is hot.

GALERIE DE PALEOBOTANIQUE. *Undergoing renovation.*

This museum offers a collection of plants from prehistoric times to the present, but like the mineralogy museum is sorely in need of updating.

PARIS MOSQUE. *1, Place du Puits de l'Ermite. The restaurant, tearoom, and Turkish bath entrances are located at 39, Rue Geoffroy Saint Hilaire. Metro: Place Monge. The Mosque is open for visits daily except Fridays, from 9am-12pm, and 2pm-6pm. The restaurant is open daily, 10am-9pm.*

The Paris Mosque was built from 1922 to 1926 as a gesture of thanks to the North African troops who fought alongside the French during World War I. It was designed to look like the mosque in the Moroccan city of Fez. Four hundred fifty artisans and technicians from Morocco, Algeria, and Tunisia worked on the building. It is beautifully decorated with mosaics, intricate wood carvings, fine rugs, and shady gardens. The minaret tower is 33 meters (109 feet) high.

The Mosque is divided into three sections. The religious section is reserved for prayer. There are guided tours every day but Friday. There is a tomb inside the Mosque for its first Imam. He is remembered not only as a religious leader and scholar, but also for his role in hiding 200 Jews during the Nazi invasion of Paris in World War II. The cultural section includes a library and bookshop and offers lessons in Arabic. The commercial section includes a Turkish bathhouse, restaurant, and tearoom.

Our favorite section includes the **restaurant and tea room**, which offer an interesting cultural and culinary experience. You walk through the entrance and feel as though you have stepped into a Moorish palace. The outdoor gardens are decorated with beautiful tiles, shady trees, and a fountain. The inside restaurant and tea room are warm and welcoming. You are served North African specialties, such as mint tea, couscous, and pastries on huge brass tray tables. It's a taste of the exotic in the middle of Paris.

OPEN-AIR SCULPTURE GARDEN. *On the Seine, along the Quai Saint Bernard. Metro: Jussieu or Gare d'Austerlitz. Open daily, sunrise to sunset. Entrance is free.*

This sculpture garden runs along the river from the Jardin des Plantes to the Institut du Monde Arabe. It is filled with works by modern artists such as Joan Arp, Constantine Brancusi, and Cesar – who sometimes appeal more to children than to adults. There are also paths for roller blading, ping-pong tables, and a playground. Sometimes after a particularly wet winter, the park becomes flooded by the rising waters of the Seine. Then some of the sculptures end up partially submerged.

INSTITUT DU MONDE ARABE. *1, Rue des Fossés-Saint-Bernard. Metro: Jussieu, or Cardinal Lemoine. Access to the building is free. The museum is open, 10am-6pm, Closed Mon. Adults and Children 12 and up: €5. Children under 12: free. There are often special exhibits with separate entrances and entrance fees.*

Fun Fact

If you are in Paris on June 24, don't miss the **Feux de la Saint John.** It's a spectacular fireworks display over the Seine in honor of the summer solstice. The best views are near the Quai Saint Bernard.

This Institute was designed to celebrate Arab culture and heritage. It is sponsored by France and the 21 members of the League of Arab Nations. The Institute includes a museum with a permanent collection of Islamic art, as well as temporary exhibits. There are films, concerts, and dance performances. The library features everything from high literature to cook books and comics. There is a fancy restaurant on the 9th floor, with spectacular views of the city. There also is a tearoom on the ground level in the courtyard.

Note: Look at the windows on the south side of the Institut du Monde Arabe. They are designed to look like Arab mosaics. But did you know they also serve a practical purpose? Like the lens of a camera or the pupil of you eye, the openings widen or narrow automatically to control the amount of light entering the building.

CLAUDE NATURE SHOP. *32, Boulevard Saint Germain. Metro: Maubert Mutualité.*

This little shop will appeal to bug lovers of all ages. It sells collectors' quality butterflies and other exotic bugs.

MAGIC SHOW - METAMORPHOSIS. *On a houseboat across from 55, Quai de la Tournelle (Apr-Sep), Metro: Maubert Mutualité Sundays at 3 pm. Family performances: €15 per person. Brunch plus show: €35 (adults); €25 (kids). Note: from Oct to Mar this boat moves upstream to by 7, Quai Malaquais across from the Pont des Arts, Metro: Pont Neuf or Saint Germain des Près.*

A floating magic show: what a winning combination! Join magician Jan Madd on his theater-houseboat for family-friendly magic shows on Sunday afternoons. Note that although there are also evening performances, those are not specially geared for families.

PIRATE SHIP. *11, Quai Francois Mauriac, Metro: Quai de la Gare. Shows daily at 3pm during summer holidays. During the school year, there are shows every Wed, Sat, and Sun afternoon at 3. Price: €3.50 (includes snack).*

This surprising ship, moored on the Seine near the Bibliothèque Nationale Francois Mitterand, is actually a real Chinese Jonque. Built in China during the 1980s, it has sailed around the world several times. Now, it is permanently stationed in Paris, where it offers live, kid-friendly shows.

GOBELINS TAPESTRY FACTORY. *42, Avenue des Gobelins. Metro: Gobelins. Guided tours Tues, Wed, Thurs at 2 pm and 2:45 pm. Adults: €8; Kids 7-25: €6: Kids under 7: free.*

Despite its name, the Gobelins Tapestry Factory has nothing to do with Halloween characters or Lord of the Rings. It is named for a Flemish tapestry maker, Jehan Gebeleen, who set up shop in 1440 along the Bièvre River where his workers could soak the wool and silks used to make their tapestries. The river water was said to enhance the quality of the fabrics. His sons and grandsons took up the business after him. By the time of King Francois I, business was booming and the factory was well known. In 1662, King Louis XIV turned the Gobelins into the royal tapestry factory. He also ordered the development of furniture and carpet workshops next to the factory. Together, they produced much of the decorations and furnishings for Louis XIV's palaces, including Versailles.

Following the French Revolution of 1789, hundreds of tapestry designs were destroyed, because they were not compatible with revolutionary ideas. The factory was also severely damaged during another popular uprising, the Paris Commune of 1871.

Today, the Gobelins and Mobilier National (National Furniture) workshops still produce tapestries, carpets, and furniture for the French government. They are used to decorate public buildings and French embassies around the world. The tapestries are based on designs by famous modern artists. They are woven on looms that are hundreds of years old. The workers begin learning their craft at the age of 16. They use only natural light, dye the colors by hand, and produce only 1 to 8 square meters of tapestry each year.

GARE D'AUSTERLITZ. *Along the Boulevard de l'Hôpital by the Quai d'Austerlitz.*

This train station is named for one of Napoleon Bonaparte's successful battles against the Austrians and Russians. It is where you come to catch trains coming and going from southwestern France, Spain, or Portugal. You can catch up on some of your correspondences at the station restaurant. The menu is conveniently printed on a postcard.

5. SAINT GERMAIN

This neighborhood gets its name from an old 6th century abbey named for one of the early bishops of Paris, Germain. **Saint Germain des Près** was an important religious center for hundreds of years. Indeed, until Nôtre Dame Cathedral was completed, the Eglise Saint Germain des Près was the most important church in Paris. During the 18th century, the neighborhood around Saint Germain became very popular with wealthy aristocrats and many of the great thinkers of the Age of Enlightenment. It is home to Paris' first official café (and the first place Parisians were able to taste a new concoction called coffee). Established in 1686, the **Café Procope** hosted such notables as Voltaire, René Descartes, Benjamin Franklin, and a young Napoleon Bonaparte.

By the 20th century, the cafés of Saint Germain des Près were attracting modern writers and intellectuals, such as Ernest Hemingway, Jean-Paul Sartre, and Simone de Beauvoir. In the 1950s, Saint Germain was home to Paris' thriving jazz scene, including many Black American performers seeking refuge from racist policies in the U.S.

Today, Saint Germain des Près still attracts intellectuals and creative types. The bookshops and cafés along the boulevard continue to attract philosophers and writers. Fashion designers have set up shop between the Boulevard Saint Germain and Place Saint Sulpice. Art and antiques dealers have their galleries in the streets near the Seine. Yet, there are treats for children, too, in the side streets of Saint Germain. These range from the magnificently restored **Musée d'Orsay** (formerly a train station) to the mysteries of a summer solstice at the **Place Saint Sulpice**.

Saint Germain Highlights

- Check out the 1000 year old church tower
- Find the portrait of Benjamin Franklin in the Cour du Commerce Saint André
- Look for the brass Paris Meridian line in the Eglise Saint Sulpice
- Find the polar bear sculpture and bedroom furniture by Macintosh at the Musée d'Orsay
- Check out the animals at Deyrolles, Paris' finest taxidermist shop
- Look at ancient coins in the Museum of Money
- Go for a Canal Boat Ride

EGLISE SAINT GERMAIN DES PRÈS, *Place Saint Germain des Près. Metro: Saint Germain des Près. Entrance is free.*

The Eglise Saint Germain des Près is the oldest church in Paris. It was first built in 543, by the Merovingian king, Childebert. He had murdered numerous rivals and relatives to get to the throne, and built the church partly to atone for his sins. He had also purchased relics from the Holy Cross, which he had placed in this church.

The Saint Germain des Près church was repeatedly attacked and damaged during the first millennium by Vikings and other invaders. For hundreds of years it was a fortified church, complete with watchtowers and a moat. The bell tower (still standing) was built in the year 1,000 AD. It was part of the defensive walls and is the oldest bell tower in Paris. Much of the church you see today dates from the 11th and 12th centuries and is a good example of the Romanesque architectural style. Some Gothic and Renaissance features were added in the 17th century. In the late 1600s, the Eglise Saint Germain des Près was turned into a prison. With the Revolution of 1789, it was changed into a saltpeter factory (used to make gunpowder). After the Revolution, the church resumed its religious role.

The famous 17th century philosopher, René Descartes, is buried in the Saint Germain des Près church. He is the author of the line, "I think, therefore I am," arguing that our human ability to think and reason is more important than mystical explanations for our existence. When he died in Sweden in 1650, a Swedish military officer stole the head off his body and sold it to a French scientist. The body is buried in the church, and the head is supposedly in the Museum d'Histoire Naturelle (Museum of Natural History) at the Jardin des Plantes.

Next to the church, along the Boulevard Saint Germain, there is a little park called the **Square Boucicault**. It is named for Aristide Boucicaut, the man who invented the first department store, the nearby Bon Marché. The

Square Boucicault covers a spot that once housed a home for lepers that was run by the church.

Behind the Eglise Saint Germain des Près is the pretty **Place Furstenberg**. This small square has hardly changed in 100 years. It was the home of Romantic painter Eugène Delacroix. You can see his home and art studio at #6. However, children will take more pleasure in admiring

his dramatic, large canvass of Liberty Guiding the People (whose central character decorates French stamps and coins) in the Louvre or his three religious paintings in the Eglise Saint Sulpice (see below).

RUE DE BUCI. *Just east of the Eglise Saint Germain des Près.* This street and the nearby cross-street, Rue de Seine, used to house an open-air market, which has unfortunately been closed. However, the street is still lined with wonderful bakeries and food shops. The cafés offer a fun vantage point from which to watch the Saint Germain crowd go by as you enjoy a beverage and rest weary feet.

RUE SAINT ANDRE DES ARTS. *Just east of the Rue de Buci, Metro: Odéon.*

This bustling street is lined with shops, small restaurants, and an artsy movie theatre. It is a fun way to get from the Rue de Buci to the Place Saint Michel. You can also take an interesting detour into the **Cour du Commerce Saint André** (heading east, on the right, shortly after you enter the street). This cobbled lane has welcomed pedestrians to its shops and restaurants for hundreds of years. It leads to the Carrefour de l'Odéon. On the right, you will see the Paris' oldest café, the Café Procope. Notice the portraits in the window. There's one you should recognize from American history books: Benjamin Franklin.

CARREFOUR DE L'ODEON. *Metro: Odéon.*

This lively intersection and square is filled with cafés and movie theaters. Towering over it all is a statue of Georges Jacques Danton, one of the leading figures of the French Revolution. Danton was a lawyer and brilliant public speaker who participated in the overthrow of King Louis XVI. Originally part of Revolutionary government, he ultimately fell into disfavor with the leaders of the Terror. Danton was accused of treason in 1794 and guillotined.

EGLISE SAINT SULPICE, *Place Saint Sulpice. Metro: Mabillon or Saint Sulpice. Open daily, 8am-7:30pm. Entrance is free.*

This church is tucked away between the Luxembourg Gardens, Carrefour de l'Odéon, and Place Saint Germain des Près. It is on a quiet square decorated with a large fountain. Topped with statues of four French bishops, the fountain's cascading waters add to the serene atmosphere of the Place Saint Sulpice. This area features an interesting mix of religious bookstores and boutiques featuring clothes by top French fashion designers like Yves Saint Laurent and Christian Lacroix.

The Eglise Saint Sulpice dominates the Place. It is named for a man who was bishop during the reign of the Merovingian king, Clotaire II in the 7th century. The outside of the church is odd and slightly out of proportion. This is largely due to the fact that it was built and rebuilt over the centuries, and combines a mish-mash of different architectural styles. The tower on the right was never completed.

The inside of Saint Sulpice is more interesting than the outside, and since the publication of Dan Brown's best-selling *The DaVinci Code* it has become a far more popular tourist destination. One of the scenes in that story takes place here in Saint Sulpice and has to do with a clue connected to the brass line, which you can see on the floor of the church leading to a white marble obelisk. It is a gnomon, a sort of sundial that indicates days of the year, instead of hours of the day. The gnomon was designed in 1744. If you look up at the stained glass windows above the meridian line, you can make out a circular hole in one of the windowpanes. On the stroke of noon, the light from the sun (provided it isn't cloudy) goes through the round hole in the window and lands on a point along the brass line. That point indicates the day's date. There is a special marble plaque indicating the spot where the light hits on the day of the Summer Solstice (June 21). Small brass plaques mark the Spring and Fall Equinoxes. On the day of the Winter Solstice (December 21) the sunlight hits a spot on the obelisk decorated with the Zodiac symbol, Capricorn. A Sagittarius symbol marks the date for November 21, and Aquarius marks the spot for January 21.

A small chapel (called Chapelle des Anges) on the right as you enter the Eglise Saint Sulpice features three famous paintings by Eugène Delacroix. One depicts the archangel Saint Michael fighting Lucifer. Another depicts the story of Heliodorus, ordered by the king of Syria to steal the treasure from a Temple. Heliodorus is chased out and attacked by three angels (one on a horse). They send him back to earth where he is swallowed up by darkness. The third painting shows Jacob wrestling with an angel sent by God, representing his struggle with accepting God's power. Jacob is injured in the leg, and he is renamed Israel.

The church's main organ is one of the largest in Paris. In a little side chapel, there is also a small organ that once belonged to Queen Marie-

Antoinette. Both Mozart and Glück played on it. The organ was sold after the queen was beheaded during the French Revolution, and later bought back by the church.

MARCHÉ DE SAINT GERMAIN DES PRÈS. *12, Rue Lobineau. Metro: Mabillon.*

This covered market once housed the Saint Germain Fair. Today it has food stalls and shops on the main level. There is a public swimming pool in the basement.

MUSÉE D'ORSAY. *1, Rue de la Légion d'Honneur (formerly Rue de Bellechasse). Metro: Solférino or Musée d'Orsay. Open 10 am-6 pm (winter), 9 am-6 pm (summer). Open until 9:45 pm on Thurs. Closed Mon. Adults: €7.50 (Sundays: €5). Kids under 18: free. Free to teachers, artists, museum employees, and journalists with presentation of professional card. Free to all on the first Sunday of each month. Audioguide rental: €5. Free children's guides, Carnet-Parcours-Jeunes, and family guide, Carnet-Parcours-Famille, are available at the entrance. Wheelchairs and strollers available free of charge.*

This magnificent museum began as a train station, known as the Gare d'Orsay. The station was built on top of the ruins of the Château d'Orsay which had been destroyed in 1871 during the Paris Commune uprising. It was inaugurated on 14 July 1900, just in time for the Paris Universal Exposition.

The Gare d'Orsay was one of the first train stations in Paris built for electric trains. It was very modern for its time, with electric elevators and more metal than was used in the construction of the Eiffel Tower. It was also very elegant and even contained a fancy hotel, which hosted wealthy passengers, banquets, and political meetings. For decades, the Gare d'Orsay was Paris' departure point for nearly 200 trains a day servicing southwestern France. However, as trains became longer, the station became to be too short to accommodate them. By 1939, the Gare d'Orsay no longer serviced passenger trains. During World War II, the station was used as a center for sending care packages to war prisoners. When the war was over, it became a triage center for returning prisoners.

The hotel was closed in 1973. In 1977, President Valéry Giscard d'Estaing signed an agreement to convert the old train station into a museum. The building was restored and remodeled. The Musée d'Orsay was opened to the public in 1986. You can still see the beautiful clocks of the train station on the outside of the building, along with the names of the French towns it formerly serviced.

Today the museum features a magnificent collection of art and architecture dating from 1848 to 1914.

You still get a feel for the beauty of the original train station as you walk in the central exhibition hall with its soaring ceiling. This area contains grand statues from the 19th century. Smaller exhibit halls on each side feature works by Ingres, Delacroix, Millet, Daumier, and Courbet. Towards the back of the main floor is an interesting wooden model of the Paris Opera and small scenes from famous operas. The upper levels feature small exhibit rooms that take you through late 19th and early 20th century painting. On the upper, Terrasse de Lille, there is a big, white statue of a polar bear that is always a hit with young children. In the exhibit galleries there are works by Dégas, Boudin, Cézanne, Renoir, Manet, and Monet. The galleries progress chronologically through the Impressionists to the post-Impressionists, such as Van Gogh, Toulouse Lautrec, and Bonnard.

The exhibit spaces in the back of the museum on the Seine side feature beautiful examples of Art Nouveau and Arts and Crafts style furniture and decorative arts. Keep going up the steps, they cover several floors. Believe it or not, many children really enjoy this section. It doesn't take much for them to imagine what it would be like to live with such cool furniture. Have them pick out their favorites. Don't miss the girl's bedroom designed by the Scottish Art Nouveau designer, Rene Macintosh. On our last visit, it made a young American girl stop dead in her tracks and cry out, "Wow! Dad! Look at that!" It's the kind of response that warms a museum-going parent's soul.

If you need a break during your visit, you can enjoy the Café des Hauteurs on the top level, which offers snacks and light meals with an impressive view of the back side of the building's giant clock – a remnant of its days as a train station. If your kids are up for a fancier setting, they might enjoy the museum restaurant, which offers a kids menu for lunch and teas and cakes for afternoon snack.

Fun Fact

During the **Great Flood of January 1910**, the water level of the Seine River rose 6 meters (20 feet) in just 10 days. It climbed 5 feet above the embankments of the river. The Gare d'Orsay was turned into a 2-block long swimming pool. Water poured into the station from its flooded, underground railway lines. The water level in the station rose so high it covered the smoke stacks of the train engines. When the flood waters inside the station reached the second floor, the force shattered the windows. Water spilled out of the Gare d'Orsay onto the streets below, further flooding the surrounding neighborhood.

Armies of engineers and volunteers managed to save the Louvre Museum, across the river, by constructing dikes. They used sand bags, cobble stones, mud, and wood floating down the Seine to hold back the flood waters.

Near the Musée d'Orsay, at 56, Rue Jacob is the former **Hotel York** mansion. This is the spot where Benjamin Franklin, John Jay, John Adams, and representatives from Britain and France signed the Paris Peace Treaty of September 3, 1783. It was this treaty that officially recognized American Independence from Britain.

DEYROLLE, *46, Rue du Bac. Metro: Bac. Open 10am-6:45pm, Mon-Sat. Closed Sun.*

This remarkable store is a big hit with kids. It is Paris' last taxidermy shop with animals ranging in size from insects to grizzly bears. There are also drawers filled with fossils and minerals. It is like walking into a natural history museum, except that you can actually purchase the displays. The shop adheres to strict rules regarding endangered species. The large animals come from zoos and farms where they died of natural causes. Deyrolle is the official supplier of specimens for France's National Education system. However, don't feel obliged to buy something. It's a great place just to observe and admire.

AU BON MARCHÉ DEPARTMENT STORE. *24, Rue de Sèvres (Metro: Sèvres-Babylone), Open Mon-Sat 9:30 am-7 pm.*

This is the world's first department store. When it was launched in 1876 by Aristide Boucicaut it was an instant success. The original building was designed by Gustave Eiffel (of Eiffel Tower fame) and Louis Charles Boileau. Today, the store has spread to more buildings, but remains a favorite place to shop. Don't miss the kids' section, called the **3 Hiboux**, in the basement that is full of toys, games, and crafts. There is also an excellent gourmet food store (La Grande Epicerie) on the ground floor.

INSTITUT DE FRANCE AND ACADEMIE FRANCAISE. *Place de l'Institut. Across the Pont des Arts from the Louvre, where the Rue de Seine meets the river.*

The Institut de France houses France's most illustrious scientific, artistic, and literary institutions. The first, the Académie Francaise was founded in 1635 to define and maintain the French language. At the time, there were many different dialects, spellings, and definitions of words in French. One of the Académie's first tasks was to produce a dictionary to standardize the language and make it more understandable to everyone. The Académie Francaise still produces a dictionary, even though people poke fun at the way it tries to preserve the French language from foreign intrusions, such "weekend" and "walkman." There are four other Académies, devoted to science, history, political science, and the arts.

Although the building is not open to visitors, try to catch a glimpse of one of its illustrious members. Known as Académiciens, they wear a fancy uniform that has not changed since the time of Napoleon Bonaparte. It comes complete with a Napoleonic hat, dress sword, and lots of gold embroideries.

MUSÉE DE LA MONNAIE (MUSEUM OF MONEY). *11, Quai de Conti. Metro: Pont Neuf. Open Tues-Fri, 11am-5:30pm and Sat-Sun, 12pm-5:30pm. Closed Mon. Adults: €3; Kids under 16: free. Free to all on the first Sun of the month. Entrance plus audioguide: €8. Special visits of the medallion workshops are organized on Wed and Fri at 2:15pm. A free guidebook "parcours-découvertes" for kids 7-12 is available at the entrance.*

If you traveling party contains any coin collectors or future financiers, this little museum is worth a detour. It's really very well done. The exhibits focus on the history of money from Antiquity to the Euro. You'll see how coins are made and get to see samples of rare coins and medallions.

PARIS CANAL BOAT RIDES. *By the Musée d'Orsay, on the Quai Anatole France. Metro: Solférino. Departs at 9:30am, daily, from late March to early November. Arrives at La Villette at 12:30pm. Adults: €16; Kids 12-25: €13; Kids 4-11: €9.*

This is a 3-hour canal boat ride that takes you along the Seine, to the Paris Marina, up through the Saint Martin Canal, and to the Parc de La Villette. You get wonderful views of major Paris sights, pass through numerous locks, under lovely foot bridges, and through a long tunnel under the Place de la Bastille. It's a unique way to experience Paris. For children who enjoy boats, it's a delightful tour, though it may be too long for small tikes. Don't forget to bring snacks or a full picnic. When you get to the Parc de la Villette, you can enjoy its wonderful science museum, museum of music, and playgrounds.

6. MONTPARNASSE

The **Montparnasse** neighborhood got its name from the 17th century students who moved here from Saint Germain des Près when Queen Margot (first wife of Henri IV) took over their favorite haunts there. There was a hill in the middle which they dubbed the Mont Parnassus – home of Apollo and the Muses in Greek mythology. After the Revolution of 1789, the area around today's Boulevard Montparnasse became a tax-free zone for wine and alcohol merchants. It thus attracted the establishment of numerous taverns and cabarets.

Whether it was the wine or the muses, Montparnasse became a beacon for artistic creativity. In the early 20th century a rich pool of artists and writers moved here to escape rising rents in Montmartre. People like Picasso, Léger, Modigiliani, Soutine, Chagall, and Man Ray rented art studios lining the side streets along the Boulevard Montparnasse, Boulevard Raspail, and Rue de la Tombe Issoire. Political refugees from Russia, including Vladimir Lenin and Leo Trotsky, would gather in the cafés along the Boulevard Montparnasse. They were joined by musicians such as Erik Satie and Stravinsky, as well as writers such as Appollinaire, Jean-Paul Sartre, and Simone de Beauvoir. After World War I, the so-called "lost generation" of American writers also settled around Montparnasse. These included Ernest Hemingway, Gertrude Stein, Alice B. Toklas, F. Scott Fitzgerald, Henri Miller, Anais Nin, and Ezra Pound.

Much of the area's Bohemian charm has been erased either through urban renewal projects in the 1970s or because of rising property prices in the city. But the old streets and sights have not all disappeared. And the kid-

Montparnasse Highlights

• Ride up to the top floor of the Tour Montparnasse
• Take in the kid-friendly brunch at the Hotel Meridien
• Check out the sea air in the Jardin Atlantique
• Eat a crêpe
• Visit the masses of bones in the Catacombs
• Play in the Parc Montsouris
• Climb on rocks and rent a remote control boat at the Parc Georges Brassens
• Shop for discount fashions in the Rue d'Alésia

friendly attractions of this neighborhood give you a chance to appreciate both the old and new aspects of this Mont-Parnassus, home of the Muses.

TOUR MONTPARNASSE. *Rue de l'Arrivée. Metro: Montparnasse-Bienvenue. Viewing galleries open 9:30am-10:30pm, Mon-Thur; 9:30am-11:00pm, Fri-Sun. Adults: €8.50, Kids: €5.80.*

Unlike many American cities, Paris does not have a skyline dotted with skyscrapers. But it does have the Tour Montparnasse. Completed in 1973, this is the tallest building in Europe. It has 59 stories. Many Parisians will tell you that the top of the Tour Montparnasse offers the best view in the city. Why? Because you can see everything but the tower itself, which they consider to be a terrible eyesore.

The view from the tower is spectacular. A 38 second elevator ride takes you up to an observation space on the 56th floor with a 360 degree view of the city. There is also a small museum, a movie that offers a bird's-eye view of Paris, and a snack bar. On the top floor, there is an open-air viewing deck. If you look southwards from the telescopes, you can even see planes taking off and landing from Orly Airport.

Most of the Tour Montparnasse is filled with offices. There is a shopping mall on the ground floor with several nice department and chain stores. There is a large, public, indoor swimming center on the lower level with pools for water lovers of all ages.

On the esplanade between the Tour Montparnasse and the Montparnasse Train Station there is an old-fashioned **carrousel** that runs just about every day of the year. In the winter the city installs a **skating rink** here as well.

HOTEL MERIDIEN-MONTPARNASSE FAMILY BRUNCH IN THE JUSTINE RESTAURANT. *19, Rue du Commandant Mouchotte.*

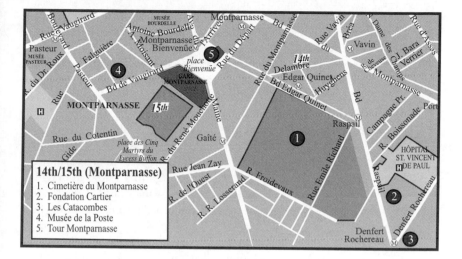

14th/15th (Montparnasse)
1. Cimetière du Montparnasse
2. Fondation Cartier
3. Les Catacombes
4. Musée de la Poste
5. Tour Montparnasse

Metro: Gaîté. Open daily for lunch, and Sundays 12pm-3:30pm for a special family brunch, Sept-Jun. Brunch: Adults: €46, Children 4-12 yrs: €23. Free for children under 4. During the week there is also a children's menu for €19.

This brunch is a favorite with French families. The all-you-can-eat buffet offers food to please both kids and adults. The dining room features a solarium that opens onto a garden. Each week offers a different theme with troops of adult clowns, dancers, and other fun makers who entertain your children with songs, games, face-painting, and other activities. Meanwhile you enjoy your meal and a break from childcare duties.

Parent Tip: The Tour Montparnasse is a great place from which to view the Bastille Day fireworks display if you have young children. It is far less crowded and harried than trying to make your way to the Eiffel Tower, where the show takes place. Beware, however, that spaces are limited. It is a good idea to get to the tower 1-2 hours before the time of the show (around 10pm, July 13).

CIMETIERE MONTPARNASSE. *3, Boulevard Edgar Quinet. Metro: Edgar Quinet or Raspail. Open daily, 9am-5:30pm.*

The best place to view this cemetery is from the top of the *Tour Montparnasse*. From the ground it is an austere place. In spite of its famous residents, it is hardly likely to excite young children. Among the luminary figures buried here are writers Charles Baudelaire, Guy de Maupassant, Jean-Paul Sartre, and Simone de Beauvoir; artists Camille Soutine, Antoine Bourdelle, Auguste Bartholdi (who designed the Statue of Liberty), Ossip Zadkine; actors Coluche and Jean Seberg; composer Camille de Saint Saëns (famous for his Carnival of the Animals); and car maker André Citroën.

SIDE STREETS AND ARTISTS' STUDIOS. *Neighborhood just north of Boulevard Montparnasse, and extending south of the Boulevard Raspail.*

the tall glass windows and skylights of artists' studios all around you. There are some lovely ones along the **Rue Nôtre Dame des Champs**, **Boulevard Raspail**, and **Boulevard Montparnasse**.

Also worth a visit is the **Rue Campagne Première**. At #9 is an impasse with numerous art studios. They were built with materials recuperated from pavilions that had been erected for the 1900 Paris Universal Exhibition. The American artist and photographer Man Ray lived up the street at #31, Rue Campagne Première. This building was also used to film the French New Wave Cinema Classic, *A Bout de Souffle* (Breathless). The young Italian painter Amadeo Modigliani lived nearby at #8 Rue de la Grande Chaumière. Down the street at #14, art students can still go to a studio to draw live models. At #100 in the nearby Rue d'Assas was the studio of the modern Russian sculptor Ossip Zadkine. It has been turned into an interesting little museum.

There is another small museum dedicated to the artists of Montparnasse at #21, Avenue du Maine in a building that once housed Russian artist Marie Vassilief's Art Academy. Many famous artists gathered here, including Picasso, Braque, Modigliani, Matisse, Zadkine, and Jean Cocteau.

Further to the south, at #101 Rue de la Tombe Issoire is the **Villa Seurat**. This little impasse features buildings constructed in the 1920s by avant-garde architects that were homes to many artists and writers.

Fun Fact

The **Rue de la Tombe Issoire** is named for a medieval tale that involves a giant and a hero. During the reign of King Louis I, Paris was under siege by the Saracen King Ysauré and his troops. According to legend, Ysauré offered to settle the battle in one-on-one combat with any fighter the French king had to offer. Ysauré was described as being 14 feet tall. Only the brave **Guillaume d'Orange** would take up the challenge. With some help from a dove and divine intervention, Guillaume slewe the Giant. Out of respect for the Saracen's courage, the King of France had him buried where he lay. The spot became known as Tombe d'Ysauré, ultimately changed to Tombe d'Issoire.

GARE MONTPARNASSE. *Place Bienvenue. Metro: Montparnasse-Bienvenue.*

This train station serves destinations to the west and southwest of Paris. These include Chartres, the Loire Valley, Brittany, Aquitaine, and Spain. Although the Gare Montparnasse was Paris' oldest train station, it was totally rebuilt after World War II, and then buried in modern buildings in the late 1960s.

The Gare Montparnasse is famous for two historic events. In August 1944, it was here that the German commander of Paris, General von Choltitz, surrendered to the French Army of Liberation led by General Leclerc. Paris was officially liberated from four years of German Occupation.

Fifty years earlier, the Gare Montparnasse was the sight of a freak train accident. On October 22, 1895, the brakes of an incoming train failed as it was pulling into the station. The train kept going, barreling beyond the tracks, into the station, and through its glass and iron facade. When the train finally stopped the locomotive and first wagon were left dangling over the sidewalk.

Today, the Gare Montparnasse is part of a modern complex. Inside the station are op-art murals by the artist Vasarely and a modern chapel built in 1969. Outside, you may notice plenty of crêpe restaurants. These are holdovers from the late 19th and early 20th centuries, when many people from Brittany (where crêpes are king) emigrated to Paris and set up shop near the station.

JARDIN ATLANTIQUE. *This park is just behind the Gare Montparnasse, but hard to find due to its elevated location several stories above street level. Entrances are located in the Gare Montparnasse and from elevators on Boulevard Vaugirard, Rue du Commandant Mouchotte, or Place des Cinq Martyrs du Lycée Buffon. Open sunrise to sunset. Entrance is free.*

This public garden was built over the roof that covers the high-speed train tracks of the Gare Montparnasse. Since many of the trains leaving the Gare Montparnasse lead to the Atlantic coast, the park was designed to elicit the beach and ocean. The lawns and benches look like waves. There are dunes and boardwalks. There are areas made to look like cliffs, boats, and sun decks. The tennis courts are blue like the ocean. There are even meteorological instruments to measure temperature, wind speed, and such. There is a playground on the southern corner of the park. The park contains a memorial museum dedicated to General Leclerc, commander of the Free French troops that liberated Paris from the Germans during World War II and to Jean Moulin, a leader of the French Resistance Movement who was killed by the Gestapo.

PASTEUR MUSEUM. *25, Rue du Docteur Roux. Metro: Pasteur. Open daily: 2pm-5:30pm. 45 minute guided tours. Adults: €2.50; Kids €1.50.*

Louis Pasteur (1822-1895) is considered by many to be the father of modern biology. His experiments showed that diseases were caused by tiny germs and did not occur spontaneously. He was the first to identify the bacteria and viruses that caused anthrax, potato blight, silkworm disease, and other human diseases. He introduced the process we call "pasteurization" – heating up perishable foods, such as milk, to kill germs without harming the food. Pasteur also introduced the first rabies inoculation, using a weakened form of the rabies virus to build up an immunity to the disease. There is a small museum dedicated to Pasteur and located in his former home and research lab. It is on the grounds of the Institut Pasteur, created to research and treat infectious diseases. It was here that researchers first discovered HIV virus that causes AIDS.

PLACE DENFERT ROCHEREAU. *Metro: Denfert Rochereau*

This square is named for Colonel Denfert-Rochereau who successfully defended the eastern French town of Belfort against Prussian attackers in 1871. Although the Prussians ultimately defeated the French and annexed the regions of Alsace and Lorraine, the town of Belfort remained a part of France. The sculpture in the middle of the Circle represents the Lion of Belfort and commemorates Denfert-Rochereau's victory. It is the work of Auguste Bartholdi – more well-known for designing one of France's most famous gifts to America, the Statue of Liberty.

CATACOMBES. *1, Place Denfert Rochereau (In a building on the SE side of the circle). Metro: Denfert Rochereau. Open Tues-Fri, 2pm-4pm; Sat-Sun, 9am-11am and 2pm-4pm. Closed Mon. Adults: €5; Kids 8-26: €2.50; Kids under 8: free. Note: This visit can be too scary for children under age 10. Also beware that you will exit several blocks south of where you entered. To return to Place Denfert Rochereau, take a right as you exit toward Avenue du General Leclerc. Take a right at the Avenue and continue several blocks north back to the Place.*

When the Romans occupied Paris (then known as Lutetia) they dug open-air rock quarries to supply stone for their roads and buildings. In the

Fun Facts

Over the years, the Paris quarry tunnels have served many purposes:
• In the late 1700s, merchants who wanted to avoid paying a tax at the city gates would sneak into Paris through secret tunnel entrances outside the city walls.
• In the early 1800s, some of the tunnels by the Rue de la Santé were found to provide a perfect environment for growing mushrooms. It was here that the popular Champignon de Paris (Paris mushroom) was developed.
• During the German Occupation of Paris in World War II, the Catacombs served as the headquarters for the French Resistance fighters.
• Today, criminals and daredevils still run through the old quarry tunnels and in and out of secret entrances. Some of them have become hopelessly lost in the unmarked tunnels. Maybe their bones have joined those in the Catacombs.

10th century, a new technique was developed for extracting rocks that involved digging the stone out from underground tunnels. Thick walls and pillars were left in place to keep the tunnels from collapsing. This went on for hundreds of years until there was a network of tunnels under the city that was over 300 kilometers (186 miles) long.

When the cemeteries in central Paris began to overflow, the decision was made to transfer their contents (more than 6 million skeletons) into some of the abandoned quarry tunnels. These became the Paris Catacombs. Today you can go through the old quarry tunnels to the Catacombs and see some of the millions of bones lined up along the walls and ceilings of the tunnels. Personally, I find it dank, dark, and creepy, but it's a big hit with many kids, especially fans of scary movies and the macabre.

RUE DAGUERR. *One block south of Place Denfert Rochereau, Metro: Denfert-Rochereau.*

This street is named for one of the fathers of photography, Louis Daguèrre. On its eastern end, near the Avenue du Général Leclerc, it is reserved for pedestrians and features a lovely open-air market.

PARC MONTSOURIS. *Between Boulevard Jourdan, Avenue Reuille, Rue Nansouty, and Rue Gazan. Metro: Porte d'Orléans or Cité Universitaire. Open sunrise to sunset. Entrance is free.*

This large park is located on the southern edge of Paris in what was once a small village, surrounded by windmill-covered hills. The area became known as Moque-souris (mock the mice) when the windmills were abandoned, leaving nothing for the mice to eat. Over time Moquesouris became Montsouris (Mount Mice). Until the 19th century, Montsouris was mainly a hangout for robbers. In the 1870s, Napoleon III transformed the land into a public park to serve the residents of southern Paris. The hills were covered with lawns, Lebanese cedars, Sequoias, Siberian Elms, and Chinese pines. An artificial lake was created in the middle of the park. On the day the park was inaugurated, the lake mysteriously emptied out. The engineer who designed it was so devastated that he killed himself.

The highest point in the park used to hold a building called the Palais Bardo. It had been made to look like a Moorish Palace and was donated to France by Tunisia for the Universal Exposition of 1867. The Palais Bardo was used as an observatory and weather station. It was destroyed by a fire in 1991, but is slated for renovation.

Today the Parc Montsouris offers pony rides, puppet shows, playgrounds, an area for roller blading, and summer concerts in the gazebo. It is famous for its wide variety of flowers. There is also a nice restaurant along the lake. On the western edge of the park there are many charming little streets with brightly colored houses and artist studios.

The **Paris Meridian Line**, which ultimately lost out to the Greenwich Meridian Line as the place from which we measure time and longitude, starts from a marker in the Parc Montsouris. You can follow the trace of the Paris Meridian by hunting for some of the 135 round copper plaques set in the ground along its path (though unfortunately many have been removed by vandals). They are the size of a CD and are stamped with the name Arago. These are memorials to François Arago, a 19th century astronomer and politician. The Meridian line runs north from the Parc Montsouris through the Paris Observatory, Luxembourg Gardens, and Palais Royal to Montmartre.

South of the park is the **Cité Universitaire**. This is a large campus of dormitory buildings and parks for students from all over the world. Many of the buildings are by famous modern architects and resemble architecture from the countries they represent, such as a Greek temple or Chinese pagoda.

RUE D'ALÉSIA. *Metro: Alésia.*

Are you traveling with a teenage girl? Do you have designer tastes in clothing but not the budget? If so, then the discount clothes stores along the Rue d'Alésia and Avenue du General Leclerc may be for you. Warning: they are chaotic, and you have to be a true bargain-hunter to find the treasures.

FONDATION CARTIER (CONTEMPORARY ART CENTER). *261, Boulevard Raspail. Metro: Raspail. Open Tues-Sun, 12pm-8pm. Closed Mon. Adults: €6.50, Children 10-18 yrs: €4.50, Under 10: free.*

This center features interesting and clever contemporary art exhibits that often appeal to children. The spot was long the site of Paris' American Center. The current building, owned by the Cartier Jewelers, was designed by architect Jean Nouvel and completed in 1994. It was constructed in such a way as to preserve a 200-year-old Lebanese Cedar, planted here by French writer and statesman, Châteaubriand. This tree is said to be the symbol of the Left Bank.

PARC GEORGES BRASSENS. *Rue des Morillons. Metro: Convention. Open daily, dawn to dusk. Entrance is free.*

Two majestic bronze bulls guard the entrance to the park, as a reminder that this was once the sight of one of Paris' slaughterhouses. Today, it is a great place for children to romp. There are playgrounds for all ages, including those with disabilities. There are puppet shows and a merry go round. There are beehives and a garden of scents. There are climbing walls made from stones recycled from old buildings. In warm weather, kids can rent remote-control boats to steer on the park's central pond, while adults can laze in the sun on rented lounge chairs.

One section of the park has been planted with Pinot Noir grape vines, harkening back to the neighborhood's pre-slaughterhouse days when it was covered with vineyards. The grapes are harvested each year and produce over 200 bottles of Clos de Morillons wine.

One of the park pavilions hosts a used book sale, including children's books, that takes place every Saturday and Sunday.

Near the Parc Georges Brassens at #2 Passage Dantzig (Metro: Convention) is an interesting building called La Rûche (the bee hive) designed by Gustave Eiffel, of Eiffel Tower fame. It was originally made as a wine pavilion to be part of the Universal Exposition of 1900. It was moved here by a wealthy sculptor and supporter of the arts. He rented it out as studio space for many starving artists, including Matisse, Chagall, Brancusi, Soutine, and Modigliani.

7. EIFFEL TOWER

This is simply a must-see! No trip to Paris with kids is complete without a visit to the Eiffel Tower.

EIFFEL TOWER. *On the Champs de Mars. Metro: Bir Hakeim. Open daily, 9 am-midnight (last elevator goes up at 11 pm, the stairs close at 6 pm). Rates: Kids under age 3 are free. Elevator to the first level-Adults: €4.10/ Children under 12: €2.30. Stairs to levels one and two-Adults: €3.80/Anyone under 25: €3. Elevator to level 2 - Adults: €7.20/Children under 12: €4.20. Elevator to level 3 - Adults: €11/Children under 12: €6.*

Note: To avoid long ticket lines during high tourist seasons visit the tower early in the morning or in the evening. Caught midday in a long line? Don't worry. It's better organized than it looks, and the lines actually move fairly quickly. If your family is active and adventuresome, the line to walk up the stairs is usually considerably shorter than the one for the elevators.

Kids love the Eiffel Tower, and who can blame them? It's big, it's cool, and seen from up close it's surprisingly beautiful. Here's how it works. The Eiffel Tower has three levels. You can take the elevator or walk up the stairs as far as the 2nd level. You must ride a special elevator to reach the 3rd level. One option is to ride the elevator up and take the stairs down from the first or second level. This offers an amazing view of the inner structure of the tower and you can take a break by reading some of the historical interest markers along the way. However, this route is not recommended for very small children or for people with vertigo.

The tower contains a small museum, a replica of Gustave Eiffel's office, a small movie theater, and a post office (mail your postcards from here and they will have a special Eiffel Tower cancellation stamp). In winter, the

Eiffel Tower Highlights

- Ride the elevators to the top of the Tower
- Take the stairs down at least one level to see the tower from the inside
- Send a postcard from the Tower's post office
- Have a meal at Altitude 95
- Go on a bike tour from the Champs de Mars
- Go on a boat tour down the Seine
- Look for the Statue of Liberty

Eiffel Tower has resurrected an old tradition of having an **ice-skating rink** on the platform of the first level. There is no extra fee to go skating and they will lend you a pair of skates free of charge. There are two restaurants: the very expensive **Jules Verne**, and the family-friendly **Altitude 95,** which offers a kid's menu, a great view, and an experience kids won't forget. You can make a lunch or dinner reservation at the Altitude 95 kiosk under the tower on the east side; by phoning ahead 01 45 55 20 04; or sending an email to: *altitude-95.rv@elior.com.*

The Eiffel Tower was built to celebrate the 1889 Paris International Exhibition, and the 100th anniversary of the French Revolution. It was designed by **Gustave Eiffel**, an architect/engineer who had already built bridges, buildings, and the interior support skeleton for the Statue of Liberty. Although it is the city's most popular landmark today, many people hated the tower when it was first built. A group of leading artists, writers, and politicians sent an editorial to a major newspaper decrying the project, saying that the tower design looked like a gigantic factory chimney.

Mr. Eiffel's tower design was part of an international competition for a commemorative tower. His was picked from more than 700 entries. Some of the losing projects included a tower with sprinklers that could be turned on in hot weather, and another shaped like a tall guillotine.

Construction of the Eiffel Tower took two years. The day it was finished, March 31, 1889, Gustave Eiffel climbed up the 1,710 steps to the top and hung a French flag. Until the Chrysler Tower was built in New York City (1930), the Eiffel Tower was the tallest building in the world.

Over time, people have tried many **stunts** from the Eiffel Tower:

1912: An Austrian tailor tried to jump from the Eiffel Tower in a homemade parachute suit. He crashed and died.

1923: Journalist, Pierre Labrie, rode a bicycle down the steps from the first level.

1925: Andre Citroën, the car manufacturer, spent 2.5 million francs to have his name written down the tower in lights, plunging his company further into bankruptcy.

1926: A young pilot tried to fly his plane under the tower, but crashed and died.

1928: A man trying out a new kind of parachute jumped from the tower to his death. The parachute never opened.

1948: Bouglione, the founder of a famous circus, coaxed an elephant up the stairs to the first level.

1949: Acrobat, Pierre Dubois, climbed up the outside of the tower to the first level. Six years later, acrobat, Alfred Thomanel, made it to the second level.

1987: Two college students rode their mountain bikes up the steps to the second level of the tower, without stopping or touching the ground with their feet.

1987: A young man from New Zealand bungee jumped off the second level of the tower.

1989: A tightrope walker crossed on a high wire from the Trocadero to the Eiffel Tower to celebrate the bicentennial of the French Revolution.

Originally, each level of the Eiffel Tower was painted a different color, ranging from dark bronze at the bottom to a golden yellow on top. Today it is all one color: light brown. The tower is repainted every 7 years. It takes 25 painters, 40 tons of paint, and nearly a year to finish the job.

In 1909, there was talk of tearing down the Eiffel Tower. Then it was discovered to be an ideal spot for a radio-telegraph center. During World War I, the tower housed a military spy center that tracked down enemy agents. The most famous of them was a woman known as Mata Hari, accused of spying for Germany. Ironically, Mata Hari was a familiar face at the Eiffel Tower. Prior to the war, she had been a dancer in the tower's first floor restaurant. After the Liberation of Paris in World War II, there was a nightclub on the Eiffel Tower where American soldiers were welcomed free of charge.

Today, the Eiffel Tower is used by numerous TV and radio stations to emit their signals. It also holds a weather station and devices to measure the city's air quality.

The Eiffel Tower is 320 meters (984 feet) tall. In hot weather it can increase by as much as 6 inches in height due to the expansion of the metal. The Eiffel Tower contains 15,000 pieces of metal and 2.5 million metal rivets. It weighs 9 million kilos (7,000 tons). On a clear day, you can see as far as the Chartres Cathedral (more than 50 miles away) from the top level. On a stormy day, there's a good chance the tower will be struck by lightening. It averages 50 lightening strikes each year.

Fun Fact

Paris hosted five **International Exhibitions** in 1855, 1867, 1889, 1900, and 1937. Each was a spectacular event, featuring special buildings, bridges, moving sidewalks, ferris wheels, and pavilions built just for the event. Some of the landmarks left over from these exhibitions include the Eiffel Tower, Grand and Petit Palais, Pont Alexandre III, Trocadero Museums, Palais de Tokyo (Modern Art Museum), Gare d'Orsay (now Musee d'Orsay) and the first metro line. Many modern items and conveniences that we take for granted were first introduced at the Paris Exhibitions. The saxophone and the sewing machine were presented at the 1855 Expo for the first time. Outdoor electric lighting made its debut at the 1878 event. The first gas-powered car was on show at the 1889 Exhibition. The one in 1900 featured some of the first motion pictures. Pablo Picasso's famous painting of a massacre in the town of Guernica, Spain was first exhibited at the Paris Expo of 1937.

CHAMPS DE MARS. *Metro: Bir Hakeim or Ecole Militaire. RER: Champs de Mars. Open day and night.*

When the Gauls were defending Paris (then known as Lutetia) against the Roman invaders in 50 BC, this was the spot where they made their final stand. The Gaul's lost the battle. The area became known as the Champs de Mars (Fields of Mars), after the Roman god of war.

When the **Ecole Militaire** (Military Academy) was built in 1751 at the southern end of the Champs de Mars, the fields were used for military drills and exercises. In the 1780s, this area also became the testing ground for some of the worlds' first hot-air balloon rides. After the French Revolution, the Champs de Mars became the sight of two gigantic parties. The first, on July 14, 1790, celebrated the one-year anniversary of the storming of the Bastille Prison. Over 300,000 people attended. However, the next year's party turned violent. Some of the revolutionaries clashed with the national guards. The guards shot into the crowd and killed dozens of people.

During the 1840s, a horse racing track was built on the Champs de Mars. The races became very popular. Eventually, they became so crowded that the city decided to build a new, bigger track in the Bois de Boulogne. The Champs de Mars course was torn down. In the 1860s, the Champs de Mars was again filled with people as the sight where Paris hosted a series of International Expositions.

In contrast to its bellicose origins, today the Champs de Mars features a Wall of Peace, a modern structure with transparent panels, where people can leave their messages about peace. It also is a favorite spot for skate boarders and roller bladers.

In addition, this is where the American-owned **Fat Tire's Bike Tours** meet, near the southeast pillar of the Eiffel Tower for bike and segway tours of major city sights. (Look for the flag.) There are 3-4 hour bike tours of the city, led by English-speaking guides. The pace is leisurely with time for photos and snacks. Kids are welcome. The tours stick to sidewalks, trails, and parks. You can rent bikes for men, women, and kids at the shop. They also rent helmets, child carriers, and trailers. Tours leave at 11 am and 3:30 pm May-August, and 11 am in September. Segway Tours, using those funny self-propelled scooter-link things, start at 10:30 am, last 4-5 hours, and are reserved for small groups with one guide. Call or visit the Website for details. The store is located at 24, Rue Edgar Faure, Metro: Dupleix (3 blocks south and west of the Eiffel Tower), Tel. 01-56-58-10-54. Email: info@FatTireBikeToursParis.com Website: www.fattirebiketoursparis.com/bikes/about-fat-tire/index.shtml.

BATEAUX PARISIENS TOUR BOATS. *Port de la Bourdonnais, at the foot of the Eiffel Tower, Metro:Bir Hakeim. Daily departures every 30 minutes, 10am-11pm. Price: Adults €9.50; Kids under 12 €4.50. Kid-friendly cruises depart at 1:45 pm and 3:45 pm, Saturday and Sunday. Try also* **BATEAU VEDETTES DE PARIS TOUR BOATS.** *Port de Suffren (Metro: Bir Hakeim) Hourly rides, 11 am-6pm. Adults €9; Kids under 12 €4. Special kid cruises on Wed, 10:30 am and 2:45 pm.*

Kids love these boat cruises. It's a great way to see many of the major sights and monuments of Paris, especially if you are jet-lagged or foot sore. The vantage point is unique. The commentaries are in English and French. The regular tour lasts 60 minutes.

Fun Fact

The **Statue of Liberty** in New York was a gift from France to the United States. It was designed by a young sculptor named **Auguste Bartholdi**. He called on Gustave Eiffel to help design the internal support structure. Bartholdi began the statue in 1874. It arrived in New York in 1885 in pieces that filled 214 packing crates. It was officially inaugurated on October 28, 1886. At the time, the Statue of Liberty was the tallest (305 feet) building in New York City. You can see a **full-size replica** of the statue's flame by the **Pont de l'Alma**, and a full-scale model of her thumb at the Musée des Arts et Métiers. There are smaller versions of the Statue on the Isle aux Cignes (upstream from the Eiffel Tower) and on the western side of the Luxembourg Gardens. By the way, do you know why the Statue of Liberty is green? The exterior was made of copper to reduce weight. (She still weighs 225 tons.)

ALLEE DES CYGNES. *Island on the Seine between Pont de Grenelle and Pont de Bir Hakeim. Metro: Bir Hakeim.*

This island is named for the swans (cygnes) stocked here during the reign of King Louis XIV. By day it is a tranquil, green space free of cars and filled with joggers and strollers. After dark it becomes more seedy. At the eastern-most tip of this island you can see a small replica of the State of Liberty that stands in New York Harbor. The statue faces east, towards the United States. The best view of this statue is from a tour boat.

PARIS SEWER TOUR AND MUSEUM. *93, Quai d'Orsay. By the Pont de l'Alma. Metro: Alma-Marceau. Open Sat-Wed, 11am-5pm (May-Sept), 11am-4pm (Oct-Apr). Closed Thur and Fri. Beware: the last tickets are sold one hour before closing time. Closed during heavy rains. Adults: €4, Children under 12: €3.*

Kids (and many adults) really enjoy and remember this unique visit. It's very well organized, with an introductory video/museum, followed by a tour led by a member of the Paris sewer system. You'll see the machinery and methods used to maintain the system. It's actually not as smelly or claustrophobic as you might imagine and offers a fascinating glimpse at the underside and mechanics of the city.

Here is some history to get you started: In 1200, King Philippe Auguste created an early version of the Paris sewers. He paved many streets, leaving a trench in the middle to evacuate sewage and water. Six-hundred-fifty years later, during Baron Haussman's huge urban renewal effort, the city dug nearly 600 kilometers (540 miles) of underground sewage tunnels. Today, there are about 2,200 kilometers (1,400 miles) of them. They run directly under every Paris street, with wider tunnels for broader avenues. Each tunnel is named for the street above it, so that anyone with a road map of Paris can find his or her way. The sewer workers are sometimes called "Master Fifi"s after a nickname for 19th century toilets. They use boats and special wagons to clean and repair the tunnels.

ECOLE MILITAIRE (MILITARY ACADEMY) *1, Place Joffre (Metro: Ecole Militaire). Not open to the public.*

On the southern edge of the Champs de Mars you can't but notice the large buildings that make up France's Military Academy. Today it houses two schools, the Ecole Supérièure de Guèrre (War College) and Institut des Hautes Etudes de Défense Nationale (National Defense University).

Although you can't visit the building, you may be interested in its history. The Military Academy was set up in 1751 by King Louis XV. It was his mistress, Madame de Pompadour who talked him into it. She suggested that he found a military academy for young men who were from noble families but had no money. It was a way of recognizing that many members of the French nobility had lost their fortunes serving their country in military campaigns. Each year, 500 young men were admitted for a three-year curriculum that trained them to be military officers. They performed military drills in the Champs de Mars. Many important military leaders graduated from the Ecole Militaire, including Napoleon Bonaparte.

Fun Fact

To cover the costs of building the Military Academy, the King levied a tax on the sale of playing cards. He also set up a special lottery jackpot.

8. LES INVALIDES

The Invalides complex was built in 1670 by King Louis XIV as a home for wounded war veterans. It follows the plans of a Roman military camp. There are straight alleys, squares, and lawns. The buildings on the eastern side were restored during the early 20th century, and still serve as a home for disabled veterans.

NAPOLEON'S TOMB IN THE EGLISE DU DOME. *Invalides complex. 129, Rue de Grenelle. Métro: Invalides, Latour-Maubourg, or Varenne. Combined ticket for tomb, Musée de l'Armée, and Musée des Plans Reliefs. Adults: €7; Kids 12-18: €5; Kids under 12: free.*

The large, golden-domed church in the middle of the Invalides complex was built by Louis XIV. It is dedicated to King Louis IX (known as Saint Louis). He is shown in a painting under the dome holding a sword out to Christ. In 1989, to honor the bicentennial of the French Revolution, the Church underwent a huge renovation. Over 500,000 pieces of gold leaf (weighing 12.64 kilos or 28 pounds) were used to restore the dome. The four statues decorating the top of the Dôme were replaced. They represent Hope, Charity, Spirituality, and Religion.

Two of the Invalides' architects, Liberal Bruant and Jules Hardouin Mansart, are buried in the church. So is Marshall Foch, who commanded the allied French, British, and American troops at the end of World War I. But the most famous tomb in the church belongs to Napoleon I.

Who was Napoleon I? Napoleon Bonaparte was born on the island of Corsica. He did not learn to speak French until he was sent off to military school on the mainland. After leading successful military campaigns in Italy, he was elected First Consul of the Republic in 1799. Napoleon established

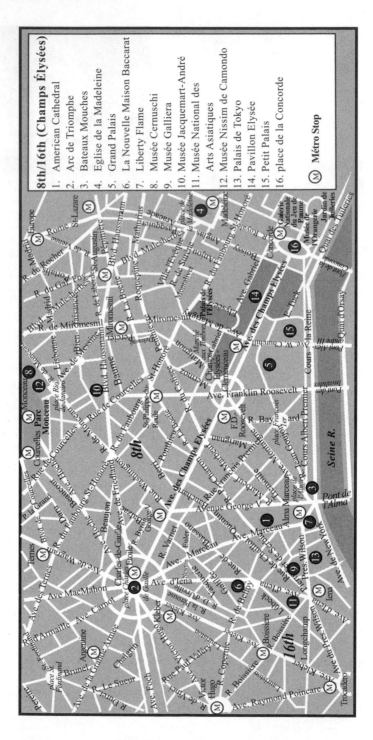

8th/16th (Champs Élysées)

1. American Cathedral
2. Arc de Triomphe
3. Bateaux Mouches
4. Eglise de la Madeleine
5. Grand Palais
6. La Nouvelle Maison Baccarat
7. Liberty Flame
8. Musée Cernuschi
9. Musée Galliera
10. Musée Jacquemart-André
11. Musée National des Arts Asiatiques
12. Musée Nissim de Camondo
13. Palais de Tokyo
14. Pavillon Elysée
15. Petit Palais
16. place de la Concorde

Ⓜ Métro Stop

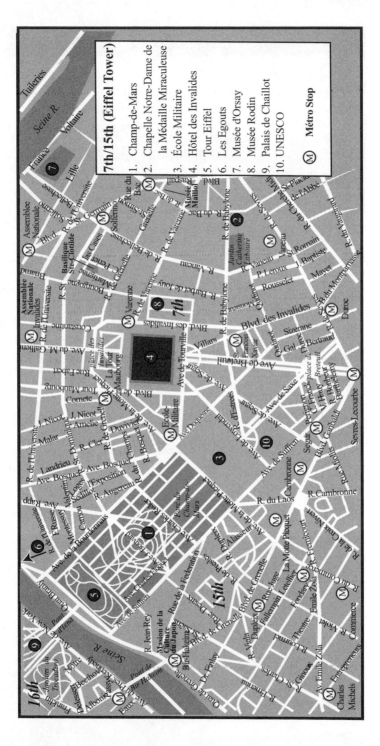

7th/15th (Eiffel Tower)

1. Champ-de-Mars
2. Chapelle Notre-Dame de la Médaille Miraculeuse
3. École Militaire
4. Hôtel des Invalides
5. Tour Eiffel
6. Les Egouts
7. Musée d'Orsay
8. Musée Rodin
9. Palais de Chaillot
10. UNESCO

Ⓜ **Métro Stop**

Les Invalides Highlights

* See Napoleon's tomb
* Pick out your favorite suit of armor, find Napoleon's horse, and check out the WWII exhibit at the Military Museum
* See the 17th century wooden models of towns, bridges, and defense towers at the Musée des Plans Reliefs
* Admire the statues and have lunch in the gardens of the Rodin Museum
* Find the movie theater made to look like a Japanese pagoda

a new constitution for France, a new code of laws, a national education system, and reformed the judicial system. He created the nation's leading universities and Academies of Art, Science, Literature, and Engineering. In 1802, Napoleon was elected Consul for life, and in 1804 declared himself Emperor. He conquered most of Europe, except Britain. In 1805, he began to suffer military defeats. In 1812 he lost 4/5 of his men in the frozen Russian winter. In 1814, he was forced from power and sent into exile on the Italian island of Elba. Napoleon returned to power in 1815, only to be forced from power once again after his military defeat at Waterloo. He was exiled to Saint Helena, an island in the south Atlantic, where he died.

In 1840, twenty years after his death, Napoleon's remains were returned to the Invalides with great pomp and circumstance. Tens of thousands of people lined the streets to watch the funeral procession.

Napoleon's remains are contained inside an enormous granite sarcophagus. It was a gift from Tsar Nicholas I of Russia, which is ironic since it was Napoleon's unsuccessful attempt to take over Russia that began his downfall. Within the sarcophagus there are 6 coffins, nestled one inside the other like Russian dolls. They are made of iron, wood, lead, lead, ebony, and oak.

Side chapels in the Eglise du Dôme contain the remains of Napoleon's brothers, Joseph and Jerome, and his son, Napoleon II. The adjacent Saint Louis church contains a collection of flags that were captured from the enemy during Napoleon's many military campaigns.

MUSÉE DE L'ARMEE (MILITARY MUSEUM). *In the Invalides complex. 129, Rue de Grenelle Métro: Invalides, Latour-Maubourg, or Varenne. Open daily 10am-5pm (winter), 10am-6pm (summer). Combined ticket for tomb, Musée de l'Armée, and Musée des Plans Reliefs. Adults: €7; Kids 12-18: €5; Kids under 12: free. Note: Due to continued updating of the museum, parts may be under construction when you visit.*

This Military Museum features exhibits ranging from prehistoric battles to 20th Century World Wars. It is quite interesting, even if you are not a military history buff. The ground floor is filled with suits of armor. The upper floors feature exhibits on the Napoleonic wars, including a display of Napoleon's horse, Vizir. There is a section dedicated to World War I, with lots of (fairly boring) maps and uniforms – the most touching is one from a man in the trenches that is caked with mud.

However, the best part of the museum is its newly renovated section dedicated to World War II. Both children and adults will be moved by its exhibits (conveniently labeled in both English and French) especially if any of your relatives were at all connected to that war. The rooms not only show artifacts and films about the fighting and military strategy. They also offer glimpses into the war's effect on ordinary people, including children. The exhibit is organized chronologically and gives a good view of just how many countries and people were affected by WWII.

MUSEE DES PLANS RELIEFS. *In the Invalides complex. 129, Rue de Grenelle. Métro: Invalides, Latour-Maubourg, or Varenne. Open daily 10am-5pm (winter), 10am-6pm (summer). Combined ticket for tomb, Musée de l'Armée, and Musée des Plans Reliefs. Adults: €7; Kids 12-18: €5; Kids under 12: free.*

If you or your kids are at all interested in models, you'll love the Musée des Plans Reliefs. It presents a collection of made-to-scale wooden models of fortresses, ports, and towns prepared for King Louis XIV as part of his strategic defense plans. They were so important that their existence was kept secret for many years.

Parent Tip: The cafeteria in the Invalides complex is pretty Spartan and crowded. If you are visiting during late spring or summer, you may want to head instead to the nearby Musée Rodin gardens for lunch or a snack. There you can enjoy your food in a quiet garden with famous sculptures and plenty of room for kids to move around.

MUSEE RODIN. *77, Rue de Varenne (Metro: Varenne), not far from the Invalides. Open Tues-Sun, 9:30 am - 5:45 pm (April-September) and 9:30 am - 4:45 pm (October-March). Closed Mondays. There is a nice, outdoor café, open during spring and summer. Adults: €5 for museum and gardens or €1 for tour of only the gardens; Kids under 18: free. Free to all on the first Sunday of each month.*

This is really a gem of a museum. It is small and surrounded by a lovely garden filled with some of Rodin's most famous sculptures. There is plenty of outdoor space for children to run around. Just remind them not to touch the sculptures. The museum has collections of drawings and sculptures by Rodin, his pal Vincent Van Gogh, and his girlfriend/partner Camille Claudel. You can visit both the museum and gardens, or opt for just a tour of the gardens.

The museum is located in a house where Rodin lived and worked. The house was built in the 18th century, and had previously belonged to the Austrian poet and writer Rainer Maria Rilke. It was used for a time as a girls' boarding school. When Rodin lived there, the building actually belonged to the French government. Rodin made a deal. He promised to donate his major art pieces to the government after his death in exchange for free housing.

Some of the major sculptures you'll see include:

The Gate of Hell: This elaborate, bronze doorway is based on the *Inferno,* a long poem by the Italian writer, Dante. It depicts characters from the poem including *Ugolino* – a crawling man imprisoned for treason and forced to starve to death with his children and grandchildren; *Paolo and Francesca* – caught in the act of kissing and killed by Francesca's husband; *Adam and Eve* – banned from Paradise; and other tortured souls trying to climb their way out of the deepest depths of Hell. Rodin worked on this piece for 20 years. It was commissioned to decorate a Museum of Decorative Arts that was never built (on the site that now houses the Musée d'Orsay).

The Thinker: This large, seated man with his head on one hand is one of Rodin's most famous sculptures. He originally designed it as a small statue for his Gate of Hell, and later turned it into a large statue. It is a portrait of Dante.

The Kiss: Rodin's most popular sculpture was originally a small piece designed for the Gate of Hell. It depicts the two lovers, Paolo and Francesca, shortly before they are discovered and stabbed by her husband.

The Burghers of Calais: This group of six figures commemorates a real story from 1347. Calais, a town on the northern coast of France, had been under siege by the English for nearly a year. To save the town from starvation, the six leading men in the town offered their lives to the English king, Edward III, in exchange for the safety of their townsfolk. The English king accepted, but his wife, Queen Phillippa, was so moved by the burghers' sacrifice that she talked the king into sparing their lives.

Statue of Honoré de Balzac: Rodin's portrait of the famous French author/playwright was commissioned by the Society of Literary Men, led by author Emile Zola. Rodin tried different versions, finally depicting Balzac as

Fun Fact

Rodin used the same model (a poor, ragged man who hauled coal for a living) for his sculptures of John the Baptist, one of the Burghers of Calais, one of the damned souls of the Gate of Hell, and his Man with a Broken Nose.

a forceful figure wrapped in a great robe. In the end, however, the statue became tangled in larger artistic and political controversies. Emile Zola, who supported the statue, also took public stands in favor of Alfred Dreyfus (a Jewish military man who had been falsely accused of treason, largely because of anti-Jewish sentiment). Members of the Literary Society who disagreed with Zola, got back at him by refusing to accept Rodin's sculpture.

LA PAGODE MOVIE HOUSE. *57 Bis, Rue de Babylone, Metro: Saint Francois Xavier*

This was originally a private house built in 1895 to look like a real Japanese pagoda. The proprietor was Aristide Boucicault, owner of the *Bon Marché* Department Store, who built this house for his wife. It was turned into a movie theater in 1931. By the year 2000, La Pagode was in such disrepair that the city forced the theater to close down. It has recently been renovated and features a nice Tea Room and Japanese Garden.

9. LES HALLES

Author Emile Zola called Les Halles the Belly of Paris. If other neighborhoods were the spiritual, intellectual, or fashion centers of the city, this was where the serious work of feeding the city took place. Les Halles was for centuries Paris' central marketplace – the realm of butchers and fishmongers.

Today the area has been transformed by modern art and architecture. Urban renewal efforts in the 1970s-80s replaced empty lots and ramshackle buildings with shiny glass and metal constructions. Entire areas have been turned into pedestrian zones, filled with shops, cafés, and art galleries. While you may argue about the architectural merits of these new constructions, your children will enjoy the car-free environment and numerous treats that await them in the belly of the beast that is Paris.

LES HALLES. *Metro: Les Halles.*

From the time of the Romans until 1969, Les Halles was Paris' central marketplace. It began as a Roman Agora, built on the major north-south road through the city. In 1183, King Philippe Auguste built two buildings for the market. They were called, "Les Halles."

During medieval times, the public pillory was placed at Les Halles where it was sure to attract plenty of attention. People condemned for petty crimes had to place their heads and hands in the pillory's holes for 3 hours a day, over a period of three days. Thus they were subjected to public taunts and humiliations. The pillory was removed after the Revolution.

In 1854, Napoleon III hired an architect named Baltard to design 12 pavilion buildings for the market. They were constructed of green metal and glass and became known as Pavillons Baltard. They housed the city's

Les Halles Area Highlights

- Play in the Jardin des Enfants des Halles, reserved just for kids
- Find the giant sculpture of a head tilted on its side
- Pick out your lunch in the Montorgeuil market street
- Go to a wooden toy workshop
- Watch the jugglers and other street performers in front of the Pompidou Center
- Check out the Stravinsky Fountain
- Look for gargoyles on the Eglise Saint Mérri
- Ride up the glass escalators in the Pompidou Center and check out its museum
- Find the Defenseur du Temps (Defender of Time) Clock

wholesale market for meat, fish, fruits and vegetables, and the like. Restaurants and bars developed around the site to cater to the Halles workers, who would eat onion soup or pigs' feet in the early hours of the morning.

By 1969, the wholesale market had outgrown the space at Les Halles. It was moved to the southern suburb of Rungis, near the Orly Airport. The attractive Pavillons Baltard buildings were torn down. Les Halles remained an empty pit for a dozen years, although many of the surrounding restaurants survived. In the 1980s, the hole was redeveloped as the Forum des Halles. It features a large shopping center, movie theater, and metro complex in three underground levels. The **Forum des Créateurs** section is reserved for young clothing designers. There is also an indoor pool called the **Piscine des Halles -Suzanne Berlioux** on the lowest level. It features palm trees and cacti, bringing a touch of the exotic to the center of Paris. (Porte Sainte Eustache, 10, Place de la Rotonde, Level -3; Metro: Les Halles).

Above ground, there is a big **merry-go-round** overlooking the Forum. It is the oldest one in Paris and has been in operation since 1872. It is open daily from 11 am to 8 pm.

The area west of the Forum has been made into a big park. There are walkways, fountains, playgrounds, lawns, and big wide areas well suited for roller blading or tossing a Frisbee. This is also where you will find a large sculpture of a tilted head and hand by artist Henri de Miller that often fascinates small children. The contrast between its modern style and the Gothic Church of Saint Eustache behind it makes for interesting photo opportunities. To the left is a giant sundial. It's curved edges make it popular with roller bladers and skate boarders.

Fun Fact

On the westernmost edge of the Les Halles Park is a column (in front of the round building that houses Paris' commodities market). Known as the **Astrology Column**, it is all that remains of a palace built on this site by Queen Catherine de Médici. She and her royal astrologer used to walk up to the top to view the stars and read her future.

JARDIN DES ENFANTS AUX HALLES. *105, Rue Rambuteau, on the northern side of Les Halles. Reserved for kids ages 7 to 11 years. Hours vary but generally run from 10am-12pm, 2pm-6pm. Cost: €0.5 per child for a 1-hour session.*

This wonderful Children's Garden is reserved for kids ages 7 to 12. Adults are not allowed inside. Instead they drop off their children for a one-hour session. (We recommend sitting in a cafe in the nearby Rue Montorgeuiland watching the people go by, if you don't know what to do with yourself.) There are gardens, tunnels, mazes, an artificial volcano, play spaces, and other fun activities. The park is staffed by friendly counselors who supervise group games and individual play. Even if your children do not understand French, they will figure out how to have fun.

EGLISE SAINT EUSTACHE. *Rue du Jour and Rue Rambuteau. Metro: Les Halles.*

This church combines Gothic architecture (note the flying buttresses) with Renaissance decorations (such as Corinthian columns). It is mainly appreciated for its music and wonderful acoustics. Both Franz Liszt and Hector Berlioz debuted some of their works here. The church choir is excellent and not to be missed on Christmas Eve. The 8,000 pipe organ is magnificent. There are free recitals every Sunday afternoon at 5:30 pm.

RUE MONTORGUEIL MARKET DISTRICT. *North of Les Halles. Metro: Les Halles or Etienne Marcel.*

This neighborhood is filled with pedestrian shopping streets. There is an open-air market in the Rue Montorgueil every day but Monday. It's a great place to pick up a picnic or snack. There are also excellent food shops and restaurants, some of which harken back to the days when Les Halles really represented the Belly of Paris. Children enjoy checking out the old shop signs that line the streets. Don't miss the giant golden snail above the Escargot Restaurant. There is a lovely **covered passageway** connecting the Rue Montorgueil and Rue Saint Denis called the Passage du Cerf. Rue Saint Denis is seedier, hearkening back to the underbelly of Paris, and its oldest profession.

FASHION DISTRICT. *Between the Forum des Halles and the Place des Victoires, mainly along the Rue du Jour and Rue Etienne Marcel. Metro: Les Halles or Etienne Marcel.*

If you enjoy names such as Kenzo, Agnes B., Comme des Garcons, Cacharel, Thierry Mugler, or Junko Shimada, you'll want to take a stroll up the Rue du Jour and along the Rue Etienne Marcel to the Place des Victoires. Note the building at #4 Rue du Jour which used to house a great fencing academy in the 17th century. The Place des Victoires is named for the King Louis XIV's military victories. That's him sitting atop the horse in the middle of the square.

WOODEN TOY WORKSHOP. *3, Rue des Prouvaires, between Rue Saint Honore and Rue Berger, south of the Les Halles Park, Metro: Les Halles or Louvre. Children's workshops on Saturdays, from 2-6 pm. Phone: 01 40 41 07 21.*

Mr. André Desmoulins loves children and wooden toys. He will show them how he makes wooden toys, especially on his favorite theme: the circus. On Saturdays children can help paint and assemble toys, by special reservation.

PLACE DES INNOCENTS. *Along Rue Berger, Between Les Halles and Pompidou Center. Metro: Les Halles.*

From the 1st century BC when the Romans occupied Paris to the late 1700s, this spot housed Paris' **central cemetery**. At its peak, it was the last resting place for half of the city's residents. So many bodies were piled up here over the years that by 1780 the level of the cemetery was 2.5 meters (over 8 feet) higher than the street level. The walls around it started collapsing and skeletons began to invade nearby cellars and streets. The local residents, who had been complaining that the cemetery was overcrowded for 200 years, finally had the satisfaction of seeing it closed. The skeletons were dug up and transferred to the vast underground tunnels in southern Paris that had once been used as rock quarries. Today, you can visit some of those tunnels at the Paris Catacombs.

In spite of all the buried bodies, the cemetery was a popular meeting place. There were shops, public scribes (who would write letters for people who didn't know how to read or write), painters, and beggars who would make fires out of old bones to keep themselves warm. When the cemetery was closed, the place was transformed into a market square.

The fountain that stands in the middle of the square today was originally built against a nearby church (now gone) called Eglise des Saints Innocents. The church was named for the biblical story of the innocent babies killed by King Herod after the birth of Jesus. The fountain's artist, Jean Goujon, was a Huguenot who managed to escape the Saint Bartholomew's Day massacre. It is the only remaining Renaissance style fountain in Paris. You can tell that a fourth side was added to the fountain when it was moved to the market square.

The Eglise des Saints Innocents was famous for having a set of little rooms called retiroirs. These were places where some women chose to live, secluded from the rest of the world. They were actually walled in, unable to come out for years at a time. There was only a small opening where passers-by could leave food or water. Occasionally, women were imprisoned there not by choice but as punishment.

Today, the Place des Innocents is filled with tourists and passers-by and lined with hip shops and cafes.

Gory Fact

Who were the **Huguenots?** They were French Protestants who followed the teachings of religious reformers Martin Luther and John Calvin starting in the 1500s. Numerous intellectuals, merchants, and nobles became Huguenots. They were widely persecuted by the Catholics (more than 3,000 were killed in 1572 in Paris during the Saint Bartholomew's Day massacre). Killings on both sides set off a **War of Religion** that lasted through most of the 16th century. It was brought to an end when King Henri IV, a Huguenot, converted to Catholicism and instituted laws of religious toleration. He rebuilt and unified the country, but was assassinated (in the nearby Rue de la Ferronerie) by a fanatical monk.

POMPIDOU CENTER. *Rue Saint Martin and Place Georges Pompidou Open daily except Tues, 11am-10pm. Metro: Rambuteau or Châtelet/Les Halles. Family-centered visits on Sundays, 1-5pm called Un Dimanche en Famille, include a tour of the museum and art projects for the whole family (in French). Cost: 3.80 E/person.*

In the 1960s, the Beaubourg neighborhood of Paris was dirty and dilapidated. President Georges Pompidou, a great fan of modern art, launched a program to build a contemporary center for the arts and culture and revitalize the neighborhood. A team of Italian and British architects, Renzo Piano and Richard Rogers, scandalized many people by putting together a multicolored, modern, monstrosity of a building, right in the heart of historical Paris. Their idea was to turn the building inside-out. All the parts that are usually hidden, such as water pipes and electrical supply systems, were not only exposed on the outside but also painted bright colors. Other parts were made to be transparent, including the snake-like escalator on the front of the building.

Although many people still think of the Pompidou Center (more commonly called Beaubourg by Parisians) as an eyesore, it has continually drawn huge crowds. In fact, it was so popular during its first 20 years of operation that it was wearing out at twice the expected rate. As a result, the

Center was closed for a few years in the late 1990s for a full face-lift and renovation.

Today, part of the Pompidou Center's charm begins before you even enter the building. There are all kinds of street musicians and performers on the wide plateau in front of the building. The plateau also houses the

Atelier Brancusi, which is a reconstruction of this modern sculptor's art studio. More than 140 of his works are on exhibit, along with drawings and photographs. The entrance is next to a giant, golden flower pot.

Don't miss the wonderful **Stravinsky Fountain** on the south side of the Pompidou Center. It depicts scenes from this modern composer's works, such as the *Sacre du Printemps* (Rights of Spring), *Oiseau de Feu* (Firebird), and *Ragtime*. The brightly colored pieces are by an artist named Niki de Saint-Phalle, and the black ones are by sculptor Jean Tinguely. They spin and spit water to the delight of children and adults alike.

The pedestrian square surrounding the fountain is a great place to relax, let children run, or enjoy a meal at the nearby restaurants and cafés. The red-brick building you can see by the fountain is a center for contemporary music, called **IRCAM**. This center often presents contemporary music concerts. There are 2 computers in the lobby on which kids can play musical games.

Once you get inside the Pompidou Center, one of the funnest treats for kids is riding up the transparent escalators and watching the people below become smaller and smaller. (Note: Although this ride used to be free, there is talk of imposing a nominal fee.) There is a great view of the city once you reach the top. You may want to grab a snack at the top-floor restaurant. Don't let its hip design by Philip Starck dissuade you. It's quite family-friendly.

MUSEE NATIONAL D'ART MODERNE. *Entrance on level 4 of the Pompidou Center. Open daily except Tues, 11am-9pm. Purchase tickets on the ground level. Adults: 7 E ; Kids under 18: free.*

This museum has an important collection of modern and contemporary art. The modern collection (on level 5) has works by the greats, such as Matisse, Leger, Picasso, Rouault, Delaunay, Kandinsky, and Calder. There is a whole section dedicated to Dada and Surrealism, including a reproduction of Andre Bretons' studio. The contemporary section (level 4) is filled with things to interest young children. Here they will find all sorts of wild and wacky paintings and sculptures. There is a reconstructed shop covered with recycled bits turned into art. There are wonderful models of futuristic buildings designed in the mid-20th century. There are examples of Op-Art. It's a good reminder for children that art can be fun and does not need to be intimidating.

The Pompidou Center also presents large temporary exhibits on the mezzanine level and level 6. There is a public library on levels 1-3 that is very popular with French students and Americans on their Junior Year Abroad. The ground level houses a special children's discovery space. This should be kid-friendly, but the exhibits have a tendency to be so overly intellectual that they are incomprehensible.

QUARTIER DE L'HORLOGE. *Just north of the Pompidou Center, between Rue Rambuteau, Rue Saint Martin, and Rue de Beaubourg. Metro: Rambuteau.*

This modern neighborhood was built as part of the urban renewal efforts of the 1980s. Its most interesting feature is the **Defenseur du Temps** (Defender of Time) – a mechanical clock built in 1979. It depicts a continual battle between the Defender of Time and the natural elements, including a phoenix (representing air), a crab (representing water), and a dragon (representing land).

EGLISE SAINT MERRI. *76, Rue de la Verrerie. Metro: Châtelet.*

The Eglise Saint Mérri is named for a 9th century Abbot named Mérri from the town of Autun. He gave up life in the abbey to live in a hut in Paris, near this church. His one companion was another monk named Frodulf – whose name some say was the inspiration for J.R.R. Tolkien's character Frodo, the hero of the *Lord of the Rings*.

This large, flamboyant Gothic-style church has wonderful gargoyles, an impressive interior with 16th century stained glass windows, a wooden organ loft, and a 13th century bell (thought to be the oldest in Paris). It was built with similar proportions to those of the Nôtre Dame Cathedral, and was called for a time Nôtre Dame la Petite (the Little Nôtre Dame). The composer Saint-Saëns (who wrote the Carnival of the Animals) played the organ here, which dates from the 17th century. There are free concerts on weekends.

PLACE DU CHATELET. *Metro: Châtelet.*

The Place du Châtelet now houses the **Théâtre Musical** and the **Théâtre de la Ville**, founded by world-famous actress Sarah Bernhardt.

But it wasn't always home to such high class entertainment. For hundreds of years this spot housed numerous thieves and murderers held in the Châtelet Prison. There were also people who were not considered criminals, but were in prison because they could not pay their debts. The debtors were considered "honest prisoners" and treated relatively well, especially if they could pay for their food and lodging. In contrast, criminals

---

Fun Fact

The name Châtelet means **little castle**. So the Grand Châtelet was the Big Little Castle and the Petit Châtelet was the Small Little Castle.

Many of the prisoners held in the Grand Châtelet were awaiting trial. They were held, interrogated, and tried in different parts of the building. The interrogations generally took the form of torture, which became increasingly nasty if the interrogators were not satisfied with the prisoner's answers. The use of torture was finally outlawed in 1780.

---

were treated very cruelly. Torture was common, and they were fed only bread and water. Some were thrown into the oubliettes – special underground cells that were dark, wet, and where prisoners were soon forgotten (oublier means to forget).

The **Châtelet Prison** was originally built in 1130. It was the larger of two defensive castles (called Grand Châtelet and Petit Châtelet) built on either side of the bridge connecting the Ile de Cité with either bank of the Seine River. In 1190, King Philippe-Auguste built a defensive wall around his city. The Châtelets were no longer part of the mainline defense for the city, so the Grand Châtelet was turned into a prison and city hall.

The **Grand Châtelet** also housed the city morgue. This is where the unidentified bodies of people who died in the streets or in the river were brought. Those that were not claimed or identified were buried in the city's central cemetery, Cimetière des Innocents. The name "morgue" came from morguer, meaning to look at something carefully.

In front of the Grand Châtelet was a bustling market square. From 1133 until 1416, it included a large butcher shop, called the Grande Boucherie. The butchers' guild paid to build a church called Saint Jacques de la Boucherie. Most of it was destroyed during the French Revolution, but you can still see the gothic-style tower from the church known as the Tour Saint Jacques next to the Place du Châtelet.

The Châtelet Prison was torn down in the early 1800s. The fountain in the middle of the Place was built in 1808 to commemorate Napoleon I's victorious campaign in Egypt. In the 1860s, during Baron Haussman's massive urban renewal projects, two theaters were built on the square, the Théâtre de la Ville and Théâtre Musical. The Théâtre de la Ville was made famous by actress Sarah Bernhardt, whose dressing room has been preserved. It features contemporary dance and theater productions. The Théâtre Musical offers a wide variety of musical productions, ranging from opera to jazz, ballet, and world music.

10. LOUVRE

The **Louvre** and **Tuileries gardens** can be very intimidating. The sheer size of the place (the Louvre is the biggest museum in the world) can be a real turnoff for children. The formal layout of the buildings and gardens can feel cold and hostile. Yet, there is much here to delight even the most flat-footed museum goers. All it takes is a little planning, and knowledge of a few fun facts and good tips.

LOUVRE MUSEUM. *99, Rue de Rivoli and 34-36, Quai du Louvre. Metro: Louvre or Palais Royal. Open daily (except Tue), 9am-6pm (until 9:45pm Wed). Closed Tues. Adults: €8.50. On Wed, Thurs entrance is €6 for adults after 6pm. Kids under 18: free. Free to teachers with ID, to people with disabilities and their companions. Free to everyone after 3 pm, and all day on the first Sunday of each month. Audioguide rental: €3. Excellent guidebooks are available in English for kids and adults in the museum bookstore. Free strollers and wheelchairs are available from the information desk under the Pyramid. Note: Hang on to your entry tickets and you will be able to enter and exit the museum all day.*

Note: Lines to enter the glass pyramid at the Louvre entrance can be very long and hot in the summer. It's a little faster if you enter through the shopping mall, from the steps leading underground by the Arc du Carrousel or via the metro entrance. However, even this method leads to long security and ticket lines inside. The quickest way to enter the Louvre and avoid lines is to use the little-known Porte des Lions entrance. This is in the Southwest wing of the Louvre, along the Seine, nearly level with the Arch du Carrousel. Look for the (female) lions on either side of the entrance.

Louvre Area Highlights

- Go on a treasure hunt for your favorite Louvre masterpieces
- Visit the old moat and walls of the medieval Louvre
- Check out the underground shopping mall and US-style food court in the Grand Louvre
- Have lunch on the Louvre's open-air terrace or in an open-air café in the Tuileries
- Stand in the alignment of the Louvre pyramid and Concorde obelisk and check out the views
- Rent a toy sailboat at the central fountain in the Tuileries
- Try out the Ferris wheel and other rides in the Fête des Tuileries
- Admire elegant fashions through the ages at the Musée de la Mode
- Buy an English-language book at W.H. Smith or Brentanos
- Have tea at Angélinas
- Visit Paris' biggest toy store, Au Nain Bleu
- Play among the Colonnes Buren in the Palais Royal gardens and look for its cannon
- See Monet's water lilies in the Orangerie Museum
- Visit the Samaritaine department store and have dinner in the top floor restaurant, Toupary.
- Look at the pet stores along Quai de la Mégisserie
- Draw a picture from the Pont des Arts.

To avoid crowds inside, you may want to consider visiting the museum in the late afternoon between 4 and 6 pm or on Wednesday evenings when it's open until 9:45 pm.

The Louvre's history stretches back 800 years. It was first a fort, then a fortified castle, a luxurious palace, and finally a world-famous museum. The first Louvre was built in 1200 by King Philippe Auguste. It consisted of a large, fortified tower built along the city walls at their most vulnerable point: the city's western edge. The purpose of this fort was to help protect Paris from the invading English Plantagenets, led by Richard the Lionheart. The early Louvre fortress also was used as a prison, an arsenal to store weapons, and place to safeguard royal treasures.

In 1360, King Charles V transformed the Louvre into a fortified castle with turrets and protective walls. It was occupied by the English for 16 years during the 100 years war with England. In the 1500s, King Francois I rebuilt the Louvre as a Renaissance Palace. His son, Henri II expanded it further, and Henri's wife, Catherine de Médicis added the Tuileries Palace (later destroyed). King Henri IV added the long galleries along the Seine.

In the 1670s, King Louis XIV moved his royal court to Versailles and abandoned the Louvre. In his absence, numerous artists, writers, philosophers, and men of science moved in. Part of the building was made into a museum to show off the royal art collections. Many of the artists living in the Louvre also exhibited their works in the arcades along the ground level at a Fair known as the Foire aux Croutes. (Croute means a crust of bread and is slang for crummy art).

In 1789, King Louis XVI was forced by the revolutionaries to leave the Palace of Versailles and move back to the Louvre. He tried to escape Paris in 1791 with his family, but they were caught and imprisoned. From 1792 to 1793, a guillotine was set up in the middle of the Place du Carrousel. The king was beheaded, and a new museum was officially inaugurated in the Louvre. When Napoleon I (Bonaparte) took over power, he moved into the Louvre and undertook further expansions and renovations. He also kicked out the last of the artists still living in the building, but added many works of art to the museum that he had brought back from his numerous military campaigns. Napoleon III (Louis Napoleon) also expanded the Louvre. You can still visit some of the lavish rooms from that period on the northern side of the museum.

Through the late 19th and most of the 20th centuries, the Louvre remained largely unchanged, serving as a major museum and housing government offices. In 1980, President François Mitterand launched a huge project to renovate and expand the Louvre. Architect I.M. Pei designed the glass pyramid and underground shopping galleries. The exhibit halls were renovated, and excavations on the eastern side uncovered remnants of the early medieval fortress that was once the original Louvre building.

Plan of attack: The Louvre is a huge museum, and is best digested in bite-sized pieces. Here are a few suggestions:

• Pick up several copies of the detailed museum map (available in English) when you purchase your tickets. You will notice that it features photographs of some of the Louvre's most famous pieces, such as the Mona Lisa, Victory of Samothrace, winged bulls of Mesopotamia, statue of Ramses II, or Gericault's Raft of the Medusa. Let each member of the family pick out several things they want to see and go on a treasure hunt.

• Begin your visit at the gift or postcard shop near the glass pyramid. Have your kids pick out a souvenir or set of postcards that

---

Fun Fact

The Louvre's **Glass Pyramid** is:
• Made of 118 glass triangles and 675 diamond shaped pieces of glass.
• Cleaned by window washers who use mountain-climbing gear (ropes, harnesses, pulleys).
• 21 meters high, and weighs 180 tons.
• Lit at night by 966 projectors.

can serve for the basis of a treasure hunt through the museum.

• Begin with the CyberLouvre in the Carrousel shopping mall. Here you can surf the Louvre's website or look at CDs of the collections to plot out your visit.

• Follow a literary lead. There are children's guidebooks to the Louvre available in English and French in the children's section of the museum's bookshop. Examples include: *Let's Visit the Louvre*, *Louvre First Visit*, *Chercheurs d'Art*, *Voyage au Coeur du Louvre*.

Still having trouble choosing? Here are some **highlights** from different sections of the museum:

Mesopotamia (Richelieu Wing, ground floor): There are two immense bulls with human heads that once guarded the Palace of Sargon, built in 720 BC. Notice that from the front they have two feet, from the side they have four, and if you look from an angle there are five!

Persia (Sully Wing, ground floor): Check out the magnificent tile friezes. One depicts archers and the other a griffin. They are from the palace of the great Persian King Darius, defeated by Alexander the Great in the 5th century BC. Darius' palace also had 72 columns, 21 meters (70 feet) high, topped with two bulls. Two are displayed. Imagine how a whole palace full would have looked.

Egypt (Sully Wing, ground and first floors): The Egyptian galleries have recently been redone and take you through different aspects of ancient Egyptian life like food, music, and religion. There are lots of mummies and sarcophagi, even mummies of animals. There are also many small objects from daily life. You will see many statues of Egyptian gods. The large red granite sculpture of a sphinx from Tanis guards one of the few American-style drinking fountains in all of Paris. There is a colossal statue of Akhenaton, the renegade pharaoh who believed in only one god and had his artist depict him and his wife Nefertiti in a realistic style (almond-shaped eyes, wide lips, big bellies and hips).

Ancient Greece (Sully Wing, ground floor, lower level, and first floor): There are many wonderful Greek sculptures and vases. The most famous statues are the Venus de Milo, still beautiful even though she's missing her arms, and the dramatic Victory of Samothrace. This statue has lost her head, has wings for arms, and has folds in her clothing that seem to be moving in spite of being made of stone. It was built to celebrate a Greek victory on the island of Rhodes and originally stood on a great rock overlooking the sea.

Ancient Rome (Denon Wing, ground floor): You'll see beautiful Roman mosaics and remarkable paintings saved from the walls of villas around Pompeii. They were buried in the ash of the Mount Vesuvius volcano when it erupted suddenly in 79 AD. There are also lovely funeral sculptures.

Medieval period (Sully Wing, lower level): The most fascinating section is the underground exhibit of the medieval Louvre itself, discovered in the 1990s during the museum's renovation. It shows the foundations of the castle, moat, and protective walls built by King Philippe Auguste in 1200. You'll also see a collection of objects that were found during the archeological excavation of the fortress, including a gold helmet belonging to King Charles VI that was thrown into a well by robbers.

Renaissance (Denon Wing, first floor and Richelieu Wing, first floor): The most famous work in this section is Leonardo da Vinci's **Mona Lisa** (or *Joconde* as she's known in French because she was married to a man named Giocondo). There are also many other famous paintings by da Vinci, Raphael, Michelangelo, Donatello, Boticelli, Bellini, and Titian. Don't miss the funny portraits of the four seasons by Giuseppe Archimbaldo (gallery 5). The faces are composed of seasonal fruits and vegetables.

Fun Facts about Mona Lisa

• Notice her famous smile? The mouth is closed. Showing your teeth was considered vulgar in her day. Most people's teeth were rotten and ugly anyway.
• Da Vinci painted this portrait in Italy, but liked it so much he brought it with him when King Francois Ist invited him to live in France.
• The painting is in a special, bullet-proof case to ward off thieves. It was stolen in 1911 and only recovered two years later.

19th century paintings (Denon Wing, first floor and Sully Wing 2nd floor): There are several huge paintings that often captivate children here. Look for the giant paintings of Napoleon I by Jacques Louis David, including the one in which he is crowning his wife, Josephine. Another classic favorite is the Raft of the Medusa by Gericault. This large painting is based on a true story of a shipwreck that left 150 men drifting on a raft for 13 days. Only 15 survived starvation, madness, and cannibalism. Notice, too, Eugene Delacroix's painting of Liberty Guiding the People. It has become a symbol of France. The painting does not actually depict the 1789 Revolution, but rather another popular rebellion in 1830.

Napoleon III's apartments (Richelieu Wing, first floor): These are preserved to reflect the rich gold and red velvet decor of this period. Here you really get a sense for what the Louvre was like as a palace.

TUILERIES GARDENS. *Between Rue de Rivoli and Seine River. Metro: Tuileries, Louvre, or Place de la Concorde. Open daily, sunrise to sunset. Entrance: Free.*

Stretched between the Louvre Museum and the Place de la Concorde is the lovely esplanade of the Tuileries Gardens. If you stroll along the middle lane of the gardens you can see the Glass Pyramid of the Louvre through the Arc du Carrousel in one direction. Then turn and look at the Obelisk in the Place de la Concorde. Notice how it is aligned with the Champs Elysées, Arch de Triomphe, and beyond that the Grande Arche de la Defense 10 kilometers (6 miles) away. The photo opportunities abound.

The name for this garden comes from the French word for roof tiles, tuiles. Before the area became part of the Louvre Palace domain, it housed a roof tile factory, a tuilerie. In the late 1500s, Queen Catherine de Medicis built herself a residence called Tuileries Palace. It was destroyed by fire in 1871, but used to stand in what is now the open section between the two longest wings of the Louvre.

The formal gardens were designed later by Louis XIV's favorite landscape architect, André Le Nôtre. He is also the one who designed the gardens at Versailles and Vaux le Vicomte. Louis XIV also added a large theater inside the Tuileries Palace, called the Salle des Machines,

> **Fun Fact**
>
> If you look carefully at the gates between the Tuileries Gardens and the Rue de Rivoli, you can find a rebus in French of the street's name. It goes like this: Riz (rice) + Veau (calf) + Lit (bed) = Rivoli.

that became the city's first public playhouse. The palace contained a concert hall where Mozart debuted two of his symphonies.

On the eastern edge of the Tuileries, standing like an entrance gate to the park, is the Arc du Carrousel. This triumphal arch was built in an imitation Roman style by Napoleon I to celebrate his military victories. You can see him on top, dressed as a Roman emperor. The golden horses pulling his chariot were stolen from Saint Mark's Cathedral in Venice, during one of Napoleon's Italian campaigns. It was an old tradition: the Venetians had stolen the horses centuries earlier from the city of Constantinople (now known as Istanbul, Turkey).

The Tuileries Gardens are great place to relax after a walk through the Louvre or down the Champs Elysées. There are playgrounds, pony rides, and miniature sailboats for rent at the main fountain. There are also several good cafés in the park between the Louvre and the Place de la Concorde, where you can grab a meal or a snack on a nice day. If you are in Paris during the summer or Christmas holidays, check out the Fête des Tuileries. It includes

Fun Fact

Why is there a **Place du Carrousel**? The first carrousels were brought back to Europe from the Middle East by the crusaders. They consisted of a game where two horsemen tried to spear a ring with their lance while riding at full gallop. Then in the 1680s, the game was changed to riding on wooden horses hanging around a center pole and trying to spear the rings outside of the circle. At first it was reserved for nobles and knights, but soon it became popular with women, children, and the general public.

Some stories say that the Place du Carrousel was named for a merry-go-round built in 1662 to celebrate the birth of Louis XIV's son. Another version claims that the square was named for military parades held here that featured members of the cavalry riding their horses in a circular formation, like a carrousel.

Either way, if you are in Paris over the winter or summer holidays, check out the Tuileries Fair. It has lots of fun amusement rides and a fancy carrousel that you can try out for yourself.

fair rides and games for all ages. A ride up the central Ferris wheel offers one of the best views of Paris.

PASSERELLE SOLFERINO. *Bridge connecting the Tuileries Gardens on the Right Bank with the Musée d'Orsay on the Right Bank.*

This pedestrian bridge was completed in 1999 to offer direct access between the Tuileries and Musée d'Orsay. However, it was quickly discovered to pose two dangers: 1) it became very slippery anytime it rained and 2) it vibrated unpleasantly whenever it was crowded. The bridge was quickly closed and repaired, so now you can enjoy it in complete safety.

ORANGERIE DES TUILERIES. *Place de la Concorde, Jardin des Tuileries. Metro: Concorde. Open daily except Tues, 10am-5pm. Closed Tues. Adults €4. Kids under 19 free. Note: the museum is undergoing renovations through May 2006.*

This former greenhouse is now a modern art museum. New renovations should make it more user friendly than ever. If you are not up to facing the crowds in the more popular Musée d'Orsay across the river, the Orangerie is an excellent alternative. It is rarely crowded and features beautiful impressionist and modern paintings by artists such as Renoir, Cezanne, and Picasso. Its most spectacular exhibit includes eight enormous water lily paintings by Claude Monet. They fill nearly 360 degrees of one room. You may recognize them from the book, *Linnea in Monet's Garden*.

JEU DE PAUME MUSEUM, *1, Place de la Concorde. Metro: Concorde. Open Tues, 12pm-9:30pm; Wed-Fri, 12pm-7pm; Sat-Sun, 10am-7pm. Closed Mon. Entrance fees vary according to the exhibits but generally run around €6 for adults. Kids are free.*

This museum features temporary exhibits of modern and contemporary art.

It is housed in a former Jeu de Paume court of the Tuileries Palace. **Jeu de Paume** was an early form of tennis popular during the Renaissance. It could be played indoors or out. It was a favorite game among nobles and courtesans. In the late 1500s, Paris had over 250 Jeu de Paume courts. The courts were made of stone tiles. The ball was made of leather. Originally, the players hit the ball with the palm of their hand, hence the name (jeu=game, paume=palm of the hand). Later, rackets were introduced into the game. Before starting the play, the server would call out "tenez" (meaning, "here you go"). Scholars believe this is the origin of the name tennis.

Some kings paid dearly for their love of Jeu de Paume. In 1316, King Louis X is said to have gulped down so much water after playing a heated match that he was struck by a fever and died. In 1498, King Charles VIII left a match at the Château d'Amboise, hit his head in a doorway, and died.

RUE DE RIVOLI. *Located along the northern edge of the Tuileries and Louvre. Metro: Concordes, Tuileries, Louvre, or Chatelet.*

The name of this road comes from a place in Italy where Napoleon I defeated the Austrians. The Rue de Rivoli features fancy antique galleries, tourist shops, and three excellent addresses:

• **Galignani Bookseller**, 224, Rue de Rivoli. Metro: Tuileries. Open 10am-7pm. Closed Sun. This is France's oldest English-language bookshop. It offers an excellent selection of books for both children and adults.

• **WH Smith**, 248, Rue de Rivoli. Metro: Tuileries or Concorde. Open Mon-Sat, 9:30am-7pm, Sun, 1pm-7pm. This is part of a major English chain of bookstores. There is a large children's section upstairs.

• **Angélina**, 226, Rue de Rivoli. Metro: Tuileries. Open daily, 9am-7pm. This is a very fancy tea room, known for its unctuous hot chocolate. It's an unforgettable treat for the well-behaved child.

MUSEE DE LA MODE, MUSEE DE LA PUBLICITE, MUSEE DES ARTS DECORATIFS. *105-111, Rue de Rivoli. Metro: Palais Royal or Louvre. Open Tues-Fri, 11am-6pm (Wed until 9pm); Sat-Sun, 10am-6pm. Closed Mon. One combined ticket allows access to all three of these museums. There are children's programs in French every day during the summer at 10am and 2pm. Adult: €6. Children under 18: Free.*

Note: As of the writing of this book these museums were undergoing renovations and only offering temporary exhibits.

These museums are lodged in the northern wing of the Louvre. They are small and treat topics that appeal easily to children.

The Musée de la Mode features clothes fashions through the ages, from the Renaissance to Sci-Fi-looking futuristic styles. Our sons were interested in spite of themselves, particularly when they reached the section on the evolution of military uniforms.

The Musée de la Publicité has some wonderful old advertisement posters from the 19th and 20th centuries. You've seen their reproductions in poster and tourist shops. Many are full of charm and humor. There are also old television ads displayed on video screens that will make you laugh even if you don't understand a word of French.

The Musée des Arts Décoratifs features every day objects, such as toys, dishes, and furniture from the 13th century to today.

EGLISE DE LA MADELEINE. *Place de la Madeleine. Metro: Madeleine. Open Mon-Sat, 7:30am-7pm; Sun, 9am-1pm and 3:30pm-7pm.*

Although it looks like a Greek temple, the Madeleine is actually a Catholic church dedicated to Mary-Magdalene, one of Jesus' most faithful followers. It was started in 1764 during the reign of King Louis XV. The church was built facing north-south, rather than the traditional east-west design, so that it would add a nice finishing touch to the Rue Royale from the Place de la Concorde. An early plan called for a church shaped like a cross and topped with a dome. However, when Napoleon I came to power, he declared that it should be a Temple to the Glory of his Grand Army. Thus it was built to look like a Greek temple, with 52 Corinthian style columns, and no obvious signs of its role as a church. The inside does look more religious.

Funeral services were held here for **Josephine Baker** (1906-1975), the famous American dancer who moved to France because she felt there was less racial prejudice against blacks (and who joined the French Resistance during World War II). More than 20,000 people attended her funeral and she was honored with a 21-gun salute – the first American woman to be buried with French military honors. Her grave is in Monaco.

PLACE DE LA MADELEINE. *Metro: Madeleine*

This square is famous for its flower market and fancy food stores, such as Fauchon, Héliard, and our favorite, the Grey Poupon mustard shop. It is also the sight of Paris' most attractive public rest rooms and shoeshine shop. They are underground by the flower market. They were built in the early 1900s in the Art Nouveau style, reflected in the tiles, floors, and restroom doors. Check them out. Opposite the church is a kiosk where you can get half-price theater and concert tickets on the day of performance.

The Passage de la Madeleine, is located between the Place de la Madeleine and Rue Boissy d'Anglas. It features pretty, luxury boutiques.

From late morning through early afternoon, you can explore the Marché de la Madeleine, between Rue Tronchet and Rue de Castellane. It

Fun Fact

Aspiring young chefs take note. The Ritz Hotel offers **special cooking classes for kids** on Wednesday afternoons (when French children are off from school). Called the **Ateliers Petits Marmitons**, they take children ages 6-12 through an unforgettable culinary experience. (In French.) There is also a group called **Les Toques Juniors** for teenagers. Kids are dressed in full chef regalia and shown how to create a meal for four that they get to take home. Each child receives a souvenir photo and a recipe book. Classes meet once a month and last 2 1/2 hours. Cost: €80 per child. Ritz Hotel, 38, Rue Cambon. Metro: Concorde or Madeleine. Tel. 01 43 16 30 50; www.ritzparis.com. Kids also can learn to **make a fancy dessert** at the Ecole Lenôtre, Pavillon Elysée-Lenôtre, 10, Avenue des Champs Elysées. Metro: Champs Elysées, Tel. 01 42 65 85 10. Cost €38.

has fun, ethnic restaurants from all over the world. Share large tables and benches with the locals for a nice lunch experience.

AUX TROIS QUARTIERS, *17, Boulevard de la Madeleine (Metro: Madeleine), Open Mon-Sat 9:30 am-7 pm.*

Founded in 1829, this department store now also doubles as a shopping mall.

PLACE VENDOME. *Metro Madeleine or Tuileries.*

The posh Place Vendôme is a center for luxury shops and hotels. It was originally called the Place des Conquètes (Place of the Conquests), then renamed Place Louis-le-Grand for King Louis XIV. His statue stood in the middle of the square until 1792, when it was toppled by a revolutionary crowd. Legend has it that one woman, wanting to see the action up close, was smashed by the falling statue and killed. The revolutionaries erected a new statue dedicated to Liberty. In the late 1790s, the square was renamed Place Vendôme for a nearby mansion. In 1806, Napoleon I decided to erect a new monument in the Place to celebrate his victorious battle at Austerlitz. He chose a column, copied from the famous Column of Trajan in Rome, and made of metal melted down from enemy cannons. The top of the column is decorated with a large statue of Napoleon I, dressed like a Roman Emperor.

The building at #12 Place Vendôme is where the composer and pianist Frederic Chopin died. The one at #16 housed a man named Antoine Mesmer, who in the 18th century was the first to popularize the use of magnets to relieve pain and illness.

AU NAIN BLEU. *408, Rue Saint Honore. Metro: Concorde or Madeleine. Open daily except Sun, 10am-6:30pm.*

Paris' biggest toy store! Need I say more?

PALAIS ROYAL. *Entrances to the gardens from the Place du Palais Royal, Place de Valois, Rue de Montpensier, and Rue de Beaujolais. Metro: Palais Royal. Open sunrise to sunset. Enrance is free.*

This is a nice place to relax after a visit to the Louvre. There is plenty of room to run and play. You can also use the gardens as a starting point for a visit through some of Paris' shopping galeries and passages, starting with the **Galerie Colbert** and **Galerie Vivienne**, just north of the gardens.

The park and palace of the Palais Royal were originally built in 1636 by Cardinal Richelieu, who was King Louis XIII's Prime Minister. It was a sumptuous palace that housed 1,200 people, most of whom had jobs involved with taking care of it.

Richelieu died in 1642. He left the palace to King Louis XIII. The king died 6 months later. Louis XIV, still a boy, moved into the palace with his mother. It was the only time the palace actually served as a royal residence. The young Louix XIV was allowed to run wild in the palace gardens. He fell into pools regularly and hunted small boar that were let loose in the gardens for his enjoyment. As king, Louis XIV built himself the magnificent palace of Versailles. The Palais Royal passed on to the king's brother and his heirs.

The princes kept up a lavish lifestyle in the Palais Royal. By the 1780s, Louis-Philippe d'Orleans, who had inherited the palace, needed more money to cover the high price of his parties and endless luxuries. He hired an architect to build apartment buildings along three edges of the Palais Royal gardens. These were then rented out, along with retail space along the galleries of the first floor. They were a huge hit with the high society of Paris. Two new theaters, the **Théâtre Français** (now Comedie Française) and **Théâtre du Palais Royal** were built along the western edge. The famous playwright, Molière, performed with his troop in the Théâtre Français. He died there after playing the leading role one night in the Malade Imaginaire (Imaginary Invalid). A fountain in the Rue de Richelieu is dedicated to him.

Before the French Revolution, the cafés of the Palais Royal became a favorite meeting place of political activists. It was from one of these that the young lawyer, Camille Desmoulins, climbed on top of a table on July 13, 1789 and urged his countrymen to take up arms against the king's tyranny. They stormed the Bastille Prison the next day.

After the Revolution, the palace was emptied of its riches. The buildings were used to house the stock market and court rooms. Numerous shops were replaced with gambling houses and pool halls. In the 19th and 20th centuries, the Palais Royal housed some illustrious artists and writers. These included the author Colette, the artist and film director, Jean Cocteau, and actor Jean Marais.

Today, the buildings along the southern wing of the Palais Royal house government offices. The courtyard is decorated with modern, black and white columns of different sizes. These were designed in 1986 by artist Daniel Buren and caused quite an uproar. Since then they have become part of the landscape, and children are allowed to run among them or jump off of them. The arcades of the gardens are once again lined with cafés, restaurants, and fancy shops, including a lovely toy store and music box shop along the northern edge of the garden. The garden features fountains and tree-lined avenues. In the summer there are temporary sculpture exhibits, outdoor concerts, and plays.

Nestled in a flowerbed on the south side of the Palais Royal gardens is a small cannon. It was never used for defense purposes, but had another important role as a timepiece. From 1786 to 1914, it would go off every day at noon, provided the weather was sunny. The canon sits on the line of the Paris Meridian. It was set up so that at midday the sun would pass through an eyepiece and warm up the fuse that shot off the canon. It was restored in 1990. Today this little cannon is set off each Saturday at noon by one of the park's guards.

SAMARITAINE DEPARTMENT STORE. *19, Rue de la Monnaie. Metro: Pont Neuf. Open Mon-Sat, 9:30 am-7 pm (Thurs until 10 pm). Closed Sun.*

This department store is named for a statue of *Jesus and the Good Samaritan Woman* that once decorated a fountain on the nearby **Pont Neuf**. The original building (Shop 2) dates from 1910 and is a beautiful example of the Art Nouveau style of that period. Note the staircase, skylight, and peacock frescoes. You'll find the usual Paris department store array of great stuff, including kids' toys. However, what really makes this store unique is the wonderful view from the top floor restaurant Toupary. In warm weather, you can also enjoy lunch and dinner on the rooftop terrace.

QUAI DE LA MEGISSERIE. *Along the Seine. Metro: Pont Neuf.*

The stretch of this road along the Seine River between the Samaritaine Department Store and Place du Châtelet is filled with pet stores. Along with the usual array of dogs, cats, birds, and reptiles are more surprising pets, such as roosters, various types of pigeons, and enormous rabbits.

RUE SAINT HONORE. Running parallel to the Rue de Rivoli, this road features an endless array of shops and boutiques. There is something for everyone, ranging from high fashion to Asian noodle restaurants, excellent pastry shops, and goofy souvenirs.

EGLISE SAINT ROCH. *296, Rue Saint Honoré. Metro: Tuileries or Pyramides.*

This church is named for a man born in 1295 in the southern French town of Montpellier. Roch was from a wealthy family, but decided to give up all his money to take care of the poor and the sick in Italy. Then he caught the plague. According to legend, a dog found him and brought him food each day. Eventually, the dog's owner found Roch and helped bring him back to health. Afterwards, the plague is supposed to have spared any town that Roch visited.

The Church of Saint Roch was built in the 17th and 18th centuries. It is one of the biggest churches in Paris. It tends not only to its local parishioners but also holds a special service every Sunday at noon for artists and musicians. There are even artist's studios in the church. There are also classical concerts every Tuesday at 12:30pm, often featuring young talent from Paris' National Conservatory of Music. Several famous men are buried at Saint Roch. One is André Le Nôtre, the landscape architect who designed the gardens at Versailles, the Champs Elysées, and Vaux le Vicômte. Others include Pierre Corneille, who wrote *The Cid*; and Denis Diderot, one of the Philosophes of the French Enlightenment.

PONT DES ARTS. *By the Louvre. Metro: Pont Neuf or Louvre.*

This graceful footbridge connects the Louvre on the Right Bank to Saint Germain des Près on the Left Bank. It was named after the Louvre, which was known as the Palais des Arts (Palace of Arts) when the bridge was completed in 1803. The Pont des Arts was the city's first pedestrian bridge and was also the first to be made of iron. However, it suffered repeated damage from boats and barges during some major floods. Finally, half of the bridge collapsed in 1979. It was rebuilt and reopened in 1984.

The bridge offers lovely views and great photo opportunities. The Pont des Arts is also a favorite spot for painters to set up their easels. Maybe your budding artist will want to give it a try, too.

MAGIC SHOW - METAMORPHOSIS. *On a houseboat at 7, Quai Malaquais (Oct-Mar) across from the Pont des Arts, Metro: Pont Neuf or Saint Germain des Près. Sundays at 3 pm. Family performances: €15 per person. Brunch plus show: €35 (adults); €25 (kids). Note from Apr-Sept this boat moves downstreatm to #55, Quai de la Tournelle, Metro: Maubert Mutualite.*

A floating magic show: what a winning combination! Join magician Jan Madd on his theater-houseboat for family-friendly magic shows on Sunday afternoons. Note that although there are also evening performances, those are not specially geared for families.

11. MARAIS

This section of town was once covered with nothing but marshy fields (marais means marsh in French) running along the northern edge of the Seine River. Today, the Marais is a lively area, and a favorite among Parisians and tourists alike. The small, cobbled streets are full of colorful shops, young designer stores, and interesting eateries (including excellent Jewish delis and bakeries). There are numerous museums that appeal to kids' interests: toys (**Musée de la Poupée**); inventions (**Musée des Arts et Métiers**); history and gore (**Musée Carnavalet** and **Musée d'Art et d'Histoire Juive**); wackiness (**Musée Picasso**); and Magic (**Musée de la Magie et de la Curiosité**).

During Roman times, there was a major east-west road that ran through the Marais on an elevated dike to protect it from floods. In the 12th century, the marshes were drained and the area became home to several religious orders as well as to a Jewish neighborhood. The Templar Knights took up residence in the section now known as the Square du Temple, and wealthy nobles began to build themselves secondary residences in the surrounding countryside. Ultimately even the kings established country palaces in the Marais.

However, the Marais' real heyday came during the 17th century, when it became a very sought after address among the noble set. The Place Royale (today's Place des Vôsges) built by King Henri IV in the early 1600s, became the center of elegance and intellectual brilliance. Wealthy aristocrats took up residence there or in nearby Renaissance style mansions, decorated by some of the great artists of the day. Leading musicians and playwrights mingled with great philosophers in fancy salons, such as the one held by Madame de Sévigné, who lived on the Place des Vôsges.

Marais Highlights

- Search for optical illusions and slights of hand at the Museum of Magic
- Explore the Museum of Jewish Art and Culture
- Pick out a Jewish pastry in the Rue des Rosiers
- Look at the funny shops in the Rue des Francs Bourgeois
- Run, play, and look for the fake bricks in the Place des Vôsges
- Tour the Doll Museum
- Look for wacky animals at the Picasso Museum
- See models of Paris, the guillotine, and a ballroom fit for a queen at the Musée Carnavalet
- Admire the inventions at the Musée des Arts et Métiers (Arts and Industries Museum)
- Follow the footsteps of Nicholas Flamel and search for the secret of the Sorcerer's Stone
- Go ice-skating (in winter) in front of the Hôtel de Ville.

The Place des Vosges used to house a royal palace and gardens. In 1559, King Henri II died in the palace of a wound to his eye suffered during a joust tournament. Henri's widow, Catherine de Medicis, was so distraught she had the whole place torn down. The remaining lot was turned into a horse market. When Henri IV became king in 1589, he had the square rebuilt with a park and fancy apartments. The tallest buildings on either side of the square were called the King's and Queen's Pavillions. The square was called the Place Royale. The name was changed to the Place des Vôsges in 1800 in honor of the first Department in France to pay its federal income taxes. The square was a favorite meeting spot for duels. In the 19th century, it became home to several important authors, including Victor Hugo, who wrote the *Hunchback of Nôtre Dame.*

Notice the buildings around the square. They seem to be made of red bricks, but if you look closely you'll see that they are actually made of stone that is covered with a thin layer of false bricks.

In the 1700s, many aristocrats began to move away from the Marais to the royal court in Versailles or to the newly fashionable neighborhoods of Saint Germain and the Faubourg Saint Honoré. By the 1789 French Revolution, the Marais had lost much of its noble luster. Many of the mansions were abandoned or destroyed. The area was resettled by artisans and laborers, and tenements filled the formerly grand abodes. Interest in the neighborhood rebounded starting in the late 20th century, when many old buildings were renovated and fashionable shops moved in.

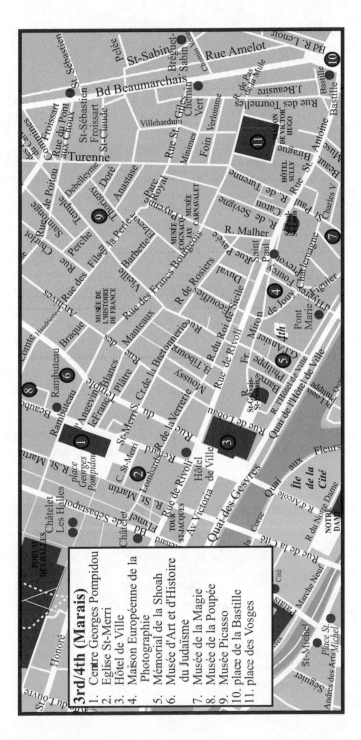

3rd/4th (Marais)
1. Centre Georges Pompidou
2. Eglise St-Merri
3. Hôtel de Ville
4. Maison Européenne de la
   Photographie
5. Mémorial de la Shoah
6. Musée d'Art et d'Histoire
   du Judaïsme
7. Musée de la Magie
8. Musée de la Poupée
9. Musée Picasso
10. place de la Bastille
11. place des Vosges

VILLAGE SAINT PAUL–THE SOUTHERN MARAIS (Situated between Metro: Saint Paul and Metro: Pont Marie)

This "village" once housed a royal residence, the Hotel Saint Paul, complete with vast gardens and a royal zoo. There is still a street named for some of the zoo's residents: the Rue des Lions Saint Paul. Although the palace and animals are now gone, the area still holds plenty to captivate the interests of both children and adults.

As you head from the Saint Paul metro to the Rue Saint Paul, you will pass the **Eglise St. Paul-St. Louis**, built from 1627 to 1641 to look like the Gesu Church in Rome. It is a classic Baroque style church with a symmetrical facade and central dome. Inside there is a painting by Eugène Delacroix representing the Christ in the Garden of Olive Trees. The shell-shaped fonts by the entrance were donated by Victor Hugo, when he lived in the nearby Place des Vôsges.

Although a visit of the church may leave your children cold, they may be entertained by the gory story of its two royal hearts. When Kings Louis XIII and Louis XIV died, their bodies were placed, like those of all the other French kings, in the Basilica of Saint Denis. However, their hearts were buried in this church. During the French Revolution of 1789, the kings' hearts were removed and sold to the highest bidder. The buyer was a painter, who used bits of the organs mixed with oil to make a particularly shiny coating for his paintings. When King Louis XVIII was restored to the throne in 1814, the painter is said to have returned what was left the kings' hearts in exchange for a gold tobacco pot.

If you walk down the Rue Saint Paul towards the Seine, you will come across a series of archways on the right. Walk through them to the little park, called the **Jardins de Saint Paul**. This park contains a large piece of the old fortress wall, complete with guard towers, that used to protect the city of Paris during the reign of King Philippe Auguste (late 1100s-early 1200s). It

Fun Fact

A Marais Skyline? In the 1920s the modern architect **LeCorbusier** proposed to level many of the dingy old streets and buildings north of the Place du Châtelet to create a neighborhood of 60-story skyscrapers. In spite of his fame and determination, the plan was never implemented. In the 1960s, André Malraux, who was Minister of Culture, successfully spearheaded an effort to preserve the Marais and have it declared a national historic site. Many of the old mansions were renovated. Several of them now house some of the city's most charming museums.

is a good place to let children run free or enjoy a snack while parents look in on the windows of the antique boutiques that line the archways.

MUSÉE DE LA CURIOSITÉ ET DE LA MAGIE, (MUSEUM OF MAGIE). *11, Rue Saint Paul (Metro: Pont Marie or Saint Paul). Open Wed, Sat, Sun, 2pm - 7pm. Magic classes (in French) are offered Sat, 11am-4pm. Adults: €7; Kids: €5.*

Note: Kids love this little museum. Beware, however, that its hours are quite limited. Without careful planning, you may end up facing a locked door and disappointed travel companions.

This is great fun for anyone who enjoys a good magic show. The museum features optical illusion tricks, automates, and old-fashioned carnival games dating from 1800 to 1950. There are also live magic demonstrations, much of which you can understand even if you don't know a word of French. To round out the visit there is a shop full of magic tricks and paraphernalia.

Parent Tip: If the Museum of Magic is a hit, you can also see a magic show at the **Double Fond** restaurant at 1, Place du Marche Sainte Catherine. Metro: Saint Paul. Special kids' shows, Sat at 3:30pm. Evening shows, Sat, 8:30pm; Tues, Thurs, Fri, at 9pm; Wed, at 10pm.

If you walk along the Seine towards the west, you will pass the **Hôtel de Sens**, a striking example of medieval Gothic architecture. In the Rue Geoffroy l'Asnie is the **Memorial to the Unknown Jewish Victim of the Nazi Holocaust**, open Sun-Fri, 10am-1pm, and 2pm-6pm. This memorial includes a wall of remembrance and a building which contains exhibits and a library about the Holocaust.

The nearby pedestrian street, Rue des Barres, climbs up between some lovely old medieval buildings and the imposing **Eglise Saint Gervais-Saint Protais**. This church is name for twin brothers who were Christian martyrs during the time of Emperor Nero. The saints were considered protectors of Paris in the 6th century. The church contains one of the oldest organs in Paris, built in 1601.

Taking a right up the Rue Francois Miron, follow your nose to #30 where you will find exotic foods and spices at a shop called **Izraël**. A walk up the Rue Vielle du Temple or Rue des Ecouffes will take you to Paris' historic Jewish section.

THE JEWISH QUARTER.

Walk along the **Rue des Rosiers** and surrounding streets and you are in the heart of Paris' Jewish Quarter. This is a great place to stop for a meal, pick up a picnic to eat in the Place des Vôsges, or grab a snack. At **Jo Goldenberg's** (corner Rue des Rosiers and Rue des Ecouffes) you can stop for a sit-down meal or go to the deli counter for a familiar array of kosher meats, chopped liver, bagels and lox, potato salad, and so forth. You'll also find Middle-Eastern eateries along the Rue des Rosiers run by North African Jews, and some excellent Jewish pastry shops. In the narrow **Rue Pavée** – said to be the first paved road in Paris – check out the remarkable facade of the Synagogue at #10. It is the work of the Art Nouveau architect Hector Guimard, famous for having designed Paris' metro entrances.

The Jewish roots of this neighborhood reach way back: The first Jews arrived in France during Roman times. Despite periods of terrible persecution over the centuries, Paris maintained a thriving Jewish community and remained an important center of Jewish learning. Parisian Jews were active in commerce, medicine, agriculture, and viticulture. Indeed it was Jewish vintners who produced wine for the Catholic Mass. Jews were only granted French citizenship in the late 18th century, and it was not until the rule of Napoleon I in the early 19th century that the Jewish religion was officially recognized.

In the late 19th century anti-Jewish sentiment ran high, culminating in the highly publicized Dreyfus Affair. This was the case of a French Jewish military captain, named Alfred Dreyfus, who was accused of being a German spy in 1894. He was given an unfair trial and condemned to life imprisonment on Devil's Island. Many members of the government and heads of the Catholic Church supported this condemnation. However, a strong protest movement was launched by well-known French writers and thinkers. After a ten year struggle, Dreyfus was finally declared innocent and set free.

The turn of the 20th century saw the arrival in France of many Jewish immigrants from Eastern Europe, North Africa, Turkey, and Greece. Then during World War II, hundreds of thousands of Jewish men, women, and children were rounded up and sent off to Nazi prison and death camps. A quarter of the Jewish population of France perished in the Holocaust.

MUSÉE D'ART ET D'HISTOIRE DU JUDAISME, (MUSEUM OF JEWISH ART AND HISTORY). *71, Rue du Temple. Metro: Rambuteau or Hôtel de Ville. Open Mon-Fri, 11am to 6pm and Sun 10 am to 6 pm. Adults: €6.10; Kids under 18: free. The museum organizes special kids' workshops (in French).*

For a fuller understanding of Jewish culture and heritage in Paris don't miss this interesting museum. The building itself has been beautifully restored. This museum celebrates not only Jewish history and religion, but also the cultural and artistic contributions of Jews in Paris. It features exhibits describing everyday life, religious festivals, and the coming together of two traditions: Sephardim and Ashkenazi. Don't miss the magnificent paintings by Marc Chagall and Amadeo Modigliani. There is also a pretty café and nice boutique. There are plans to restore the gardens, originally designed by Louis XVI's favorite landscaper, LeNôtre.

HÔTEL DE VILLE (PARIS CITY HALL). *Place de l'Hôtel de Ville. Metro: Hôtel de Ville.*

Take your children to the Hôtel de Ville and ask them if they'd like to stay there for the night. It's rather imposing with its wedding cake architecture and decor. We're just kidding, of course. A *hotel* in French can mean a place where you can book a room to spend the night, but it can also mean a mansion (hôtel particulier), a hospital (Hôtel Dieu), or a city hall (Hôtel de Ville) as in this case.

This history of this building dates back to medieval times, when the water merchants of Paris, called "Nautes," were among the most wealthy and powerful residents of the city. They controlled the commerce in and out of Paris on the Seine River. They set up a harbor on the shore near the current site of the Hôtel de Ville. It was the most important harbor in the city. In 1246, they set up a city council that met nearby. In the mid-1300s they moved their council room into a building called the Pillar House that was where the Hôtel de Ville stands today. In the 15th century, that building was falling apart so they built a new town hall in its place. This building was destroyed by the Commune de Paris revolt in 1871. It was quickly rebuilt in the ornate style that you see today. Today the building is decorated with statues representing different French cities. If you look carefully at the façade you'll also find a statue of a white sphinx.

The Hôtel de Ville houses the official version of the **Paris City Seal**. This depicts a boat floating on water (in honor of the water merchants). Above it are fleurs de lys and crenellated castle towers. On either side are two branches: laurel representing courage, and oak representing strength. A Latin inscription along the bottom reads, "fluctuat nec mergitur" or "It floats, but does not sink." Even in times of difficulty, the city will not be defeated. Look for examples of the city seal throughout Paris. They are everywhere – from parking meters to school buildings and trash cans.

The square in front of the Hôtel de Ville used to be called the Place de Grève. It was a lively spot, and the sight of public balls, markets, and festivities. A big bonfire would be lit there every June 21 to celebrate the summer solstice. On more gruesome days, the Place de Grève was used for public executions. It also was where unemployed or unhappy workmen would gather to publicly voice their complaints. Today the French expression faire la grève (do the grève) means to go on strike.

In the winter, the city sets up an **ice-skating rink** on the square in front of the Hôtel de Ville. In the summer, usually late June, the city's annual café waiter and waitress race starts and ends here. The participants run 8 kilometers (5 miles) through the streets of Paris carrying a full platter of drinks in their work clothes (no running shoes). It's quite impressive!

CENTRAL MARAIS. *Metro: Saint Paul or Chemin Vert.*

A walk up the Rue Vieille du Temple, Rue Pavée, and along the Rue des Francs Bourgeois takes you past shops filled with funky gadgets, cartoon characters, or clothing by hip designers.

When you are ready for more sight-seeing, you face the choice of three terrific museums:

MUSÉE CARNAVALET, *29, Rue de Sévigné. Métro: Saint-Paul or Chemin-Vert. Open Tues-Sun, 10am to 3:40 pm. Closed Mon. Entrance to the permanent collections is free, but there is a fee for special exhibits.*

The Musée Carnavalet is devoted to the history of Paris, from prehistory through the early 20th century. Although this may sound stuffy, you might be surprised at how many of the objects can arouse your child's curiosity and imagination. There are wooden canoes made by prehistoric fishermen and discovered along the Seine when construction was underway for the new Parc de Bercy. There is a room filled with old shopkeepers' signs. Have fun guessing what kind of trade they represented. There are models and maps of Paris through the ages. There's a set of locks from the Bastille prison (ask the guard to give you a demonstration), a portrait of Dr. Guillotin who designed the guillotine, and a chess set that King Louis XVI played in prison before his execution. There's the cradle in which Napoleon Bonaparte slept as a baby. There are replicas of a 16th century room, a room during the Revolution, and Marcel Proust's bedroom. There is a jewelry store and a ballroom from the Hotel Wendell guaranteed to delight any fan of Cinderella. To finish the visit, the gift shop offers nice games, books, and souvenirs.

Gory Fact

Did you know that the **guillotine** was actually developed as a more humane form of capital punishment? Prior methods included hanging, the rack, quartering (pulled apart by horses), being burnt at the stake, being buried alive, and the chopping block. **Dr. Guillotin** worked with a German harpsichord maker named Tobias Schmidt to make his machine. He tested it on sheep. King Louis XVI was the one who suggested that an angled blade would be more efficient. Little did he know that within a few short years it would be used on his own neck. Legend has it that Dr. Guillotin was himself a victim of the guillotine. It's not true. He died in his 70s of natural causes.

MUSÉE PICASSO. *Hôtel de Salé, 5, Rue de Thorigny. Metro: Saint Paul. Open Wed-Mon, 9:30am-5:30pm. Closed Tues. Adults €6.70. Kids under 18: free. Free to all on the first Sun of each month. Family-centered guided tours offered on Sun, 11am and 3 pm (in French).*

This museum contains a huge collection of works by Pablo Picasso, whose long career lasted from 1894 to his death in 1973. Born in Malaga, Spain, Picasso spent much of his younger artistic life in Paris and later life in Provence. When he died, his heirs donated paintings, drawings, and sculptures to the French government in lieu of an inheritance tax. The French government created this beautiful museum to house the collection. More works were added in 1990, when Picasso's widow Jacqueline died. The pieces are organized chronologically, taking you through different periods of the artist's style: blue, rose, cubism, surrealism.

Young children may not get excited about the influence of African art on Picasso, his experiments with planes, or the fundamentals of cubism. But they do respond well to the humor and wackiness of many of the pieces – sometimes more than adults. Kids also enjoy hunting for depictions of children (e.g. Harlequin Boy, Girl Jumping Rope) and animals (e.g. crouching cat, bicycle goat). Don't be afraid to move at the pace of a short attention span. There's a lot here and some of the best is saved for the last galleries. The reward at the end of the journey is a lovely café and interesting gift shop.

The building that houses the Picasso Museum was once a private mansion known as the **Hotel de Salé** (Hotel of Salt). In spite of this name it was neither a hotel nor filled with salt. Instead it was a fancy residence. The salty part comes from the fact that this building's first owner was in charge of collecting the royal tax on salt.

MUSÉE DE LA POUPÉE. *located in the Impasse Berthaud, just off the Rue Beaubourg (Metro: Rambuteau). Open Tues-Sun, 10am-1pm, 2pm-6pm. Closed Mon. Adults: €6; Kids: €3.*

This charming little museum is nestled in a lane, just half a block from the back of the Pompidou Center. It has a collection of dolls dating back to the mid-1800s and up through the 1960s. They are arranged with accessories and furniture to reflect the time period in which they were made. There are also two rooms devoted to temporary exhibits, often set up around fun themes like the history of the Barbie doll or plastic squeeze toys. The museum has a gift shop with doll accessories and dollhouse furniture. There is also a repair shop that can offer estimates of the age and value of collectors' dolls.

Many of the dolls in the Musée de la Poupée have faces of a type of porcelain called **biscuit**. Do they look like they are made of dough? Actually, the name comes from the fact that the porcelain is cooked twice: *bis* = twice, *cuit* = cooked.

THE NORTHERN MARAIS - FOLLOWING THE FOOTSTEPS OF NICOLAS FLAMEL.

Do you have any Harry Potter fans in your midst? Do they remember how Harry, Hermione, and Ron searched the school library for clues about Nicolas Flamel during their first year at Hogwarts? Here's your chance to hunt him down yourself, and maybe discover the secrets of the Sorcerer's Stone:

Nicolas Flamel was a real person, born in Pontoise (west of Paris) in 1330. He was a bookseller who set up shop near the Place des Innocents. It is said that one night, Flamel dreamt that an angel appeared to him with a mysterious book, saying that some day he would discover its secrets. A few days later, a stranger walked into Flamel's shop with the very book from his dream. It was about alchemy and supposedly held two secrets: 1) how to change ordinary metal into gold and 2) how to live forever. Flamel studied the book for years. Then in 1382, he claimed to have successfully turned mercury into gold. He did it again in 1386. Was it true? No one knows for sure, but what is certain is that Flamel did become a wealthy man.

Did he also discover the secret to eternal life? Who knows? According to legend, he and his wife Pernelle only pretended to die in 1417, and have lived in many different countries around the world ever since. His tombstone is in the Cluny Museum.

For your Flamel tour start at the **Tour Saint Jacques**, located just off the Place du Châtelet (Metro: Châtelet). This Gothic-style bell tower is all that remains of a church called Saint Jacques de la Boucherie. The church was built in 1523 for the butchers and tanners who worked in the nearby Les Halles (Paris' former central market). One of its most regular and generous patrons was Nicolas Flamel, who lived nearby. The church was destroyed during the French Revolution, but the bell tower was saved. Note: For the past several years the tower has been under repair, so you may have to catch glimpses of it through the scaffolding.

The Tour St. Jacques was also the starting point for the religious pilgrimage to St. Jacques de Compostelle (Saint James the Apostle of Compostella) in Spain. Pilgrims would gather here from the North of France, England, and Flanders (now Belgium). They would follow a path across the Seine river and down the Rue St. Jacques. They would continue towards the town of Etampes, then southwest through Orleans, Bordeaux, and over to Spain. The pilgrim's symbol was the scallop shell, and you can find images of that shell all along the pilgrimage route. For example, there is one on the facade of the church Saint Jacques du Haut Pas (corner Rue Saint Jacques and the Rue de l'Abbe de l'Epee, near the Luxembourg Gardens) and another on a wall across from the Chartres Cathedral. This pilgrimage was important not only for religious reasons, but also because of the cultural, scientific, and economic exchanges that it promoted between France and Spain.

Since 1891, the Tour Saint Jacques has served as a weather station for Paris. The tower holds meteorological instruments to measure the air quality, pollution levels, and other readings. There is a statue under the tower of the great French philosopher and scientist, Blaise Pascal. It commemorates the meteorological experiments he conducted there in 1648. Today, weathermen still climb up to the top of the tower every day to take meteorological readings. They use the stairs, because there is no elevator.

From the Tour Saint Jacques, if you head due north you will find a little pedestrian street (one block west of the larger pedestrian street, Rue Saint Martin). Look up at the street sign. This is the **Rue Nicolas Flamel**. Notice that the first cross street you meet is called the **Rue Pernelle**, named for Flamel's wife and companion in eternity.

Here you may want to stray a bit from Nicolas Flamel to admire the Eglise Saint Mérri, visit the Stravinsky Fountain, check out the Pompidou Center, or visit the Doll Museum.

The trail of Nicolas Flamel resumes up the Rue Beaubourg (heading north). Take a right when you reach the **Rue de Montmorency**. You have just stepped back into medieval times. Notice the house at #51. It has been on this spot since 1407, when it was built by Nicolas Flamel as a home for the poor. The tenants were given free room and board, and shops were rented out on the ground level to cover the costs. All that was asked in exchange was that the boarders live an honest life and offer a prayer each day for Flamel and his wife. Said to be the oldest house in Paris, it now contains a restaurant called the Auberge Nicolas Flamel.

Another house at #3 Rue Volta, near the Musée des Arts et Métiers, competes with Flamels' house for the title of oldest house in the city. It was long thought to date back to 1298. However, recent evidence indicates that the Rue Volta house was built in the 1500s.

MUSÉE DES ARTS ET MÉTIERS, *60, Rue Reaumur (Metro: Arts et Métiers). Open Tues-Sun, 10am-6pm (Thurs. until 9:30 pm). Closed Mon. Adults: €6.50; Kids are free. The museum is handicap accessible and free to individuals accompanying persons with disabilities.*

This cool museum is a nice way to round out your Nicolas Flamel tour. It is just 4 blocks up the Rue Beaubourg from Flamel's house. The museum is chock full of scientific and artistic inventions, like the first calculator (1642), telegraph (1794), and automobile (1770). It was recently remodeled, so the exhibit rooms are airy and well done. There are numerous interactive computer stations to explore different sections. Much of the fun, however, comes from seeing models of early airplanes, drawbridges, and skyscrapers. There are early measuring tools, cameras, and bicycles. You'll see Volta's battery and Watt's steam engine. There's Edison's phonograph and Foucault's pendulum.

In the final room of the museum, a converted chapel, you'll see large-scale models of the Statue of Liberty (including a full-size replica of her thumb), the first autobus, early airplanes, and the Vulcain motor used in the French space shuttle, Ariane. Although this museum offers no direct links to the experiments and inventions of Nicolas Flamel, it's surely the kind of place he, too, would have enjoyed.

QUARTIER DU TEMPLE. *(Metro: Arts et Métiers or Temple).*

Although you might associate the names Square du Temple, Rue du Temple, and Rue Vielle du Temple with the Marais' Jewish heritage, they actually hearken back to the days of the Christian Crusaders in the Holy Land. These names are legacies of the once powerful **Order of the Knights of the Temple**. Also known as the **Templars**, their name was derived from the fact that their headquarters in Jerusalem were on a spot thought to have once held the Temple of Solomon. This Order was founded in 1169, and its members were both knights and monks. Their tight discipline and military skill earned them favors with the French king who charged them with guarding pilgrims in the Holy Land, including his own troops. Over time, however, the kings came to resent the increasing power and wealth of the Templars – who came to own half of Paris, including the Marais. In 1307, King Philippe le Bel had the pope declare that all the Templars were heretics. Their leader was burnt at the stake, and members were hunted down and killed all over France. The king confiscated their assets.

After they were massacred, the Templars' headquarters at the Tour du Temple were converted into a prison. It is here that King Louis XVI, Marie-Antoinette, and their children were held in 1792 after trying to escape from Paris. The king spent his final days in this prison before being executed on January 21, 1793. The queen was transferred to the Concièrgerie Prison until her turn came to face the guillotine on August 2, 1793. The building was torn down by Napoleon I. The empty lot was eventually transformed into a little park, the Square du Temple, by Napoleon III.

Today, the Temple neighborhood is the city's garment district. The Carreau du Temple, near the Square du Temple, is a covered market hall full of new and used clothing. It is a favorite spot among teens to look for clothing, especially bargain-priced leather jackets.

12. BASTILLE

On July 14, 1789 the storming of the **Bastille Prison** marked the launch of the French Revolution. Ever since, the neighborhood has maintained a reputation for feistiness. For many years, the Saint Antoine neighborhood east of the Bastille was home to woodworkers and craftsmen. Many of them made up the core of those ready to revolt against repressive governments, both in 1789 and during later rebellions.

During the 1980s-1990s, this area became home to artists, young designers, and cybercafés seeking less expensive living and retail space. Today, the old mingles with the new around the Bastille. Small woodworking shops sit next door to new internet cafés. An old train route has been converted into suspended gardens. Houseboats still pass slowly through the locks of the city's canals, and a new park welcomes strollers to their banks.

PLACE DE LA BASTILLE. *Metro: Bastille.*

The Bastille was originally a military fort. It was built in the 1370s to protect the eastern edge of the city from invaders. The fort's walls were 5 feet thick, and built to resist attack. Over time, they proved to be more useful at keeping people in than out, and the Bastille was transformed into a prison.

By the 1700s, most of the people shut inside the Bastille had been sent there by royal decree. Some were political prisoners. For example French philosopher, Voltaire, was sent to the Bastille because of his ideas on religious tolerance. Other prisoners were people whose families had appealed to the king to have them locked up. It was a system some people used to rid themselves of a family member who was spending too much money, causing embarrassment, or otherwise in the way.

Bastille Area Highlights

- Hunt for traces of the old Bastille prison
- Walk, bike, or rollerblade above the crowds along the Promenade Plantée
- Find the giant sundial in the Espace Reuilly
- Watch a canal boat go through a lock, or take a ride on a canal boat and experience the locks for yourself
- Visit the weavers, glassblowers, and boutiques in the Viaduct des Arts
- Check out the exotic foods and spices at the Place d'Aligre Street Market

By 1789, the Bastille had become a symbol of royal tyranny to many Parisians. That's why it was one of the first targets of the revolutionaries. On July 14, members of an armed uprising attacked the Bastille, killed the guards, freed the prisoners (who numbered only seven), and launched the French Revolution. In the weeks that followed, the building was set on fire and torn down. Some of the stones were recovered and used in the building of the Pont de la Concorde. One enterprising businessman gathered up stones and other remnants of the building to sell as souvenirs. He even carved some into miniature copies of the Bastille Prison. You can see examples of these at the Musée Carnavalet in the Marais.

King Louis XVI, who was on the throne at the time, was so frightened by the storming of the Bastille that he gave in to some of the revolutionaries' demands. Some of his powers were limited, and he agreed to name General Marquis de Lafayette (who had helped George Washington win the American Revolution) as mayor of Paris. Many European philosophers, poets, and reformers were very impressed by the Bastille attack. It became a symbol of the triumph of modern ideas. It was also the beginning of the end of absolute monarchy in France – though not of politically upheavals and periods of tyranny.

If you visit the Place de la Bastille today, you'll see an outline of the old prison on the pavement in the middle of the Place. A plaque at #4, Rue St. Antoine marks where the entrance was. The Bastille metro station (line 5) has an exposed fragment of the prison's foundation.

The tall column you can see today in the middle of the Place de la Bastille is called the **Colonne de Juillet** (July Column). You would think it was named for the July 14 storming of the Bastille Prison in 1789. But it's not. Instead, it commemorates the people of Paris who died during smaller uprisings in July 1830 and 1848. The victims of those uprisings were buried under the Column, and their names are engraved on a brass plaque near the base. The statue on top represents Liberty.

PROMENADE PLANTÉE. *Access from numerous stairs and elevators along the Avenue Daumesnil and Rue du Sahel. Metro: Bastille, Gare de Lyon, Daumesnil, Bel-Air, or Porte Dorée. Entrance is free.*

The Promenade Plantée is a lovely park planted along a 4 kilometer stretch in eastern Paris that used to be covered with train tracks. The old railroad line, built in 1859, ran along

Fun Fact

In the early 1800s, **Napoleon I** wanted to erect a great monument in the middle of the Place de la Bastille to celebrate his mighty Empire. The original design called for a huge bronze elephant, atop a magnificent fountain. However, an unsuccessful military campaign against Spain cut into the funds for the monument, so it had to be built of plaster instead of bronze. Within a few years, Napoleon's Empire was collapsing, and his great elephant monument was rotting and infested with rats. By 1846, the poor elephant was so dilapidated it was torn down. However, the monument lives on in Victor Hugo's *Les Misérables*, where it serves as a hiding place for the young hero, Gavroche.

a viaduct heading east from the Place de la Bastille (now replaced with the Bastille Opera House) to the Bois de Vincennes. When the underground metro system was built, the train was discontinued. The tracks were still used for a time to move or store trains. In the 1970s, however, they were abandoned. The property was sold to the city and left empty. In the 1990s, the city hired architect Philippe Mathieu to transform the space into a park.

Today, the Promenade Plantée offers a third-story view of the streets and buildings, along flower-lined paths and gardens. It is a great place for families, since there are no cars or streets to cross. In some sections of the park the paths split into two: one reserved for walkers and people pushing strollers, and the other reserved for bikes and rollerbladers.

About midway along, the Promenade Plantée passes through a large park called the Jardin de Reuilly. It features wide green lawns and playgrounds. Do you know what time it is? Look for the giant sundial, and see if you can figure it out. This park also contains a public swimming pool. Called the **Piscine de Reuilly**, it is located at 13, Rue Hénard, Metro: Montgallet.

And check out the building at #85, Avenue Daumesnil. It's covered with fancy decorations that you can admire from the Promenade Plantée's bird's-eye view. There are even copies of Michelangelos' *Slave Sculptures*. Does it look like an art museum? It's actually a police station.

VIADUCT DES ARTS. *Under the Promenade Plantée, Along Boulevard Daumesnil. Metro: Bastille or Gare de Lyon.*

The area under the Promenade Plantée is called the Viaduct des Arts. It is made up of graceful, brick archways that have been converted into art studios, designer stores, craftsmen's workshops, computer stores, and other shops. The one at #119, Avenue Daumesnil is a workshop for France's top art school, the Ecole Nationale des Beaux-Arts. You can watch the students at work on their paintings, sculptures, glassblowing and other art projects.

PORT DE L'ARSENAL MARINA. *Canal south of Place de la Bastille. Metro: Bastille or Quai de la Rapée.*

This port connects the Saint Martin Canal to the Seine. It is a popular stopping point for leisure and houseboats from all over Europe. Nearly 900 pleasure boats use this port each year. The area along the marina has been converted into a large park. There are rose gardens, playgrounds featuring wonderful boat-like structures, a restaurant, and a small open-air theater.

The port and canals were all created under Napoleon I, mainly to provide a greater supply of fresh water to the citizens and fountains of Paris. However, as the city began to tap more underground springs meet the demand for drinking water, the canals' primary function shifted. They became important shipping routes for the transportation of merchandise. Today, you can still watch many barges filled with sand, coal, or other merchandise as they make their way through the canals to the Seine.

Every 7-8 years, the canals are cleaned out. As part of this process workmen have to remove all of the fish. They stun them temporarily with chemicals or an electric shock and transfer the fish to other places. They are returned safely when the cleaning is complete.

CANAUXRAMA (CANAL TOUR BOAT RIDES). *Near #50, Boulevard de la Bastille. Metro: Bastille. (Tel. 01.42.39.15.00). Daily departures at 9:45 am and 2:30 pm. Weekend and Holiday rates €13 for everyone, regardless of age. During the week, Adults: €14; Kids 6-12: €8; Under 6: free.*

Do you enjoy watching the boats go through the canal? How about going for a canal boat ride of your own? Tour boats leave from the Port de l'Arsenal for a 2 hour 40 minute tour up the Canal Saint Martin to the Parc de la Villette, where you can go visit the spectacular playgrounds and Science Museum. Don't forget to bring along a picnic. There is a special sound and lights show as you go through the tunnel under the Place de la Bastille. For the real, die-hard canal boat fans, you can even take a full-day tour down to the Marne River or rent a canal boat for parties and special occasions.

ROLLERS ET COQUILLAGES. *Nomades Store. 37, Boulevard Bourdon. Metro: Bastille. Free kid-friendly group outings meet in front of the store every Sunday, 2:30-5:30 pm.*

The Nomades store will outfit your whole family (ages 7 and up) with rental roller blades, helmets, and pads. Then you can join the group Rollers et Coquillages Sunday afternoons for a 3-hour ride along Paris sidewalks and parks. If you prefer to go on your own, take your skates and head for the Promenade Plantée. There you will find smooth, flat paths. Some of them are specially reserved for rollerblading.

PARIS À VELO C'EST SYMPA, *37, Boulevard Bourdon, Metro: Arsenal, Tel. 01 48 87 60 01. Be sure to call ahead to make sure that the kids' equipment you may need will be available.*

This is just one of many shops where you can rent bicycles, helmets, and other equipment for a nice cycling tour in Paris. The Bastille neighborhood offers several excellent routes that keep you well away from traffic. The **Promenade Plantée** has special paths reserved for bikes and roller blades. There are also bike paths north of the Place de la Bastille along the **Saint Martin Canal**. On Sundays during the year, and every day from July 15-August 15, the parkways along the Seine River are closed to motorized traffic. Here you can enjoy some of Paris' best sights at a leisurely bicycling pace.

PLACE D'ALIGRE MARKET. *Place d'Aligre. Between Rue de Charenton and Rue du Faubourg Saint Antoine. Metro: Ledru Rollin. Open 9am-1pm Tues-Sun. Closed Mon.*

This square contains both a covered market, originally constructed in 1777, and street vendors that spill onto the side streets. It features very interesting and exotic types of foods, including plenty of Caribbean and North African specialties. You also can find used clothes and flea market items, here. It is a colorful and exotic experience.

GARE DE LYON. *Cour L. Armand. Metro: Gare de Lyon*

This train station services routes going to the south of France, the Alps, and Italy. It was built in 1895, as part of the massive construction projects for the Paris Exhibition of 1900. The large clock tower on the outside is a familiar rendez-vous point for lost travelers. It is decorated with statues representing Paris and Marseilles. There are 40 murals inside the station representing many of the cities and towns along the routes served by the station. On the ground floor there are also paintings symbolizing Navigation, Steam Power, Electricity, and Mechanics. The Gare de Lyon's restaurant, **Le Train Bleu**, is famous for its excellent food and its 1901 Belle-Epoque-style decor.

APACHE – KID-FRIENDLY CYBERCAFE. *84, Rue du Faubourg Saint Antoine. Metro: Ledru-Rollin.*

The ground floor of this store offers plenty of toys, gadgets, and other fun stuff for kids. Head upstairs and you will come to the city's only kid-centered Internet zone. For a small fee kids can surf the net or take a workshop (in French) to help them navigate the electronic superhighway more efficiently.

AU CAFE CHANTANT (SINGING CAFE). *36, Rue Bichat, 75011, Metro: République.*

On Sunday afternoons at 3 pm, this Singing Café puts on special shows for children. These may feature clowns, jugglers, puppeteers, or other kid-friendly entertainers.

13. BERCY

Bercy is one of Paris' most recent, up-and-coming new neighborhoods. And yet, it is here that builders recently discovered the traces of Paris' earliest known inhabitants. In the 1990s, Bercy was transformed from an area filled with empty wine warehouses to a lovely new park and shopping district. During the construction, workers stumbled across several 7,000-year old dugout canoes. These once belonged to the people who fished and hunted along the marshy banks of the Seine during prehistoric times.

Modern Bercy has much to offer children. There is a great park filled with gardens, bridges, a maze, and play areas. There are magical museums that will transport them to an exotic music room, old-fashioned carnival, or Venetian palace. Family-friendly stores and restaurants round out the visit in a pedestrian section that makes you feel as though you have left the bustle of the city for a quieter village.

PARC DE BERCY. *Along the Seine in Eastern Paris, between Boulevard de Bercy and BercyExpo. Metro: Bercy or Cour Saint Emilion. Entrance is free.*

According to legend, in 1704, King Louis XIV attended mass in a church in Bercy. He noticed a man who seemed to remain standing while everyone else knelt in prayer. Louis sent his guards to arrest the man for his lack of respect. It turned out the man was kneeling, but was so tall he towered above the crowd. The king was amused and invited the man for a talk. He discovered that the tall man was a vintner and offered to let him come to Bercy each year to sell his wine free of taxes. Bercy attracted more and more wine merchants, and within 100 years was the biggest wine market in the world.

Bercy Area Highlights

- Try to figure out how they mow the grass growing up the sides of the Bercy Sports Arena
- Go through the maze, see what's growing in the childrens' garden, and throw crumbs to the ducks in the Bercy Park
- Ride old carrousels, see player pianos, and step into a Venetian palace at the Musée des Arts Forains
- Take a trapeze lesson at the Club Med World
- Have a snack and enjoy the shops along the pedestrian zone of Cour Saint Emilion
- See a movie at the Ciné Cité Bercy – the biggest cinema in Paris

For over 200 years, Bercy was Paris' wholesale wine district. It was a bustling neighborhood covered with wine warehouses, cobbled streets, and railway tracks leading down to ships along the Seine. There were also plenty of restaurants and dance halls. In 1910, Paris experienced a huge flood. The entire Bercy neighborhood was covered with water. When the waters finally receded, wine barrels were discovered stuck on roofs and trapped in the tops of trees.

In the 1970s, the wine market was moved out to the suburbs. The Bercy buildings were abandoned. Then in the 1980-90s, the area was revitalized. A large pyramid-shaped sports center was built on the western edge of Bercy, known as the **Palais Omnisport de Bercy**. It was soon joined by a new Government Finance building, a new building for the American Center, and modern apartment buildings – all designed by famous architects. The old wine warehouse district was turned into a large park.

The Bercy Park is filled with wide expanses where children can run, explore, and discover. It features a variety of small gardens. One is a vegetable patch tended by children. Others include a vineyard, a botanical garden, a garden of scents, and a wonderful maze that kids love to run through. There are ponds, large grassy areas, some very old trees, and small bridges. There are little buildings that house temporary exhibits or gardening workshops. The alleyways are named for famous wine regions.

On the northern side of the Bercy Park is a remarkable building designed by architect Frank Gehry. It was originally built to house the American Center, which had moved from its old space in Montparnasse. For decades it had featured art exhibits, dance, and theater productions to promote Franco-American cultural exchanges. Unfortunately, the Center went bankrupt shortly after moving to its new building, which is being transformed into a new Museum of Cinema.

On the eastern edge of the Bercy park is a new development called Bercy Village. It includes a pedestrian section filled with kid-friendly shops, restaurants, and cafés. There is a large movie complex called Ciné Cité. It often plays kid-friendly films, including American ones in English. This section also houses three museums lodged

in old wine warehouses and dedicated to carnavals, Venice, and music. Though interesting they are hard to visit due to their somewhat unpredictable hours. It's best to call ahead to see if they are open.

MUSÉE DES ARTS FORAINS (CARNAVAL MUSEUM), SALONS DE MUSIQUE, AND SALONS VENITIENS. *53, Avenue des Terroirs de France. Open Sat-Sun, 2pm-7pm and during school holidays for groups of 15 or more at a time. The hours are sporadic, so you should phone ahead (Tel. 01.43.40.16.22). Adults: €12; Kids: €4. Fee includes visit to all three museums.*

The Musée des Arts Forains will take you back in time to the days of old-fashioned carrousels and carnivals. The organ plays while kids get to ride on antique merry-go-rounds. Some feature elaborately decorated animals. One is made of old-fashioned bicycles. There are also old-fashioned carnival games. From this museum you can step into the Salons de Musique. Its rooms feature old player-pianos and other instruments that were once used to make music for shows and movies. There are also wax figures of Vaudeville stars from the early 1900s. In the Salons Vénitiens you will feel as though you have just stepped off a gondola in the midst of the Venice Carnival. The rooms look like those of a Venetian palace. There is a carrousel of gondolas and reconstructed Venetian bridge.

CLUB MED WORLD. *39, Cour Saint Emilion. Metro: Cour Saint Emilion. Buffet meals during the week. Sunday Brunch, 12pm-4pm. No membership required. Adults: €30; Kids: €17. Special activities are extra, generally €3-10/hour.*

Need a vacation from your vacation? If so, take a break from the cultural sights and head for this urban Club Med. The Club offers different sports and activities for all ages. Depending on the program, kids and adults can try out trapezes, rock climbing, trampolines, juggling, and other new challenges. There are mini-club workshops for kids, ages 6-12. If you go for Sunday brunch, the kids can eat at the mini-club with friendly instructors, then try out some of the Club's kid-friendly activities.

14. BOIS DE VINCENNES

The Bois de Vincennes borders the eastern edge of Paris. Like the Bois de Boulogne, it is a remnant of the large ring of forests that once encircled the city, when it was known as Lutetia. Once the domain of kings, the Bois de Vincennes is now a favorite among Parisian families when they need a breath of fresh air. It features large woods, lakes, bike trails, a big zoo, a small farm, a castle, a museum, a tropical garden, terrific playgrounds, a horse racing track, and even a baseball field.

CHÂTEAU DE VINCENNES (CASTLE). *Metro: Château de Vincennes. Open daily,. You must join a guided tour. Long visit (90 minutes - includes the castle and tour of the guard walls) leaves at 10:15 am, 11 am, 2:15 pm, 3 pm, 3:45 pm, 4:30 pm. Adults: €6.10, Kids: free. Short visit (45 minutes includes the castle) leaves as 11:45 am, 1:30 pm, 5:15 pm. Adults: €4.60; Kids: free.*

This castle has roots that go back more than 800 years. Today you can take a tour of the castle and its protective walls. Highlights include the 17th century palace rooms, the gothic Holy Chapel, and the walk around the defense walls. The great donjon tower (or keep) has been renovated on the outside, and it is now undergoing major repairs of the interior sections.

Its history goes like this: The woods of Vincennes were for many years the hunting grounds of French kings. In the late 12th century, King Philippe Auguste built a wall around the Vincennes woods to preserve the deer, boar, and other animals for his hunting pleasure. He also built himself a small manor house, which he used as a hunting lodge. Over time, Philippe Auguste's building was transformed into a fortified castle, designed to keep out invaders from the East.

Bois de Vincennes Highlights

- Visit the Vincennes castle
- Go to the zoo and climb up its big rock
- Take a bike ride
- Visit the Palais Dorée aquarium
- Try out the playgrounds and fun rides in the Parc Floral
- Rent a rowboat and paddle around the lake
- See a horse race or go horseback riding
- Visit the farm
- Go to the Foire du Trone Fair

In the 13th century, King Louis IX (also known as Saint Louis) lived in this castle. Legend has it that when people had disputes, they could present their cases to the king who would receive them outside under a great oak tree. Here he would hear their complaints and pass a judgment, with the understanding that it would be obeyed immediately. Saint Louis, being zealously religious, added a Holy Chapel to the castle, following a design similar to the Sainte Chapelle that he built on Ile de la Cité.

The large central tower, known as a keep in English and a donjon in French, was built in 1337. It originally contained the best rooms in the palace, including the royal apartments.

During France's Hundred Years War with England the Vincennes Castle became a property of the English king (including King Henry V who died here), who had managed to gain control over much of northern France. The castle remained in English hands until the reign of the French King Charles VII. Helped mainly by the encouragements and successful battles of Joan of Arc, Charles VII was finally able to regain control of Paris and its surrounding castles. This didn't help Joan much. When she was captured by the Burgundians and sold to the English in 1431, he did nothing to help save her. She was condemned as a witch by the leaders of the Sorbonne University, who were allies of the Burgundians. Joan of Arc was burned at the stake at the age of 19. She was declared a saint in 1920.

The famous "Sun King", Louis XIV, spent his honeymoon in the Vincennes Castle. He considered setting up his permanent residence here, but decided instead to build a new palace at Versailles.

In 1738, the Vincennes Castle was turned into a porcelain factory. The original founders of the factory were two porcelain workers who had gotten into trouble at their former worksite in Chantilly. They sought refuge in Vincennes and created a new industry there. The porcelain factory was eventually transferred to Sèvres in 1756.

Fun Fact

When is a **donjon** not a donjon? In French, the term donjon refers to a central castle tower that is known in English as the keep. In medieval fortresses and castles this was often where the kings or nobles lived, because it was the most well defended part of the castle. A donjon can also mean a prison, as it does in English. At Vincennes, the great donjon served both as a royal residence and later as a prison, so either meaning works.

In the early 16th century, part of the great keep of the castle was transformed into a royal prison. Thus the donjon became a donjon and remained so until shortly before the French Revolution of 1789. When King Louis XIV became angry with his finance minister, Nicolas Fouquet, for building himself a sumptuous palace at Vaux-le-Vicomte, it was here that Fouquet was first imprisoned. The king put him under the watchful eye of one of his best musketeers, the one called d'Artagnon.

In the early 1800s, Napoleon I transformed much of the Vincennes castle into a military arsenal and barracks. There is still a military garrison stationed next to the castle today. Napoleon also used the donjon to put away state prisoners.

In 1940, the castle was taken over by the occupying German Army. They were pushed out in 1944 by the Allied forces, but not before German troops had shot the 26 Resistance fighters they had captured and set fire to the castle buildings.

ZOOLOGICAL PARK. *53, Avenue de Saint Maurice, or corner of Avenue du Lac and Avenue Daumesnil. Metro: Porte Dorée. Open daily 9am–6pm (until 6:30 on Sun). Entrace is €5 for kids and adults. Note: As of the publication of this book the future of this zoo was somewhat in question and the interior galleries were "temporarily" closed. There is still much to see outside – for the time being.*

This zoo was founded in 1934. It contains thousands of animals, mostly birds and mammals. The zoo tries to house its animals in large, naturalistic settings. Many represent endangered species such the white rhino, Asian elephant, and lemurs. If you are lucky, you'll see some of the animals at feeding time. The pelicans eat at 2:15pm, the otters at 3pm, and the seals are fed at 4pm.

There is a huge artificial rock on the eastern side of the zoo. It is 65 meters (215 feet) high and is covered with mountain goats, vultures, and hawks. You can take an elevator ride up the inside of the rock, or climb the 352 steps to the top. There are several observation decks that offer a birds-eye view of the zoo, the park, and the eastern side of Paris. If you look towards the east from the rock, one of the first sets of buildings you'll see is a special center that trains seeing-eye dogs as companions for blind people.

The Vincennes Zoo's Forest African elephant was the subject of an interesting recent discovery about elephants. Named Coco, she is the only one of this type in captivity in the world. Researchers analyzed her DNA and discovered that contrary to what had been believed previously, Forest African elephants are not the same species as the more common Savanna African elephants. This means that there are three distinct types of elephants in the world: Asian, Forest African, and Savanna African.

PARC FLORAL. *By the Esplanade du Château and Route de la Pyramide. Metro: Château de Vincennes. Then take bus # 112 or walk about 10 minutes. Open daily 9:30am-8pm. Adults: €3; Kids 6-18: €1.50; Kids under 7: free. Ask for the free map and the program to free "Pestacles" performances at the entrance.*

This park is a real treat! When you first walk in you are greeted by several different gardens. There are flower gardens, pine gardens, and a garden of four seasons that blossoms all year. If you head towards the left, you come to a small museum that features exhibits on the ecosystems around Paris and a butterfly garden. The day we were there, we got to see what kinds of fish live in the Seine River. If you keep going past the crêpe restaurant and big pond, you'll come to the children's section. It features wonderful playgrounds, complete with castles and those climbing webs that we like to call Eiffel Towers. There also are some really fun activities for which you will need to purchase tickets. They are organized according to age and size. Look at the horizontal bars at the entrance. They indicate the minimum and maximum heights for each ride. The activities include such favorites as pedal-powered horse chariots, race cars, and a hilarious mini boat ride for babies.

Parent Tip: If tired little feet are threatening to spoil your visit, hop onto the park's little white train. It has stops all around the Parc Floral.

The park features several eateries, ranging from light fare at the crêpe restaurant to a full (and still family-friendly) meal in the big restaurant by the pond. It also has several buildings called **Maisons de Paris Nature**, that are dedicated to sensitizing Parisians about the natural world around them.

There are two theaters in the park. One features a marionette show. The other has live performances and concerts. In the summer, there is a whole kid-centered festival called Les Pestacles that offers free shows every Wednesday afternoon at 2:30. These range from mime, to clown, theater, singing, and musical performances.

If you enjoy miniature golf, don't miss the one in this park. Each hole features one or several of the major monuments of Paris. Can you get your ball through the Eiffel Tower or up the Montmartre hill? See if you can recognize all the sights. Hint: the course is laid out as if it were a big map of the city.

AQUARIUM–PALAIS DE LA PORTE D'OREE. *293, Avenue Daumesnil. Metro: Porte Dorée. Open Wed-Mon, 10am-5:15pm. Closed Tues. Adults: €4; Kids under 18: €2.60. One adult with 1-2 children between the ages of 4 and 12: €5.*

This aquarium is located in the basement of a building, which was constructed in 1931 as part of a Colonial Exposition meant to show off art and artifacts from the French colonies in Africa and the Pacific. The building, called the Palais de La Porte Dorée, also was meant to showcase the so-called civilizing influence of colonialism on the occupied peoples. Many of the building's decorations reflect this colonial hubris. For example, there are allegories to the French ideals of Liberty, Justice, Science, and Industry being brought to the colonies.

Today we see these images as biased and offensive. At least, children will enjoy looking at all the animals depicted in the scenes along the facade and in the main lobby. Until recently the Palais de La Porte Dorée housed a museum of art and artifacts from North Africa, Sub-Saharan Africa, and Pacific Islands. These are currently in storage awaiting the completion of a new museum on the Quai Branly. The rooms here will house a new center dedicated to the history of immigration in France. Meanwhile, the aquarium remains open and home to different sorts of fish big and small. There are brightly colored fish from tropical waters like the clown fish of *Finding Nemo* fame. There are electric eels, piranhas, and primitive looking fish that have barely evolved since dinosaurs ruled the earth. Best of all, there's the big stuff: crocodiles, tortoises, and even sharks.

HIPPODROME DE VINCENNES (HORSE RACES). *2, Route de la Ferme. Metro: Château de Vincennes, then take Bus #112 or RER: Joinville le Pont (line A) plus Free shuttle bus from the train station. Adults €3-5 depending on the race.; Kids: free. Races begin at 1:45pm.*

Do you have any horse lovers in your group? Why not got to the races? This 19th century racecourse features trotters. You can look around and see the stables, tribunes, and place where the jockeys are weighed. Best of all you can see beautiful horses in action. Pick a favorite, even if you're not going to bet any money on it. There is a playground to entertain smaller children, if you need it.

RENTING BICYCLES. Bikes are a great way to explore and enjoy this vast park. You can rent bicycles at the **Lac des Minimes** (*Tel. 01 30 59 68 38*); **Lac Daumesnil** (*Tel. 01 47 47 76 50*); or the **Bicyclub** in the Parc Floral (*Tel. 01 47 66 55 92*).

LAC DES MINIMES, *on the northeastern side of the Bois de Vincennes,* *RER: Fontenay sous Bois* and **LAC DAUMESNIL,** *on the western edge of the* *park, near Metro: Porte Dorée.*

Both of these lakes were artificially created and decorated with fake islands and grottos. They are very pretty. You can watch the ducks and swans float by. Children enjoy exploring the lake in a rented rowboat or paddleboat. You can also visit the islands by crossing the charming little bridges. Both of these lakes have a restaurant on their islands. On the southern side of the Lac Daumesnil, there is a Buddhist center. The building was created for the Colonial Exhibition of 1931. It contains an enormous, golden statue of Buddha.

PARIS FARM. *Route du Pésage or Route de la Ferme. Near the* *Hippodrôme. Metro: Château de Vincennes then take Bus #112 or RER:* *Joinville le Pont. Open Sat-Sun and holidays, 1:30pm-7pm. Adults: €2; Kids* *6-18, €1; Kids under 6: free.*

A visit to the farm is always fun, even if it is on the edge of a big city. This one is run by a young couple, who make it a point to help children understand where their food comes from. If your timing is right, you may be able to help feed the animals or pick fruits in the orchard. Or you may catch the farmers in time to watch them sheer the sheep or milk the cows. Visit during the late spring or early summer and you'll see the new lambs, ducklings, and other baby animals.

FOIRE DU TRONE. *In the Bois de Vincennes, near the Lac Daumesnil.* *Metro: Porte de Charenton. During the summer months.*

In the 9th century, monks used to hold a fair on this spot every year. Here we are over 1,000 years later, and the tradition continues. The Foire du Trône is still held every year, between Easter and the end of May. The fair is named for the thrown (trône) that once stood in the Place du Trône (now called Place de la Nation) in honor of the marriage of King Louis XIV and Marie-Therese. There are plenty of thrill rides, merry-go-rounds, carnival games, food, and other amusement park attractions.

HORSEBACK RIDING. For information, contact the **Club d'Equitation Bayard,** *Tel. 01 43 65 46 87.*

TENNIS. One of the best places to find an open court in the Paris area is at the **Centre de Tennis de la Falguère**, Route de la Pyramide, Metro: Château de Vincennes.

BASEBALL DIAMOND. *Route de la Pyramide, among the athletic* *fields north of the Hippodrome.*

This is one of the few baseball fields in Paris. Baseball is not widely known in France, but there is a local baseball association that sponsors regular games.

15. CHAMPS ELYSÉES & CONCORDE

The **Avenue des Champs Elysées** is one of the most famous avenues in the world. It was named for the Elysian Fields of Greek mythology, where heroes get to go after they die. Today, the Champs Elysées is more of a shopper's paradise. A popular old French tune describes it this way, "Whether it's sunny or rainy, midnight or midday, there's something for everyone on the Champs Elysées."

With its wide, tree-lined sidewalks, the Avenue des Champs Elysées also follows the perspective formed by the Louvre, Tuileries Gardens, **Place de la Concorde** and Arc de Triomphe. Lovely vistas and photo opportunities abound.

ARC DE TRIOMPHE. *Place Charles de Gaulle-Etoile. Access to the arch through the metro or underground passageway from the Champs Elysées. Do not attempt to cross the traffic circle. Metro: Charles de Gaulle/Etoile. Museum and viewing platform open daily, 9:30am-11pm (April-September); 10 am-10 pm (October-March). Adults: €7, Kids ages 12-25: €4.50. Kids under 12: free.*

The Arc de Triomphe graces the center of the Place Charles de Gaulle-Etoile and the top of the Champs Elysées hill. It is directly in line with the Louvre, Arch du Carrousel, and Concorde Obelisk to the east. To the west it is aligned with the modern, Grande Arche de la Défense. The perspective offers great photo opportunities.

Champs Elysées & Concorde Highlights

• Climb up to the top of the Arc de Triomphe
• Find the frieze that depicts the French national anthem
• Look at the cars in the Renault show room/museum
• See a movie in the plush Champs Elysées theaters
• Visit the stamp collectors near the Place de la Concorde
• Watch the rats go through their maze at the Palais de la Découverte
(Science Museum)
• Admire the glass domes of the Grand and Petit Palais
• Have your photo taken on the Pont Alexandre III
• Imagine living inside one of the statues on the Place de la Concorde
• Play in the Parc Monceau

The Arc de Triomphe was built by Napoleon I to celebrate his military victories. It was meant to look like an ancient Roman triumphal arch, only bigger. Work on the project began in 1809. In 1810, Napoleon married his second wife, Marie-Louise. He wanted to celebrate with a procession under the arch. But since it wasn't finished, they had to settle for a parade under a wooden replica. When Napoleon was ousted from power in 1814, the arch was still unfinished. It was finally completed in 1836.

Napoleon was not the first to think of building a monument on this hilly crossroad, known as l'Etoile (or "Star," since it's at the intersection of several major streets). Fifty years earlier, King Louis XV had plans drawn up for a monumental elephant to be built on this spot. This elephant monument would have been as big as a palace. It was designed with fancy rooms, staircases, and fountains that would pour out of the elephant's trunk. Alas, it was never built. You can see a drawing of the plan in the small museum inside the Arc.

For over a hundred years, the Arc de Triomphe has been one of the most recognizable monuments of Paris, and it has come to represent a symbol of patriotism and national glory. Great funeral and military parades have taken place up and down the avenue. When Napoleon's ashes were brought back to France after his death in exile, they were paraded under the arch before being laid to rest in the Invalides. Victor Hugo's funeral procession also passed through the Arc de Triomphe. The avenue also has been the scene of some of France's greatest triumphs and some of its worst humiliations. In 1870, when Germany defeated France and took over the regions of Alsace and Lorraine, the Kaiser and his troops marched down the Champs Elysées. All the shops put up signs saying, "Closed for National

Mourning," and the statues in the Place de la Concorde were covered in black veils. During the German occupation of Paris in World War II, German troops marched through the arch every day. The Allied forces held victory parades through the Arc de Triomphe in 1919 at the end of World War I, and again in 1945 after the Liberation of Paris in World War II.

In 1920, the ashes of an unknown soldier killed in World War I were laid to rest under the Arc de Triomphe. A memorial flame was placed to mark the spot in 1923. It is re-lit every day at 6 pm. Each year there is a memorial service under the arch to remember all the French soldiers who have fallen in war. It takes place on the anniversary of the signing of the Armistice ending World War I: the 11th hour of the 11th day of the 11th month (celebrated in the U.S. as Veteran's Day, November 11).

The sides of the Arc de Triomphe are decorated with battle scenes. The most famous depicts a woman representing Liberty who is guiding the troops to victory. It is called La Marseillaise, which is the name of France's national anthem. There are also sculptures representing Peace and Triumph.

You can visit the inside of the arch and climb up the 284 steps to the top. The entrance is inside one of the legs of the arch. There is a small museum and a roof top terrace that offers terrific views of the city.

Fun Fact

The **Marseillaise** is the French national anthem. It was written in 1792 by a soldier and musician named Claude-Joseph Rouget de Lisle. He was stationed in Strasbourg, a city in eastern France. His commanding officer asked him to write a marching song for the Army of the Rhine. He did. Although it was written in Strasbourg, the song got the name Marseillaise, because it was adopted by pro-revolutionary troops as they marched from Marseilles to Paris in 1789. According to legend, the troops were still singing the song as they approached the king's palace in the Tuileries. The Marseillaise became the song of the Revolution, and in 1795 it was adopted as the national anthem. Ironically, Rouget de Lisle did not support the Revolution. He was arrested for remaining loyal to the king, and barely escaped losing his head to the guillotine.

CHAMPS ELYSÉES. *Stretches from the Arch de Triomphe to the Place de la Concorde. Metro: Charles de Gaulle-Etoile, George V, Franklin Roosevelt, Champs Elysées-Clemenceau, or Concorde.*

In the early 16th century, Queen Marie de Médicis ordered that the marshy fields west of her Tuileries Palace be drained and transformed into a tree-lined promenade. It was named the Cours de la Reine (Queen's Course). In 1667, King Louis XIV asked his favorite landscape architect, André Le Nôtre, to redesign the area. In 1709, the course was renamed Champs Elysées after the Elysian Fields of Greek mythology, where heroes go after they die.

For many years, much of the Champs Elysées path was lined with houses, cafés, and cabarets. Cows grazed in nearby fields. In 1814-1815, invading Russian and Prussian troops camped out in the fields and gardens along the Champs Elysées, leaving the place a wreck. In the 1830s, the Champs Elysées started to undergo a massive facelift. Gardens were rebuilt. Sidewalks, fountains, and gas street lamps were added. Famous architects were hired to build fancy dance halls, theaters, circuses, restaurants, and mansions.

By 1900, the Champs Elysées had become Paris' most fashionable address. It was lined with luxury shops and cafés, and filled with elegant folks dressed in their finest clothes. The avenue's popularity was boosted even more with the completion of the first metro subway line in 1902. This line ran directly under the Champs Elysées, from the Place de la Concorde to the Arc de Triomphe.

Today, the Avenue des Champs Elysées is still a popular place for a stroll, shopping, and great national events. It was the scene of a big celebration for France's bicentennial in 1989 and for the French men's World Cup Soccer victory in 1998. Each year the avenue is the site of the annual Bastille Day military parade, and the final stage of the Tour de France bicycle race. During the Christmas holiday season, the whole avenue is lit up and decorated until it positively glitters.

Fun Fact

North of the Rond Point des Champs Elysées is the home of France's President, known as the **Palais de l'Elysée**. It was built in 1718 as a royal palace and was used by kings mainly to house their guests. During the Revolution it was turned into a printing house, a ballet school, and eventually shops and apartments. Napoleon I used the Elysée Palace to house family and guests. It became the official presidential residence in 1873. It is closed to the public except during official visiting days in September, when people wait in line for up to three hours for a tour.

As you walk up and down either side of the Avenue des Champs Elysées, you will encounter a wide mix of shopping opportunities. There are occasional reminders that this avenue was once the heart of high fashion, with designer and high-end boutiques. There are gourmet eateries, like

Fouquet's that continue to attract French movie stars. However, mixed in with these are more familiar-looking American imports, such as Planet Hollywood, Virgin Records, Disney Store, and the ubiquitous Mac-Do (as the French call MacDonalds). There are several, large movie theaters. These are known for their comfortable seats. If you are in the mood for a movie, the chances are good that they'll be playing the latest Hollywood hits. To catch one in English, ask if it is in *version originale*. The *version française* will be dubbed in French.

If you enjoy checking out the latest models of European cars, there are several showrooms on either side of the avenue. The Renault showroom on the south side of the features a small exhibit of older models.

Below the Rond Point des Champs Elysées, where the avenue intersects with Avenue Gabriel and Avenue Matignon, is the oldest **marionnette show** in Paris. The small theater is located in the park on the left as you face the Place de la Concorde. The main character, Guignol, has been delighting audiences young and old on this spot since 1818. Shows take place daily during summer holidays (Wed, Sat, Sun during the school year) at 3pm, 4pm, and 5pm. Cost: €3.

Close by, at the lower end of the Champs Elysées, also on the left as you face the Place de la Concorde, is the Carée Marigny. This is where Paris' **stamp collectors** have been meeting to talk, buy, and sell their stamps for more than 125 years. Open every Thurs, Sat, and Sun.

Note the two magnificent horse sculptures at the entrance to the Champs Elysées by the Place de la Concorde. These are called the Chevaux de Marly (Horses of Marly), brought here from the Château de Marly during the French Revolution.

PALAIS DE LA DECOUVERTE (SCIENCE MUSEUM). *On the western side of the Grand Palais, along the Avenue Franklin Roosevelt. Metro: Champs Elysées/Clemenceau. Open: Tues-Sat, 9:30 am-6 pm, Sun, 10 am-7 pm. Note: the ticket offices shuts down 30 minutes before closing time. Closed Mon. Adults: €6.50. Kids 5-18: €4, Kids under 5: free. Supplement for the planetarium show: €3.50. Planetarium shows at 11:30am, 2pm, 3:15pm, 4:30pm (also at 5:45 Sat, Sun, and during school holidays).*

The Palais de la Découverte (Palace of Discovery) started out as a temporary exhibit for the 1937 Universal Exposition in Paris. It featured the latest scientific discoveries and techniques. The exhibit was such a hit that it was made into a permanent museum, with lots of hands-on experiments and demonstrations.

Today, the museum features exhibits and activities about astronomy, physics, geo-science, biology, math, and chemistry. The explanations and demonstrations are all in French, so you may be a little lost if you're not familiar with the experiments. But if you like science, it's well worth a try. Check out the rat school demonstration (Ecole des Rats) where real rats have to push levers, open doors, and find their way through a maze to food. The static electricity exhibit will make your hair stand on end. You can take a voyage into the center of a cell in the human biology section, or a virtual trip into space at the planetarium.

The building alone is pretty impressive. There is an excellent gift shop which is part of the Nature et Découverte chain (very much like the Nature Store chain in the US).

GRAND AND PETIT PALAIS. *Facing each other on the Avenue Winston Churchill by the Pont Alexander III (Metro: Champs Elysées-Clemenceau). The Petit Palais is open daily except Mon, 10am-5:40pm. Hours for the Grand Palais vary according to different temporary exhibits.*

Note: As of the writing of this book the Petit Palais was closed for renovations.

London's is lost to history, but Paris still has two crystal palaces, the Grand and Petit Palais. They were both built of glass and metal for the Paris Exhibition of 1900. The Grand Palais has a simpler design and is more in keeping with the Art Nouveau style of the time. The Petit Palais is more elaborately decorated, in the Rococo style, using lots of colonnades and classical statues. Both buildings were designed to show off French art at the 1900 Exhibition. Today, the Petit Palais continues to hold a collection of French art from the Renaissance through the 19th century, including nice impressionist paintings. The Grand Palais is used for blockbuster temporary exhibits on everything from Ancient Egypt to contemporary cartoons. They both make a great backdrop for family photos.

PONT ALEXANDRE III. *Between the Invalides and the Grand Palais. Metro: Invalides or Champs Elysées-Clemenceau.*

Another great photo opportunity, this is Paris' most elaborately decorated bridge. It was started 1897 to commemorate a new alliance between France and Russia and finished in time for the Paris Exposition of 1900. The first stone was laid by Czar Nicholas II of Russia, and the bridge is named for his father. On either side in the middle of the bridge are two statues representing the Seine and the Volga Rivers. At each end are statues of the mythical Greek winged horse Pegasus. They are covered in real gold leaf, as are many of the decorations on the bridge. The lamp posts were added in 1925. Their globes are made of hand-blown glass.

PARC MONCEAU. *Along Boulevard de Courcelles. Metro: Monceau. Open daily 7am-10pm (summer), and 7am-8pm (winter).*

In 1787, the Duke of Chartres (father of King Louis-Philippe) built himself a garden in the village of Monceau. The head landscaper was a theater lover and built arrangements that looked like sets for a play. He added naturalistic features typical of English gardens such as little rivers, water falls woods, boulders, and artificial grottos. There were also exotic touches such as a Chinese pagoda, an Egyptian pyramid, ruined Greek columns, and a Nomad's tent. In the 1860s, Napoleon III revamped the park and opened it to the public. A series of columns from an unfinished royal tomb were transported here, and numerous rare trees were planted throughout.

Today, the park preserves a certain romantic charm. There is a fine playground and plenty of room for kids to play. There is a special path for rollerblading.

The Parc Monceau is home to the biggest tree in all of Paris. It is a Platane d'Orient (Oriental Sycamore). At its widest, the tree's trunk measures more than 7 meters (23 feet) in circumference.

PLACE DE LA CONCORDE. *Metro: Concorde.*

This square was originally called Place Louis XV since it was started during his reign. The original design called for a magnificent statue of the king in the center. By the time the statue was completed, however, the king's popularity had declined sharply. The Place Louis XV was finally completely in 1774. Its namesake died a few months later of smallpox.

In 1770, even though the Place Louis XV was not finished, the king decided to hold a magnificent public party on the site with free wine flowing from the fountains and a huge fireworks display. This was all fine and well until one of the fireworks went astray, setting off a huge fire and series of explosions. One hundred thirty three people were killed.

Following the French Revolution, the square was renamed Place de la Revolution. The statue of Louis XV was toppled and melted down. A new statue to Liberty was erected in its place. In 1792, a guillotine was placed in the center of the Place. Over 1,000 people were beheaded there, including King Louis XVI and his wife, Marie Antoinette.

The square was renamed Place de la Concorde in 1795. When the monarchy was restored in the early 19th century, it was again called Place Louis XV, then Place Louis XVI. Finally, under King Louis Philippe, the name was changed back for good to Place de la Concorde.

The tall obelisk in the center of the Place was a gift from Egypt to France 1831 in thanks for the work of French archaeologist Champollion, who deciphered the secret to understanding hieroglyphics. The obelisk was from the Temple of Ramses II in Luxor where it was used to measure the sun's shadows. It dates from the 13th century BC. The obelisk is made of a solid piece of pink granite and is 23 meters (77 feet) tall. The four sides are covered with hieroglyphs describing the reigns of Ramses II and Ramses III. It took two years to transport the obelisk from Luxor to Paris. That trip is depicted in scenes along the base.

The **obelisk** still functions as a sundial. Look for the markings on the ground and see where the shadow of the monument's point hits them. That tells you what time it is.

There are two large fountains on the Place, representing river and maritime navigation. There are also eight large female statues. These represent some of France's main cities: Marseilles, Lyon, Lille, Strasbourg, Bordeaux, Nantes, Rouen, and Brest. In the late 1800s, people lived inside the bases of these statues, as depicted in Victor Hugo's novel *Les Misérables*. Note the small doors and windows.

16. L'OPÉRA, GRANDS MAGASINS & GRANDS BOULEVARDS

If there is a Phantom of the Opera, he must have a taste for luxury. He lives in a building made to look like a palace. The streets around it are filled with fancy shops and a Grand Hotel. And it's a quick walk to the city's biggest department stores.

Children, too, like the Opera neighborhood. Along with the luxury are fascinating tales in the Opera building, wonderful toy sections in the Grands Magasins department stores, and plenty of adventures along the Grands Boulevards.

PALAIS GARNIER OPERA HOUSE. *Place de l'Opéra (Metro: Opéra). Tours of the Opera House, including basements and backstage, are offered daily from 10 am to 4:30 pm (winter), 10 am to 5:30 pm (summer). English guides are available. Adults: €10; Kids 10-25: €6; Kids under 10: €3.80. You can also tour the grand staircase, performance hall, and museum on your own. Adults: €6; Kids: €3. The performance hall is closed to the public if there is a rehearsal.*

Although the idea of taking children to the Opera House may strike you as absurd, we were surprised at how much our boys and other kids around us enjoyed visiting the building. To them it offered all the glitter and

L'Opéra & Area Highlights

• Go behind the scenes and into the basements on a tour of the Opera House
• Buy a book in English at Brentano's
• Check out the toys and other cool stuff in the Grands Magasins
• Have lunch on top of the Galeries Lafayette
• See a real fashion show
• Discover Paris' shopping galleries and passageways
• Visit the Musée Grévin wax museum
• Be a star on the tour of the Grand Rex movie theater

adventure of a real palace. For a treat, take a guided tour (some are offered in English). It includes visits to grand staircase, *Grand Foyer*, performance hall, and mysterious lower levels, including the underground lake. You'll hear about the famous Phantom and some of the other secrets held within the magnificent bowels of this monumental building. There is also a small museum with a collection of costumes, set designs, and other articles from famous operas and ballets.

The history of this building dates back to the 1850s, when Emperor Napoleon III was leading a massive renovation of Paris to make the city more grand and beautiful. As part of this plan he invited architects to design a new opera house for the city. He received over 160 different proposals, and chose the one by Charles Garnier.

Garnier's Opera building was modeled on an Italian palace, and became known as the Palais Garnier (Garnier Palace). The design was so fancy and complicated that it involved 33 kilometers (20 miles) worth of drawings. The building was started in 1860 and finished in 1875. The construction workers ran into problems early on because the ground on which the opera was being built was marshy and unstable. There was even an underground spring running beneath it. Much of the water was drained with steam-powered pumps. The spring was diverted, and some of the water was used to create a lake under the building. The lake serves as a counterweight to help support the load of the 17 stories of Opera house above it. It lies in one of the building's sub-basements and is stocked with trout.

When it was built, the Palais Garnier was the largest theater in the world. It had 2,531 doors; 7,593 keys; 14 furnaces; 16 miles of gas pipes; 9 reservoirs; 2 huge water tanks; changing rooms for 538 people; and 100 closets for musical instruments. There was an entire section reserved for Napoleon III, including a private entrance, salons, guard rooms, and a stable that could hold 50 horses. Today, the stage can fit as many as 450 performers and the performance hall can seat more than 2,000 spectators. There are four balcony levels in the performance hall and seven basement levels below the stage.

The Garnier Opera House is richly decorated inside and out. The entrance is lined with statues representing poetry, music, dance, and drama. In 1860, vandals threw ink on the naked figures in the dance sculpture. In 1960, the statues were removed and replaced with copies to protect them from car pollution. The originals are now in the Musée d'Orsay. There are still traces of ink on the dancers.

The roof of the building is decorated with a statue of Apollo, the Greek god of music and arts. He is holding a lyre (small, harp-like instrument). The tip of this instrument is made of metal and serves as a lightening rod for the building. Garnier used the image of Apollo's lyre throughout the Opera. Look for it throughout the building decorating details of the ceilings, seats, staircases, chandeliers, curtains, and even doorknobs.

The original chandelier in the center of the performance hall weighed 20 tons. On May 20, 1896 the counterweight that held up the chandelier gave way in the middle of a performance and fell on the crowd below. Amazingly, only one person was killed, although many were injured. The current chandelier weighs 8 tons and contains more than 400 lights.

The ceiling of the performance hall was redone in 1964. It features a painting by Marc Chagall that shows some of the monuments of Paris as well as characters from some of Chagall's favorite operas. The main curtain for the stage is also painted on canvas, even though it looks like it is made of fabric. It rises straight up when the performance begins.

Do you know about the **Opera's phantom?** He comes from a book written by Gaston Leroux in 1910. Leroux loved to write mysteries. He was also fascinated with the Opera building's details and its legends – many of which he incorporated into his story of the *Phantom of the Opera*. It is about a man who lives hidden in the Opera like a phantom. He covers his deformed face with a mask and gives secret voice lessons to a beautiful young singer named Christine. The phantom falls in love with Christine and kidnaps her. Two men go to her rescue but are trapped by the phantom. Christine pities the phantom and lets him kiss her. In gratitude, the phantom releases her and the two men. Christine marries one of her rescuers, and the phantom dies of a broken heart.

The Opera also has had smaller, four-legged inhabitants – rats – due to all the underground passages and water. At one point the rat problem became so bad that the director of the Opera hired a rat-catcher. According to legend, he would come to the Opera house every two weeks covered in a special perfume that the rats couldn't resist. Like the Pied Piper, he would lead them down to the underground lake, where all the rats would drown.

Most of the city's operas are now performed at the Bastille Opera House. The Palais Garnier mainly features ballet and dance performances. In fact, the Opera is famous for its ballet school. The promising young dancers are referred to as the Petits Rats de l'Opera (Little Opera Rats). Unlike the 4-legged ones, these little rats are graceful and well loved.

BRENTANO'S BOOKSTORE. *37, Avenue de l'Opera. Metro: Opera or Pyramides. Closed Sun*

If you or your children have run out of reading materials, this is a good place to stop. Brentano's is an American bookstore that has been around for over 100 years. It offers a huge selection of English-language books on two floors. It has a large children's section and hosts a children's book club (in English).

GRANDS MAGASINS–DEPARTMENT STORES.

Le Printemps, *64, Boulevard Haussmann. Metro: Havre-Caumartin or Auber. Open Mon-Sat, 9:30 am-7 pm (Thurs until 10pm), Closed Sun.*

Galeries Lafayette, *40, Boulevard Haussmann. Metro: Chaussee d'Antin. Open Mon-Sat, 9:30 am-6:45 pm, (Thurs until 9 pm), Closed Sun.*

Paris invented the first department store and still shows the rest of the world how to do them well. The Printemps and Galeries Lafayette chains have stores throughout the city and across France. However, the Boulevard Haussman stores are the best. The buildings themselves are quite beautiful. There are elaborate, art-nouveau style skylights, stairways, and decorations. Each one has a top floor caféteria. The Galeries Lafayette also has a nice rooftop café open in warm weather. The views of the Opera and other rooftops of Paris are spectacular.

Inside these stores, you'll find fantastic toy sections with play areas for smaller tots. Of course there are many fashions, perfumes, and cosmetics to choose from. If you need gifts for folks back home, don't miss the souvenir and gourmet food sections. You will also see plenty of electronics and video games. Remember, however, that French appliances function on a 220 volt current, whereas those in the US are made for 110 volts. You can purchase an adapter to compensate, or opt for those that are battery powered. Note that French televisions, DVDs, and videos function on a different standard than those in the US. Finally, remember that if you purchase a computer or video game in France, it will likely be in French.

If you are in Paris during the winter holidays, don't miss the lights and decorations along the **Boulevard Haussman.** The windows feature wonderful toy displays. The streets sparkle with lights and stars. Once, I heard a little boy look up at them and exclaim, "Oh Mommy, I never realized how dark it was until I saw all these lights."

Is your child a natural fashion critic? Future clothing designer? You're in the fashion capital of the world. Here's a great opportunity to see the latest trends up close. The Galeries Lafayette Store on Boulevard Haussman features free 1-hour **fashion shows** every Tuesday at 11am (all year), and Fridays at 2:30 pm (April through October).

If you are in Paris in August or early September, take your children to see the "Back to School" section of the Grands Magasins. It's fun to compare the French version of school supplies with those back home. Besides, a Parisian pencil case, agenda, or portfolio can make a nice souvenir or gift for friends and teachers.

Fun Fashion Fact

The **beret** – a flat, round, black hat – is one of the classic fashion symbols of France. It was originally worn by people from the Basque and Bearnais regions in southwestern France. Today, anyone from students to old men can be seen wearing a beret. It's also part of several French military uniforms, including the *chasseurs alpins* (Alpine military patrol on skis) and parachute brigades.

France holds an annual **beret tossing competition**. The world distance record is 42 meters (nearly 1,400 feet).

GRANDS BOULEVARDS. *East of the Opera, including Boulevard des Capucines, Boulevard des Italiens, Boulevard Montmartre, Boulevard Poissonière, and Boulevard Bonne Nouvelle. Metro: Richelieu Drouot, Grands Boulevards, and Bonne Nouvelle.*

If you are going to be in Paris for New Year's Day, don't miss the parade down the Grands Boulevards. It comes complete with floats, giant balloons, clowns, the works!

These boulevards were once the sight of a protective wall built to defend the city from its enemies. In the 1670s, King Louis XIV decided the country's borders were well protected. He had the wall torn down, and in its place he created these wide boulevards. At the time they were on the edge of Paris, and they looked out over pastures and countryside. The boulevards were lined with high class cafés and theaters. Wealthy nobles built themselves mansions along the boulevards surrounded by large parks.

During the 19th century, the fancier shops and noble residents began to move west. The Grands Boulevards became more bohemian. There was a lively theater and music hall scene. Artists such as Maurice Utrillo and Edouard Manet painted street scenes along the boulevards. In the 20th century they were also popularized in song by singers such as Maurice Chevalier and Yves Montand.

Today, the Grands Boulevards feature theaters, cinemas, shops, and American-style eateries. In fact, if you are homesick for American food, this is where you can find some familiar names and menus (e.g., TGI Fridays, Hard Rock Café, Ben and Jerry's, the ubiquitous McDonalds).

SHOPPING GALLERIES AND PASSAGES. *Running perpendicular to the Grands Boulevards with entrances on Boulevard des Italiens and Boulevard Montmartre. Metro: Richelieu Drouot.*

Long before there were shopping malls, Paris had its indoor shopping galleries and passages. These were built in the second half of the 19th century to offer Parisians a chance to shop protected from the elements and street traffic. There were over 100 of them. Many were elaborately decorated with fancy skylights, tile floors, columns, and statues. Some had motifs from Egypt or Ancient Rome. Today, there are about 20 galleries and passages that are still open to the public. They remain one of the city's best shopping treats. The ones near the Grands Boulevards have much to please kids of all ages. There are stores featuring comic book characters, dollhouse furniture, teddy bears, and hip clothing. There are also nice cafés and irresistible pastry shops. So make like a 19th century Parisian and stroll through the shopping galleries away from the traffic, bad weather, and general bustle of the big city.

The first set of passages you will come to if you are arriving from the Avenue de l'Opéra is at #5 Boulevard des Italiens. It is called the **Passage des Princes**, and should not be missed. The whole place was recently renovated and transformed into a "Village of Toys." All the stores sell toys or games for your own little princes and princesses.

As you reach the Boulevard Montmartre, you will encounter two sets of passages, facing each other across the boulevard. At #10 Boulevard Montmartre, on the north side of the street, you can enter the **Passage Verdeau**. It is filled with fun shops, including the biggest collection of dollhouse furniture and other miniatures in the city. It has an excellent pastry place, a shop that sells rocks and minerals, and one of the oldest cane stores still in existence. This passage also contains a charming hotel (Hotel Chopin) and has Paris' wax museum (see below). Once you reach the end of the Passage Verdeau, cross the small side street to enter the **Passage Jouffroy**. Here there are excellent tearooms, used book stores, and shops. It then leads to the Rue Cadet which has a very nice outdoor market.

On the south side of the Boulevard Montmartre, across the street from the Passage Verdeau, is the **Passage des Panoramas**. This one was developed by an American businessman. It was originally decorated with giant circular paintings called panoramas. It was also the first passageway to be lit with gas lamps. The Passage des Panoramas has several parallel galleries, like a tic-tac-toe board. It eventually leads to the Rue Vivienne. If you follow the Rue Vivienne several blocks south to #6, you will come to the **Galerie Vivienne**. In here don't miss the wonderful toy shop called Si Tu Veux, featuring games, toys, teddy bears, and costumes. The Galerie Vivienne leads right into the **Galerie Colbert**. Both of these galleries have recently undergone a facelift and are very pretty. The Galerie Colbert has a wine paraphernalia store with a remarkable array of corkscrews.

MUSÉE GRÉVIN (WAX MUSEUM). *10, Boulevard Montmartre. Also opens onto the Passage Verdeau. Metro: Grands Boulevards. Open daily 10am-6pm. Adults: €17; Kids 6-14: €10; Kids under 6: free.*

Shortly before the French Revolution, a man named Jean Christophe Curtius opened a wax figure display called the Caverne des Voleurs (Robbers' Cavern). One of its principle pieces was the wax figure of a famous bandit, known as Cartouche. Curtius' niece, Marie Gresholtz, was a sculptor who married Francois Tussaud. They emigrated to London, where they set up Madame Tussaud's Wax Museum. Meanwhile, the Caverne des Voleurs was such a hit that Alfred Grévin and a man named Arthur Meyer expanded it to include historical figures and contemporary people. It was renamed, Musée Grévin.

Fun Fact

Have you heard of the French Robin Hood? His name was Louis Dominic Bourgignon, nicknamed **Cartouche**. He lived in Paris in the 1700s. Cartouche was the head of a band of more than 200 robbers. They stole from the rich and gave to the poor. Their hangout was the Taverne Saint Nicolas on the Ile de la Cité. Cartouche was seen as a hero by many Parisians. He was caught by the police but escaped from prison by digging a tunnel. He was later caught again and publicly executed in front of the Hôtel de Ville.

In the late 1800s, the Musée Grévin played an important role in promoting early telecommunications. When the first telephones were invented, the owners of the museum had two of them installed so that visitors could try them out by calling each other from different parts of the building. The Musée Grévin also sponsored early demonstrations of Thomas Edison's phonograph and the first x-rays. Then in 1892, the Musée Grévin presented the first public demonstration of moving pictures. The show was called the Théâtre Optique and included three short films. They were shown regularly until 1900.

Today, the wax museum's figures include famous actors, sports figures, politicians, historical figures, and even French chefs. Some are staged to represent historical events, including gory scenes from the French Revolution. These are a big hit with kids.

Most of the Grévin museum's wax figures are dressed in clothes that actually belonged to the people they represent. In fact, the designers start with the clothes and model the wax figures to fit into them. The hairpieces are made of real hair and placed in softened wax one strand at a time. Some of the wax figures (mostly politicians) have been stuck with pins and needles by people who believe in voodoo magic.

The museum also features a fun magic show. There is a sound and lights show dating from the Paris World Exhibition of 1900. Finally, don't miss the hall of funny mirrors. It gets a laugh every time.

LE GRAND REX. *1, Boulevard Poissonière. Metro: Bonne Nouvelle or Grands Boulevards. Self-guided, 50-minute tours offered every 5 minutes, 10 am-7 pm, Wed-Sun during the school year and daily during the summer. Ask for an English version. Adults: €7.50; Kids 6-12: €6.50. You can get a combined ticket for the visit + a movie for an additional €5 per person. Note: the visit includes dark hallways and special effects that may scare smaller children.*

The Grand Rex is a beautiful, grand, art-deco style movie theater built in 1932. It has welcomed many movie stars over the years and still has twinkling stars that shine from the ceiling of the main theater. You can go for a movie or opt for a self-guided, backstage tour (ask for an English headset). The tour, called Les Etoiles du Rex (Stars of the Rex), takes you up a glass elevator behind the giant screen. If there is a movie playing, you will catch a glimpse of it from the back. The tour introduces you to cartoon and real movie legends, shows you special effects, lets you feel and hear surround sound at its fullest, and shows films clips of the Rex's history. You even take part in a mini-movie production. At the exit, you can purchase a video of your own movie or buy photos that have been snapped by a candid camera during your tour. Giggles guaranteed.

PARIS STORY. *11, Bis Rue du Scribe. Metro: Opera. Open daily, 9am-7pm. Adults: €8; Kids 6-18: €5; Kids under 6: free. Special sessions for kids ages 8-12 are held each Saturday at 3pm and 5pm. Cost: €12 (snack included).*

Two-thousand years of Paris' history, legends, and monuments are told in this panoramic film. Headphones available in 12 different languages, including English.

GARE SAINT LAZARE (TRAIN STATION). *Place du Hâvre. Metro: Saint Lazare.*

This is the oldest of Paris' train stations. It was built in 1837. The Gare Saint Lazare is where you come if you need to catch a train for Giverny and other parts of Normandy. There are also trains for England (through Dieppe, other British-bound trains go from the Gare du Nord). The station has a hotel called Le Terminus. It was built for the Paris Exposition of 1889.

You may recognize the Gare Saint-Lazare from Impressionist paintings of it by **Edouard Manet** (whose art studio was nearby at #58, Rue de Rome) or by **Claude Monet** (who used to catch the train here to reach his house in Argenteuil and later at Giverny). Outside, in front of the station are two funny modern sculptures. One is called l'Heure de Tous (Everyone's Time). It is composed of pile of clocks. The other, called Consigne à Vie (Baggage Check for Life) is a pile of suitcases. Both were created in the 1980s by the artist Arman.

17. TROCADERO

If you want a photo of your family in front of the Eiffel Tower, the Trocadéro terrace is a must stop for you. It is on a hill, directly across the river from the Eiffel Tower, flanked by two rows of golden statues.

This neighborhood is also the sight of several wonderful museums, a lovely shopping street, and an informal memorial to the late Princess Diana.

The **Place du Trocadéro** is named for a Spanish Fort that was captured by the French in 1823. A magnificent museum was built on the Trocadéro hill for the Paris International Exhibition of 1878. It looked like the Taj Mahal in India. It was torn down and replaced with the current Palais de Chaillot (the two curved buildings surrounding the Trocadéro) for the Paris Exhibition of 1937.

MUSEE DE L'HOMME. *Palais de Chaillot. 17, Place du Trocadéro. On the right as you face the Eiffel Tower. Metro: Trocadéro. Open Wed-Mon, 9:45 am - 5:15 pm. Closed Tues. Adult: €4.57, Kids under 18: €3.05.*

As of the writing of this book many of the ethnographic exhibits of the museum were closed, awaiting transfer to a new home. What remains are temporary exhibits and presentations on the history of man. The formerly kid friendly Totem Restaurant has been replaced with a more expensive Café de l'Homme, which still offers a spectacular view of the Eiffel Tower.

MUSEE DE LA MARINE. *Palais de Chaillot. 17, Place du Trocadéro. In the same building as the Musée de l'Homme. Open Wed-Mon, 10am-5:50pm. Ticket office shuts down 30 minutes before closing time. Closed Tues. Adults: €9. Kids 8-25 yrs: €5. Kids under 8: Free. Audioguide: €4. A kid's guide with games (in French) is available free of charge at the entrance. Family tours (in French) Sun. at 3pm.*

Trocadero Highlights

- Have your photo taken with the Eiffel Tower in the background
- Check out Napoleon's golden boat and other amazing ships at the Musée de la Marine
- Watch the roller-bladers and fountains in the Trocadéro Gardens
- Go window shopping along the Rue de Passy
- Visit Balzac's House
- Look for the statue of Benjamin Franklin
- Visit the Museum of Modern Art
- Look for the replica of the Statue of Liberty's flame
- See Monet's Impressionist paintings at the Musée Marmottan
- Take a boat tour and find the statue of the Zouave

This is a must-see for anyone big or small who likes boats of any kind. The museum has a remarkable collection of large ship models designed for King Louis XIV. There are also models of Columbus' Santa Maria, famous cruise ships, submarines, and many others. You can see a full-size replica of Napoleon's imperial boat. There are live demonstrations by people who make or repair ship models. Special exhibits cater to kids' tastes, with topics such as pirates or ships featured in the Adventures of Tintin.

The **TROCADERO GARDENS** were created for the 1937 Paris Exhibition. The statues lining the fountains celebrate joy and youth. The fountains are very impressive when the canons (big jets) are turned on. These gardens have become a favorite rendez-vous spot for roller-bladers. You can watch them perform their stunts, framed by the majestic view of the Eiffel Tower. The gardens contain playgrounds and plenty of space for running around. There is a big, double-decker carrousel at the bottom of the hill.

Note: Do not let your children play in the Trocadéro Fountains, even if it is a hot day. Not only is it against the rules, but it is also dangerous to be in the pool when the giant water jets turn on without warning.

If you head south and west from the Place du Trocadéro, you will come to a statue of **Benjamin Franklin** and a street that bears his name. This statue commemorates the fact that Franklin lived in the nearby Rue Raynouard when he was America's Ambassador to France. In 1776, Franklin successfully persuaded the French King Louis XVI to help support the American colonists in their War of Independence against Britain. Louis XVI, who had his own bones to pick with the British, agreed to furnish troops, naval support, supplies, and military commanders to the American effort. The French help proved to be critical to the Americans. Their naval support and commanders such as General Lafayette were invaluable. Moreover, when General George Washington won the Battle of Yorktown – which would turn around the war in his favor – half of his troops were French. In 1783, Benjamin Franklin returned to Paris to negotiate a Peace Treaty with Britain, which officially recognized America's independence.

It was from his house in the Rue Raynouard that Franklin watched the world's first hot air balloon flight by the French Montgolfier brothers. It was also on the rooftop of this house that he tested the city's first lightening rod. Ben Franklin loved Paris, and Paris loved him. Elegant men and women copied his hair and fashion styles. Franklin became a popular boy's name. Today he is honored with this statue and one in the Louvre Museum, which was a gift from the United States to commemorate Franklins' 200th birthday.

PASSY NEIGHBORHOOD. *Southwest from the Place du Trocadéro, down the Rue Franklin to the Place de Costa Rica, and Rue de Passy. Metro: Passy.*

This is a very chic neighborhood. The Rue de Passy is a great street for window-shopping, particularly if you favor classic fashions (known in French as Bon Chic, Bon Genre). Think preppy with a French flair. The nearby Rue de l'Annonciation has a lovely outdoor market. It is a nice place to pick up a picnic lunch or some delicious pastries for a snack.

MAISON DE BALZAC. *47, Rue Raynouard, Metro: Passy. Open Tues-Sun, 10am-5:30pm. Closed Mon. Adults: €4. Kids age 14-26: €2. Kids under 14: free. Free to all every Sun, 10am-1pm.*

If you or your high-schooler ever had to read the works of Honoré de Balzac you may enjoy this visit. Balzac was a famous French author who lived from 1799 to 1850. He wrote more than 90 books and short stories, such as Cousine Bette and Le Père Goriot. Balzac was an avid worker, often writing for 14 to 16 hours a day. He slept little and drank lots of coffee. Although an excellent writer, Balzac was a terrible businessman. He was always broke, and had to rent the top floor of this house under a false name, Madame veuve Breugnol (the Widow Breugnol) to avoid his creditors. Balzac gave his friends a secret password so that the housekeeper would let them in.

You can visit the author's old rooms, see his coffee set, and admire the carved decorations in the dining room. In his library, even the door was covered with bookshelves, so that when it was closed you couldn't tell which way was out. One of Balzac's favorite tricks on first-time visitors was to invite them into the library and pull the door shut, trapping them until they could find the hidden exit.

MUSÉE MARMOTTAN - MUSÉE MONET. *2, Rue Louis Boilly. Metro: La Muette. Open Tues-Sun, 10am-5:30pm. Closed Mon. Adults: €7. Kids ages 8-25: €4.50. Kids under 8: free.*

Fun Fact

Did you know that art critics originally used the name **Impressionism** as an insult? They thought the works by Monet and his friends were sloppy and unfinished. The painters liked the name, however. It reflected their attempts to capture the feeling of a scene. They were breaking with traditional methods taught in art school by using bold colors, big brushstrokes, and painting outdoor scenes of everyday life. Although many of the Impressionist painters struggled to make a living, today Impressionist paintings sell for a fortune. Success was ultimately their revenge.

This is another fun stop for any child who enjoyed the book, *Linnea in Monet's Garden*. It is an excellent place to see some of the most important examples of Impressionist art. It is rarely crowded and a good alternative if you are not up to facing the crowds at the Musée d'Orsay. The permanent collection includes 65 paintings by Claude Monet that were donated by his son, Michel. This is where you can see Monet's Impression, Soleil Levant (Impression, Sunrise) that gave Impressionism its name.

On the lower level of the museum there is a room full of water lilies and other paintings from Monet's garden at Giverny. As you explore this part of the museum, encourage your kids to follow Linnea's example. Have them stand just a foot or two from a painting, where all you can make out are brush strokes and colors. Then have them move back to see how the subjects and details of the painting become clearer. Are some of them still hard to make out, even from a distance? Some art historians attribute this to the fact that in his later life, Monet suffered from cataracts and was losing his eyesight.

The museum also features works by Monet's friends, Renoir, Sisley, Berthe Morisot, Pissarro, and Gauguin. They were part of his private collection.

The Musée Marmottan is housed in a private mansion, formerly owned by an art historian named Paul Marmottan. Mr. Marmottan also collected medieval art objects and furniture from the time of Napoleon I. These are exhibited in the museum's upper floors.

Parent Tip: After a tour of the Musée Marmottan head for a break in the **Jardin du Ranelagh**. It is located behind the museum, across the street. There are playgrounds, roller-bladers, pony rides, a puppet theater, and an antique Merry-Go-Round that's still turned by hand.

MUSÉE D'ART MODERNE DE LA VILLE DE PARIS. *11, Avenue du Président Wilson. Metro: Iéna or Alma Marceau. Open Tues-Sun, 10am-6pm (until 10 pm on Wed). Closed Mon. Fees vary depending on the temporary* *exhibits offered. Free for everyone each Sun, 10am-1pm. Kids' tours and workshops (in French) offered daily during summer holidays and on Wed and Sat at 2:30pm and 4:30pm.*

This museum has recently re-opened after a major renovation. It has plenty to offer kids, remembering that they often enjoy modern art as much or more than adults. The permanent collections include works such as Matisse's dancer cutouts, Chagall's The Dream; and pieces by Fernand Leger, Picasso, and Robert Delaunay. There are also excellent temporary exhibits.

MUSEE GUIMET (ASIAN ART). *6, Place d'Iéna. Metro: Iéna. Open Wed-Mon, 10am-6pm. Closed Tues. Adults: €6. Kids under 18: free. Free to all every Sun. Audio-guide: free. Numerous special workshops are offered for kids on the art of calligraphy and other topics.*

This museum offers one of the most important Asian art collections in the world. The building was recently renovated, so it offers bright, airy exhibit spaces. The works are organized chronologically by culture: Chinese, Japanese, Korean, Indian, Thai, Khmer, Burmese, Vietnamese, Tibetan, Nepaliese, Pakistani, Afghan, and more. From the top floor rotunda, you can admire beautiful Chinese screens, and a take in the wonderful view of the Eiffel Tower.

PONT DE L'ALMA. *Between Place de l'Alma and Place de la Résistance, Metro: Alma Marceau*

This bridge was built by Napoleon III and named for one of his successful battles in the Crimea in 1854. It is famous for its statue of a **Zouave soldier**, used to measure high water points. Boatmen know that if the Seine's water rises as high as the Zouave's waist during periods of flooding, it is not safe to navigate under the bridges. During the Great Flood of 1910, the Seine's waters rose all the way up to the Zouave's chin.

Who is the Zouave? In 1830, a group of Zouaoua tribesmen from the hills of Algeria and Morocco joined the French army as an auxiliary battalion. Their uniform was based on their brightly colored traditional clothes, including a red sash, blue vest, baggy pants, and red fez (a brimless cap with a tassel). Called Zouaves, they were brave and well trained. They developed a reputation as dashing daredevils. The Zouaves remained an important part of the French military up to World War I.

In 1860, an American named Elmer Ellsworth, a friend and former law clerk of Abraham Lincoln, put together two local militia groups composed primarily of New York firemen. They adopted the Zouave uniform and training drills. With the outbreak of the Civil War, these groups joined the Union forces

Ellsworth was shot in Alexandria, Virginia trying to tear down a Confederate Flag. On orders of Abraham Lincoln, Ellsworth's body was laid in state in the White House. Ultimately, dozens of American Zouave Units were formed and fought for the North.

On the Place de l'Alma side of the bridge there is a full-size replica of the golden torch that sits atop the Statue of Liberty in New York Harbor. This torch sculpture was a given to Paris by a consortium of American companies to celebrate the bicentennial of the French Revolution in 1989. It happens to be located near the tunnel in which Princess Diana had her fatal car crash, and for years was covered with flowers and other mementos as an unofficial monument to her memory.

BATEAUX MOUCHES–TOUR BOAT RIDES. *Pont de l'Alma. Right Bank. Metro: Alma Marceau. Daily departures at 11am, 11:30am, 12:15pm, 1pm, 2pm, 3:15pm, and every 30 minutes from 4-10pm. Adults: €7; Kids 4-12: €4; Under 4: free. Daily lunch cruise (except Mon) at 12:30pm features a kid's menu. Adults: €50; Kids under 12: €30. (Note: Although there are also evening dinner cruises, they are formal affairs and not recommended for children.)*

Always a welcome treat, the Bâteaux Mouches boat rides offer a unique view of many of the city's major monuments and bridges. Regular tours last one hour. There are commentaries in French and English. The lunch tour lasts 2.5 hours. Either tour is a great way to rest weary feet or recover from jet lag. It is also the best vantage point from which to admire the Zouave statue on the Pont de l'Alma and the small replica of the Statue of Liberty on the Ile Aux Cignes.

The Bâteaux Mouches were first introduced to Paris as a form of public transportation for the 1867 Universal Exposition. They were a huge hit. By 1900, there were over 100 Bâteaux Mouches ferrying 25 million passengers each year to points along the Seine. With the growth of the subway and bus lines, demand for these boats as a form of public transportation died. They were eventually converted to tour boats. However, in the 1990s demand for a public transportation boat returned, and the Bâtobus was born.

By the way, although mouches means fly in French, don't let the locals convince you that these boats were named for a water bug. The truth is Mouches was the name of the neighborhood in the city of Lyon where the original Bâteaux Mouches were designed.

18. MONTMARTRE

Ah, **Monmartre**. The name conjures images of Bohemian artists, accordion players, and Amélie Poulain. There is clearly something tender and charming about this little village of a neighborhood, perched atop one of the tallest hills in Paris. Montmartre has preserved its cobbled streets, little houses, even a vineyard and two windmills. There is much to enchant both adults and children here. So climb to the top of the hill and enjoy the wonderful views and secrets hidden among the winding streets of this village on a hill.

According to legend, the name Montmartre comes from Mont des Martyrs (Martyrs' Hill). This refers to the martyr Saint Denis and his two companions, Rustique and Eleuthère, who were early Christian evangelists. They were captured and condemned to death by Roman soldiers in the year 250 AD. The path they are said to have followed on the way to their execution atop the Montmartre hill is now the Rue des Martyrs (Martyrs' Road). A second explanation for Montmartre's name comes from the fact that during the Roman Occupation of Paris there was a temple on top of the hill that was dedicated to Mars, the god of war. Hence the name would come from Mont Mars.

There are several different ways you can approach a visit to Montmartre. You can start at Metro: Anvers, walk up the hill to the Sacré Coeur Basilica, then wind your way through the side streets to the west and back down the hill to Metro: Anvers or Pigalle. Conversely, you can start at Pigalle and follow the footsteps of Saint Denis up the side streets, then over to the Basilica and back down the hill to Metro: Anvers. If you are pressed for time or not up to walking up and down steep hills, you can hop on the tourist

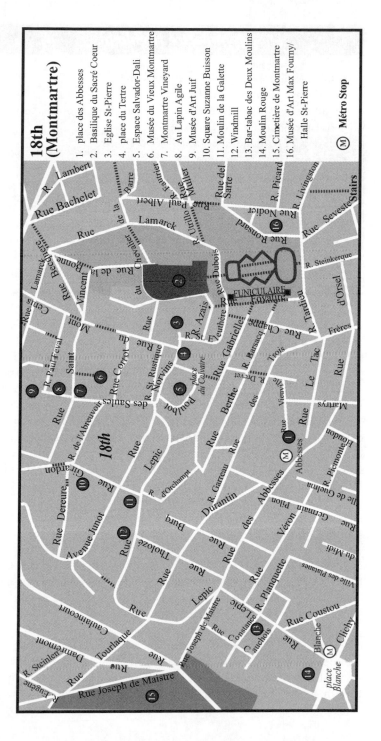

18th
(Montmartre)

1. place des Abbesses
2. Basilique du Sacré Coeur
3. Eglise St-Pierre
4. place du Tertre
5. Espace Salvador-Dali
6. Musée du Vieux Montmartre
7. Montmartre Vineyard
8. Au Lapin Agile
9. Musée d'Art Juif
10. Square Suzanne Buisson
11. Moulin de la Galette
12. Windmill
13. Bar-tabac des Deux Moulins
14. Moulin Rouge
15. Cimetière de Montmartre
16. Musée d'Art Max Fourny/
    Halle St-Pierre

Ⓜ Métro Stop

Montmartre Highlights

- Ride the funicular up the Montmartre hill
- Check out the view from the Sacré Coeur
- Find the spot that used to house a Roman Temple of Mercury
- Visit the funny Dali Museum
- Have your portrait done at the Place du Tertre
- Find the Montmartre vineyards
- Look for the man who could walk through walls
- See Montmartre's two remaining windmills
- Admire the Art Nouveau subway entrance and church on the Place des Abesses
- Retrace the footsteps of the saint who carried his chopped off head up the hill
- Take a ride on the Montmartrain tourist train.

train, called Montmartretrain, for a 40 minute tour from Place Pigalle to the Sacré Coeur and back (Adults: €3.50; Kids: €2). There is also a public bus that runs through the neighborhood, called the Montmartrebus. For the price of one metro ticket, you can ride in a circle through Montmartre and past many of the major sights. The Montmartrebus has stops at the Place des Abesses and along many side streets.

GOING UP TO THE SACRÉ COEUR CHURCH. As you return to the square at the bottom of the Montmartre Hill, below the Sacré Coeur, you face several choices for reaching the top. You can opt for the lovely staircases that wind their way up in front of you. You can choose the slightly straighter stairs that run up the hill on both the right and left sides. Or you can head to the left and take a ride on the **funicular**. For the price of a regular metro ticket, you can glide up the hill on this diagonal train track. The ride is fairly short, and some parts take place in tunnels. However, the view when you are out in the open is fun, and kids love it.

BASILIQUE DU SACRÉ COEUR (BASILICA OF THE SACRED HEART). *Place du Parvis Sacré Coeur. Metro: Anvers or Château Rouge. Open daily: 9am-6pm. Entrance to the church is free, but you must pay to visit the crypt or to climb up to the top of the dome. Adults: €4.50; Kids: €2.50.*

One of the most recognizable sights on top of the Montmartre hill is the giant white Basilique du Sacré Coeur. This church was built to commemorate the victims of the Paris Commune uprising in 1870. Construction lasted from 1873 to 1912. It was made in the Byzantine style with the shape of a short cross, decorated with domes and mosaics. The church is made of a special type of limestone that bleaches itself every time it rains. This explains why the Sacré Coeur looks so white and bright. In contrast, the inside of the church is quite dark. You can climb up to the top of the dome for a magnificent view of Paris and the surrounding area. There is also an excellent view from the terraces in front of the church. The belfry contains the largest bell in the world. It weighs 20,000 kilos (19 tons) and is 8 feet in diameter.

The small cobbled streets west of the Sacré Coeur take you into the heart of old Montmartre. Just beyond the Basilica is the old church of Saint Pierre de Montmartre. It dates from the early 12th century and was built on the spot that once held a Temple to Mercury during Roman times. In 1793, it was the sight of early telegraph experiments and ultimately served as a telegraph station until 1844.

Fun Fact

All French bells have names, and **Françoise Marguerite** is the name of the bell in the Sacré Coeur. It is also nicknamed the "Savoyarde," because it was made in the town of Annecy in the Savoy Region of France. The bell was carried to Paris in 1895 on a cart pulled by 11 pairs of oxen and 3 horses. It took 28 horses to pull the cart up the Montmartre hill. The bell is so large that it vibrates for 3 minutes after it has been struck. The sound can travel several miles.

PLACE DU TERTRE. *One block west of the Sacré Coeur Basilica. Metro: Abesses or Lamarck Caulaincourt.*

In the 1880s, many of the old buildings in the center of Paris were torn down as part of the period's great urban renewal projects. Low-income Parisians fled to the outskirts of the city, including to the Montmartre neighborhood. At the time, Montmartre was like a small village with narrow streets, fields, vineyards, and windmills. There were also cafés and dance halls, such as the famous Moulin Rouge. Until World War I, the area attracted many starving artists, musicians, and writers who flocked here to live the bohemian life. Some of their names included painters Amadeo Modigliani, Henri Toulouse-Lautrec, Paul Cézanne, Auguste Renoir, Camille Soutine, Maurice Utrillo, Pablo Picasso, Georges Braque, and Juan Gris; composers Hector Berlioz and Jacques Offenbach; and poets Henrich Heine and Guillaume Apollinaire.

The Place du Tertre does its best to keep alive the spirit of Montmartre's artistic heyday. It still resembles a village square surrounded by shade trees, shops, and small houses. Here you can purchase reproductions of the works of Montmartre's famous painters as well as other souvenirs. You can also support today's generation of starving artists who display their works in the Place or may offer to do your portrait. It is a fun place to grab a bite in a café and soak in the artistic atmosphere. If you have budding artists in the family, they may want to pull out the paper and drawing supplies for some artistic inspiration of their own.

Fun Fact

On December 24, 1898 a young car builder was at the wheel of the first gas-powered automobile to make it up the windy streets to the Place du Tertre. His name was **Louis Renault**, founder of the French car company that still carries his name. Every year on May 30 there is an antique car race up the Rue Lepic to the Place du Tertre to commemorate the event.

ESPACE MONTMARTRE – DALI MUSEUM. *11, Rue Poulbot (near Place du Tertre). Open daily 10am-6:30pm. Adults: €7; Kids 8-18: €5; Kids under 8: free.*

This little museum is literally dug into the hillside of Montmartre. It features the wild and wacky works of surrealist artist, Salvador Dali. While some kids will just find this gross, those with a taste for fantasy will get a kick out of his melting clocks and other odd scenes. After all it is not unlike the futuristic comics that many children enjoy.

Don't miss the great view of Paris from the Place du Calvaire, across from the museum.

MUSÉE DU VIEUX MONTMARTRE. *12, Rue Cortot. (2 blocks north of Place du Tertre) Open Tues-Sun, 11am-5:30 pm. Closed Mon. Adults: €5.50; Kids 10-18: €3.50; Kids under 10: Free.*

This small museum is located in a house that belonged to an actor who was part of Molière's theater troupe in the 1700s. There are rooms that are reconstructed to give you the feel of Bohemian Montmartre: a music room, the inside of a café, an office. There are paintings by Montmartre artists and many old-fashioned posters that you will recognize, like the Chat Noir (Black Cat). There are sometimes interesting temporary exhibits, such as a recent one of children's drawings dating from World War I.

EXPLORING SIDE STREETS. The area by the Sacré Coeur and Place du Tertre can get quite crowded during high tourist season. Luckily, you don't have to go very far into the side streets of Montmartre to escape the crowd and enjoy the quieter charm of the neighborhood.

If you take the Rue des Saules from the Rue Norvins, Rue Saint Rustique, or Rue Cortot you will run into several Montmartre landmarks. At the top of the street is the **Auberge de la Bonne Franquette**. This is a restaurant where Cezanne, Toulouse-Lautrec, Renoir, Sisley, Pissaro and other pals used to hang out. Later painters like Van Gogh and Maurice Utrillo immortalized this restaurant in their paintings. There are two other favorite artist restaurants as you head down the Rue des Saules. On the left is a pink restaurant, **La Maison Rose**, that was owned by Suzanne Valadon, artist and mother of Maurice Utrillo. Lower on the right is another restaurant with a painting of a rabbit jumping out of a pan. Called the **Lapin Agile**, it was a cabaret that also attracted plenty of artists in its day. It still features food and live music.

To the right, as you go down the Rue des Saules is the famous **Montmartre vineyard**. This is all that is left from the days when wine grapes covered the entire back side of the Montmartre hill. Each year on the first Saturday in October, the Montmartre neighborhood celebrates its local wine. The grapes are picked, then taken to the basement of the district's town hall to be pressed, aged, and bottled. The total wine production is about 700 bottles. The wine is called Clos Montmartre. Profits from the wine's sale pay for neighborhood events and festivities.

A walk down the Rue Saint Vincent along a small cemetery, leads to the Place Dalida, named for a popular singer of the 1960s-80s who lived in Montmartre. Down the Rue Girardon you come to a park called the **Square Suzanne Buisson**. The park is named for a Resistance leader captured by the Nazis during World War II. It is supposed to mark the spot where Saint Denis washed off his head in a fountain after his execution. A statue of Saint Denis carrying his head overlooks a reflecting pool in the park.

The nearby Avenue Junot used to be filled with windmills and is now lined with art studios and apartments. At the Place Marcel Aymé you will come across an odd **statue of a man walking through a wall**. It depicts a

Fun Fact

There were once 30 **windmills** on Montmartre. Now there are only two, both along the Rue Lepic. The Moulin Radet was moved here in the 17th century from another part of the city. **Moulin de la Galette** is over 600 years old. For 50 generations it belonged to a family of millers, called the Debrays. In 1814, Paris was under attack by the Russians. Four Debray brothers and one of their sons joined the battle to defend their city. All four brothers were killed. The son was pinned to the ground by a sword that went through his body. Somehow he survived his wounds. Since he loved dancing, the young Debray converted the family mill into a dance hall. It appears in many paintings by Montmartre artists, including Renoir and Toulouse Lautrec.

character from a novel by Marcel Aymé. The novel is a story about a man named Dutilleul who discovers he can walk through walls, and uses this skill to scare his bosses and become a burglar. Although he arrested and sent to jail, Dutilleul passes through the prison walls, has lunch in a restaurant, and calls the prison guard to help him pay the tab. In the end, he falls in love with a young woman and loses his magical powers.

The charming **Place Emile Goudot**, further down the hill, was home to artists Pablo Picasso, George Braque, and Juan Gris before World War I, at the time when they were experimenting with a new style called cubism. They lived in a building called the **Bâteau Lavoir**, which is still filled with art studios today.

Further down the hill still is the pretty **Place des Abesses**. This square is notable for its beautiful metro entrance. The glass awning is one of only two left that were designed in the Art Nouveau style by Hector Guimard. There is also an Art Nouveau style church across the street called Eglise Saint Jean de Montmartre.

FOLLOWING THE TRACES OF SAINT DENIS. *This path takes you through Montmartre, from the Pigalle Metro, up the Rue des Martyrs, Rue Yvonne Le Tac, past the Place Emile Goudeau, Moulin Radet to the Square Suzanne Buisson.*

Saint Denis was the first Bishop of Paris. He is also the patron saint of France. There are different stories about who he really was. Some versions say he was Greek, others that he was from Rome. In either case, he was sent to Paris to spread the word of Christianity around 250 AD, during the Roman occupation of Gaul. He was evidently very good at his work. Along with his two companions, Rustique and Eleuthère, Denis converted many people to Christianity. This made the Roman Emperor furious. He wanted his subjects to worship the Roman gods. The Emperor sent troops to Paris to stop the Christians. Roman soldiers arrested Denis, his companions, and many other Christians throughout the city. Denis and his companions were tortured and sentenced to death. According to the legend, the night before the execution was scheduled to take place, Christ (or in some versions a group of angels) appeared to Denis in his jail cell to give him Holy Communion.

The next day Denis, Rustique, and Eleuthère were marched up Mount Mercury (now known as Montmartre) to be executed in front of the temple of Mercury. However, the impatient Roman guards took matters into their own hands and beheaded the three prisoners well before they reached the top of the hill. According to the legend, while Rustique and Eleuthère fell to the ground, Denis picked up his head and continued walking up the hill. He washed the head off in a fountain, then walked another six kilometers (4 miles) until he reached the house of a holy woman named Catulla. Denis handed her his head, then collapsed. Catulla had him buried near her house.

Today it marks the spot of the great Saint Denis Cathedral, located north of Paris in a suburb called Saint Denis.

You can retrace the footsteps of Saint Denis as a way to enjoy some of the sights of Montmartre. Start at Metro: Pigalle. Walk one block east to the Rue des Martyrs and take it north, up the Montmartre Hill. This is supposedly the path that was taken by Denis and his companions on their way to the execution. When you reach the end of the street, take a right into the Rue Yvonne Le Tac. At #11, you will come to the Chapel of the Martyrs. This supposedly marks the spot where Denis, Rustique, and Eleutère were beheaded. In the 7th century, this chapel was considered to be a place of asylum. Any criminal who made it inside the building could seek refuge and pardon. The chapel was considered to be very sacred, and it received important visitors, such as Thomas of Canterbury and Thomas Aquinas.

Fun Fact

Husband's beware! The Chapel of the Martyrs was once thought to have holy spirits that could reform a bad husband. Unhappy wives would bring a piece of their husband's clothing to the chapel. It was supposed to guarantee that, within the year, the women's husbands would either reform or die.

Next, go back down the Rue Yvonne Le Tac the way you came, until you reach the Place des Abbesses (described above). Climb up the Rue de Ravignan, admiring the Place Emile Goudeau and Bâteau Lavoir along the way. Turn left into the Rue Norvins, past the Place Marcel Aymé (described above) with its sculpture of the man who could walk through walls. Take the Rue Girardon to the Square Suzanne Buisson. This pretty garden features a fountain and a statue of Saint Denis with his head in his hands. It is supposed to mark the spot where Denis rinsed off his head before continuing his journey north. It is also a nice place to play or relax in the shade, if you need a break from walking uphill.

To follow the rest of Saint Denis' path, you would need to go another four miles north and east from this spot. This would take you beyond Paris and into the suburb of Saint Denis to the great Saint Denis Basilica. This magnificent, gothic cathedral is well worth a visit. It contains the tombs of the French kings. You don't actually have to walk the whole way. There is an excellent subway station, called Basilique de Saint Denis that you can get to from the Pigalle or Anvers metro, by changing and heading north at the Place de Clichy metro stop.

To continue your tour of Montmartre, meanwhile, go past the Place Dalida and up the Rue de l'Abreuvoir to the Rue de Saules, where you can admire the Montmartre vineyard, Maison Rose, and Lapin Agile. A hike back up the Rue de Saules gets you to the Rue Cortot's Montmartre Museum. Meander down to the Place du Tertre, Espace Montmartre, and Place Poulbot. Then head for the Sacré Coeur. You can ride the funicular down the hill or opt for the stairs. At the bottom, kids will enjoy the fancy merry-go-round.

GARE DU NORD TRAIN STATION. *Located south and east of Montmartre, on the Rue Dunkerque. Metro: Gare du Nord.*

This station serves trains going to and from northern France as well as Belgium, the Netherlands, Scandinavia, and trains bound for Britain through Lille (including the Eurostar that goes through the Chunnel). The facade is decorated with statues symbolizing the principal cities and regions served by this station.

GARE DE L'EST TRAIN STATION. *Located just a few blocks south and east of the Gare du Nord, on the Place du 8 Mai 1945. Metro: Gare de l'Est.*

This is where you come to catch trains bound for eastern France, Germany, Switzerland, and Austria. It was originally called the Gare de Strasbourg, and the streets around it still carry the names of cities and regions in eastern France. The statues decorating the facade represent the cities of Strasbourg and Verdun. The clock is decorated with symbols representing the Marne, Meuse, Seine, and Rhine rivers. Inside, near the ticket booths, is an enormous painting by Alfred Herter (painted in 1926) representing World War I soldiers heading for the front in 1914.

RUE DU PARADIS. *Located one block south and west of the Gare de l'Est. Metro: Gare de l'Est.*

This interesting street is lined with crystal and porcelain shops. It makes for fun window shopping. At # 30 Bis Rue du Paradis there is a neat little museum, called the **Musée Baccarat**. This place absolutely glitters with chandeliers and crystal. Open Mon-Sat, 10am-6pm. Adults: €7, Kids: €3.50.

19. LA VILLETTE

It's a little hard to imagine that this massive urban park with its modern museums and structures used to be just a little village. But that is where the name, Villette (small village) comes from. Originally a Roman hamlet on the road to Belgium, **La Villette** took on greater importance in the 1800s, when it became the home of Paris' main slaughterhouse. When that work was moved to the suburbs in the 1970s, a massive new plan was devised to transform the site into a series of public parks, museums, and entertainment halls.

The result is a huge green space, dotted with gardens, waterways, playgrounds, and architectural "follies." There is much to spark the interests and joys of children here, starting with the magnificent science museum, leading through a slide shaped like a dragon, across a canal, all the way to an excellent Museum of Music.

CITÉ DES SCIENCES ET DES INDUSTRIES (SCIENCE MUSEUM). *Parc de la Villette, 30, Avenue Corentin Cariou. Metro: Porte de la Villette. Open Tues-Sun, 10am-6pm (Sun, until 7pm). Closed Mon. Adults: €7.50; Kids 7-12 yr: €5.50. Kids under 7: free. Planetarium: €2.50. Argonaute submarine: €3 or free with ticket for the museum; Cité des Enfants: €3.80 per person. Audioguide rental: €1.50.*

This "Science City" is made to spur your child's curiosity and natural urge to touch and experiment. To get the most out of it and avoid language barrier frustrations: rent the audioguide, available in English.

The Cité des Sciences et des Industries was inaugurated on March 13, 1986 – coinciding with the day Halley's Comet was passing over the earth. It is an interactive science and technology museum for kids of all ages. It's

---

La Villette Highlights

- Explore the human body, the ocean, the solar system, or virtual reality at the Cité des Sciences
- Try hands-on activities at the Cité des Enfants
- Eat in a cafeteria featuring a giant aquarium
- See an IMAX movie at La Géode
- Go for a wacky virtual ride at the Cinaxe theater
- Visit a real submarine
- Play on a giant dragon slide
- Bounce, pedal, get sprayed with water, and play in the delightful gardens of the Park
- Go on a canal boat ride
- Look for the red "follies"
- Check out the ancient instruments and many musical sounds at the Musée de la Musique

---

more than a museum. It is a huge, hands-on space for experimenting with science and trying out different technologies. There are myriad activities and exhibits about sound, optical illusions, light, and visual signals. There are sections on health, the ocean, geology, stars and galaxies, plants, volcanoes, and virtual reality. An area called la Cité des Enfants features hands-on activities designed for kids ages 3 to 12. It is divided into two sections: one reserved for 3-5 year olds and the other for 5-12 year olds. The little ones get to do things such as manipulate a crane, pump water, feel their way through a course, or watch a film slowing down their movements. Older kids can do things such as experiment with a sound studio, visit the inside of a human body, make a robot move, or watch a giant ant farm.

The Techno Cité section of the museum is reserved for kids 11 years and older. Here there are plenty of computer opportunities as well as activities like trying out a helicopter engine, seeing how the gears of a car work, checking out a racing bike prototype, or designing their own puzzle which they then learn how to mass produce.

The Cité des Sciences also contains a planetarium and a 3-D movie theater called Cinema Louis Lumière. The lower level cafeteria features its own aquarium. Real scientists and technology experts talk about their jobs at the Cité des Métiers. Outside, you can take a self-guided visit (with free audioguide) through the Argonaute, a real military submarine. It will give kids an appreciation for the claustrophobia of life on board.

LA GÉODE IMAX MOVIE THEATER. *Next to the Argonaute submarine and Cité des Sciences et des Industries. Open Tues-Sun. Closed Mon.*

Shows projected every hour from 10 am to 9 pm. Adults: €9; Kids: €7. Ask for English-language headphones.

This theater is already cool just from the outside, where its mirrored spherical surfaces reflect the sky and passers-by. Inside it shows IMAX movies. You are literally surrounded by images that transport you under the sea, into outer space, through King Tut's tomb, up and down a roller coaster, or into a tropical rain forest. It's so realistic that it is not recommended for children under age 3 or women who are more than 6 months pregnant.

Note: Want to avoid a stiff neck at La Géode? Try the theater's top row seats.

LE CINAXE. *From the Géode, this theater is around the Cité des Sciences building, on the left. Buy tickets at the Géode box office. Open Tues-Sun, 11am-5pm. Closed Mon. Shows projected every 15 minutes. Adults: €5.40; Kids: €4.50.*

Get ready to shake, rattle, and roll. The seats of this theater are mounted on a platform that sends you lurching and laughing along with the crazy ride being projected on the movie screen. It is not recommended for kids under 4, pregnant women, people with heart problems, epileptics, and people with fragile backs or necks. For the rest, it's 15 minutes of wacky fun.

JARDIN DU DRAGON. *Near the Cité des Sciences et des Technologies, on the south side.*

This dragon is irresistible if you are a kid. It contains a giant slide plus several smaller ones that offer plenty of opportunities to climb and squeal.

BIG PLAYGROUND. *Near the Grande Halle, along the path called Galérie de la Villette. If you are coming from the dragon or science museum, you will need to take the bridge across the Canal de l'Ourcq.*

Technically, this area is known as the Jardin des Vents (Garden of Winds), Jardin des Dunes (Garden of Dunes), and Jardin des Miroirs (Garden of Mirrors). To a kid, and anyone who is young at heart, it is really a giant playground. These gardens are filled with clever and delightful activities. Large sections (divided by age groups) are covered with moonbounce type surfaces where kids can jump to their hearts' content. They are connected by wobbly sidewalks. Watching you try to negotiate these will be guaranteed to make the rest of the family laugh. Kids also love trying out the pedal-powered windmills that they can manipulate with their hands or feet. There are mini-mountains to climb and a garden filled with mirrors.

OTHER GARDENS. *In the Parc de la Villette.*

In the vast 3-kilometer stretch – about 2 miles – between the Porte de la Villette side of the park and its Porte de Pantin entrance, you will find several interesting little gardens. They are full of charm and surprises. The Jardin des Equilibres features games where kids try out their skills of balance. The Jardin de Bambous is like walking through a bamboo forest. The Jardin de la Treille (Trellis Garden) has 90 small fountains decorated with trellises of climbing vines and plants. The Jardin des Frâyeurs Enfantines (Garden of Childhood Fears) takes you through dark paths filled with strange music and sounds of the forest. The Jardin des Brouillards (Garden of Fog) sprays you with jets of mist on warm days.

There are also two wide fields, called Prairies, where kids can run, kick a ball, and generally let loose. The benches, lampposts, trash cans, and other park furniture were designed by Philippe Starck. During the summer, the Triangle Prairie is transformed into a free, outdoor movie theater. It plays old movies (often American classics) making it feel like an old-fashioned drive-in theater without the cars. Films are shown in July and August at 10 pm, Tues-Sun.

PARIS CANAL BOAT RIDE. *Dock near the bridge crossing the Canal de l'Ourcq by the Jardin des Brouillards (Garden of Fog). Metro: Porte de Pantin. Tel. 01 42 40 96 97. One rides depart hourly. A 3-hour ride all the way to the Seine departs at 2:30pm and arrives at the Musée d'Orsay at 5:30 pm. Adults: €16; Kids 12-25: €13; Kids 4-11: €9; Under 4: free.*

Enjoy a ride through Paris' canals and locks from the Canal de l'Ourcq. A 1-hour trip takes your through part of the canals and back again. It is ideal for younger children. A 3-hour trip goes all the way through the canals to the Seine River and over to the Musée d'Orsay. For kids who love boating, it's a great thrill. You go through locks and tunnels, and see some of Paris' most famous sights. Make sure to bring along a picnic or snacks. Reserve in advance during high tourist season. The tours sell out quickly.

Parent Tip: Once you are near the canals at La Villette, keep a sharp eye on active toddlers. There are no railings along the water's edge.

If you look at a map of Paris, the Seine River makes a curve like a frown through the city then turns back north and forms several S-shapes on its way west towards the English Channel. The city's canals allow barges to bypass the center of Paris and take a shortcut past some of the Seine's winding meanders.

CANAUXRAMA CANAL BOAT RIDES. *Depart from 13, Quai de la Loire on the Bassin de la Villette. Metro: Jaurès. This is 4 metro stops down from Porte de Pantin, past the Canal de l'Ourq and at the southern end of the Bassin de la Villette. Phone: 01 42 39 15 00. Departures at 9:45 am or 2:45 pm. Tours last 2hrs 40min. Adults: €14; Students: €10; Kids 6-12: €8; Kids under 6: free.*

These boats take you down through the canals and locks from the Bassin de la Villette to the Place de la Bastille and back again. The ride is long for short

Fun Fact

Rumor has it that the canals are filled with goldfish abandoned there by owners who no longer want to take care of them. How many can you find?

attention spans, but for those who enjoy boats, the passages through tunnels and locks are fascinating. The sights along the way take you through some truly Parisian neighborhoods and under picturesque footbridges. You'll feel like you've stepped onto the set of *Amélie Poulain* or any other charming Parisian film. Bring along a picnic. Reserve in advance, during high tourist season.

GRANDE HALLE. *Near the Lion Fountain at the Porte de Pantin end of the park.*

This is one of the few buildings remaining from La Villette's slaughterhouse days. Today it features temporary shows and exhibits. This is also where the youth-based trade shows are held featuring information about college studies, jobs for youth, and training opportunities for young people. For the average family visit, the Grande Halle is mainly interesting for the fact that it contains a café and a crêpe/waffle stand.

FOLLIES. *Red buildings made to look like modern sculptures scattered throughout the Park.*

There are 26 of these wacky modern constructions throughout the park. Their red color is meant to provide a bright contrast to the green of the gardens and big open fields. Each one is based on the design of a 10.8 meter square cube to which all sorts of sculptural and practical elements have been added. No two are alike. See how many you can find. Each has a special purpose. Examples include a music kiosk, a jazz theater, a fire house, a video studio, a daycare center, a first aid station, an information center for the Zenith rock concerts, an observation station, and others. There is one near the Cinaxe that has a caféteria, and another between the Jardin des Bambous and Jardins des Equilibres that serves as a café.

Are your kids artistically inclined? Do they enjoy building things out of blocks and Legos? Have them try a hand at designing their own Follies. What would theirs be for?

MUSÉE DE LA MUSIQUE. *In the Cité de la Musique building, 221, Avenue Jean Jaures. Metro: Porte de Pantin. Open Tues-Sun, 10am-6pm. Closed Mon. Adults: €6.50; Kids 6-18: €3.20; Kids under 6: free. There is a free children's guide for kids ages 6-12 available when your purchase your tickets.*

This is a very interesting museum for any child who plays a musical instrument or enjoys music. It offers not only lots to see, but also many sounds. The exhibits are easy to follow and enjoy thanks to the free headsets (available in English) supplied at the entrance. There are also live presentations by musicians demonstrating all types of different instruments from around the world. The museum has a collection of rare and ancient instruments. You can see a real Stradivarius violin or instruments that belonged to famous composers and hear what they sound like. There are also set designs from famous operas and models of musical theaters that are surprisingly popular with children. There are plenty of interactive exhibits that allow you to hear musical sounds ranging from classical, to music from around the world, '70s synthesizers, and techno music. You may actually have to drag your kids away. If you need more, there are also films about music, concerts that are often specifically targeted to young people, and an excellent gift shop.

Outside the museum, you can refuel at the Café de la Musique. It is conveniently situated facing the Place de la Fountaine aux Lions, which offers plenty of car-free space to run while kids wait for their food.

20. BELLEVILLE & THE BUTTES CHAUMONT

This part of the city is not well known by locals or visitors. Snobby Parisians turn their noses up at **Belleville** and the **Buttes Chaumont**, considering them too working class. Yet it is here that you find the Paris reflected in black and white photos, the songs of Edith Piaf, and the classic children's film, *The Red Balloon*.

If you've seen The Red Balloon, you'll recognize the hilly, cobbled streets of Belleville and the Buttes Chaumont. A tour through this area will also reveal charming lanes, dotted with little houses. It will take you past an exotic array of smells and tastes from Asia, Eastern Europe, and North Africa. You will also have your choice of green spots: the recently renovated Parc de Belleville, the romantic **Parc des Buttes Chaumont**, and the serene **Père Lachaise cemetery**.

TAKING A RED BALLOON TOUR. This tour takes you up the *Rue de Belleville*, through some of the back streets and lanes of the neighborhood, and back to the *Parc de Belleville*. It involves hills, cobbled streets, and lots of walking. Bring drinks and snacks.

If you'd rather walk downhill than up, start at the Pyrénées metro station. Walk to the Belleville park, and make your way downhill to the Belleville or Couronne metro stations.

In the story *The Red Balloon*, a lonely little boy named Pascal finds a magic helium balloon that follows him everywhere through the Belleville neighborhood where he lives. It even waits for him outside of his school.

Belleville & Area Highlights

- Follow an imaginary red balloon through the sides streets of Belleville
- Discover the African Market the Rue de Belleville
- Check out the magnificent view of Paris from the Rue Piat
- Look at today's air quality and learn about preventing air pollution at the Maison de l'Air
- Run up and down the hills and don't miss the giant slides in the Parc de Belleville
- Look for the tomb of Héloise and Abélard in the Père Lachaise cemetery
- Go across a suspension bridge and explore the grottos at the Parc des Buttes Chaumont
- See a puppet show

Eventually, however, a gang of boys chases Pascal and pops his balloon. Then all the balloons of Paris leave their owners and float over to Pascal. The balloons join together and carry him off on a tour around the world.

You may not be able to float above Paris with a magic balloon, but a Red Balloon tour through Belleville will give you a taste of the charms and many cultures that make Paris unique. Start at the Belleville metro station. Head up the Rue de Belleville (note: don't confuse it with the Boulevard de Belleville running perpendicular to it). Notice all the different ethnic shops and restaurants. This neighborhood has a long tradition of attracting immigrants from Asia, Eastern Europe, the Maghreb, and Africa. The result is a potpourri of cultural diversity. There are Jewish delis and synagogues. You can pick between wonderful North African couscous restaurants or a wide variety of Asian ones. If you come here on a Tuesday or Friday morning, you can walk through the African market. Look for dried bats, prickly fruits, and other exotic items.

Notice the building at #72, Rue de Belleville. This is where the famous French singer, Edith Piaf, was born in 1915. Today, the neighborhood attracts many artists, musicians, and young people who have been priced out of more central neighborhoods of the city.

Take a right when you reach the Rue Piat. In a short block you will reach the top of the Parc de Belleville. Check out the panoramic view of Paris. It is much nicer now than when our hero Pascal was a little boy in the 1950s. Many of the buildings have been cleaned and the park has been completely redone.

We'll come back to the park, but for now our Red Balloon is urging us along. Peek down the Rue des Envièrges, which is featured in the movie. Now walk along the Rue du Transvaal. Take a right down the Passage Plantin. Take a short right down Rue des Couronnes, short left, then quick left again up the Rue de la Mare to the Rue de Saviés. At the end, take a right into the Rue des Cascades. At #42 there is a small building above the stairs called the Regard Saint Martin, which was once used to monitor the quality of the local water. It is decorated with an image of Saint Martin riding on his horse. Further down the Rue des Cascades is another water monitoring building at #17. If you are tired now, you may want to head back to the Parc de Belleville.

Who was **Saint Martin**? He was a Roman soldier born in Hungary in the late 4th century. According to legend, one day as he was riding his horse he came upon a poor beggar trembling with cold. Martin took off his cloak, split it in two with his sword, and offered half to the beggar. That night, Christ appeared to him in a dream and thanked him. The next morning, Martin decided to quit the army and convert to Christianity. He founded a monastery near the French town of Tours.

If you still have energy to follow our imaginary balloon a little farther, you can take a short left onto the Rue de Menilmontant, then another left into Rue de l'Ermitage. A right turn into the Villa de l'Ermitage leads into the hidden lanes of Belleville. Here you may feel as though you've stepped into a country village. Go left at Rue des Pyrénées, quick right into Rue de l'Est, left in Rue de Pixerecourt, and then check out the tiny Passage de la Duée. A left into the Rue de Duée takes you to the Villa Georgina on your right. Notice all the pretty gardens.

Just beyond the Villa Georgina is the Rue du Telegraphe. The building at #40 is where the city's first telegraph was tested in 1793.

Now it is time to wind your way back to the Belleville Park. Retrace your steps to the Rue de l'Est. Where the Rue de l'Est meets the Rue des Pyrénées take a right, then a left into the Rue de l'Ermitage. Here you can take the steps back up to the Regard Saint Martin, make your way back along Rue de Saviés and Rue de la Mare. Now you can take a left into the Rue des Couronnes along the park, until you reach the steps that take you into the Parc de Belleville. You can make your way past the vineyards and up the hill to the Maison de l'Air. Although this Museum of Air did not exist when the Red Balloon movie was made, it seems to be a fitting end to a tour led by a floating, magical balloon.

MAISON DE L'AIR. *27, Rue Piat. Metro: Pyrénées. Open Tues-Sun, 1:30pm-5:30pm (until 6:30 on weekends in the summer). Closed Mon. Adults: €2; Kids: €1. Free kids' workshops on Wed and Sat afternoons during the school year.*

This new museum was developed by the City of Paris to help build public awareness about the air around us. There are lots of hands-on activities. You can feel, smell, and touch air. You can learn about clouds, the ways different animals fly, and how plants use air to spread their seeds. There is a weather station that monitors the air quality in Paris and exhibits on what we can do to promote cleaner air around us.

PARC DE BELLEVILLE. *Between Rue Piat, Rue des Couronnes, and Rue Julien Lacroix. Metro: Pyrénées, Belleville, or Couronne.*

The Belleville hill used to be covered with vineyards, windmills, and rock quarries. The Parc de Belleville, recently remodeled, was designed to pay homage to the neighborhood's heritage. It takes advantage of the natural topography and wonderful panoramic view of Paris. As you look from the top of the park, by the Maison de l'Air, you have before you a sweeping view of Paris, and a lovely set of fountains cascading down the hillside. To the right, there are rocky outcroppings. These serve as a reminder of the days when Belleville was pockmarked with gypsum quarries. To the left, from the top of the park, lies a small patch of vineyards – also a souvenir of old Belleville.

Children enjoy following the fountains down the hill through the park. On hot days, they can take off their shoes and paddle around in the water. Toward the lower part of the park, on the left if you are facing downhill, is a terrific play area. It includes several long slides that are built right into the hillside. To reach the top of the slides, you run through steps and climbing structures set in a sort of castle-like fort. It's free and loads of fun.

> **Fun Fact**
>
> In the 1700s, the Belleville hill was an important source of gypsum that was used to make plaster. It's where we get the name Plaster of Paris.

PÈRE LACHAISE CEMETERY. *Main entrance on the Boulevard Ménilmontant between Metro: Père Lachaise and Philippe Auguste. You can obtain a map from the guard station at the entrance indicating the locations of famous tombs. Open daily, 7:30am-6pm Mon-Fri; 8:30am-6pm Sat-Sun (Mar-Oct). 8:30am-5:30pm (Nov-Feb). Entrance is free.*

Note: If you are visiting the cemetery with small children who are bored by the tombs, have them count how many **stray cats** they can find. The park is full of them. Just make sure you don't try to touch them.

Even for those of us who don't particularly relish a visit to the cemetery, the Père Lachaise is a fascinating place. It will particularly appeal to older children, including the surly teenager who complains about every church and museum but enjoys more macabre sights. The Père Lachaise is not unlike a giant park, filled with sculptures (albeit funerary ones) and stray cats. But it is unlike any other cemetery we've ever seen. Fans of classic rock and roll will go just to see the tomb of Jim Morrison (lead singer for the Doors, who died of a drug overdose in Paris). There is plenty of graffiti to show you the way. The tomb has something of a cult following.

There are many other important tombs at the Père Lachaise. In fact, there are more than 70,000 tombs in all. Permanent residents include composers Frédéric Chopin and Georges Bizet; ill-fated lovers Héloise and Abélard; writers Alfred de Musset, Molière, Appollinaire, Oscar Wilde, Honoré de Balzac, Marcel Proust, Gertrude Stein, and Colette; painters Jacques-Louis David, Dominic Ingres, Eugène Delacroix, Camille Pissaro, Georges Seurat, Jean Baptiste Corot, Amedeo Modigliani, and Max Ernst; actors Sarah Bernhardt, Simone Signoret, and Yves Montand; singer Edith Piaf; dancer Isadora Duncan; urban planner Baron Haussman; astronomer and French abolitionist François Arago, and members of the French branch of the Rothchild family (known for their fine Bordeaux wines).

The Père Lachaise Cemetery was created by Napoleon I in 1804. So how can there be a tomb for someone who died in 1142? To boost the cemetery's popularity, Napoleon transferred some of France's best-loved forefathers here from other resting places. Thus the remains of medieval lovers Héloise (d. 1164) and Abélard (d.1142) or the 17th century playwright Molière (d.1673) are in this cemetery.

There are also several important memorials in the Père Lachaise cemetery. On the southeastern side of the cemetery along the Avenue Circulaire there is a moving memorial to those who died during World War II fighting in the Resistance movement or as victims of the Nazi death camps. Across from this memorial is the Mur de Fédérés. This is the spot where, during the Paris Commune uprising, the last of the Communards fighters were hunted down, lined up against the wall, and shot by government guards. They were buried where they fell in a mass grave.

PARK DES BUTTES CHAUMONT. *Entrances from Rue Botzaris, Rue Manin, and Rue de Crimée. Metro: Buttes Chaumont or Botzaris.*

This park was developed in the 1860s by Baron Haussman for Napoleon III, who wanted to create a green space for the people living in the northern neighborhoods of Paris. At the time, the area served as a dumping ground for trash and run-off. The soil was heavy with clay and not conducive to growing plants. In fact the name, Chaumont, comes from "Mont Chauve" or bald hill, for the fact that there was no vegetation on it. It took three years, tons of dirt (literally), lots of digging, plenty of dynamite, and many plants to transform this spot into the lovely garden it is today. Engineers created a lake, an artificial cliff and grotto, roads, terraces, and footpaths. They built a suspended bridge, a waterfall, a music kiosk, and an imitation Greek temple.

The park was inaugurated in 1867 as part of the festivities associated with the Paris Expo of 1867. It contains a nice restaurant towards the top of the hill, the kid-friendly Weber Café, and a snack bar by the lake. Like all large Parisian parks there is a merry-go-round and a puppet show. The classic French puppet character, Guignol, and his friends have been delighting children on this spot for 150 years. The theater building had to be rebuilt after a freak storm on 26 December 1999, which destroyed trees and buildings all across France. There are daily shows at 3 pm and 4:30 pm. Cost: 2.50 E.

Unlike many other green spaces in Paris, you can walk and frolic in the grass at the Buttes Chaumont. Kids love rolling down the hills, climbing up the great rock to the Belvedere, and making their way back down through the fake grottos.

21. BOIS DE BOULOGNE

This huge park fills most of the western edge of Paris. Along with the Bois de Vincennes on Paris' eastern edge, it is all that remains of the thick ring of forests that once surrounded Lutetia. The Bois de Boulogne was originally called the Forest of Rouvray, where early French kings hunted wild boar, bear, wolf, and deer. Today, it offers countless fun activities for kids and families. There are gardens, playgrounds, lakes, and museums. It is here that you can find Paris' only campgrounds, two equestrian centers, two hippodromes, and the Roland Garros stadium which hosts the French Open Tennis competition each year in May.

THE BOIS DE BOULOGNE. *Access to the eastern side by little train from Metro: Porte Maillot. Walk to northern side from Metro: Les Sablons. Access to Lac Supérieur from Metro: Henri Martin. Access to southern side from Metro: Porte d'Auteuil.*

In the early 13th century, Isabelle de France (sister of King Louis IX) founded the Abbey of Longchamp in this forest. In the 14th century, pilgrims returning from Boulogne-sur-Mer obtained permission to build a church in the forest, called Notre Dame de Boulogne. Ultimately, the forest took on the name and became the Bois de Boulogne. In the 16th century, King Francois I built himself a hunting castle in the Bois de Boulogne. At the turn of the 17th century, King Henri IV created a silkworm farm in the Bois, planting 15,000 mulberry trees to feed the worms. His first wife, Marguerite de Valois, came to live in the Boulogne castle when he annulled their wedding. The Allée de la Reine Marguerite is named for her. During the 17th century, numerous wealthy nobles built palaces in the Bois de Boulogne.

Bois de Boulogne Highlights

- Take the little train from the Porte Maillot
- Check out the funny mirrors, rides, petting zoo, terrific playgrounds, and other amusements at the Jardin d'Acclimatation
- Rent bikes and explore the park
- Go bowling
- Go for a pony or horseback ride
- See a traditional French country cheese producer, a woodworker's shop, an Alpine chalet, and other artifacts representing rural French life at the Musée des Arts et Traditions Populaires.
- Visit the Shakespearean Garden in the Pré Catalan
- Smell the roses and wind your way up to the Belvedere in the pretty Parc de Bagatelle
- Rent a row boat on the Lac Inférieur or take a short boat ride to its island
- Rent a remote control boat on the Lac Supérieur
- Have a swim in the Piscine d'Auteuil
- Go to the horse races or tennis competition
- Stay in one of the cabins at the Bois de Boulogne campsite

These were mostly destroyed during the French Revolution, when the area also became a hide-out for people condemned by the revolutionaries.

Napoleon I rehabilitated the Bois de Boulogne after the Revolution, with new trees and alleyways. However, after his defeat at Waterloo, the invading English and Russian troops camped out in the Bois and trashed the place. In 1852, Napoleon III oversaw the restoration of the area, which he wanted to make into a Parisian version of London's Hyde Park. He employed enormous engineering efforts to create three rivers and two lakes. Rocks were hauled in from Fontainebleau (100 kilometers south of Paris) to create a great waterfall and romantic grottos. More than 400,000 trees were planted along with countless plants and flowers. He oversaw the building of the Longchamp Race Track, the Jardin d'Acclimatation, and the Pré Catelan field with its Shakespearean garden and theater. The Emperor's Kiosk, restored in the 1980s, was built as a quiet retreat for Napoleon III.

By the late 19th century, the Bois de Boulogne had become very fashionable. It was where people like the characters in Marcel Proust's novels would come to see and be seen. Today, the Bois de Boulogne attracts families, joggers, cyclists, and many others who want to enjoy its myriad activities and green spaces. Note that at night, the families go home and the dark alleys become something of a pickup scene.

Thousands of trees in the Bois de Boulogne were uprooted or destroyed by a freak storm on December 26, 1999. After several years of clean up and restoration efforts, the park is slowly recovering.

JARDIN D'ACCLIMATATION. *Entrance at intersection of Boulevard des Sablons and Avenue du Mahatma Gandhi on the N edge of the park. Walk from Metro: Sablons or take the free train from Metro: Porte Maillot. Open daily, 10am-6pm (until 7pm, Jun-Sep). Adults and Kids 3-18: €2.50; Kids under 3: free. People with disabilities: free. Ask for a free map at the entrance.*

Note: The amusement rides and arcades in the Jardin d'Acclimatation require special tickets. For the best deal, go ahead and buy a carnet of 20 or 30 tickets. You'll have no trouble using them up!

We've been here with kids ranging from babies to teenagers, and they have all loved it. Start with the hall of funny mirrors on your left as you enter. This will get everyone into the proper mood. It's not that they will need much prompting in this delightful amusement park. There are plenty of familiar amusement rides and arcade games. There are also some charming old-fashioned rides, such as the enchanted river with its self-propelled boats or the bouncing horse course that will remind you of the magic carrousel in Mary Poppins. If you can drag your kids away from the rides (or more likely, when they run out of tickets) there are plenty of free amusements. There is a small collection of zoo animals plus a petting zoo featuring lots of familiar farm animals. There are vegetable gardens and fruit trees to explore.

The Jardin d'Acclimatation also features several large playgrounds, organized by age group. Toddlers can enjoy their own specially designed playgrounds and a mini-beach with lots of sand and a wading pool. There are free puppet shows at the marionette theater. Older kids will love all the climbing apparatuses reserved for them, including the huge web-like climbing structures that our kids like to call Eiffel Towers.

Some of the fun things for kids here include:

- Riding the little train
- the hall of funny mirrors
- amusement rides and games
- minigolf
- puppet shows
- farm animals at the petting zoo
- great playgrounds
- bowling
- pony or horse rides
- hands-on science experiments at the Explor@drome

There are also several cafés and food stands, along with a picnic area.

Bowling de Paris. *In the Jardin d'Acclimatation along the Avenue du Mahatma Gandhi. Open daily, 9am-well past midnight. Cost: €2.50-6.50. Shoes: €2.*

Go bowling? In Paris? Why not? Bowling actually seems to be more popular here than in many American cities. There are more than 25 bowling alleys in Paris. This is one of the most popular ones. It can get rather packed on weekends. There's glow-in-the-dark bowling on weekend nights. You can also play pool or video games.

Musee en Herbe. *On the left, near the main entrance to the Jardin d'Acclimatation. Open daily, 10am-6pm (Sat, 2pm-6pm). Costs for exhibits and workshops range from €3 to 4/person.*

This is a small, kid-centered museum. It features hands-on activities, often centered around special temporary exhibits. Some can be quite charming and well suited for toddlers and rookie museum goers.

Explor@Dome. *Inside the Jardin d'Acclimatation, by the Neuilly entrance, on the NW side of the park. Open daily, 10am-6pm. Adults: €5; Kids: €3.50. Note: you will also have to pay the entrance fee for the Jardin d'Acclimatation.*

This is an interactive, kid-centered, science museum. You can do things like create your own fog or tornados. You can look at optical illusions. There are also plenty of IMAC computers set up for kids to explore the possibilities of digital multimedia (web page designs, digital photography, and more).

MUSÉE NATIONAL DES ARTS ET TRADITIONS POPULAIRES. *6, Avenue du Mahatma Gandhi. Located next to the main entrance to the Jardin d'Acclimatation, but has its own entrance. Metro: Les Sablons or take the little train from Metro: Porte Maillot. Open Wed-Mon, 9:30 am-5:15 pm. Closed Tues. Adults: €4; Kids: free. Free to all on the first Sun. of each month. There is a free treasure hunt book for kids at the entrance.*

This museum presents elements of rural life in France, ranging from 1000 years ago to today. There are re-creations of an Alpine chalet, cheese makers shop, woodworker's studio, fishing boat, and more. There are costumes, songs, and legends from different parts of France. There are exhibits on how grapes become wine, or wheat becomes bread. The displays are a little quaint and old-fashioned, but the temporary exhibits can be charming.

BIKE RENTALS. These are located across from the main entrance to the Jardin d'Acclimatation. There are special bike lanes and paths throughout the Bois de Boulogne. It's a great way to enjoy the park.

HORSEBACK RIDING. There are two equestrian centers in the Bois de Boulogne. The **Centre Hippique du Bois de Boulogne** is located along the Route de la Muêtte in the Jardin d'Acclimatation. And the **Société Equèstre de l'Etrier** is on the Route des Lacs à Madrid, between the Allée de Longchamps and the Avenue Mahatma Gandhi. For information on horseback riding lessons at either of these centers contact the Société d'Equitation de Paris, Tel. 01 45 01 20 06.

PRÉ CATALAN. *In the middle of the Bois de Boulogne, off the Allée de la Reine Marguerite, at the same level as the Lac Inférieur.*

This area features big grassy fields and some ancient trees. There is a giant Sequoia from California, a 200 year old purple Hêtre, and a huge oak tree known as a Rouvre oak in French which is where the forest got its original name of Rourvray.

There is also a lovely Shakespearean garden in the Pré Catalan. It contains plants and herbs that are mentioned in the Bard's plays. From May to October the garden becomes an open-air theater, featuring works by Shakespeare. These are often performed in English by British theater companies.

BAGATELLE PARK AND PALACE. *Between the Allée de Longchamps and Route de Sèvres. Open daily, 8:30am-6:30 pm (summer); 9am-4:30pm (winter). Adults: €3. Kids: €1.50. Free for kids under 7.*

This is one of the few aristocratic buildings in the Bois de Boulogne to have survived the French Revolution. It is famous for its rose gardens. There is also a nice Belvedere that you reach by winding up a snail-shell shaped path. The little palace was a folly built for Queen Marie Antoinette.

Fun Fact

The small palace in the **Parc de Bagatelle** was built for Queen Marie Antoinette as a folly. She had a bet with her brother-in-law, the Count d'Artois. He claimed he could build her a palace in less than 3 months. It was finished in 64 days.

LAC INFERIEUR AND LAC SUPERIEUR. *Towards the middle of the Bois de Boulogne on its eastern side. Near the Porte de la Muêtte. Metro: Avenue Henri Martin.*

The Lac Supérieur is the smaller of these two lakes. Its most interesting feature is that fact that on warm afternoons, you can rent a remote-controlled toy powerboat to play with on the lake. On the Lac Inférieur you can rent full-sized rowboats. For a nominal fee, you can also take the ferry to the lake's main island. There are two islands on the lake, connected by a little suspension bridge. They feature large grassy fields for children to play. Look for the peacocks that wander freely. There is a nice, but expensive, restaurant on the bigger island.

HIPPODROME DE LONGCHAMP. *On the SW side of the Bois de Boulogne, along the Route des Tribunes. Free buses from Metro: Porte d'Auteuil. Adults: €4 Mon-Fri, €6 Sat-Sun. Kids: free. Races start at 2pm.*

Do you have a child who loves horses? Why not go to the horse races? This race track was built by Napoleon III in the 1870s. It features thoroughbred races. On the northern edge you can see the old windmill that was part of the 13th century Longchamps Abbey. On Sundays there are free pony rides for kids ages 3-7 and a kids' activity area.

HIPPODROME D'AUTEUIL. *On the SE side of the Bois de Boulogne, along the Route des Lacs. Metro: Porte d'Auteuil. Closed in August, December, January. Adults: €4, Mon-Fri, €6, Sat-Sun. Kids: free. Races start at 2pm.*

Another fun activity for young horse fans. This is a steeple-chase race course. It also features a kids' area and free pony rides on Sunday afternoons.

PISCINE D'AUTEUIL (PUBLIC SWIMMING POOL). *Near the Hippodrome d'Auteuil on the Rue des Lacs de Passy and Allée des Fortifications. Metro: Ranelagh.*

There are two pools, including one that is outdoors. It is a nice place to cool off on hot summer days. Note: Boys and men are required to wear Speedo-style swimsuits.

ROLAND GARROS TENNIS STADIUM. *2, Avenue Gordon Bennett. On the southern edge of the Bois de Boulogne. Metro: Porte d'Auteuil. You can purchase tickets for the French Open: Tel. 01 47 43 48 00 or www.frenchopen.org.*

This red-clay tennis stadium is named for a French pilot who was the first aviator to fly solo across the Mediterranean Sea. It hosts the annual French Open Tennis Tournament in May. This is a real treat for tennis fans. Although the final matches are always played on the center court, if you go during the earlier rounds you can see more games and many of the world's top players.

BOIS DE BOULOGNE CAMPGROUND. *Allée du Bord de l'Eau. Special shuttle bus available to and from Metro: Porte Maillot. Mobile home reservations 4/5 people: €76/night. For reservations, Tel. 01 45 24 30 81 or email:resa@mobilhome-paris.com*

This is a really original way to experience Paris, combining a visit to the city with a stay in the woods by the river. The campground offers not only spots for tents and RVs but also rents family-friendly mobile homes. These feature 2 bedrooms, one with a double bed and one with two twins, plus a convertible couch in the living room. There is a kitchenette and bathroom. Linens and kitchen equipment are furnished with the rental. The facilities at the campsite include cash machines, a Laundromat, a grocery store, and an office where you can purchase tickets for Disneyland, Parc Asterix, Aquaboulevard, and other visits in and around Paris.

22. MORE FUN

The family-friendly possibilities of Paris are endless. Now that you've explored some of the major monuments and sights, why not head for some of the lesser known adventures.

AQUABOULEVARD. *4, Rue Louis Armand. Metro: Balard or Porte de Versailles. Open daily, 9 am-11 pm (later on weekends). Adults: €20; Kids under 12: €10. Family pass for 2 adults and 1 child or 1 adult and 2 children: €25.*

Note: Like every other pool in France, the Aquaboulevard center requires that men and boys wear speedo-style swimsuits. You can usually purchase them there, if they haven't run out.

This is a huge aquatic park and sports center. Most of it is indoors, with big skylights and windows. The water park is decorated with palm trees and beaches. There are water slides, fountains, wave pools, hot tubs, and outdoor pools. You can also take part in the center's other sports activities, such as fitness training, a golf range, squash courts, etc. If you get hungry, there is an American-style food court. Kids love it! You'll have a hard time dragging them away.

PARC ANDRE CITROEN. *Located along the Quai André Citroën, Rue Saint Charles, and Rue Balard, Metro: Javel or Balard. Open daily: 8:30am-5:30pm (until 7 pm during the summer). Entrance to the park is free.*

In 1915, as World War I was raging, André Citroën built a weapons factory on the Seine along the *Quai de Javel* (now called *Quai André Citroën*). In 1919, he converted it into an automobile assembly plant. The Citroën plant produced cars until the 1970s, when the factory moved to a larger space near the town of Rennes. The old buildings were torn down. Meanwhile, the area around the plant was developing rapidly, sprouting new skyscrapers to house luxury offices, hotels, and apartments. This development, and plans to use the Citroën site, came to a screeching halt with the oil crisis and economic downturn of the 1970s. Finally, in the 1980s, the decision was made to transform the area into a big public park.

The city hired several young architects to create a series of gardens, greenhouses, and open spaces that would be the Parc André Citroën. The Jardin Blanc (White Garden) specializes in white-flowering plants and features a children's playground. The Jardin Noir (Black Garden) has lots of dense vegetation and shade arranged along narrow, maze-like paths. Smaller gardens are dedicated to the five senses: smell, touch, hearing, feeling, and tasting. They offer plenty of rocks and playground structures to climb on as well as interesting plants and flowers. There is a wide lawn in the middle of the park overlooking the Seine. Two large greenhouses border an esplanade that features a fountain composed of jets of water that pop out of the ground at irregular intervals. This place is a real treat on hot days! Kids love running through the dancing jets, seeing if they can make it past them before they get sprayed. Technically it's not allowed, but the guards look benevolently the other way. Bring a bathing suit or change of clothes for the kids.

Fun Fact

In the 1770s, this area was called Javel. The Count of Artois had a factory here where he experimented with creating new products out of chemicals. In the 1780s, his factory developed its most successful product: a combination of hypochlorite and potassium chloride that helped keep white fabrics clean. It was called Eau de Javel (Javel's Water) – known in English as chlorine bleach.

HOT AIR BALLOON RIDES. *In the Parc André Citroën. Open Apr-Oct; 9:20am-6:30pm. Adults: €12; Kids 12-17: €9; Kids 3-11: €5; Kids under 3: free.*

The brightly colored Ballon Eutelsat takes you up 150 meters (nearly 500 feet) for an exciting view of the city. Unlike Phineus Fogg, you won't get a chance to race around the world in 80 days. The balloon is tethered to the ground by a good, strong cable.

FLEA MARKETS. If you love hunting through flea markets, why not share the pleasure with your kids? But remember, it's only fun if they get to hunt, too. We give our boys some spending money (€10-15) to find their own treasures. Some of their finds have included a French Monopoly game, some race cars, a box of retired Legos, a catapult game, and some nifty little pocket knives.

Paris' main flea markets are located on the outer edges of the city.

The biggest, the **Marché aux Puces de Saint Ouen**, is on the northern edge of Paris. Metro: Porte de Clingancourt. Walk up the Avenue de la Porte de Clingancourt under the highway, then head left into the Rue des Rosiers. Open Sat, Sun, Mon, 10am- 6pm.

The Saint Ouen flea market was originally set up in 1880. It started with a few antique stores and stalls that were rented out to chiff-tir merchants, people who collected and sold used items. Over time it expanded. Today, the Puces de Saint Ouen market includes thousands of shops and stalls covering a vast area. There's an interesting array of fancy antique stores, vintage shops, military surplus, and stalls filled with all sorts of junk. In the middle of all the shops and stalls are cafés and restaurants, such as Chez Louisette, where singers belt out old French tunes.

On the south side of Paris is the **Marché aux Puces de la Porte de Vanves**. Located along the Avenue Georges Lafenèstre and Avenue Marc Sangrier. Metro: Porte de Vanves or Porte d'Orleans. Open Sat, Sun, 7am-5pm.

The Porte de Vanves market is known for its furniture and household items. There are also old toys, games, and our kids' favorite - mini pocket knives. It attracts a younger crowd than the antique stores of Saint Ouen and is generally thought to be more hip.

The **Puces de Montreuil** are on the eastern edge of Paris, along the Avenue du Professeur Lemière. Metro: Porte de Montreuil. Open Sat, Sun, Mon, 8am-6pm.

The Montreuil market is famous for its used clothing stalls. It's a favorite with young people looking for bargains, who claim to come across secondhand designer clothes.

Within the city limits, the **Place d'Aligre** market, known mainly for its food stalls, also offers flea market bric-a-brac and vintage clothes. Metro: Bastille or Ledru Rollin. Open daily except Mon, 7am-1pm.

AIR AND SPACE MUSEUM – LE BOURGET. *Located at the Le Bourget Airport, 8 kilometers (5 miles) north of Paris. By car, take highway A1 north to the Le Bourget exit. By Metro, take line 7 to La Courneuve/8 mai 1945, then transfer to bus #152. By RER, take line B to Gare du Bourget, then transfer to bus 152. Open 10am-5pm. Closed Mon. Adults: €7; Kids: free.*

This fascinating Air and Space Museum is located in what used to be Paris' main airport, Le Bourget. It is here that Charles Lindbergh landed his plane, Spirit of Saint Louis, after being the first person to fly across the Atlantic Ocean in 1927. Today, Le Bourget is no longer open to commercial aviation. When the nearby Roissy/Charles de Gaulle airport was opened in 1973, Le Bourget was slowly converted from an airport to a museum

The museum has been continually expanded and now displays more than 180 planes. It features the oldest flying machine, a glider dating from 1879. There is one of the Wright Brothers' planes that was produced in France, where the brothers built and tested planes in the early 1900s. There are Blériot airplanes that were the first to cross the English Channel and to fly across the Mediterranean. There are fighter planes, air circus planes, and hot air balloons. There is a section devoted to the development of the Concorde, France's supersonic passenger plane, and to the development of France's space shuttle, Ariane. The museum also has a new planetarium. It is a great outing for anyone who enjoys aviation or space exploration

LA DÉFENSE. *West of Paris, Metro or RER: La Défense-Grande Arche.*

Note: for a free map of the area, you can go to the Information Office at 15, Place de La Défense, in a cube-shaped building on the left side of the esplanade as you face Paris. This office also sells kid-friendly guidebooks describing the fountains and sculptures of La Défense. Note: Below the esplanade there is a huge underground shopping mall called Les Quatres Temps (Four Seasons).

La Défense was named for a desperate defensive stand that the French took against the invading Prussians on this site in 1870-71. The French were ultimately defeated. They had to pay a huge tax and surrender the territories of Alsace and Lorraine to Prussian (later German) control. France did not recover these regions until the end of World War I.

This suburb of tall skyscrapers contrasts sharply with the old buildings of central Paris. Everything is modern, from the towers (many designed by famous architects) to the fountains, and sculptures. Although it seems stark at first glance, this area is very popular with children who can run to their hearts' content along the car free esplanade. It is also a favorite spot among roller bladers and skate boarders.

Kids enjoy looking at the funny modern sculptures along the esplanade and between the skyscrapers. These include a giant thumb by French sculptor César, 25 columns connected by wires by the Japanese artist Miyawaki, the red "Stabile" (as he called his standing mobiles) by Alexander Calder, a giant bronze bust of Toscano by Polish artist Mitoraj, a science fiction-type piece by Italian Delfino, a colorful fountain by French artist Agam, a ceramic cloud sculpture by Atila, a bronze Earth by Derbre, a perched Sleepwalker by Henri de Miller, and a Mechanical Bird by Philolaos. The Takis Fountain has 49 flexible lights reflected on its mirror-like surface. The Fountain of Dialogue features two bronze figures talking to each other. The tragic Ophelia from Shakespeare's Hamlet is depicted in a bronze bas-relief by a Catalan sculptor named Fenosa. There is a big frog water fountain. There is a sculpture featuring two long steel rods, one that looks like a rugby helmet, and a series of interconnected heads and hands. A sculpture of Lady Moon is made of white marble, in contrast to two figures by Miró that stand out in their bright multi-colored splendor. Another statue by César represents Icarus falling from his attempt to fly too close to the sun next to a sculpture of granite waves and pyramids.

The Agam Fountain comes to life with lights, music, and dancing jets of water every Sat. at 3pm and 8pm; Sun. at 3pm; and in the summer on Fri. and Sat. at 9pm

GRANDE ARCHE DE LA DÉFENSE. *Metro: La Défense/Grande Arche, Open daily 10am-7pm. Elevator access to the viewing deck on top of the arch, exhibits, restaurant, and bookshop. Adults: €7.50; Kids 6-18: €6; Kids under 6: free.*

In the 1980s, the French president François Mitterand launched a new project to build an International Center For Communications in the Paris suburb of *La Défense*. The site picked for the new center was along the same axis as the *Louvre, Place de la Concorde*, and *Arch de Triomphe*. He launched an international competition to design a building worthy of this location. There were over 400 applications. One, by the *Louvre* pyramid architect I.M. Pei suggested a V-shaped skyscraper. Another plan featured two towers, one black and one silver. The winning design was a giant modern arch by the Danish architect, Johan Otto Von Sperckelsen. It became known as the *Grande Arche* and was inaugurated on July 14, 1989 in celebration of the bicentennial of the French Revolution.

The *Grande Arche* houses French government offices, private businesses, and a human rights organization. There is a European Information and Documentation Center in the building. The tent-like structure hanging in the middle of the arch was added to cut down the force of the wind tunnels. There are four glass elevators under the arch that can whisk you from the ground to the top level in just 60 seconds. On top, there is a large open-air viewing deck with breathtaking views of Paris and its western suburbs. The view is particularly spectacular at night. There is also a restaurant on the top floor and art galleries that feature temporary exhibits.

Fun Fact

The **Grande Arche** is so tall you could fit the entire Nôtre Dame Cathedral under it. It measures 100 meters (330 feet) high by 100 meters wide, and the whole thing weighs over 30,000 tons. It took more than 2,000 workers to build the structure. The arch contains nearly 2,500 glass panels weighing 800 kilos (1,760 pounds) each. It takes a special team of mountain-climbing window washers three months to clean all of them. The building is covered with panels of white marble that was imported from Italy.

DOME IMAX MOVIE THEATER. *On the Place du Dôme, to the left if you are facing the Grande Arche at La Défense. Open daily, noon-7 pm. Adults: €9: Kids: €5.*

The huge 8-story sphere next to the Automobile Museum is the Dôme IMAX movie theater. It features OMNIMAX movies every hour. You get a 180-degree view of the screen and sit in seats inclined at an angle of 30 degrees. Shows typically feature topics such as nature, historical places, adventure, and technology.

BASILIQUE DE SAINT DENIS (CATHEDRAL). *1, Rue de la Légion d'Honneur, in Saint Denis, a suburb north of Paris. Metro: Basilique de Saint Denis. Open daily 10am-7pm (summer), 10am-5pm (winter). Adults: €5.50; Kids: free.*

This magnificent Gothic cathedral stands on the site where Saint Denis is said to have stopped, after carrying his severed head in his hands all the way from Montmartre. It started out as a small chapel, built in the 6th century by King Clovis to honor Saint Denis. During the 7th century, King Dagobert replaced the chapel with a larger church and abbey. Dagobert insisted on being buried here, and from then on all the French kings were buried in the St. Denis church. King Dagobert also instituted an annual fair at Saint Denis that became hugely popular. People would come from all across France and northern Europe to attend the fair. Thanks to this the town developed and prospered.

Over the years, as kings came and went, the church was filled with magnificent tombs and funerary sculptures. King Charlemagne enlarged the church in the 8th century. Then in the 12th century, under the direction of the Abbot Suger, the church was rebuilt as the great cathedral you see today.

The Saint Denis Cathedral features wonderful gargoyles and stained glass windows. However, its most interesting features are the royal tombs. Altogether 42 kings, 32 queens, and 63 princes and princesses were buried here. During the French Revolution, the tombs were ransacked and damaged, and the bones were thrown into a common pit. The tombs were later restored and the bones were placed in the crypt of the church. There is a big plaque on the wall of the crypt listing the names of all the royals whose remains are contained there. On a wall in one of the small chapels hangs a replica of the Oriflamme. This was the banner of the church that was carried into battle by Joan of Arc.

STADE DE FRANCE (SPORTS STADIUM). *Rue Francis de Pressense, in Saint Denis. Metro: St Denis-Porte de Paris; or RER line D1: Stade de France-St. Denis or RER line B3/B5: la Plaine-Stade. There are daily tours in English 2:30 pm, except if there is a game or concert. The tour office is open daily, 10 am-6 pm, at Gate H.*

This impressive new sports stadium is located on the outskirts of Paris in the northern suburb of Saint Denis. It looks like a flying saucer (especially at night) that landed just in time to host the finals of the 1998 Soccor World Cup Games (which the French team won). It can seat as many as 100,000 people. The stadium has 18 sets of stairs, 45 kilometers of bleachers, and more than 1,000 handicap-accessible seats. It contains more than 32,000 tons of steel. The stadium can be adapted to host different sports events and rock concerts. Guided tours take you through the stadium, up 200 steps to the top, and into the locker room.

DOG CEMETERY. *4, Pont de Clichy, West of Paris, on an island in the Seine between the suburbs of Clichy and Asnières. Metro: Mairie de Clichy. Open Wed-Mon, 10 am-7 pm (summer) or 10am-5 pm (winter). Closed Tues.*

Thirty-eight percent of French households have a dog, and 25% have a cat. The French are so fond of their pets they have an entire cemetery devoted to them. Created in 1899, the Cimetière des Chiens (Dog Cemetery) is on an island in the Seine. Along with many dogs, the cemetery includes lots of cats, some birds, a few monkeys, and other assorted pets – over 100,000 in all.

The Clichy Dog Cemetary has some famous residents:

Barry was a St. Bernard dog who lived in a monastery in the French Alps. He was famous for rescuing people lost in the snow and saved many lives. Barry was mortally wounded while trying to help a man in a blinding snowstorm. The man mistook Barry for a wolf and stabbed him with a knife.

Rin Tin Tin was a famous German Shepherd movie star. He was found as a puppy by a French soldier at the end of World War I. The soldier became his trainer and launched his film career. Rin Tin Tin starred in more than 20 movies, where he amazed audiences with his cliff-hanging scenes and other stunts. He had his own limo, chauffeur, cook, and wore a diamond-covered collar.

Fun Fact

There are more than **200,000 dogs** living in Paris. In fact, the French own more dogs per capita than anyone else. Dogs are accepted in public places: shops, restaurants, grocery stores, buses. The city spends millions of euros each year cleaning up after people's dogs. The mayor finally imposed a fine on people who don't clean up their dogs' messes.

BUTTE AUX CAILLES NEIGHBORHOOD. *Between the Boulevard Blanqui and Place d'Italie on the north, Avenue d'Italie on the east, Rue Barrault on the west, and Place de l'Abbé Georges-Hénocque to the south. Metro: Corvisart, Place d'Italie, or Tolbiac.*

Tucked behind the modern high-rises of the Avenue d'Italie is this lovely old neighborhood. It has preserved its charming streets and small houses, and feels more like a village than an urban neighborhood. The central Place Paul Verlaine is surrounded by cobbled streets, cafés, and shops. In the middle of the Place is a statue commemorating the first hot air balloon ride in 1783, which started in western Paris and landed here.

This neighborhood has a history of political activism and still features a cooperative restaurant, Le Temps des Cerises, that is worker self-managed. In the 19th century, the area attracted many writers and artists, such as Gustave Flaubert, Honoré de Balzac, Victor Hugo, and Camille Corot. It still houses numerous art studios and galleries. There are also cyber cafés and artsy boutiques.

For kids, one of the most appealing features of this neighborhood is the public swimming pool, the **Piscine de la Butte aux Cailles**. It is located in an Art Deco brick building at #5, Place Verlaine. Metro: Place d'Italie. It has both outdoor and indoor pools. They are fed from an underground spring that has water that stays naturally warm (28 degrees Celsius, 82 degrees Fahrenheit) all year.

23. DAY TRIPS

VERSAILLES

A fancy palace, spectacular gardens, musical fountains, and fireworks: this is Louis XIV's Château de Versailles. Come taste of the luxury and splendor that was life at court during the reign of the France's Sun King.

The **Versailles Tourist Office** is located at 2, bis Avenue de Paris in town. Open 9am-7pm (summer); and 9am-6pm (winter). During the summer there is also an information tent in front of the palace.

Story of the Sun King

King **Louis XIV** took the throne in 1661. With his famous statement, "L'Etat, c'est moi!" (I am the State), he declared that he alone would rule the country. Though not a brilliant man, Louis XIV was a master at building his royal image and absolute power. He chose the sun as his symbol, calling himself the Sun King and associating his image with that of Apollo, the Greek god of the sun and the arts. Louis decorated his palace at Versailles with many images of the sun, the god Apollo, and himself dressed up as the Sun God. Louis XIV was also a great patron of the arts. He supported playwrights such as Molière and Racine, composers, such as Lully, as well as architects, painters, and sculptures. He also founded the royal academies of language, arts, architecture, and science.

The Sun King surrounded himself with great pomp and luxury. He set new standards of elegance. Members of the royal court competed for favors and special privileges. The king's days were regulated like clockwork from his awakening (*levée*) to the time he went to bed (*couché*). The roles of the

Versailles Highlights

• Visit the king's chambers, queen's chambers, and count the mirrors in the *Galerie des Glaces*
• See the *Grandes Eaux Musicales* when all the fountains dance to Baroque music
• Stay for a fireworks display by the Neptune Fountain
• Look for the statue of Enceladus, buried under a pile of rocks by the Greek god, Zeus.
• Take the little train to the Grand and Petit Trianon
• Go for a bike ride through the park
• Rent a rowboat on the Grand Canal
• Make like kings and queens and ride in a horse drawn carriage

courtiers were also tightly defined with elaborate rules about what it took to be in the king's favors.

Each morning, Louis XIV awoke to an elaborate ceremony called the *levée*. The First Valet would wake him. Then a crew of doctors, family, and favored friends would appear as the king was washed, combed, and shaven. Another crew of servants would arrive to help him dress. Important officials would be allowed in as the king ate his breakfast. This means that by the end of the morning meal, as many as 100 people would have already come through the king's bed chamber!

The first two decades of Louis XIV's reign were fairly successful. He reorganized the country's finances, trade, and manufacturing and created France's first postal system. In Paris, Louis instituted a police force and police chief. He had the streets cleaned and lit to make them safer. He established several institutions where poor beggars were fed, taught a skill, and expected to work. The king also reformed the military and led numerous successful campaigns against the Spanish, Dutch, English, and the German states that brought further glory to his rule.

Louis XIV made it clear from the beginning that his authority to govern came directly from God. He was a staunch defender of the Catholic Church and re-launched a series of persecutions against the French Protestants. Louis XIV also led a struggle against the Jansenists – members of a splinter Catholic movement that believed that human will was not free and that redemption was limited to only a few select people.

By the 1680s, Louis XIV's wars and extravagant expenditures had taken a huge toll on the country. Poverty increased, as did general public discontent. Life at Versailles became more dull and strict, and courtiers

Gory Fact

If you see a portrait of Louis XIV as an older man, notice how the upper half of his mouth has a sunken look. Medical historians explain that a bad dentist did severe damage to Louis' upper jaw and palate while pulling out some teeth. The damage was so bad that when the king tried to drink soup, it would come out through his nose.

increasingly left for a livelier aristocratic scene in Paris. In 1700, France became entangled in a long and difficult war with Spain. A poor harvest and harsh winter in 1708-09 killed even more people than the war. Combined, these factors sapped much of the king's spirit and popularity. The deaths of Louis XIV's sons and grandsons in 1711-1712 caused him enormous grief. The Sun King died in 1715, five days before his 77th birthday. His great-grandson and heir, the future Louis XV, was only 5 years old.

VERSAILLES PALACE. *Place des Armes, in Versailles, 20 kilometers southwest of Paris. By car take highway A13 towards Rouen to exit Versailles-Château. By public transportation take RER line C-line to Versailles Rive Gauche station (this station is only a few blocks from the Palace). There are also regular trains from Gare Montparnasse to the Versailles-Chantiers train station, or from Gare St. Lazare to Versailles-Rive Droite train station. The Palace is open Tues-Sun, 9am-6:30pm (May-Sep), 9am-5:30pm (Oct-Apr). Closed Mon. The pricing system in the palace is complicated and confusing. It varies depending on which parts you want to see. The king's apartments are a separate visit from the rest of the palace. If you go to Entrance A, you can opt for a combined ticket, including the king's rooms, queen's rooms, and Hall of Mirrors (Galerie des Glaces). Adults: €7.50; Kids: free. The audioguide (highly recommended) is €3.*

To avoid summer crowds, you may want to do this visit backwards. Start with the park and gardens. Have lunch by the Grand Canal. Go for a boat or bike ride. Save the palace for the late afternoon. The western light will be filling the Hall of Mirrors and the crowds will be thinner.

History of the Palace

The palace of Versailles was originally built by King Louis XIII as a small hunting lodge. Louis XIV had already planned to expand Versailles when he saw Nicholas Fouquet's palace at Vaux-le-Vicomte. Fouquet's palace was so splendid that the king had him arrested. Officially, Fouquet was imprisoned for using state funds for his own luxurious life style. Unofficially, his main crime was to have dared to outshine the Sun King. Louis XIV immediately hired Fouquet's architect Le Vau, painter Le Brun, and landscape designer Le Nôtre to make him an even grander palace at Versailles.

The builders and designers had their work cut out for them at Versailles. The land was marshy and unstable. Workmen had to bring in mountains of earth to build up the land. Fully grown trees were uprooted and replanted to make a forest, many of them dying along the way. A long and complicated system of pipes, pumps, and windmills was installed to drain the swamps and bring water for a grand canal and the multitude of fountains set up to decorate the gardens.

Louis XIV moved into the new palace in 1682. He made his whole court move from Paris to Versailles with him. It was a good way for the king to show his absolute power and keep an eye on members of his court. He loved to organize elaborate parties and festivities. Louis XIV filled his palace and gardens with musicians, writers, painters, acrobats, and other entertainers. Even the canals were filled with elaborately decorated boats for the amusement of the king and his court. The gardens were decorated with statues and fountains. In spite of all the installations, there was never enough water to run all of the fountains at one time. So when the king took a stroll through the gardens, workmen would whistle back and forth to signal which fountains to turn on and off along the king's path.

The new palace was built to be large, imposing, and extravagantly decorated. It included 700 rooms and 67 staircases. There were over 2,000 windows and 6,000 paintings. The chandeliers, throne, and some of the furniture were made of solid silver. Gold gilding (a thin layer of solid gold paint) covered much of the wall and ceiling decorations. Gold thread was

Fun Facts

- A secret passage led from the queen's private cabinets to those of the king. It was through here that Marie-Antoinette escaped revolutionary rioters in October 1789.
- Louis XIV's bathtub was enormous and made of solid marble. Today it is preserved in the Orangerie.
- The largest room in the palace is the spectacular Hall of Mirrors. It is 240 feet long, 32 feet wide, and two stories high. There are 17 mirrors and 17 windows.
- There are over 200,000 trees at Versailles. Thousands had to be replanted after a freak storm in December 1999 uprooted many of them.
- The orchards contain 150 different varieties of apples and pears.
- Over 200,000 flowers are planted in the gardens each year.

woven into the wall coverings. There were 5,000 pieces of furniture and decorative objects.

Versailles was one of the first royal palaces to be permanently furnished. Prior to that, most furniture was moved along with the king each time the royal court went from one palace to another. After the French Revolution of 1789, all the furniture was sold to the highest bidder. The paintings and antiquities were sent to the Louvre. The silver and metal pieces were melted down. The books were transferred to the national library. The palace was turned into a museum and never again served as a royal residence.

Versailles' heyday was during Louis XIV's reign. However, the palace was also the sight of later important historical events. In 1776, it was in the Versailles Palace that King Louis XVI met with Benjamin Franklin and agreed to send troops and supplies to support the American War of Independence. In 1789, dissenting members of the Etats-Generaux (made up of representatives from the nobility, clergy, and middle-class) met at Versailles to form the first National Assembly. This group formed the basis of France's representative democracy. It also established the Declaration of the Rights of Man and the Citizen, which served as a model for the American Constitution and Bill of Rights. Many years later, the great Hall of Mirrors at Versailles served as the sight for the signing of the 1918 peace treaty that put an end to World War I.

However, by the 1920s, the Versailles Palace was in terrible disrepair. It was thanks to American donations, notably by the Rockefeller family, that the building was saved and restored.

VERSAILLES GARDENS. *Open daily from sunrise to sunset, except during stormy or extreme weather. Entrance to the gardens is free except during special events like the Grandes Eaux Musicales or Fêtes de Nuit. If you want to park your car in the garden's lots you will have to pay €3.50.*

There are over 50 fountains decorating the gardens around the Versailles Palace. Many refer to Greek and Roman mythology:

The **Bassin de Latone** is named after a character in mythology who was seduced by the god Zeus and gave birth to Apollo and his twin sister Diana, goddess of the hunt. One day Latone took her children to have a drink from a spring in a land called Lycia. The locals teased and insulted her. Latone called for Zeus' help. He exacted revenge on the Lycians by turning them into frogs and lizards. This may be a symbol of Louis XIV's revenge over the nobles who tried to overthrow his rule during the Fronde period, when the king was just a child.

The **Bassin d'Apollon** is a huge fountain featuring Apollo driving his magnificent golden chariot, pulled by four horses, across the sky. The figure of Apollo was meant to remind his subjects of Louis XIV's power and splendor.

On the north side of the palace is another spectacular fountain, the **Bassin de Neptune**. This is where the Nuits d'Eté shows are held (see below). You can recognize Neptune, god of the seas, by his trident (three-pronged spear).

Hidden among the plants and alleyways is another great fountain. It represents **Enceladus**, a mythical Greek giant who tried to climb Mount Olympus and overthrow Zeus, king of the gods. Zeus sent down a barrage of stones to hold him back. In this fountain you can see the golden figure of Enceladus partially buried under the huge rocks.

The **Bassin du Dragon** at the end of the Allée de l'Eau is not based on Greek or Roman mythology but is still a delight. Here you will see statues of little children riding on swans and fighting off a big dragon. The jet coming from the dragon's mouth can shoot up nearly 30 meters (over 90 feet).

GRAND CANAL. *In the Versailles Gardens.*

In the days of Louis XIV, this canal was filled with golden boats – even a special gondola from Venice. Some of the boats carried musicians who entertained the king and his guests as they ambled round the water. Today, you can rent a more modest rowboat. Though less fancy than the king's, it will still offer nice views of the Palace and gardens.

BICYCLE RENTALS. *Two locations: 1) at the vehicle entrance to the park, on the Boulevard dela Reine; and 2) in the park, by the Grand Canal. Open daily 10am-6:30pm. Closed in December and January.*

These bike rental spots offer a large supply of bicycles, including kid-sized ones and child carriers. It is a great way to explore the vast park around the palace and make your way to the Trianons or Hameau de la Reine. There are plenty of car-free lanes, so you won't have to worry about traffic. Just watch out for the little tourist train that makes the rounds between the palace, Grand Canal, and Trianons.

GRAND TRIANON, PETIT TRIANON, HAMEAU DE LA REINE. *On the Versailles grounds, north and west of the Palace. Access from the Avenue du Trianon, Petit Canal, Allée de la Reine, or Allée des Deux Trianons. Open daily 9am-6:30 pm (May-Sep), 9am-5:30 pm (Oct-Apr). Adults: €7; Kids: free.*

These three buildings were built as royal residences. The Grand and Petit Trianon were designed as retreats where the king could escape from the royal court from time to time. The Grand Trianon is still used today to house visiting dignitaries. It features a large, formal garden. The Petit Trianon originally included a garden and greenhouses full of exotic plants. The original plants were moved to the Jardin des Plantes during the reign of Louis XVI. Today, the gardens around the Petit Trianon feature romantic ponds and alleyways.

As you walk north and a hair west from the Petit Trianon towards the Grand Lake, you will come to the Hameau de la Reine; built for Marie Antoinette, the wife of Louis XVI, it was a folly for her. She would go there dressed up as a milk maid and pretend to be in a small country village, surrounded by a real working farm. Your children can also enjoy the feel of a real country farm here. The Ferme du Hameau still features farm animals that children can admire and enjoy. There are special kids' workshops here (each afternoon during the summer, and on weekends during the school year at 1:30pm and 4:30pm) where children can help feed or care for some of the animals.

GRANDES EAUX MUSICALES. *Sat-Sun during the summer at 11 am and 3:30 pm. Adults: €5; Kids: 10-18: €3; Kids under 10: free.*

This show emulates the festivities at Versailles during Louis XIV's reign when the fountains would dance to the concerts by Lully and other baroque composers. The king would invite his guests to stroll among the gardens as different fountains became animated to the music. Today, the music is piped in, but the effect is still lovely.

FETES DE LA NUIT. *By the Neptune Fountain on N side of the park. Sat evenings in Jul, Aug, Sep at 10:30 pm. Seats range from €10-40. Kids under 8: free.*

In Louis XIV's day, the gardens were filled with musicians, dancers, plays, and other forms of entertainment. The Fêtes de la Nuit give you a taste of this. There are characters dressed in period clothes. There is plenty of music, and the fountains are on in full force. It's quite spectacular. At the end of the show there is a magnificent fireworks display.

LITTLE TRAIN. *Starts from the Palace (N-side terrace), with stops at the Grand Canal, Petit Trianon, and Grand Trianon. Adults and Kids 12 and up: €5.50; Kids 3-12: €3; Kids under 3: free.*

The little train is always a favorite with kids, especially if they are tired of being on their feet. It takes you from the palace to the royal residences and on to the Grand Canal. Hang on to your tickets and you will be able to get on and off all day.

CARRIAGE RIDES. *Start from the Palace (N-side terrace, near the little train). Available Tues-Sun. Closed Mon. Adults: €6.50; Kids: €5.50.*

If you are in the mood for a royal treat, hop on board one of the horse drawn carriages for a charming tour of the grounds and park. Your kids will be delighted.

CHARTRES

The **Chartres Tourist Office** is located on the Place de la Cathedral, one block from the front of the cathedral (*Tel. 02 37 18 26 26*). Open Mon-Sat, 9am-7pm; Sun, 9:30-5:30 (summer) and Mon-Sat, 10am-6pm; Sun, 10am-1pm, 2:30pm-4:30pm (winter).

You can rent audioguides to the old town here. The first costs €5.50 and subsequent ones are €3. In July and August, you can get a schedule and guide to the town's free outdoor concerts and shows. They take place every Tues, Thurs, and Sat night at 9:15pm.

Chartres Highlights

• Find the cathedral's two labyrinths
• Go on a tour of the cathedral with Malcolm Miller
• Use your binoculars to check out the gargoyles and stained glass windows
• Climb up to the top of the cathedral tower for a great view
• Take the little tourist train through the old side streets by the cathedral
• Visit the surprising Maison Picassiette

You can see the two towers of the Chartres Cathedral rising over the plains well before you actually reach the town itself. It is a magnificent building and the best preserved Medieval cathedral in all of France. Much of the old town has also maintained its 12th-13th century flavor. Thus a visit to Chartres is a trip back in time to gargoyles and gabled houses. Just don't forget to bring your binoculars.

NÔTRE DAME DE CHARTRES CATHEDRAL. *Located 88 kilometers (53 miles) southwest of Paris. By car, take the A11 highway towards Le Mans to the Chartres exit, and follow signs to Centre Ville, then to the Place de la Cathédrale. Trains leave regularly from the Gare Montparnasse for a 1-hour ride to Chartres. You can rent an audio-guide to the cathedral in the bookshop: €3 (short version), €4 (long version). Visits of the tower cost Adults: €4; Kids: free.*

The town of Chartres has been an important religious center for countless generations. In ancient Gaul, before the Christian era, there was a well-known Druid temple here. When the Romans took over Gaul in the 1st century BC, they built a temple to the Dea Mater (Mother Goddess). In 876, King Charles the Bald gave the town of Chartres relics from a piece of the robe of the Virgin Mary. The town built a church, called Nôtre Dame de Chartres (Our Lady of Chartres) to house these relics. It was built in the Romanesque style and became a popular destination for religious pilgrims devoted to the cult of Mary. However, a big fire in 1194 destroyed much of the church, along with a good chunk of the town. However, it did not damage the relic of the Virgin Mary's veil. The townspeople saw this as a sign from God that they should rebuild the church, and they raised huge sums of money and manpower – resulting in a great cathedral that combined the remaining Romanesque elements with new Gothic features.

From the outside, you can see the mix of "old" Romanesque elements and "new" Gothic ones. The cathedral's main entrance, known as the Royal Portal, predates the big fire and is in the Romanesque style (note the rounded archways). It depicts Christ surrounded by his disciples and the evangelists. The statues date from the 1140s-1150s. The door on the right is dedicated to Mary, and the one on the left depicts the Ascension. If you look at the cathedral's two towers you'll notice that they are not the same. The one on the right is the old tower. It was built in the 1140s, and is the tallest remaining Romanesque-style church tower in the world. The new tower, Clocher Neuf, is on the left side. It was built in the flamboyant Gothic style (so named because it resembles flames!) in the early 13th century. Note the peaked arches and flamboyant decorations. The Clocher Neuf is 115 meters tall. The top spire was originally made of wood but was toppled by lightening in the 16th century. It was rebuilt in stone. You can climb the 378 steps to the top of the Clocher Neuf for a very impressive view. Be warned, however, that it is not for people who are afraid of heights.

During the French Revolution, when anti-church sentiments were very strong, the cathedral narrowly escaped total destruction. In 1791, the revolutionary government set up a task force to figure out how to demolish this huge structure. The members spent so much time discussing potential plans that they never got around to carrying them out.

Parent Tip: Is your child an aspiring artist? Future photographer? Amateur architect? Encourage your kids to explore the details and decorations of the cathedral. Have them draw their favorite gargoyle or take photos of their favorite statues. Talk about how the flying buttresses help support the weight and height of the cathedral walls. Help them imagine how hard it would be to build such a structure without a single power tool.

Once you step inside the cathedral, notice the enormous labyrinth on the floor made of black and white stone. The center is supposed to represent paradise. Pilgrims used to crawl on their knees along all 306 yards of the labyrinth until they reached the center. Many churches once had labyrinths such as this one, but this is one of the few that still remains.

Then look up and admire the stained glass windows. There are 176 of them in all. They have miraculously survived the tests of time and war. During the First and Second World Wars, the windows were carefully taken down and hidden in a safe place to protect them from bombardments. Each window panel is 4ft/4ft square. They appear much smaller from the ground. The windows are famous for their bright blue color, known as Chartres Blue, contrasted with bright reds. They depict scenes from the Bible, lives of the saints, and different Medieval trades. The three windows on the facade are the oldest and date from before the great fire. They represent the family tree of Jesus, Christmas, and Easter. The other windows are more modern(!): they date from the 13th century. The three rose windows represent the Apocalypse, the Virgin Mary, and the Last Judgment.

As you walk around the inside of the church, take a look at the sculptures surrounding the Choir (the U-shaped area behind the pulpit). They date from the 16th century and represent scenes from the life of Christ. On the left side as you face the Choir is the Chapelle Saint Piat where the Virgin Mary's robe is housed. Did Mary really wear this cloth? It is not certain, but dating techniques have indeed shown that the cloth is about 2,000 years old. The robe used to be much longer than it is today, but during the Medieval period pieces were cut off and sold.

Once you have visited the inside of the cathedral, don't forget to check out the statues and gargoyles on the outside of the building. Remember that these were originally painted in vivid colors. You can occasionally still see traces of colors around the eyes or other small details in the sculptures. If you go behind the cathedral, you will find a lovely garden with terraces overlooking the town. This is also where you will discover the cathedral's second labyrinth. It is made of low hedges and located on one of the garden terraces. It is a great place to let children run and play.

TOURS OF THE CATHEDRAL WITH MALCOLM MILLER. *1-hour public tours offered Mid-March to Mid-November, at noon and 2:45 pm, Mon-Sat. Adults: €10; Kids 10 and up: €5; Kids under 10: free (provided they behave – otherwise they are tossed in the well, he warns jokingly). Private groups may also organize special tours with Mr. Miller.*

Even if you (or your kids) are not a big fan of guided tours, try to catch this one with the English-speaking guide, Malcolm Miller. Mr. Miller is known world round for his lively presentations and deep knowledge of the cathedral. He has been guiding people through the stories and surprises of the Chartres cathedral for over 45 years. Mr. Miller uses a great deal of humor in his tours and manages to make his passion for the place contagious to listeners of all ages.

OLD TOWN OF CHARTRES, *South and east of the cathedral.*

If you are in Chartres during the month of December, don't miss the town's living advent calendar. Each evening at 6 pm a different window of the town is opened featuring music, theater, or stories to celebrate the Christmas season. Contact the tourist office for details.

The small streets near the cathedral give you a nice feel for life in a medieval town (minus the bad smells). Notice the way the old half-timbered houses jut out above the streets. At # 29 Rue Chantault, you'll find the town's oldest house, which dates from the 12th century.

Make your way to the Place de la Poissonerie, site of the former fish market. See if you can find the House of the Salmon, decorated with wooden carvings of the fish. You can meander down towards the Eure River through old streets. Or try out some of the steep passageways known as Tetres and often lined with stairs. There are five of them leading down the hill to the river. Along the Eure there are pretty walkways and lovely houses. By the **Pont de la Courtille** you can rent paddle-boats, rowboats, and canoes for an enjoyable outing on the river.

TOURIST TRAIN. *Departs from the Place de la Cathedral in front of the Tourist Office, Mar-Nov, starting at 10:30 am. Adults: €5.50; Kids: €3.*

This little train is a good alternative for tired feet or grumpy children. It takes you for a 35-minute ride through the streets of old Chartres. Commentaries are in English and French.

HOT AIR BALLOON TOURS. *Reservations at the Tourist Office. Place de la Cathedral, Tel. 02 37 18 26 26. Adults: €130; Kids: €99. Discounts apply if several people reserve together. Website: www.air-magic.com*

If you really want an unforgettable way to visit Chartres, you can reserve a ride in a hot air balloon! The trip follows the Eure River region, including a fly over of the Chateau de Maintenon,

MAISON PICASSIETTE. *22, Rue du Repos, Chartres. From the old town, cross the Eure River to the Place Morard. Take the Rue du Faubourg la Grappe to Rue de Sours, and left into the Rue du Repos. Open Apr-Oct; Wed-Mon, 10am-12pm and 2pm-6pm, Closed Tues and Sun. Adults: €4.10; Kids 12-18: €2.10; Kids under 12: free.*

This surprising house is nestled in a modest, modern neighborhood of Chartres. It belonged to a man named Raymond Isidore, who was a town street sweeper. He spent 25 years collecting bits of broken glass and china that he used to make mosaic decorations all over the house and garden. There are even reproductions of the Chartres Cathedral and the *Mona Lisa*.

CHANTILLY

The **Chantilly Tourist Office** is located in the center of town at 60, Avenue du Maréchal Joffre (*Tel. 03 44 67 37 37*). Open daily, 9am-6pm.

This town is renowned for two things that make it a sure hit with many children: horses and Crème Chantilly (whipped cream). Kids love the horse museum, lodged in the former stables of the Château de Chantilly. The Château itself looks straight out of a fairy tale. It is surrounded by a real moat, lovely gardens, and deep woods. Chantilly is also famous for its horse races and equestrian center where over 3,000 pure bred horses are trained for high level competition.

MUSÉE VIVANT DU CHEVAL. *Grandes Ecuries, by the Château in Chantilly. Located 50 kilometers (about 30 miles) north of Paris. By car take the A1 highway north to the exit for Saint Witz, then the N16 or D924 to Chantilly. By train leave from the Gare du Nord in Paris for the Chantilly-Gouvieux Station. You can also take an RER commuter train from Châtelet-Les Halles in*

Chantilly Highlights

• See the royal stables, horses, and horse shows at the Musée Vivant du Cheval (Horse Museum)
• Look for the gallery of monkeys and famous pink diamond in Château de Chantilly
• Ride an electric boat on the Grand Canal in the Château gardens
• Have an afternoon treat topped with Crème Chantilly

Paris, Line D, to Chantilly. The ride lasts 30-40 minutes. To get from the station to the Château de Chantilly, you can take a taxi, ride the free Cariane bus, or go on foot (it's a 20 minute walk). The museum is open daily except Tues, 10:30am-5:30pm (April-Oct). Open Tues afternoons, June-Aug. Winter hours (Nov-Mar) are Mon, Wed-Fri, 2pm-5pm; Sat-Sun, 10:30am-5:30pm. Closed Tues. Adults: €8.50; Kids 13-18: €7.80; Kids 5-12: €6.50; Kids 4 and under: free. Special shows include an additional fee. Note: The stables are not heated, so bring warm clothes if the weather is cold.

This remarkable "living museum" showcases not only the royal stables and paraphernalia surrounding horses, but also features live horse demonstrations and shows. It is not to be missed if your group includes any horse lovers. The museum is housed in the royal stables of the Château de Chantilly. These were designed in 1719 by a prince named Louis Henri de Bourbon. According to legend, he was something of a horse fanatic and even believed that he would be reincarnated as a horse after his death. The stables are over 600 feet long and once housed as many as 240 horses. There were also 500 hunting dogs and nearly 100 hunting birds. The museum tour includes a visit to the old stables, including a central fountain where the horses went to drink. There are exhibits ranging from toys to hunting and horse racing, veterinary medicine, and how to make horseshoes. This living museum also features 30 live horses, representing famous breeds from around the world. There are live demonstrations of horse showmanship and tricks scheduled at different points during the day.

If you are in the Paris during the month of June you can catch the **annual Jockey Club race** at the Chantilly race track (first Sunday of the month) or the Prix de Diane Hermes (second Sunday of the month). If you are in the area over the Christmas Holidays, don't miss the special "Magical Afternoons with Santa Clause" at the Musée Vivant du Cheval. At 2:30pm and 4pm during the winter break, Santa Clause and his helpers distribute treats and spread plenty of holiday cheer. Then the horses perform tricks, accompanied by clowns and heroes from popular children's tales.

CHANTILLY PALACE AND ITS GARDENS. *Located 50 kilometers (about 30 miles) north of Paris. By car take the A1 highway north to the exit for Saint Witz, then the N16 or D924 to Chantilly. There are commuter trains from the Châtelet/Les Halles RER station as well as regular trains (called Trains Grandes Lignes) from the Gare du Nord in Paris. Either train takes you to the Chantilly-Gouvieux train station. The ride lasts about 30-40 minutes. From the Chantilly train station you can walk about 25 minutes, take a taxi, or ride a free city bus to the Palace. The Château de Chantilly is open daily except Tues, 10am-6pm (Mar-Oct); and 10:30am-12:45pm, 2pm-5pm (Nov-Feb). Closed Tues. The gardens are open daily, including Tues.*

Fees for entry to the castle and park are: Adults: €8; Kids 12-18: €4; Kids 3-11: €3; Kids under 3: free. If you only want to visit the gardens the fees are: Adults and Kids 12-18: €4; Kids 3-11: €2. Entrance to the park plus boat ride: Adults: €10; Kids 13-17: €9; Kids 4-12: €6; Kids under 4: free. Or you can get a ticket for the palace, gardens, boat ride, and ride on the little train for: Adults and Kids over age 13: €15; Kids 4-12: €9; Kids under 4: free.

The Castle

The first fancy residence to be built on this spot was a villa for a wealthy man named Cantilius, during the Roman occupation of France in the first century AD. The name Chantilly is supposed to be derived from his name. The Renaissance castle that you see here today dates from the early 16th century. Although part of the castle was destroyed during the French Revolution of 1789, it was restored to its original splendor in the late 1800s. The building and its setting are so lovely that they have often been used as the backdrop for movies.

The Château de Chantilly is famous for its collection of paintings, rare books, ceramics, drawings, and furniture. It is filled with masterpieces by artists such as Raphael, Gericault, Ingres, and Delacroix. Although these may not impress your average 10-year-old, there are plenty of elements that kids enjoy. First of all, if they have not been through a fancy palace, it is worth

Fun Fact

The Château's famous **pink diamond** was stolen in 1926. Several months after the theft, a housekeeper was cleaning a room in a little hotel in Paris. She came across a suitcase accidentally left behind by the last guest. Inside the suitcase was a shiny, red apple. When the housekeeper tried to bite into the fruit, she hit something hard that chipped her tooth. It was the priceless pink diamond. The gem was returned to the palace with great fanfare and celebration.

taking them to see the princely bedrooms, ballrooms, galleries, and such. There is a room that kids enjoy called the **Grande Singerie**, which is entirely decorated with monkeys. The **Galerie des Batailles** is decorated with huge scenes of the successful military battles led by one of the castle's owners, the Prince de Condé. The **Galerie des Peintures** is crammed full of paintings, placed one right next to the other in the display fashion popular in the 19th century.

The **Cabinet des Gems** features an amazing pink diamond, nicknamed the Grand Condé. The Prince de Condé used to wear it on the handle tip of his cane. The room also displays a series of tiny portraits and collection of ladies' fans.

The Galerie des Cerfs was used as the formal dining room in the late 19th century. It is decorated with tapestries from the Gobelins Tapestry Factory in Paris. They depict stag-hunting scenes. The Galerie des Logis has paintings that depict the history of Chantilly, including its horse races.

There is a music room and a gallery filled with 44 gray and gold stained glass windows depicting the Greek myth of Cupid and Psyche. The panes tell the story of Psyche, whose beauty brought out the rage and jealousy of Venus, the goddess of love. Venus asked her son, Cupid, to exact revenge on Psyche, but instead he fell in love with her. Venus was furious and determined to punish both of them, but the king of the gods, Jupiter, took the two lovers under his protection. In the end, everyone made peace during a grand banquet.

The Castle Gardens

The French gardens at Chantilly were designed by the renowned landscape architect, André Le Nôtre, who also designed the ones at Versailles, the Tuileries, and Vaux le Vicomte. They date from the 1640s and include the formal gardens, fountains, Grand Canal, and its waterfall. Gryffinder fans will note the statues of female griffins that guard the castle. The English gardens date from the late 18th and early 19th centuries. They feature romantic getaways, little temples, and Island of Love (Ile d'Amour), a swan lake, and Chinese decorations.

Fun Fact

Cooking has always been serious business at Chantilly. In the 17th century, the Chantilly Palace hosted King Louis XIV. When some of the food did not appear on the table as planned, the head steward and chef of the castle, named Vatel, committed suicide by plunging a sword through his heart. A later cooking accident in the 18th century had a happier ending. One of the cooks spilled sugar into his stirred cream, thereby inventing Crème Chantilly (whipped cream).

The Hameau (Hamlet) in the English gardens is made up of five little farm houses built in 1774. They served as inspiration to Queen Marie Antoinette who had an Hameau built for herself at the Palace of Versailles. Kids will enjoy losing you in the hamlet's small labyrinth. In the dining room of the Grande Chaumière (the central building) there is a trompe l'oeil painting made to look as though you are sitting in the woods. The Hameau's buildings are meant to represent a charming, country farm. Today, they house a lovely café, Au Gouter Champêtre, open Apr-Oct. It is a great spot to take a break and enjoy a treat covered in Crème Chantilly.

Beyond the gardens stretches the forest of Chantilly. It is a very popular place for hikes and picnics. You can walk around the 4 lakes and visit the Château de la Reine Blanche. This former mill was converted to a hunting lodge in the late 19th century.

ELECTRIC BOAT RIDES. *Grand Canal, in the gardens of the Château de Chantilly. Open daily, Apr-Oct, 10am-6pm. Entrance to the park + boat ride: Adults and Kids over 12: €8; Kids 4-12: €5; Kids under 4: free.*

In the 16th and 17th centuries the princes who lived at Chantilly and their guests would ride along the Grand Canal in fancy boats. Today you, too, can enjoy the views and the water by taking a ride in one of the canal's quiet, electric boats. The tour lasts 30 minutes.

You can also visit the park and gardens in a **horse-drawn carriage** or on the little white **tourist train**. There are some **playgrounds** by the Maison du Hameau and by the boat rentals.

NUITS DU FEU – FIREWORKS. *In the gardens of the Château de Chantilly. Held one weekend in June at 11:30 pm. Call 03 44 45 18 18 or check the Pariscope or Officiel des Spectacles weekly events magazines for the exact date and prices.*

This spectacular fireworks show has been an annual tradition at the Château de Chantilly since 1672.

FONTAINEBLEAU
"A bright new day – the sky is blue
The storm is gone; the world is new
This is the Castle of Fountainblue –
All this, dear children, belongs to you"
– *Madeleine and the Gypsies* by Ludwig Bemelmans

Whether or not your children are fans of the Madeleine stories, they will find plenty to do and enjoy in Fontainebleau. It is a great spot to explore a palace, hike through the woods, go for a bike ride, or try your hand at rock-climbing.

The **Fontainebleau Tourist Office** (4, Rue Royale) is open Mon-Fri:

10am-6:30pm and Sun: 10am-4pm. *Tel. 01 60 74 99 99.* It offers maps and audioguides to the forest. Staff members organize kid-friendly nature walks and painting expeditions (in French). You can pick up the free "livret jeux" for kids that is full of information and games about the town, forest, and palace (in French). For €4.60 you also can rent an audioguide (In French or English) that will take you on a 1.5 hour tour of the historic town center.

Note: You can download a map of Fontainebleau at: www.fontainebleau-tourisme.com/PDF/fontainebleau-plan.pdf.

FONTAINEBLEAU FOREST. *Located 65 kilometers southeast of Paris. By car, take the A6 highway or N7 road south to the Fontainebleau exit. Trains leave the Gare de Lyon every 60 minutes for the Fontainebleau-Avon Station, located in the heart of the woods. The ride takes about 50 minutes. You will want a map. They are available at the train station and at the tourist office. You can also rent an (English or French) audioguide, which will give you a 1.5 hour tour of the woods at the tourist office for €4.60/person.*

The Fontainebleau Forest is considered one of the prettiest in Europe. It is filled with beech, oak, and pine trees. Some have been around for centuries and are among the oldest in Europe. The terrain is quite varied and spectacular. There are vast stretches of sand and dunes. These are left over from the Tertiary Era, when the great shallow sea that had covered the area around Paris receded, leaving behind a thick later of fine, white sand. There are also spectacular rock formations, some of which offer great hiking and rock-climbing opportunities. Several of these rocks are said to look like animals: there's a diplodocus in the Massif des Trois-Pignons, an elephant near the Route des Gorges d'Apremont, and a turtle along the N6 road near the Carrière du Carrousel. The observation deck at the Rocher Cassepot on the north side of the forest offers an impressive view. With a pair of binoculars you can see all the way to the Eiffel Tower and Tour Montparnasse in Paris.

There are many kid-friendly hiking possibilities. You may want to try the **Gorges du Fanchard** (take N7 road to D301 and park at the Carrefour de la Croix Franchard. This hike takes you through rocks and trails to the Belvedere of the Druids. The **Gorges d'Apremont** walk (from Carrefour de Bas Bréau on the Barbizon side of the forest) takes you up the rocky terrain for a great view then down to the Caverne des Brigands (Robbers' Cave). Another hike to the Rocher des Demoiselles leaves from the Route de Recloses (D63, on the right from the N7 after the Carrefour de l'Obelisque de Fontainebleau) is also a fun hike for adventurous small fry.

The forest is full of well-marked trails for hiking, biking, and horseback riding. There are also 22 little Maisons de la Nature (Nature Houses) scattered throughout the woods. They have maps and information about the area's fauna and flora.

Biking in Fontainebleau Forest

This is a fun way to discover the Fontainebleau Forest and make your way to the Palace. There are numerous paths you can follow, marked with street signs when different paths intersect. Here are some addresses for bike rentals:

• **Fontainebleau-Avon Train Station** (*Tel. 01 60 22 36 14*). If you are coming from Paris, you may want to try the Train+Vélo formula starting from the Gare de Lyon. Ask for it at the train station ticket office in Paris. This formula combines the price of the train ticket to and from Paris, along with the bike rental. It is a good way to get from the Fontainebleau train station and forest to the Fontainebleau Palace, 2 kilometers away.

• **Fontainebleau Tourist Office**, *4, Rue Royal in town, directly across from the Fontainebleau Palace (Tel. 01 60 74 99 99)*. Here you can purchase maps of the local marked trails (parcours balisés) through the forest and to the castle.

• **Top Loisirs**, *10, Passage Ronsard, in Fontainebleau (Tel. 01 60 74 08 50)*.

Rock Climbing

Rock climbing trails in the Fontainebleau Forest are color-coded to indicate the level of difficulty:

White: specially designed for kids
Yellow: beginners
Orange: medium
Blue: longer, more challenging
Green: difficult
Black on white: experts only

This is a fun family sport, and the Fontainebleau woods offer the best outdoor rock-climbing in the Paris vicinity. You can sign up with a group or private climbing guide, who will provide instruction and equipment. Contact these organizations for more information on climbing opportunities in Fontainebleau:

• **Au Vieux Campeur**, *48, Rue des Ecoles, in Paris, Metro: Maubert Mutualité*. This store features equipment and information for sports and outdoor enthusiasts. They have guidebooks and information on rock-climbing in Fontainebleau and around France.

• **Association des Amis de la Forêt de Fontainebleau** (*Tel. 01 64 23 46 45*). They can give you information about trails, gear, and how to join a group outing.

• **Fontainebleau Tourist Office**, *4, Rue Royal in town, directly across from the Fontainebleau Palace (Tel. 01 60 74 99 99)*, sells books with maps of the forest and trails to climbing rocks.

• **Club Alpins Français**, 24 av. Laumière, in Paris, Metro: Laumiere (*Tel. 01 42 02 75 94*)

Horseback Riding

There are special trails in the woods designated for horseback riding and several equestrian centers in the area. For more information contact:
• **Centre Equestre de Recloses-Fontainebleau**, *Rue Clos de la Bonne 77760 Recloses (Tel. 01 64 24 21 10)*
• **Le Relais du Picotin**, *Château Saint Louis-Route de Sens in Poligny, next to Fontainebleau Forest (Tel. 01 64 28 84 16; Email: lerelaisdupicotin@free.fr. Website: lerelaisdupicotin.free.fr)*
• **Fontainebleau Tourist Office**, *4, Rue Royal in town, directly across from the Fontainebleau Palace (Tel. 01 60 74 99 99).*

If you enjoy watching horses in action, you can go to the **horse races** at the Hippodrome de la Solle, located on National Road 6 between the towns of Fontainebleau and Melun. *Tel. 01.60.71.15.86.* Adults: €3.50, Kids: free. Scheduling information is available on line at www.lescourseshippiques.com and further information on touring the hippodrome or attending a race can be obtained at the Fountainebleau Tourist Office.

FONTAINEBLEAU PALACE. *Located about 65 kilometers southeast of Paris. By car, take the A6 highway south to the Fontainebleau exit, then N37 road. Trains leave the Gare de Lyon train station every 60 minutes for Fontainebleau-Avon. The ride takes about 50 minutes. The Fontainebleau train station is in the middle of the forest, about 2 km from the Fontainebleau Palace. You can walk, bike, or catch the AB public bus to the Palace. Open Wed-Mon, 9:30am-5pm. Closed Tues. Adults: €5.50. Kids: free. Free to everyone on the first Sun of each month. Audioguides to the palace and gardens are available either at the tourist office or at the palace for €4.60. A free jeu-parcours children's guidebook with games and pictures is distributed to kids at the ticket office.*

The Fontainebleau Palace served as a residence for French kings and emperors from the 12th to the 19th centuries. Of all of France's castles and palaces, this is the only one to have served so long and uninterrupted a time as a royal home. It began in the 12th century, as a small fortified residence in the middle of the Fontainebleau Forest, where the hunting was especially good. Only the old donjon (or keep) remains from the old 12th century hunting lodge. Look for it in the **Cour Ovale** (Oval Courtyard).

In the early 16th century, King Francois I decided to transform the hunting lodge into a magnificent palace. Heavily influenced by the new ideas and styles of the Italian Renaissance, he brought in Italian artists, architects, and craftsmen to turn his Fontainebleau home into a "New Rome." The renovations began in 1528. The palace was rebuilt with grand rooms and galleries that were elaborately decorated. Fontainebleau became the king's favorite palace. He held magnificent festivals, costume balls, and hunting tournaments there. The palace's ballroom gives you an idea of the luxury and splendor of Francois I's court.

Over time, the artists and architects associated with Fontainebleau began to add a French touch to their Italian Renaissance style. They launched a new art movement known as "Mannerism" since it was done in the manner of the greats, such as Michelangelo and Leonardo da Vinci. Their group came to be known as the Ecole de Fontainebleau (Fontainebleau School).

After Francois I's reign, subsequent kings further improved the Fontainebleau Palace. Henri IV added courtyards, canals, ponds, a jeu de paume court (early version of tennis), and gardens. Louis XIII added the horseshoe shaped double staircase that leads to the palace entrance. Louis XIV's landscape architect, André LeNôtre, designed the formal gardens.

When Emperor Napoleon I ruled France in the early 19th century, he settled at Fontainebleau, preferring it to Versailles. You can still see his bedroom with its military camp bed, and the throne room that Napoleon created from a former royal bedroom. It was in the great entrance hall of the Fontainebleau palace that Napoleon said good-bye to his loyal guards on his way to exile on the Italian island of Elba. The hall is now called the **Cour des Adieux** (Court of Farewells).

The **Chapelle de la Trinite** in the palace was where Louis XV married Marie Leszczinska in 1725. It is also where the future Emperor Napoleon III was baptized in 1810.

There are several fun ways to explore the gardens and town around the Fontainebleau Palace. You can go for a ride in a horse-drawn carriage. You can also opt for a ride on the little tourist train that goes around the gardens and town. If you make your way to the carp pond, you can rent a rowboat and enjoy views of the gardens from there.

Fun Fact

The Palace's **Carp Pond** dates from the reign of Henri IV (1589-1610). It used to contain a fountain with water that was said to be so pure, it was reserved solely for the king's use. The pond also had a small pavilion where food was served to the king and members of the royal court during their strolls through the gardens.

VAUX LE VICOMTE

If imitation is the greatest form of flattery, then Vaux le Vicomte has been flattered indeed. This is the little palace that prompted King Louis XIV to build his magnificent (and overly pompous) Palace of Versailles. Along the way, it launched the careers of great artists and caused the downfall of its owner. Many visitors will tell you that they actually prefer Vaux le Vicomte to Versailles, because it is smaller and more manageable.

PALACE OF VAUX LE VICOMTE. *Located 55 kilometers (34 miles) south of Paris in Maincy. By car, take the A4, A5, or A6 highway south to the Melun exit, then follow the signs to Vaux le Vicomte. By train, take the RER D2 line from Châtelet/Les Halles or Gare de Lyon to Melun. From Melun take a taxi for the 5 kilometers (3 miles) to Vaux le Vicomte. (Make sure to arrange for a return pickup.) There are also tour bus trips to Vaux le Vicomte from Paris. Contact Paris-Vision (Tel. 01 42 60 30 01) or Cityrama (Tel. 01 44 55 61 00). Open daily, Apr-Oct, 10am-6pm. (The palace visit closes for lunch, 1pm-2pm). Entry fee includes access to the palace, gardens, and Musée des Equipages (Carriage Museum). Adults: €12.50; Kids 6-16: €9.90; Kids under 6: free. Audioguides are available for €3. Free kids' guides, for kids 6-9 and 10-15, are available (in French) at the entrance. Candlelight visits offered Fri-Sat nights, see below.*

Vaux le Vicomte was built by a man named **Nicholas Fouquet**, who was Minister of Finance during the reign of King Louis XIV. Fouquet was wealthy and powerful. He was also a great patron of the arts. When he decided to build himself a palace, Fouquet hired the best architect (Le Vau), painter (Le Brun), and landscape designer (Le Nôtre) the country had to offer. His family's motto was, "The sky is the limit," and he did his best to live up to it.

It took five years and 18,000 workers to build the palace and gardens at Vaux le Vicomte. When they were completed in 1661, Fouquet celebrated with a sumptuous party. He invited the Sun King himself (as Louis XIV was known) to attend. Food was served on plates of solid gold. Molière wrote a play called *Les Fâcheux* (The Nuisances) specially for the event. There was music by Lully. Ballet dancers performed among the flower beds. Actors recited poetry from the statues. Jewel-covered elephants dazzled the crowd. To top off the evening there was an elaborate fireworks display.

Vaux le Vicomte Highlights

- Visit the palace's kitchens made famous by its greatest chef, Vatel
- See the Carriage Museum in the former stables
- Go for a ride in one of the animal-shaped boats on the Grand Canal
- Tour the gardens in an electric "Club Car"
- Look for the giant statue of Hercules
- Watch the fountain displays dance to music
- Tour the palace by candlelight

Fun Facts

• When Louis XIV decided to have Fouquet arrested, he turned to one of his most trusted guards: none other than **d'Artagnon**, the aging head of the royal **Musketeers**.

• Alexander Dumas (and Leonardo di Capria) fans take note. If you've seen the 1990s film version of *The Man in the Iron Mask*, this place may look familiar. Much of the movie was filmed here at Vaux le Vicomte.

Fouquet's fancy party completely backfired on him, however. Rather than being impressed by Fouquet's displays, the 23-year old king was furious! Vaux le Vicomte was more magnificent than any of the royal palaces. The Sun King, unwilling to be outshined by one of his own subjects, had Fouquet arrested for stealing state funds. Fouquet was condemned to life imprisonment in a high security retreat in the Alps. In the meantime, Louis XIV confiscated Fouquet's wealth. The king also hired the architect, painter, and landscape designer from Vaux le Vicomte and set them to work building him an even grander royal palace. The result was the Palace of Versailles.

Today, the palace and gardens of Vaux le Vicomte are well worth a visit. They are on a more human scale than Versailles, yet offer much of the same elegance. The palace is full of lavishly decorated rooms, including a bedroom reserved for the king, a magnificent dining room, and a fairy-tale-like ballroom. In the kitchens, wax figures bring to life the behind the scenes activities involved in preparing the sumptuous meals. The man in charge of the kitchens during Fouquet's time was a famous steward named Vatel. Vatel later worked at the Château de Chantilly where he oversaw preparations for a series of meals in honor of King Louis XIV. When the food did not come out as planned, he was so devastated that he killed himself.

Although no longer a cause for suicide, food is still a big deal at Vaux le Vicomte. There are gourmet cooking demonstrations on weekend afternoons, and you can by some local delicacies at the museum gift shop.

For younger kids, you can turn a tour of the palace into a treasure hunt. See how many examples they can find of Fouquet's initial "F"; his emblem, the squirrel; and his family motto, "Quo non ascendat" (The sky is the limit).

MUSÉE DES EQUIPAGES (CARRAIGE MUSEUM). *Located in the former stables of the Vaux le Vicomte Palace. Entrance is included in the price of the ticket for the palace and gardens. Open daily 10am-6pm, Mar-Oct.*

This museum features some 30 horse-drawn carriages. They are displayed in realistic settings, with wax figures to help bring the scenes to life. Most date from the 19th century, but there is also a very interesting Roman cart.

GARDENS OF VAUX LE VICOMTE.

Outside, you can explore the formal, French gardens with their pretty fountains and topiary trees carved to look like animals and other forms. Look all the way down the central promenade and you will see a giant statue of the Greek hero, Hercules. You can take a royal stroll around the gardens or rent a "**Club Car**" (4-person electric cart) to toot around the park. You can also rent a **Nautil** (boat in the form of a marine animal) for a ride on the Grand Canal from May through September. On warm afternoons there are **pony rides** for little tikes.

LES JEUX D'EAU – MUSICAL FOUNTAINS. *In the gardens of Vaux le Vicomte on the second and last Saturday of the month, 3pm-6pm. Entry fees are the same as the regular visit.*

Every other Saturday afternoon, all the fountains of Vaux le Vicomte come to life with lights and music. It is a lovely show that evokes the lavish splendor that was life at the royal court of the 17th century.

SOIREES AUX CHANDELLES - CANDLELIGHT VISITS OF THE PALACE. *Saturday evenings, May-Oct, and also Friday evenings in July and August, from 8pm-midnight. Adults: €12.50; Kids 6-16: €9.9; Kids under 6: free.*

This is a special visit for kids who are old enough to stay up past 8 pm and appreciate a step back in time. The rooms and gardens of Vaux le Vicomte are lit with more than 2,000 candles. Baroque music fills the air. It is quite enchanting.

GIVERNY & LES ANDELYS

Venture just an hour west of Paris along the Seine River and you come to the lush, green, rolling hills of Normandy. The region is famous for its apples, creamy butter, camembert cheese, and D-Day beaches. It is also home to two terrific day-trip destinations: Giverny and the Château Gaillard. The first features a magical garden so filled with color it will make you feel like you've walked right into an Impressionist painting. The second holds the echoes of Richard the Lionheart and great battles between the French Capetiens and English Plantagenat kings.

CLAUDE MONET'S HOUSE AND GARDENS. *Rue Claude Monet, in Giverny, 80 kilometers (50 miles) west of Paris. By car, follow the directions for the A13 highway toward Rouen (via the Pont de Saint Cloud on the west side of Paris) to the Bonnières exit, then the D201 to Giverny. For a more scenic route along the Seine River you can get off the A13 earlier, following the green road signs to Vernon, and take the N15 road through Rosny and Bonnières to Vernon and Giverny. The house and parking lots are well marked. By train, go from the Gare Saint Lazare to Vernon, 45 minutes away. From the Vernon train station you can catch a bus or take a taxi for the 5 kilometer (3 mile) ride to Giverny (fare:*

about 12 E each way). You also can rent bikes in the cafés across from the station. By bike, take the Rue d'Albufera and cross the bridge over the Seine. At the traffic circle don't follow the sign to Giverny. Take the first right and first left to the bike path that will take you safely to Giverny. There are also tour bus trips to Giverny from Paris. Contact Paris-Vision (Tel. 01 42 60 30 01) or Cityrama (Tel. 01 44 55 61 00). Claude Monet's house and gardens are open daily, Apr-Oct, Tues-Sun, 19:30am-6pm. Closed Mon and Nov-Mar. Adults: €5.50 (house and gardens), €4 (gardens only); Kids 12-18: €4, Kids 7-11: €3 (house and garden); Kids under 7: free.

If your children are fans of the book *Linnea in Monet's Garden* by Christina Bjock and Lena Anderson, they will really enjoy this visit. You can follow Linnea's footsteps by boarding a train at the Gare Saint Lazare (immortalized in paintings by both Claude Monet and his friend Edouard Manet) for Vernon. There you can buy food for a picnic to be enjoyed along the shores of the Seine River, just like Linnea. Ride to Giverny by bike, bus, or taxi. Explore Monet's house and gardens, and see how many scenes you recognize from the book. Did you forget your copy? Don't worry, you can purchase the book (as well as Linnea dolls and paraphernalia) in the gift shop at Monet's house, at the Musée d'Art Americain in Giverny, at the Louvre, or in many of the English bookshops in Paris.

Giverny & Les Andelys Highlights

• Follow the traces of Linnea and Mr. Bloom to Monet's House
• Say hello to the turkeys and explore the flowered alleyways of Monet's garden
• Admire the lily pond from the Japanese Bridge
• Visit Monet's pink house
• Paint your own impressionist pictures
• See the Museum of American Art in Giverny
• Imagine yourself as a medieval knight living in the Château Gaillard
• Have a glass of cider and slice of camembert cheese

Monet's Life at Giverny

In the 1870s, Claude Monet was one of a handful of French painters who spearheaded a new art movement, known as Impressionism. They broke with traditional artistic methods, using bold colors and broad brushstrokes. They played with the effects of light on a subject and concentrated on capturing the mood or impression of a scene rather than its exact details.

Monet moved to the pink house at Giverny in 1883 and lived there until his death in 1926 at the age of 86. He claimed that the only two things he was any good at were gardening and painting, and this house offered plenty of opportunity for both. Monet was passionate about his painting, often getting up at 5 am and working on several different paintings at once. If he didn't like the way a picture turned out, he would burn it in a fit of anger. Yet it was here in Giverny that Monet created many of his most famous works.

Although Monet became relatively wealthy from selling his paintings later in life, he was still a struggling artist when he rented the Giverny house with his large, blended family. His wife, Camille, had died of tuberculosis, leaving Monet with two young sons. Earlier, their friend Alice Hoschédé had come to live with the Monets along with her five children, because they had been abandoned by her bankrupt husband. After Camille died, Alice ran the household and raised all seven of the children. She and Monet later married.

Monet and the children planted many different types of flowers in the garden at Giverny. They also planted a vegetable garden, installed a turkey house, and raised pigeons. The children caught fish and frogs in the nearby stream. They had picnics in the fields. When Monet's paintings started to sell well, he bought the house. He transformed a little barn next to the house into an art studio. In 1893, Monet bought land across the railroad tracks from his garden. It was here that he installed a water garden, digging out two ponds fed by a local stream. The garden's steep, green bridge was built to look like one that Monet had seen in a Japanese print. Eventually the pond, water lilies, and reflections in the water became a favorite subject for his paintings.

Visiting the House & Gardens

"It's just like in the book!," exclaimed a 6-year-old friend on one of our trips to Claude Monet's house in Giverny. Sure enough, if you've seen Linnea in Monet's Garden you'll recognize Monet's pink house, his art studio, the big garden filled with flowers and alleyways, the Japanese footbridge, and the pond full of water lilies. Children love this place, even if they have never heard of Linnea, Monet, or Impressionism. They can't resist the urge to explore the paths, hide behind gigantic flowerbeds, and listen to the gobble gobble of the white turkeys. See if they can find the underground passageway to the water lily pond. Do they recognize the Japanese Bridge from his paintings? How about the little green rowboat?

At the end of your visit, you'll find Linnea, copies of water lily paintings, and other souvenirs in the gift shop. This was formerly Monet's big studio. Today it is an excellent place to pick up gifts for folks back home.

Parent Tip: Monet used to refer to all the colors of his garden as his artist's palette. Follow his example, and bring along some paper and paints, crayons, or colored pencils. There are plenty of nice spots from which to create your own masterpieces.

Also, don't forget your cameras. You won't want to miss the chance to photograph your kids in front of the nasturtiums, on the **Japanese Bridge**, or on the green steps of the pink house. Encourage your children to try their hand at photographing the flowers and lily pond, too. Like Linnea, they can experiment with close-up shots and wider angles.

Monet's **pink house** at Giverny is very interesting, too. It offers a glimpse of daily life in the home of a great painter. You'll see the original furniture, decorations, and dishes. There's also one of Monet's art studios, his reading room, and his bedroom. There are lots of Japanese prints on the walls from which he drew inspiration. You can also see how Monet's love of color extended to the inside of his house. Bright blues and yellows dominate throughout the entire house. Don't forget to look out the windows for nice views of the gardens.

MUSEE D'ART AMERICAIN (MUSEUM OF AMERICAN ART). *99, Rue Claude Monet, in Giverny. Open Apr-Oct, Tues-Sun, 10am-6pm. Closed Mon. Closed Nov-Mar. Adults: €5.50;Students, Seniors, and Teachers: €4; Kids 12-18: €3; Kids under 12: free. Free to all on the first Sun of the month. Audioguide: €1. The museum offers painting classes for children and adults in July and August.*

In the 1890s, as Monet's fame and that of other French Impressionist painters spread, many American painters came to live in Giverny and the surrounding area. This relatively new museum, built in the 1990s, showcases their work. The permanent collection features paintings from 1870 to 1920. Temporary exhibits embrace themes such as depictions of trains in Impressionist paintings or views of the Seine. The museum is bright, airy, and not terribly big – excellent qualities for a kid-friendly visit. There is a nice café and a terrific gift shop featuring a good kids' section.

Fun Facts

• Normandy is famous for its soft, white **Camembert** cheese and sparkling apple cider. Tradition has it that people in Normandy have been making Camembert since the 13th century. They say it takes five liters (21 cups) of milk to make one cheese. Try some on a fresh baguette of bread.

• For a full Norman treat, wash your Camembert down with a glass of **cider**. Cider production in Normandy is supposed to date back nearly 2000 years. It comes in two forms: Brut is dry; Doux is sweet. Note that you can get both alcoholic and non-alcoholic varieties.

PACY TRAIN STATION AND EURE VALLEY TOURIST TRAIN. *Pacy-sur-Eure Train Station, located 15 kilometers SW of Vernon. By car it is off the same highway exit #16 as Vernon, but in the opposite direction on the D 181. It is also accessible from highway exit # 15 via the N13 road. Tourist train rides available. Adults: €8; Kids: €6. For information: Tel. 02 32 36 04 63.*

This train station features several old-fashioned trains and locomotives and offers rides on one of them through the Eure Valley between Pacy and Breuilpont or Pacy and Cocherel. It is a pretty ride and fun for train fans big and small.

CHATEAU GAILLARD, *in Les Andelys, 100 kilometers from Paris. By car, take the A13 highway towards Rouen. Take exit # 17 toward Gaillon and follow the signs to Les Andelys. From there, go up the hill to the castle. By train go from the Gare Saint Lazare to Gaillon on the Paris-Rouen line, then take a taxi to Château Gaillard. Open Mar 15-Nov 15, Thurs-Mon, 9am-12pm, 2pm-6pm. Also open Wed, 2pm-6pm. Closed Tues all day and Wed morning. Closed from Nov 16-Mar 14.*

This old castle fortress is spectacular for both its setting – perched dramatically above a meander of the Seine River, and for its age – dating back nearly 1,000 years. Although today it is in ruins, you can still imagine the imposing figure that Château Gaillard must have cut with its 17 towers and triple set of protective walls, each 8 feet thick. Adults admire the beauty of this place. Children love it, because they can run amid the old stones pretending to be kings, queens, or battling knights.

To truly appreciate this visit, roll your time clock back to the year 1187. This is the time of Eleanor of Aquitaine, Richard the Lionheart, and Robin Hood. Normandy is under English control. Richard the Lionheart is both King of England and Duke of Normandy. Although they have fought together in the Crusades, he and the French king Philippe-Auguste are bitter rivals. Richard has been captured by the Austrians on his way back from the Crusades. Philippe-Auguste has taken advantage of Richard's absence to attack and regain control over some of the Normand territories. Once freed, Richard is determined to regain and protect his holdings in Normandy. He builds a fortress in Les Andelys right on the border of France and Normandy. The castle, called Château Gaillard, is built using techniques learned in the Holy Land for making defensive walls and structures. It is completed in less than a year.

Richard's Château Gaillard stood up to years of fighting between the French and English. Then in 1199, Richard was killed in a battle. His successor and younger brother, King John, was not a skilled fighter and lost many of England's former territories. In 1203, Philippe-Auguste decided to take on the Château Gaillard once and for all. The castle was well defended and filled with elite English troops. Philippe's French troops surrounded the castle and set up a siege for eight months. Finally, a handful of them managed to get into the castle. Legend has it that the French fighters climbed in through the latrines. Other reports claim they got in through a small chapel window. In either case, the French finally captured the Château Gaillard from the English, and they eventually reconquered the rest of Normandy.

The Château Gaillard survived for several hundred more years. However, during the Wars of Religion between the French Catholics and Protestants in the late 16th century, the castle was overpowered and destroyed.

Standing among the ruined stones today, you can still appreciate why Les Andelys was such a choice spot for a castle. The castle dominates the Seine and offers dramatic views of the Normand countryside. For kids, the Château Gaillard is like a great play set, with plenty of room to roam, explore, and let young imaginations run wild.

THEME PARKS

If you or your child's idea of a real vacation isn't complete without life size cartoon characters, thrill rides, or an African safari, don't worry. The Paris area abounds with theme parks, ranging from the American-style Disneyland to a miniature tour of major French monuments.

DISNEYLAND PARIS. *Located 32 kilometers E of Paris in the town of Marne-la-Vallee. By car, take highway A4 towards Nancy-Metz to exit 14. The parking lots are huge. Don't forget where you've left your car, and be prepared to hike 10-15 minutes to the park entrance. By public transportation, take the RER line A4 commuter train to the Marne la Vallee- Chessy stop. You can also take a special shuttle bus to the park from either Orly or Charles-de-Gaulle airports. Buses leave every 45 minutes. High-speed TGV trains also service the Marne-la-Vallee station from many major French cities. Open year-round, 9am-11pm (July-Sept) 9am-8pm (Fall, Spring), 10am-8pm (Nov-Dec). 1-day pass for both Disneyland and Walt Disney Studios, Adults: €49; Kids 3-11: €39; Kids under 3: free. 1-day passes for just Disneyland Paris, Adults: €40; kids 3-11: €30; kids under 3: free. Multi-day passes are also available. You can rent cameras, video cameras, strollers, and wheelchairs at the entrance. Further information and special discounts are available online at www.disneylandparis.com*

Note: Buy your Disneyland tickets ahead of time and save yourself a long line. Advance tickets are available at the Paris Tourist Office, Virgin Record stores, FNAC stores, and hotels in the Disneyland resort (these may offer discounts). You can also purchase a combined RER-train and park entrance ticket at RER stations in the city.

If you've never had a chance to go to the American Disney theme parks or want to compare the French and American ones, here's your chance. Disneyland Paris is hugely popular with Europeans, including French families. They look on it as a way to get a big dose of American culture without having to cross the Atlantic or give up red wine with lunch.

Just like in the American parks, Disneyland Paris features a Main Street with its afternoon parade of Disney characters. Sleeping Beauty's castle towers over the whole scene. There is a new, daily fireworks display. From Main Street you can catch the train or old-fashioned cars to go to other parts of the park. The park is divided into different sections: each with a special theme. Fantasyland is designed for younger children. This is where you'll find "It's a Small World" and favorite Disney characters like Snow White, Dumbo, and Peter Pan. Adventureland caters to thrill seekers with the Pirates of the Caribbean, Swiss Family Robinson, and Indian Jones' Temple of Peril. Frontierland evokes the American Wild West with wild rides and a haunted house. Discoveryland has a new Space Mountain: Mission II, Honey I Shrunk the Audience, and the Orbitron Flying Machines.

Not surprisingly, Disneyland Paris gets very crowded during the summer tourist season. Your best bet during this time is to arrive early, as the park is opening, and head straight for the most popular rides. Another strategy is to wait until the end of the day to try the favorite sections, when many people are leaving or watching the Main Street Parade. You can also obtain a Fast-Pass for the most crowded rides. These are available by the entrance and give you a specific time when you can go to a particular ride. You will then get to bypass the long line and go through the much shorter Fast-Pass line.

Parent Tip: First Aid, Baby Stations, and the **Lost Children's Center** are all located at the end of Main Street, by the Plaza Garden Restaurant.

Disney Village, located outside of the amusement park, has shops, restaurants, shows, and hotels. It feels very American and is a good place to grab a meal if you are feeling homesick. You'll recognize some of the American chain restaurants, such as Rainforest Cafe or Planet Hollywood. Not surprisingly, the hotels and restaurants are very family-friendly. Each of the hotels has a different American theme: New York, Newport Bay, Santa Fe, Sequoia, and Cheyenne. At the Davy Crockett Ranch you can rent a bungalow or park your RV.

WALT DISNEY STUDIOS. *Located next to Disneyland Paris. Open Mon-Fri, 10am-10pm; Sat-Sun, 9am-8pm. Adults: €40; Kids 3-11: €30; Kids under 3: free.*

This newer addition to Disneyland Paris features shows and attractions about movies, cartoons, and television. The buildings and some of the attractions were designed to look like the original MGM Studios in Florida. The result tends to be high on cement and low on greenery. This park is still growing, with plans for some super thrill rides. In place already is a Rock'n Rollercoaster featuring music from the band Aerosmith.

PARC ASTERIX. *Located 35 kilometers N of Paris, near Charles de Gaulle Airport. By car, take highway A1 north to the Parc Asterix exit, located between exits 7 and 8. By public transportation, take RER line B3 from Paris to the Charles de Gaulle/Roissy station where you can catch the Parc Asterix shuttle bus that leaves every 30 minutes. You can purchase a combined RER-Park Entrance tickets for a discount at RER stations in Paris. High-speed TGV trains from across France also stop at the Charles de Gaulle/ Roissy Station, where you can catch the Parc Asterix shuttle. Open daily, April-August and every weekend in Sept-Oct, 10am-6pm (Mon-Fri), 9:30am-7pm (Sat-Sun and daily in August). Adults: €31; Kids 3-12: €23; Kids under 3: free. The nearby hotels offer special family rates for lodging plus park entrance. Strollers and wheelchairs are available in the park free of charge. Baby changing station and place to warm up bottles located under the big rock with Asterix on top.*

Note: Due to its proximity to the Charles de Gaulle/Roissy Airport, you may want to save a visit to Parc Asterix for the end of your trip. You can visit the park on the day before your flight home (there are places to check your bags at the park entrance). Spend the night at a hotel near the park or near the airport, and catch your flight out the next day. It's a great way to combine fun and convenience.

If you want to see a truly French theme park, this is the one for you! Parc Asterix is based on the popular French comic book characters Asterix and Obelix. Their (very funny) adventures are set in the 1st century BC, during the Roman Occupation of Gaul (France). If you've seen any of the comic books, you'll really enjoy recognizing the characters and buildings from the stories. If you haven't seen the books, you'll want to after this visit (Note: they are available in French, English, and numerous other languages). We love this park not only because we are big Asterix fans, but also because it is a more manageable size than Disneyland Paris, yet still offers plenty of fun.

Parc Asterix is divided into several sections, starting with Gaul, Classical Rome, and Ancient Greece. Then you pass through time to Medieval France, the Renaissance, and on to 19th century Paris. There are plenty of activities for kids and adults of all ages. There are some great thrill rides, including a huge wooden roller coaster, plenty of loop de loops, and a bobsled ride. There are several different boat rides, ranging from a steep roller coaster one to a hilarious bumper boat ride on the River Styx. There are also lots of funny rides, playgrounds, merry-go-rounds, automates, and shops. You can also take in any number of shows. Examples include a dolphin show in Ancient Greece, a Three Musketeer sword fight in Medieval Paris, a mystery about thieves stealing the Mona Lisa, a magic show in Gaul, and acrobats in the Roman Amphitheater.

Since this is France after all, there are plenty of eateries throughout the park, ranging from a little crêpe hut in the Gaul village to full restaurants by

---

Fun Fact

When you get to the **Arcimbaldo Restaurant**, notice how it is composed of fruits and vegetables. Where have you seen this before? The Renaissance painter Arcimbaldo's portraits of the four seasons (4 faces made up fruits and vegetables of each season) are in the Louvre. They are just around the corner from the *Mona Lisa* – who is also featured in one of the park's shows.

---

the Medieval and Renaissance sections. There are family-friendly hotels near the park with shuttle service to the park and to the Charles de Gaulle/Roissy airport.

MER DE SABLE (SEA OF SAND) AMUSEMENT PARK. *Located 45 kilometers NE of Paris. By car, take the A1 highway north towards Lille to exit 7 for Ermenonville. By public transportation take RER line B to Charles de Gaulle/Roissy Airport, where you can catch a special shuttle bus to the park. There is a special discount rate that includes the RER ride and entrance to the park, available at RER stations in Paris. Open daily, Apr-Sep, 10:30am-6:30pm. Adults: €16.50; Kids 3-11: €13.50; Kids under 3: free.*

This is the oldest theme park in the area. It was created in 1963 by a French actor named Pierre Richard, who was fond of stunts and circus tricks. The name of the park comes from the fact that it is set in a natural sandy desert, left over from 50 million years ago when the area around Paris was covered by a shallow sea. It's quite a remarkable sight, complete with dunes and dromedaries. The Mer de Sable is smaller, less crowded, and less expensive than Disneyland or Parc Asterix. It is also targeted primarily at younger kids, under the age of 10. Many of the rides and attractions have an American Western theme, including a wild-west train ride and plenty of horses. There is a river raft ride, a pirate ship, and an irresistible boat ride through the jungles that features hundreds of little stuffed animal puppets. There are villages from the American West, Morocco, and China. You can see an equestrian show each afternoon featuring lots of stunts.

PARC DE THOIRY (ANIMAL SAFARI). *Located 40 kilometers W of Paris in the parkland surrounding the Thoiry Castle. By car take the A13 highway southwest to the A12, then to the N12 towards Dreux. Take the Thoiry exit, follow the D76, then the D11 to Thoiry. Open daily: 10 am to 6 pm (Spring-Summer) and 10 am to 5 pm (Autumn-Winter). Adults: €20; Kids 3-18: €14; Kids under 3: free.*

This is a fun visit for animal lovers young and old. It's a surprising mix of African Safari and French formal gardens set up by the Viscount and

Viscountess de La Panouse some 30 years ago. The La Panouse family still lives in part of the castle.

The Thoiry Park visit is divided into two sections. The safari section is a natural reserve where wild animals such as giraffes, lions, elephants, wildebeests, zebras, antelopes, ostriches, rhinos, and bears wander freely. You view them from the safety of your car or the park's bus. The animals will come right up to your car, so you can get great close-up views. They will even occasionally sit on the hood of your car or try to poke their heads in, so keep the windows rolled up.

The other section, by the Thoiry Castle, is more like a traditional zoo. Here you can walk through the nicely laid out park to observe snow leopards, river otters, various types of birds and monkeys, and other animals. Many of the exhibits are set up with tunnels or windows so that you have a good view of the animals. In the middle there is an excellent children's playground where kids can run and parents can take a break. If you are tired, a little train, the Mandrill Express, will take you back to the entrance for a small fee.

Back by the castle there is a pretty botanical garden and plans to build an indoor Amazonian Forest exhibit. You can visit the inside of the Thoiry Castle for an additional fee. It was built in 1559 and still features the original furnishings. You'll also find a self-service restaurant and tearoom next to the Castle.

FRANCE MINIATURE. *25, Rue du Mesnil in Elancourt, SW of Paris. By car take the A13 highway, then the A12 towards St. Quentin en Yvelines/ Dreux. Follow the signs for Elancourt-France Miniature. By train, buy a combined train+bus+France Miniature ticket for the La Verrière train station from either the La Défense or Paris Montparnasse train stations. Then get the 411 bus in La Verrière which stops at France Miniature. Open daily from 10 am - 7 pm, Apr-Oct. Open until 11:30 pm on Sat, Jul-Aug for special fireworks displays. Adults: €12.50; Kids: €8.80.*

This park is a big hit with kids. It features miniature models of more than 150 French monuments and natural features. They are exquisitely detailed and arranged on a huge map of France that includes rivers, mountains, and coastlines. There are little fishing boats in the ports, cars on the highways, and people in the market. There are miniature trains that pass by models of French villages. There are famous sights like the Mont Saint Michel in Normandy, the Pont du Gard in Provence, and the Loire Valley castles.

There are also many of the Paris monuments that your kids will enjoy picking out. Make sure you admire the miniature Eiffel Tower. It took 15,000 hours to build. France Miniature is a great way to learn about French geography. It will leave your kids wanting to come back to France to explore more.

24. SLEEPS & EATS

Apart'hotel Chains

The apart'hotels combine the freedom and space of an apartment with hotel services such as laundry and concierges. Apartments come as efficiencies that sleep 2-4, 1-bedroom apartments that sleep 2-4, and in some cases a 2-bedroom apartments that sleep 4-6 people. The apartments are clean, modern, and efficient.

Generally, the living room has a two-person sleeper sofa (sometimes two day beds), color TV with cable or satellite channels, small stereo, phone, and table. Bedrooms have either double beds or two twins. You can ask for a crib or extra bed. The bathrooms come equipped with a hair dryer. The kitchen has a refrigerator, microwave oven, stovetop, coffeemaker, dishwasher, and all the necessary utensils. Bed and bath linens are provided.

CITADINES APART'HÔTEL***. This chain has numerous locations throughout the city. Rates range from €130-280 per night depending on size and location:

Saint Germain des Prés, 53 ter, Quai des Grands Augustins, 75006 Paris. Metro: Saint Michel. Tel. 01 44 07 70 00; Fax 01 44 07 29 50. Email: resa@citadines.com. Studios and 1-bedrooms.

Jardin des Plantes-Austerlitz, 27, Rue Esquirol, 75013 Paris, Metro: Campo Formio or Place d'Italie. Tel.01 56 61 5400; Fax 0145 86 59 76; Email: resa@citadines.com. Studios and 1-bedrooms.

Bastille and Marais, 37, Boulevard Richard Lenoir, 75011 Paris, Metro: Bréguet Sabin or Bastille. Tel. 01 53 36 90 00; Fax 01 53 36 90 22; Email: resa@citadines.com. Studios and 1-bedrooms.

Bastille and Promenade Plantée, 14-18 Rue de Chaligny, 75012 Paris. Metro: Reuilly Diderot. Studios, 1-bedrooms, 2-bedrooms.

Les Halles, 4, Rue des Innocents, 75001 Paris. Metro: Les Halles. Tel. 01 40 39 26 50; Fax 01 45 08 40 65; Email: resa@citadines.com. Studios and 1-bedrooms.

Louvre, 8, Rue Richelieu, 75001 Paris. Metro: Palais Royal-Musée du Louvre Tel. 01 55 35 28 00; Fax 01 55 35 29 99. Email: resa@citadines.com. Studios and 1-bedrooms.

Montparnasse, 67, Avenue du Maine, 75014 Paris. Metro: Gaite or Vavin or Montparnasse. Tel. 01 53 91 27 00; Fax 01 43 27 29 94; Email: resa@citadines.com. Studios and 1-bedrooms.

Montmartre, 16, Avenue Rachel, 75018 Paris. Metro: Blanche. Tel. 01 44 70 45 50; Fax 01 45 22 59 10. Email: resa@citadines.com. Studios and 1-bedrooms.

Opéra-Drouot, 18, Rue Favart, 75002 Paris. Metro: Opéra. Tel. 01 40 15 14 00; Fax 01 40 15 14 50. Email: resa@citadines.com. Studios, 1-bedrooms, duplexes.

Opéra Vendôme Préstige, 2, Rue Edouard VII, 75009 Paris. Metro: Opéra, Auber, or Madeleine. Tel. 01 40 06 56 00; Fax 01 40 06 96 50. Email: resa@citadines.com. Studios, 1-bedrooms, 2-bedrooms.

Eiffel Tower, 132 Boulevard de Grenelle, 75015 Paris. Metro: La Motte Piquet Grenelle or Cambronne. Tel. 01 53 95 60 00; Fax 01 53 95 60 95. Email: resa@citadines.com. Studios and 1-bedrooms.

Trocadéro, 29 bis, Rue Saint Didier, 75016 Paris. Metro: Trocadéro or Victor Hugo. Tel. 01 56 90 70 00; Fax 01 47 04 50 07. Email: resa@citadines.com. Studios, 1-bedrooms, 2-bedrooms.

Place d'Italie, 18, Place d'Italie, 75013; Metro: Place d'Italie. Tel. 01 43 13 85 00; Fax 01 43 13 86 99; Email: italie@citadines.com. Studios and 1-bedrooms.

République, 75 bis, Avenue Parmentier, 75011 Paris. Metro: Parmentier or République. Tel. 01 55 28 08 20; Fax 0143 14 90 30. Email: resa@citadines.com. Studios and 1-bedrooms.

PIERRE ET VACANCES*. This chain offers 3 locations. Rates range from €180-250 per night depending on size and location:

Montmartre: 10, Place Charles Dullin, 75018 Paris, Tel. 01 42 57 14 55; Fax 01 43 54 48 87; Email: montmartre@pierreetvacances.com. Studios, 1-bedrooms, 2-bedrooms.

Bercy, 1-7 Cours du Minervois, 75012 Paris. Metro: Cour Saint Emilion. Tel. 01 53 02 11 00; Fax 01 53 02 11 10, Email: paris@pierreetvacances.com. Studios and 1-bedrooms.

Buttes Chaumont, 3-5 Cours du 7ième Art, 75019 Paris. Metro: Buttes Chaumont or Botzaris. Tel. 01 53 38 24 24; Fax 01 53 38 24 00; Email: butteschaumont@pierreetvacances.com. Studios, 1-bedrooms, 2-bedrooms.

Family-friendly Restaurant Chains

BÎSTROT ROMAIN: These restaurants offer good food at a great price. Adult menus offer ample options, such as salads, appetizers, well-garnished main courses, and tasty desserts – including vast quantities of chocolate mousse. Kids get crayons and an activity sheet. A kids menu proposes a choice of lasagna, chicken nuggets, or hamburger; unlimited supplies of French fries or pasta; chocolate mousse or ice cream; and a drink – all for €8. Adult menus are about €17.

Champs Elysées - 26, Avenue des Champs Elysées, 75008; Metro: Franklin Roosevelt, near the Rond Point des Champs Elysées.

Champs Elysées - 73, Avenue des Champs Elysées, 75008; Metro: Franklin Roosevelt

Champs Elysées -122, Avenue des Champs Elysées, 75008; Metro: George

Les Halles - 30, Rue Saint Denis, 75001; Metro: Châtelet; near Les Halles and Pompidou Center

Les Halles - 10, Rue Coquillière, 75001; Metro: Les Halles or Louvre Rivoli; on the NW edge of Les Halles.

Opéra and Grands Boulevards - 9, Boulevard des Italiens, 75002; Metro: Opéra

Montparnasse - 103, Boulevard Montparnasse, 75006, Metro: Vavin

Saint Germain des Près - 7, Rue Gozlin, 75006; Metro: Saint Germain des Près

Opéra - 2, Rue de la Chaussée d'Antin, 75009; Metro: Chaussée d'Antin; near the big department stores.

La Défense - 37, Le Parvis de la Défense; Metro: La Défense-Grand Arche

Parent Tip: You'll find red meats much less cooked in France than in either England or the US. Even if you ask for it well done, "bien cuit," it will be pretty red. For children, you may want to specify very well done, "très bien cuit."

HIPPOPOTAMUS RESTAURANT AND GRILL. This family-friendly chain specializes in grilled meats including beef, chicken, lamb, and even ostrich. You can also opt salads or vegetarian dishes. Kids get a fun sheet and crayons. The €7.50 kid's menu offers a salad; choice of burger, fish sticks, or chicken nuggets; fries; ice cream or chocolate mousse; and a drink.

Adult menus range in price from €10.50-25 depending how many courses you want to include. Early bird specials offer a 30% discount for meals ordered between 2:30 and 7:30 pm.

Les Halles, 29, Rue Berger, 75001; Metro: Les Halles

Opéra, 1, Boulevard des Capucines, 75002; Metro: Opéra

Bastille, 1, Boulevard Beaumarchais, 75004 Paris; Metro: Bastille

Latin Quarter, 9, Rue Lagrange, 75005; Metro: Maubert Mutualité

Montparnasse, 119, Boulevard Montparnasse, 75006; Metro: Vavin

Montparnasse, 68, Boulevard Montparnasse, 75014; Metro: Montparnasse

Montparnasse, 12, Avenue du Maine, 75015 Paris; Metro: Montparnasse

Champs Elysées, 6, avenue Franklin Roosevelt, 75008, Métro: Franklin Roosevelt

Champs Elysées, 20, rue Quentin Bauchart, 75008; Métro: George V

Champs Elysées, 42, Avenue des Champs Elysées, 75008; Metro: Franklin Roosevelt

Arc de Triomphe, 46, Avenue de Wagram, 75008; Metro: Ternes

Bercy, Cour Saint Emilion-Bercy Village, 75012; Metro: Cour Saint Emilion

Aquaboulevard (aquatic and sports center), 4, Rue Louis Armand, 75015; Metro: Balard

La Défense, 2, Place de la Défense; Metro: La Défense-Grande Arche

OH! POIVRIER! This chain offers warm and cold gourmet sandwiches, as well as salads and quiches. The €9 menu includes a sandwich, slice of pie, and drink. Or for €8 you can get a gourmet basket with bread, and a selection of roast beef, cheese, and salad; turkey, bacon, cheese, salad; chicken with BBQ sauce; or salmon tartar with tomatoes and salad.

Saint Germain des Près, 25, Quai des Grands Augustins, 75006; Metro: Saint Michel

Montparnasse, 143, Boulevard Raspail, 75006 Paris, Metro: Vavin, near intersection of Boulevard Raspail and Boulevard Montparnasse

Montparnasse, 2, Avenue du Maine, 75015; Metro: Montparnasse, near the train station.

Champs Elysées, 20, Rue du Colisée, 75008 (Metro: Franklin Roosevelt)

Opéra, 2, Boulevard Haussman, 75009; Metro: Chausée d'Antin or Richelieu Drouot

Aquaboulevard (aquatic and sports center), 4, Rue Louis Armand, 75015; Metro: Balard

AMERICAN CHAINS. You will find several familiar American restaurant and snack chains in Paris, including the ubiquitous **McDonalds** (or Mac Do as the French call it); **TGI Fridays**, 8, Boulevard Montmartre, 75009, Metro: Grands Boulevards, **Hard Rock Café**, 14, Boulevard Montmartre, 75009, Metro: Grands Boulevards; **Chicago Pizza Factory**, 5, Rue de Berri, 75008 Paris; Metro: George V; *Tel. 01 45 62 50 23;* **Planet Hollywood**, 78, Avenue des Champs Elysées, 75008, Metro: George V; and **Baskin Robbins Ice Cream** (numerous locations around the city). These are familiar and predictable.

Ile de la Cité & Ile Saint Louis

HÔTEL DU JEU DE PAUME****; *54, Rue Saint Louis en l'Ile, 75004 Paris; Tel. 01-43 26 14 18; Fax 01 40 46 02 76; www.jeudepaumehotel.com; Metro: Pont Marie, Saint Michel, Nôtre Dame. Rates: €165 (single); €250-305 (double); €500 (2 room, 2 bath, kitchenette apartment); breakfast: €18.*

This lovely luxury hotel is located in a building that used to hold a *jeu de paume* court (early form of tennis), built in 1634. It features beautiful wooden beams and old stone walls. The hotel is set back from the street, so it is nice and quiet. There is a pretty private garden where you can eat breakfast on warm mornings. This is the only hotel on Ile Saint Louis that we found that was family-friendly and had family-sized rooms

RESTAURANT: LE MONDE DES CHIMIÈRES, *69, Rue Saint Louis en l'Ile, 75004 Paris, Metro: Pont Marie; Tel. 01 43 54 45 27; Open Tues-Sat, lunch and dinner. Closed Sun-Mon.*

This cozy little place offers a warm welcome and good traditional French food – all at a reasonable price. Inside the stone walls and wooden beams, you get platters such as sole meunière, garlic chicken, grilled langoustines, filet mignon, and duck in orange sauce. The express lunch menu offers an appetizer and main course or main course and dessert for only €12. There are also menus for €18 and €24.

RESTAURANT: LES FOUS DE L'ILE, *33, Rue des Deux Ponts, 75004 Paris, Metro: Pont Marie. Tel. 01 43 25 76 67; Open Tues-Fri for lunch and dinner, Sat for dinner only, Sun for lunch. Closed Mon.*

This restaurant has an artsy décor and offers nice daily specials and delicious pastries. The lunch menu is €12. Dinner runs around €23-28. The Sunday brunch menus are at €15, €19, and €22. In the afternoon, you can go for tea and a snack.

LE FLORE EN L'ILE, *42 Quai d'Orleans, 75004 Paris, Metro: Pont Marie. Tel. 01 43 29 88 27. Open daily, breakfast, lunch, and dinner.*

This is a good spot to stop for Berthillon ice cream (see below), a snack, or a full meal. The outdoor tables offer a great view of the back of Notre Dame Cathedral and the Seine River.

ICE CREAM: GLACES BERTHILLON, *Main store: 31, Rue Saint Louis en l'Isle, 75004 Paris, Metro: Pont Marie; Open Wed-Sun, 10am-8pm. Other stands open more regularly throughout the Ile Saint Louis.*

This is some of the best ice cream in Paris. Although the scoops are small, they are bursting with flavor. The tough part is picking among the wide selection, including flavors such as vineyard peach, black currant, mirabelle (yellow plum), pain d'epice (spice cake), poire william (pear liquour), and wild strawberries.

Latin Quarter

HÔTEL DES GRANDES ECOLES***, *75, Rue du Cardinal Lemoine, 75005 Paris. Tel. 01 43 26 79 23; Fax 01 43 25 28 15; Email: Hôtel.Grandes.Ecoles@wanadoo.fr; www. hôtel-grandes-ecoles.com; Metro: Cardinal Lemoine or Place Monge; Rates: €105-130 (doubles), additional bed: €15; breakfast: €8; parking: €30.*

This is one of our all-time favorite Parisian hotels. It offers the best of both worlds: a quiet country lane-type atmosphere, nestled in the heart of the lively Rue Mouffetard neighborhood and Latin Quarter. You are close to major sights, with easy public transportation access to the rest of the city. Yet, you are off the main roads in a quite corner with a lovely garden. The rooms are distributed among several 3-story buildings. Five of the double rooms are large enough to fit 1-2 extra beds comfortably, and in some there is even a large curtain to separate the adult bed from the kids. When the weather is nice you can eat breakfast or have an afternoon drink on the terrace.

HÔTEL DES ARÈNES***, *51, Rue Monge, 75005 Paris; Metro: Place Monge or Jussieu; Tel. 01 43 25 09 26; Fax 01 43 25 79 56; Email:hôteldesarenes@wanadoo.fr; Rates: €90 (double); €120 (triple). Children under 5 stay with parents at no extra cost. Children ages 5-12: €30 supplement. Buffet breakfast: €10 (free for kids).*

This hotel overlooks the gardens and ruins of the former Roman Arena, built in the 1st century AD. Make sure to get rooms on the Arena side and not on the street, which can be very noisy. The location is excellent: in the Latin Quarter near the Jardin des Plantes, Rue Mouffetard market street, and an easy walk to Nôtre Dame Cathedral. The rooms, though not huge (this is Paris, remember), are efficient and comfortable. Although there are no family suites, you can ask for a triple or for adjoining doubles that can be made into a suite.

HÔTEL DU LEVANT***, *18, Rue de la Harpe, 75005 Paris; Metro: Saint Michel; Tel. 01 46 34 1100, Fax 01 46 34 25 87; http://peprso.club-internet.fr/hlevant; Email: hlevant@club-internet.fr; Rates:€111-150 (doubles); €165-206 (triples); €206-220 (quadruple); €285-303 (4-5 person suite). Rates include the buffet breakfast or continental breakfast in the room.*

This hotel is a real gem, especially considering its location in such a central, touristy spot. It is very family-friendly and has been run by the same family for four generations. They take great pride in keeping it clean, tastefully decorated, and up to date. It is situated on one of the pedestrian side streets near the Place Saint Michel, where college students and professors mingle with tourists. The staff members are very friendly. The rooms are quite pretty and several are well-designed to accommodate a family of four or five. Most of the rooms are air-conditioned. The ones on the top floor are especially charming.

HÔTEL RÉSIDENCE HENRI IV***, *50, Rue des Bernardins, 75005 Paris; Metro: Maubert Mutualité; Tel. 01 44 41 31 81; Fax 01 466 33 93 22; Email: reservation@résidencehenri4.com; Rates vary according to the season and special deals: €123-145 (single/double room); €153-190 (2 person apartment); €183-220 (3 person apartment); €213-250 (4-person apartment). Buffet breakfast: €9.*

This handsome hotel combines convenience and quiet in a great location. The hotel is set back from the main road on a nice little square. It feels intimate, because there are only 7 rooms and 7 apartments. Each features high ceilings, with decorated friezes and moldings, that give the place a feeling of elegance. The apartments feature 2 rooms, plus a kitchenette with a refrigerator, microwave, stovetop, and utensils.

HÔTEL LE JARDIN DE CLUNY (Best Western)***, *9, Rue du Sommérard, 75005 Paris; Metro: Maubert Mutualité or Cluny-La Sorbonne; Tel. 01 43 54 22 66; Fax 01 40 5103 36; www.bw-paris-hôtels.com/jardin/; Email: hôtel.decluny@wanadoo.fr; Rates: €180-200 (double); €260 (family rooms). However you may get a significant discount booking early, on-line. Buffet breakfast: €10.*

This hotel combines old features with modern comforts. Although you are in a very central location, the hotel is on a small side-street and away from the noise of the main avenues. The rooms are well-appointed, air-conditioned, and efficient. There are only 2 rooms on each floor, so you can comfortably rent two adjacent doubles to accommodate a family of four. Some rooms are reserved for non-smokers. There is a pretty garden courtyard in the middle of the hotel. For breakfast you can eat in your room or head downstairs to the Louis XIII style dining room. It features vaulted stone ceilings and copies of the Woman with a Unicorn tapestries that you can see in the nearby Cluny Museum.

HÔTEL MERCURE PARIS LA SORBONNE***, *14, Rue de la Sorbonne, 75005 Paris; Metro: Cluny-La Sorbonne; Tel. 01 56 24 34 34; Fax 01 56 24 19 60; Email: H2897@accor-hôtels.com; Rates: €160-200 (double); €220 (triples); €220 (duplex-quadruple). Buffet breakfast: €13.*

Tucked away in the heart of the Latin Quarter, across the street from the historic Sorbonne University, this hotel welcomes families with bright, modern rooms. There are several large enough to fit a family of 4. Each features air-conditioning and the usual 3-star amenities of satellite TV, hairdryer, safe, and minibar. You are a stone's throw from the Cluny Museum and Luxembourg Gardens. At the end of a day of touring you can sit back and relax with a cold drink in the cafés of the charming Place de la Sorbonne around the corner from this hotel.

HÔTEL RÉSIDENCE LE VERT GALANT***, *41-43, Rue Croulebarbe, 75013 Paris; Metro: Place d'Italie or Les Gobelins; Tel. 01 44 08 83 50; Web: www.vertgalant.com; Rates: €87-97 (double); €107 (double with kitchenette). Extra bed: €10. Garage: €10. Buffet breakfast: €8.*

This is a very nice little hotel. It is a little off the beaten track. However, you still have excellent bus and metro access to all the major sights. What's more, there is a lovely public park across the street with excellent playground facilities. You are also only a few blocks away from the Butte aux Cailles indoor/outdoor public swimming pool. Many of the rooms open onto the hotel's private garden, as does the breakfast room. The larger rooms feature fully equipped kitchenettes. The owners also run an excellent restaurant, located next door. Called l'Auberge Etchegorry it features delicious Basque specialties from southwestern France. It is located in a building that used to house a popular cabaret, frequented by author Victor Hugo (*Les Misérables* and *Hunchback of Nôtre Dame*). Menus range from 18 to 36 E.

HÔTEL DES TROIS COLLEGES**,*16, Rue Cujas, 75005 Paris; Metro: Luxembourg or Cluny; Tel. 01 43 54 67 30; Fax 01 46 34 02 99; Email: hôtel@3colleges.com; Rates: €70-110 (single); €90-120 (double); €150 (triple). Continental breakfast: €8.*

This is a really nice hotel, conveniently located near the Luxembourg Gardens and Cluny Museum. It's remarkably quiet and discreet, considering you are in the heart of Paris' Latin Quarter. The welcome is very warm, and the rooms are bright and cozy. The largest ones are on the top floor, including the hotel's lovely triple. They are under the rafters and offer great views of the rooftops of Paris. On the lower floors, you can opt for two double rooms across from each other at the end of the corridor. There is a tearoom adjacent to the hotel where you can get breakfast with orange juice and homemade jams.

HOTEL SAINT JACQUES**, *35, Rue Des Ecoles, 75005 Paris, Metro: Maubert-Mutualité. Tel: 01 44 07 45 45. Fax: 01 43 25 65 50. www.paris-hotel-stjacques.com. Rates:€95-124 (double); €152 (triple). Breakfast €8.50.*

This is a very friendly hotel in a great Latin Quarter location. The building is in a former mansion, and the owners have taken pride in restoring many of the original details, including ceiling paintings and door details. The rooms have high ceilings and big windows. The upper floors offer terrific views of the rooftops of Paris, Nôtre Dame Cathedral, and the Panthéon.

HÔTEL AU ROYAL CARDINAL**, *1, Rue des Ecoles, 75005 Paris; Metro: Cardinal Lemoine or Jussieu; Tel. 01 46 33 93 62; Fax 01 44 07 22 32; Rates: €92-103 (double); €126 (triple); €130 (quadruple). Breakfast: €5.*

This hotel is more affordable than most in this neighborhood and offers 8 triple rooms and 2 quadruples. The rooms are a little cramped and don't have that nice, updated feel that you find in higher end hotels. Still, you get a functional room, with soundproofed windows, TV, safe, and a hairdryer. Some even have a little balcony overlooking the street. The service is very friendly, and the location is very convenient – in the heart of the Latin Quarter, and a short walk to Nôtre Dame.

HÔTEL TIMHÔTEL-JARDIN DES PLANTES**, *5, Rue Linné (across from the Jardin des Plantes), 75005 Paris; Metro: Place Monge or Jussieu; Tel. 01 47 07 06 20; Fax 01 47 07 62 74; www.timhotel.com/hotels/ vf/jardin.html; Rates: vary by season. Summer rates are approximately: €109 (double); €135 (triple); €210 (family). Buffet breakfast: €8.50.*

This hotel has pretty rooms with nice amenities (modern bathrooms, TV, hair dryer), but they are fairly small. The staff is kid-friendly. There is a sauna and rooftop terrace. The hotel's main attraction is the fact that it is located across the street from one of the entrances to the Jardin des Plantes, with its gardens, playground, zoo, and natural history museums.

HÔTEL MARIGNAN*, *13, Rue du Sommérard, 75005 Paris; Metro: Maubert Mutualité or Cluny-La Sorbonne; Tel. 01 43 54 63 81; Fax 01 43 25 16 69; www.hôtel-marignan.com; Rates for high season: €40-47 (single); €90 (double w/private bathroom); €110 (triple w/private bathroom); €130-150 (quadruple/quintuple with private bathroom). Extra bed: €20. Rates include breakfast. Note: They do not accept credit cards.*

This hotel feels like a youth hostel. It will take you back to the days when you bummed around Europe with a backpack on your back. The friendly owners, a Franco-British couple, are happy to help you get around the city, lend you a guidebook, or give advice. The hotel offers a free washer and dryer – a real luxury when you are traveling with kids – and access to a communal kitchen and dining area. The rooms have a hostel-like feel to them, too, with plaid bedspreads and cheap, utilitarian furniture. Some of the rooms do not have private bathrooms, so you have to share the ones in the hallway. The family-size rooms, however, have private facilities that were recently renovated. The hotel is located in the heart of the Latin Quarter, on a quiet side street.

HÔTEL ESMERALDA*, *4, Rue Saint Julien Le Pauvre, 75005 Paris; Tel. 01 43 54 19 20; Fax 01 40 51 00 68; Metro: Saint Michel or Cluny/La Sorbonne; Rates: €95-110 (double); €110 (triple); €120 (quadruple). Continental breakfast: €6. Note: This hotel does not accept credit cards!*

This is the same Hôtel Esmeralda as the one featured in the book *Linnea in Monet's Garden.* It's a real treat for fans of the story, who will recognize the drawing of Esmeralda (tragic heroine from Victor Hugo's *Hunchback of Nôtre Dame*) in the stairway. The place oozes with Left Bank charm, including exposed beams and old stones. The rooms are small and have a feel of shabby gentility. However, the price is hard to beat in such a wonderful location. You are directly across from Nôtre Dame Cathedral, around the corner from Shakespeare and Company English Language Bookshop, and in the heart of the Latin Quarter. Some of the rooms have a view of Nôtre Dame. There is a park across the street with room for kids to run.

RESTAURANT: BRASSERIE BALZAR, *49, Rue des Ecoles, 75005 Paris; Metro: Cluny – La Sorbonne; Tel. 01 44 07 14 91; Open daily.*

This is a classic, Parisian institution that has been welcoming French intellectuals from the nearby Sorbonne for ages. There are tall ceilings, big mirrors, and a 1930s style feel. Underneath their somewhat cold, professional exterior, the waiters are actually quite friendly to kids. The restaurant has joined the Flo Brasseries chain of high-end restaurants, which means the food is traditional and reliable. There is a big aquarium to distract bored children. Count on spending €32-45 per person. There is a kids' menu for €13.50 that features a choice of fish or meat dishes, ice cream or chocolate mousse, water or juice, and a grenadine cocktail.

RESTAURANT: MARTY, *20, Avenue des Gobelins, 75005; Tel. 01 43 31 39 51; Metro: Les Gobelins or Censier Daubenton.*

This is a big, traditional Parisian brasserie with beautiful mahogany wood features and a décor from the 1920s. The food is excellent. The specialty is fish and seafood, but there are also plenty of meat and poultry alternatives. There is a €14 kid's menu. The lunch menu at €18 includes a glass of wine. There are dinner menus for €30 and €50.

RESTAURANT LA MOSQUÉE, *39, Rue Geoffroy Saint Hilaire, 75005 (across from entrance to Jardin des Plantes); Metro: Place Monge.*

Walk through the entrance of this restaurant and you'll feel like you've been transported to a Moorish Palace. It is decorated with white walls, carved wood, and beautiful blue and green tiles. The seats are covered with plush pillows and the tables composed of enormous, brass platters. The menu offers North African specialties such as couscous, brochettes (shish kabobs), tajines (stews), and brick (ground meat and egg fried inside a turnover made of phillo pastry). Main courses range in price from €9-25.

If you are only searching for a snack after visiting the Jardin des Plantes and Natural History Museums, check out the lovely tea room next to the restaurant. Here you get sweet mint tea served in a glass or chilled drinks, along with baklava and other North African pastries (each for €2). On warm days, you can eat in the garden surrounded by flowers, fig trees, and fountains.

RESTAURANT: JARDIN DES PÂTES, *4, Rue Lacépède, 75005; Tel. 01 43 31 50 71; Metro: Place Monge; Open daily: 12pm-2:30pm; 7pm-11pm.*

This Garden of Pasta is a hit with kids who can choose from a wide assortment pastas and sauces. For the gourmet eater, there are many types of vegetarian pasta to choose made from rye, whole wheat, multi-grain, rice, oat, and other types of flour. There are also soups and salads and desserts. This location is half a block from the Jardin des Plantes. The restaurant also has another location at 33, Boulevard Arago, 75013 Paris, Metro: Les Gobelins.

RESTAURANT: LE TANGO DUE CHAT, *6, Rue Saint Séverin, 75005 Paris. Tel. 01 43 54 69 69. Metro: Luxembourg.*

This restaurant is tucked in a pedestrian street right across from the Saint Séverin church. It offers classic French cold weather fare, including specialties from the Alps, such as fondue, raclette (melted cheese poured on to potatoes), tartiflette (oignons, potatoes, bacon, in a creamy sauce), and oignon soup. Desserts are also classic, including chocolate mousse and fruit tarts. Very reasonably priced menus at €10 and €14.

RESTAURANT: LES DÉLICES D'APHRODITE, *4, Rue de Candolle; Metro: Censier Daubenton, Tel. 01 43 31 40 39. Open Mon-Sat.*

There are plenty of mediocre Greek restaurants in the Latin Quarter. This is one of the good ones. The ingredients are fresh and carefully chosen, including classics such as tzatziki, tarama, and moussaka. The lunch menu is €15. You can get a plate of assorted Greek appetizers for €16. Dinners run €25-30.

RESTAURANT: LE VOLCAN, *10, Rue Thouin (near Place de la Contrescarpe), 75005 Paris. Metro: Cardinal Lemoine or Place Monge; Tel. 01 46 33 38 33; Open daily for lunch and dinner.*

In a neighborhood where restaurants tend to come and go, this one has been around for ages. You won't get anything fancy here, but you will get good basic food, such as onion soup, steak and fries, chicken breast in cream sauce, and *confit de canard* at a good price. There are also selections of Greek and Nordic foods. The menus offer an appetizer, main course, and dessert for €10, €15, and €25.

RESTAURANT: LE BÎSTROT DES CIGALES, *12, Rue Thouin, 75005 Paris; Metro: Cardinal Lemoine or Place Monge.*

This charming place offers light, southern French food in a provençal-inspired décor. You can almost hear the *cigales* (cicadas) from which it takes its name. You get a nice choice of fresh foods to reflect the season. In the summer this means cold soups, salads, brushettas, and some heavier dishes, too. The lunch menu is €10.50. Dinner menus are €18 and €22.

RESTAURANT: L'ETOILE DU BERGER, *42, Rue de la Montagne Sainte Genevieve, 75005 Paris; Metro: Cardinal Lemoine.*

This restaurant looks a little like a Swiss Chalet. The food is exactly what you'd want to eat after a day of hiking or skiing in the Alps: cheese fondue, raclettes (melted cheese poured over potatoes); and tartiflette (another delicious cheese and potato dish). It's also good comfort food when the weather in Paris is cold or rainy. You won't walk away hungry. Dishes run about €16-20.

Light Fare

RESTAURANT: PIZZA PEPPA BELLA, *25, Rue Francisque Gay, 75006; Metro: Saint Michel (small side street 1 block south of Saint Michel Fountain); Open daily for lunch and dinner.*

This restaurant makes assorted pizzas in a wood-burning oven. They may or may not be the best in Paris as a sign in the window claims, but they are pretty good. There are also numerous pasta dishes to choose from. The price is certainly right, especially in this touristy neighborhood. Pizzas and pasta dishes run €10-12. There is a €12 lunch menu that includes pizza, pasta, or the daily special plus a drink. The daily special is €9. For €16, you can get an appetizer, pizza, and dessert. You can order pizzas to take out if you want to have a picnic by the Seine or in the Luxembourg Gardens.

CAFÉ DESCARTES, *1, Rue Thouin, 75005. Tel. 01 43 26 17 70. Metro: Place Monge.*

This place offers good salads, sandwiches, and other typical café fare at the top of the Ste. Genevieve hill. It is around the corner from where Ernest Hemingway lived when he wrote his classic autobiographical story of living in Paris, *An Immoveable Feast.* You are in walking distance of the Rue Mouffetard, Institut du Monde Arabe, and Arenes de Lutèce.

GREEK DELI: MAVROMMATIS, *47, Rue Censier, 75005; Metro: Censier Daubenton.*

Located just around the corner from the Rue Mouffetard market street, this is a great place to pick up take-out Greek food. There are creamy dips and spreads, freshly stuffed grape leaves, grilled shish kabobs, and other Greek delights.

GOURMET DELI: LES COMPTOIRS DE LA TOUR D'ARGENT, *2, Rue du Cardinal Lemoine, 75005 Paris. Metro: Maubert-Mutualité or Cardinale Lemoine.*

If you would like a touch of the luxury of dining at the famous Tour d'Argent restaurant (located across the street) without having to endure the cost and endless courses, drop in here. The ready-made foods are prepared with the same art and finesse as the ones in the restaurant.

RESTAURANT/TEA ROOM: TEA CADDY, *14, Rue Saint Julien le Pauvre, 75005 Paris; Metro: Maubert Mutualité, Cluny/La Sorbonne, or Saint Michel; Tel. 01 43 54 15 56; Open noon-7pm, Closed Tuesdays.*

This little restaurant offers light fare, including breakfast, at affordable prices. There are salads and scrambled eggs; hot dogs and grilled sandwiches; salmon torte and eggs Florentine – all for about €10. For a snack, you can try the scones, muffins, toast, and pastries.

BAKERY/CAFÉ: COLUMBUS CAFÉ, *21, Rue Soufflot, 75005 Paris; Tel. 01 43 25 41 41; Fax 01 43 25 41 42, www.columbuscafé.com.*

Once in a while, you want to grab a snack or cup of coffee without sitting down in a café or fast food joint. That's when this shop may appeal to you. It is a lot like an American Starbuck's. There are assorted coffees and cappuccinos, fresh juices, muffins, brownies, cookies, and the like.

CHOCOLATE SHOP: JADIS ET GOURMANDE, *88, Boulevard Port Royal, 75005 Paris; Metro: Port Royal.*

This shop is filled with chocolates that not only taste wonderful but also look beautiful. There are chocolate pianos, chocolate coins, and chocolate letters that you can pick to spell out the names of your loved ones. There are also creatively attractive gift boxes that are bound to be a hit with folks back home.

Light Fare along the Rue Mouffetard

Along with wonderful market offerings, there are many places to pick up a light meal or snack along this lively street:

LE PAIN QUOTIDIEN, *138, Rue Mouffetard, 75005 Paris; Metro: Censier Daubenton.*

This is a great spot to pick up breakfast or a light meal. The bakery and other items are very fresh. Breakfast will run you about €6-7. For lunch, you can pick up a sandwich for €4-8 or salad for €10. There is also a brunch for

Fun Fact

Parisians take their bread seriously. Maybe that's why it's so good. Some food historians argue that it was the impossibly high price of bread that led to the French Revolution. They claim that one of the reasons a Paris mob stormed the Bastille Prison on July 14, 1789 was to get to the supplies of wheat that were stored there. A few months later, another mob – composed mainly of women and children – marched on the king's palace at Versailles, because they were tired of being hungry. This is when Queen **Marie Antoinette**, upon hearing that the people were angry at not having enough bread to eat, is supposed to have answered, "Well, then let them eat cake!"

€18 on Saturday and Sunday, but you'll need to get there early to beat the crowds. You can also buy terrific ice cream here, which changes to reflect the fruits and flavors of each season.

STEFF, LE BOULANGER, *123, Rue Mouffetard, 75005; Metro: Censier Daubenton.*

This bakery is known for its wonderful breads, made the old-fashioned way and sometimes filled with nuts, raisons, or olives. The plain old baguette is delicious, too. It's also a good place to pick up a sandwich and pastry.

LES PANETONS, *113, Rue Mouffetard, 75005; Metro: Censier Daubenton.*

This bakery, along with its sister pastry shop next door, Le Moule à Gateaux, uses plenty of butter to make mouth-watering pastries and desserts. The croissants are deliciously puffy, and get my vote for the best around. You can also get fresh sandwiches, quiches, and breads. The cakes and pies are out of this world.

SHANGHAI EXPRÈSS, *105, Rue Mouffetard, 75005; Metro: Censier Daubenton.*

I had to include this little Asian deli, because it never fails to win high praises from kids. You can choose from a wide assortment of grilled skewers, steamed dumplings, and dishes such as cashew chicken or sweet and sour pork.

LA MAISON DES TARTES, *67, Rue Mouffetard, 75005; Metro: Place Monge.*

This shop specializes in both sweet and savory types of pies, with a wide assortment of quiches and fruit tarts.

GELATI D'ALBERTO, *45, Rue Mouffetard, 75005; Metro: Place Monge. Open daily in the summer, noon-midnight. Closed Mondays in Spring and Fall. Closed November-February.*

The owner of this shop, Alberto, has been written up in numerous newspapers and magazines for daring to set up an Italian ice cream shop in the middle of Paris. It has been a big success. It seems that people can't resist his rose-shaped scoops of strawberry, wild currant, or even Nutella flavored ice cream.

Saint Germain des Près & Musée d'Orsay

HÔTEL DES MARRONNIERS***, *21, rue Jacob, 75006 Paris; Metro: Saint Germain des Près or Mabillon; Tel. 01 43 25 30 60; Fax 01 430 46 83 56; http://www.hotel-marronniers.com/; Rates: €138-153 (double); €188 (triple); €228 (quadruple). Buffet breakfast: €10 downstairs or €12 rooms service.*

This hotel is located in the heart of Saint Germain des Près. From here it is just steps to the old Saint Germain des Près church, Rue de Buci stores, fancy clothing designer shops, and historic cafés. To reach the entrance, you walk through a little courtyard filled with flowers and chestnut trees. Since it is set back from the street, the rooms are nice and quiet. Some have a view of the Saint Germain church. After a warm welcome at the front desk you proceed to your room, which can only be described as… unforgettable! It's hard to tell whether you've just stepped into the royal bedroom of the king's palace, or onto the theatrical set of some silly farce. Each room has a main color theme (like RED! or BLUE!). The decorators have had no fear of using an abundance of matching fabrics and wallpaper (even on the ceilings).

HÔTEL LEFT BANK – SAINT GERMAIN (Best Western) ***, *9, Rue de l'Ancienne Comédie, 75006 Paris; Metro: Odeon; Tel. 01 43 54 01 70; Fax 01 43 26 17 14; Email: lb@paris-hôtels-charm.com; http:// book.bestwestern.com/bestwestern/priceAvail.do ; Rates: €220-250 (doubles); €250 (triple). One child under 12 is free with 2 paying adults. Rates include buffet breakfast.*

This hotel offers charm and a great location. It is situated in the heart of Saint Germain des Près. It is around the corner from the Rue de Buci street market, not far from the Luxembourg Gardens and Cluny Museum. You can walk to Nôtre Dame Cathedral, the Musée d'Orsay, or the Louvre. The rooms feature exposed wooden beams and antique furniture, and they are decorated in warm red and golden tones. From the upper floors there are beautiful views of the rooftops and church towers of Paris. Some of the adjacent double rooms can be set up as a 2-room suite.

HOTEL PERREYVE**, *63, Rue Madame, 7006 Paris. Tel. 01 45 48 35 01. Fax. 01 42 84 03 30. perreyve@clubinternet.fr Rates: €70-105.*

The big advantage of this hotel is its location in a quiet side street right near the Luxembourg Gardens. The rates are also quite reasonable for this neighborhood. There is one triple room or you can choose two doubles next door to each other.

RESTAURANT: POLIDOR, *41, Rue Monsieur le Prince, 75006; Metro: Cluny – la Sorbonne or RER: Luxembourg; Tel. 01 43 26 95 34; Open daily for lunch and dinner.*

This restaurant has been around for over 150 years and continues to provide good food at a reasonable price in a friendly atmosphere. You sit at big, family-style tables covered with red-checkered table clothes. There's hâchis parmentier (ground beef with mashed potatoes), ham and lentils, stuffed cabbage, salmon steak, and more. The lunch menu is only €12 and dinner menu is €19. Daily specials run €9-11. There are two down sides. They do not accept credit cards, and the restroom is the old-fashioned hole in the ground style.

RESTAURANT: LA TABLE D'AUDE, *8, Rue de Vaugirard, 75006 Paris; Metro: Odeon or RER: Luxembourg. Open Tues-Fri, Closed in August.*

This jolly restaurant caters to every age group. It offers specialties from southwestern France, and is most famous for its cassoulet – a casserole composed of white beans, sausages and pork meats, and vegetables. There are lunch menus for €11, €16, and €18. Dinner runs €25-35.

RESTAURANT DU MUSÉE D'ORSAY, *Level 2 of the Musée d'Orsay; Metro:Solférino; Open Tues-Sun, for lunch, 11:30am-2:30 pm. Thurs, open for dinner. Tea and snacks offered from 3pm-5:30pm. Closed Mon.*

If your child has never eaten in a fancy restaurant this might be a good place to start. The soaring ceiling, big mirrors, and golden details recall the days when Orsay was a train station with a luxury hotel and dining room. Yet it is family friendly, so it's a good place for kids to practice their good restaurant behavior. The lunch offerings include a big buffet for €15. The daily special runs about €13, or €15 with dessert. The kid's menu offers a choice of ham or fish, plus ice cream and a drink for €7.

Note: The Musée d'Orsay also has a nice (though often crowded) café on Level 5, called the **CAFÉ DES HAUTEURS.** There are sandwiches, quiches, salads, and snacks for afternoon tea. It offers a remarkable view of the reverse side of one of the building's giant clocks. A snack bar is located on Level 6.

RESTAURANT: CAFÉ MINOTTI, *33, Rue de Verneuil, 75007 (Metro: Solférino); Open daily for lunch and dinner.*

This airy, friendly restaurant is a great place to stop after hours of wandering through the Musée d'Orsay or Saint Germain neighborhood. Legend has it that the Three Musketeers lived down the street. If they were around today, they would undoubtedly approve of this restaurant. The food is very fresh and delicious. The secret here is good, basic ingredients that change regularly to reflect the seasons. For example in summer you might choose the chilled ratatouille or melted goat cheese salad. There are simple omelets, sandwiches, and pasta dishes to please kids' tastes. The chef will adapt a selection to your child's tastes, too. Dishes range from €18-25.

RESTAURANT: LE CAFÉ DES LETTRES, *53, Rue de Verneuil, 75007; Tel. 01 42 22 52 17; Metro: Solferino; Closed Sun. evening.*

This Swedish restaurant is filled with books and decorated with paintings by young, local artists. It is in the same building as the *Maison des Lettres* where writers and Nobel Laureates come to meet. In nice weather you can eat in the outdoor courtyard, well away from street noise and traffic. The menu features plenty of smoked salmon, herring, and shrimp. There are also salads, sandwiches, and our kids' favorite: Swedish meatballs. On Sunday, there is a smorgasbord brunch from 12 to 4 pm. Main courses a la carte run between €12-24. Daily specials at €15 and €20. Sunday brunch is €25.

Light Fare

BAKERY: POILÂNE, *8, Rue du Chèrche Midi, 75006 Paris; Metro: Saint Sulpice or Saint Germain des Près; Open Mon-Sat.*

This may be the most famous bakery in Paris, thanks to Lionel

Poilâne's dark, round bread. You can get open-faced sandwiches on Poilâne bread in many fancy cafés around the city, but here you get it straight from the oven. The pastries and other varieties of bread are also excellent.

GRANDE EPICERIE IN THE AU BON MARCHÉ DEPART-MENT STORE, *22, Rue de Sèvres, 75007 Paris. Metro: Sevres-Babylone; Open Mon-Sat.*

On the ground level of this historic department store (the first in the world) you will find a huge assortment of gourmet foods. There are several deli and bakery counters where you can get prepared foods. There are also plenty of packaged delights for a snack or to take home as gifts. While you are here, take your children to the 3 Hiboux section in the basement. It is filled with kids' crafts, games, and toys.

PETIT HONG KONG, *1 Rue Haute Feuille, 75006 Paris. Metro: St. Michel*

This is one of many Asian delis that you see all over Paris. It gets a mention here because of the convenient location, wide choice, and fact that it is a hit with kids. You can eat in or take out and have a picnic in the nearby Luxembourg Gardens.

ICE CREAM AND PASTRIES: PIERRE HERMÉ, *72, Rue Bonaparte, 75006 Paris. Metro: Mabillon or Saint Sulpice.*

A good address, especially known for its exotic ice cream flavors, such as lime with basil.

ICE CREAM AND PASTRIES: CHRISTIAN CONSTANT, *37, Rue d'Assas, 75006 Paris. Metro: Rennes.*

Another great address with irresistible pastries and a wide selection of delicious ice creams.

Montparnasse

HÔTEL DELAMBRE***, *35, Rue Delambre, 75014 Paris; Metro: Vavin or Edgar Quinet; Tel. 01 43 20 66 31; Fax 01 45 38 9176; www.hôteldelambre.com; Email: hôtel@hôteldelambre.com. Rates: €85-105 (doubles); €150-160 (mini-suite); extra bed: €12; buffet breakfast: €9 (free for kids under 12).*

This is a great little hotel. It is located in the heart of the Montparnasse neighborhood, with easy access to metro and buses. There are some wonderful rooms for families. We liked the L-shaped mini-suite on the top floor, under the gables with lovely views of the rooftops of Paris. There are also some nice adjoining double rooms on the lower floors. They are in short supply, however, so be sure to reserve well in advance of your trip. As an added convenience, there is a Laundromat next door to the hotel.

HÔTEL LE BRÉA***, *14, Rue Bréa, 75006 Paris (Metro: Vavin or Nôtre Dame des Champs). Tel. 01 43 25 44 41; Fax 01 44 07 19 25; Email: brea.hôtel@wanadoo.fr; Rates: €120-160 (single); €140-160 (double); €160* *(triple); Extra bed: €16. Buffet breakfast: €12 (downstairs) or €14 (rooms service).*

This pretty hotel is located in the heart of Montparnasse and is only a 5-minute walk from the Luxembourg gardens. The lobby and rooms are decorated with taste and warm, Provençal colors. The rooms are divided into standard and superior categories, with the superior ones being a bit larger. All of them were renovated in the late 1990s, and they feature new bathrooms and air-conditioning. The rooms with two twin beds are definitely bigger than the ones with a double bed. There is a nice sunroom and attractive breakfast room. The Rue Bréa in which the hotel is located is lined with wonderful kids' stores.

HÔTEL: LA VILLA DES ARTISTES (Best Western)***, *9, Rue de la Grande Chaumière, 75006 Paris; (Metro: Vavin) near intersection of Boulevard Montparnasse and Boulevard Raspail; Tel. 01 43 26 60 86; Fax 01 43 54 73 70; Rates: €126-176 (doubles); €215 (triples); €240 (quadruples). Buffet breakfast: €9.*

This pretty hotel is very popular with American families. Maybe it's because the parents spent their Junior Year Abroad days in Reid Hall, 1 block away. Perhaps it's the combination of comfort and convenient location: you are in Montparnasse, surrounded by artists' studios, and a 5-minute walk to the Luxembourg Gardens. Yet you are set back from the hustle and noise of the nearby avenues. The hotel takes its name Villa des Artistes seriously. It helps promote contemporary painters with exhibits of their works. It is also decorated with reproductions of paintings from many of Montparnasses' great early 20th century painters. The rooms are separated into standard and deluxe categories. The main difference is that the deluxe rooms are air-conditioned and a bit bigger. There is a pretty little outdoor garden with a fountain where you can eat breakfast in warm weather.

HÔTEL DAGUÈRRE*, *94, Rue Daguèrre, 75014 Paris; Metro: Gaité or Denfert Rochereau; Tel. 01 43 22 43 54; Fax 01 43 20 66 84; Email: paris@hôteldaguerre.com; Rates: €77 E (single); €83 (double); €114 (4-person suite). Extra bed: €15.50. Buffet breakfast: €11.*

This hotel recently had a face lift. It is located down the street from a little toy store (Les Cousins d'Alice) and a few blocks from the part of the Rue Daguèrre that is reserved for pedestrians and an open-air market. You are a bit off the beaten path here, but close to Montparnasse, the Catacombes and numerous subway and bus lines. The hotel owners offer a warm welcome to families. The rooms are small, but nice.

RESTAURANT WADJA, *10, Rue de la Grande Chaumière, 75006 Paris; (Metro: Vavin); Tel. 01 46 33 02 02; Closed Sun all day and Mon lunch.*

I must confess that I used to eat here in my starving student days when the tables were set family style, and the waiters greeted you by tossing a big chunk of bread directly onto the table. Since then, the place has gone more upscale. But the secret to it's continued popularity is still the same: offer good food at a reasonable price. The €14 menu offers choices such as salad with stingray; roasted chicken with olive polenta; and rhubarb pie. Each month, the restaurant features specialties from a different region of France.

LA COUPOLE, *102, Boulevard Montparnasse, 75014, Metro: Vavin or Montparnasse. Tel. 01 43 20 14 20. Open daily 8 am-1 am.*

This is a big, classic Paris icon. It was once a favorite haunt of the artists, writers, and dancers who made Montparnasse such an artistic haven – Man Ray, Josephine Baker, Marc Chagall, Pablo Picasso, Ernest Hemingway, and many others whose spirit still lingers. The dining room columns are decorated with paintings in an early 20th century modern art style. It is quite kid-friendly and popular with families. Anyone celebrating a birthday gets a special tribute from the waiters, who turn down the lights and emerge from the kitchen singing Happy Birthday. The food is classic and reliable. The fixed priced menus are €18 for lunch and €23 and €33 for dinner, including a small carafe of wine. The kids' menu is €13.50 and includes a special kiddie cocktail, choice of main fish or meat-based dish, and choice of several desserts.

FAMILY BRUNCH AT RESTAURANT JUSTINE, *in the Meridien Montparnasse Hôtel; 19, Rue du Commandant Mouchotte, 75014 Paris; Metro: Gaite; Served on Sundays from 12pm to 3:30 pm.*

On Sundays, this restaurant serves up a big brunch buffet for families. Adults pay €40 (includes a glass of champagne, or coffee, or tea). Kids ages 4-12 pay €20 for their own special buffet. Kids under 4 eat for free. Each Sunday has a different kid-friendly theme; for example Spiderman, Harry Potter, The Jungle Book, and more. Friendly staff members are there to entertain children with balloon tricks, face-painting, songs, magic tricks, or other activities.

RESTAURANT/CRÊPERIE: LA PATACRÊPE, *19, Rue Daguèrre, 75014 Paris; Metro: Denfert Rochereau; Tel. 01 43 20 20 79; Open daily except Monday evening; Dinner menus: €15 amd €19; Lunch menu: €9.60; Kid's menu: €6.50.*

This nice crêperie is located in a courtyard off of the pedestrian market street, Rue Daguèrre. It is decorated with pretty Breton paintings and ceiling fans. The food is good. The menu offers an ample range of salads and crêpes, with a nice terrace for warm weather meals. You are far away from traffic, so restless children can move around safely between courses.

RESTAURANT/CRÊPERIE: TY BREIZ, *52, Boulevard de Vaugirard, 75015 Paris; Metro: Montparnasse or Pasteur. Open for lunch and dinner. Closed Sun-Mon, and in August.*

This is reputed to be the best crêpe restaurant in Paris. It's also very family-friendly. Kids get a crêpe, dessert, and drink for €7.50. Adults can count on €15 for a crêpe, drink, and dessert.

PÂTISSERIE/VIENNOISERIE, *145, Boulevard Raspail, 75006 (Metro: Vavin).*

This bakery at the intersection of Boulevard Raspail and Boulevard Montparnasse offers delicious light foods for breakfast or a picnic lunch. There are nice quiches, brushettas, pizzas, and tortes with puff pastry dough. The breakfast pastries are yummy, too.

MAX POILANE, *29, Rue de l'Ouest, 75014. Metro: Gaité. Open Mon-Fri, 10-7.*

The Poilâne family has become famous for its delicious country-style bread. Here you can try it with a variety of hot and cold sandwiches. There are also salads and other snacks. Prices range from €3-7.

LES BONBONS, *6, Rue Bréa, 75006 Paris. Metro: Vavin. Closed on Mondays and in August.*

You'll feel like a kid in a candy shop!

Eiffel Tower & Champs de Mars

HÔTEL DERBY ALMA (Best Western)****, *8, Avenue Rapp, 75007 Paris; Metro: Alma Marceau or RER: Pont de l'Alma; Tel. 01 44 18 77 77; Fax 01 44 18 77 78; Email: info@derbyalmahôtel.com; http:// book.bestwestern.com/bestwestern/productInfo.do?propertyCode=93513#null; Rates (lower rates apply in Jan, Feb, Aug, Nov, Dec; higher rates apply in Mar, Apr, May, Jun, Jul, Sep, Oct, 28Dec-1Jan): €235-265 (double); €295-335 (triple suite); €375-385 (quadruple suite). Full buffet breakfast: €18.*

This hotel offers the comforts and spaciousness of a four-star hotel. It is located on the lovely Avenue Rapp, famous for its remarkable Art Nouveau apartment buildings. The neighborhood is upscale and residential, and you are only a stone's throw from the Eiffel Tower, which you can admire from many of the rooms. From here, it is also an easy walk or bus ride to major sights, such as the Trocadéro, Champs Elysées, Invalides, and Saint Germain des Près neighborhood. The hotel welcomes many families with large rooms and suites. All the rooms are air-conditioned and very tastefully decorated. Two of the floors are reserved for non-smokers. There is a copious English-style breakfast with cereal, eggs, sausages, assorted breads, and pastries.

HÔTEL: EIFFEL PARK (Best Western)***, *17 Bis, Rue Amélie, 75007 Paris; Metro: La Tour Maubeuge; Tel. 01 45 55 10 01; Fax 01 47 05 28 88; Email: reservation@eiffelpark.com; http://www.eiffelpark.com/; Rates: €175 (double).Breakfast: €12.*

This hotel is situated in a nice, quiet street in the tony residential section of the 7th arrondissement. It is close to the Eiffel Tower and Invalides. You can go to the Pont Alexandre III and cross the Seine towards the Champs Elysées. The rooms are bright and airy. Each one is decorated differently, but tastefully. They are all air-conditioned. The upper floor rooms have lovely views over the rooftops of Paris. There is a cozy breakfast room, or you can eat on the terrace in nice weather. Some of the adjacent double rooms can be connected and made into a 2-room suite.

RESTAURANT: ALTITUDE 95, *Level 1, Eiffel Tower; Metro: Bir Hakeim or RER: Champs de Mars – Tour Eiffel; Tel. 01 45 55 20 04; Open daily for lunch and dinner.[Note: You should make a reservation if you are visiting during tourist season. You can either call ahead or make a reservation at the Altitude 95 kiosk at the foot of the tower. With a lunch or dinner reservation, you can access the tower's elevators without having to stand in line for tickets.]*

This is a treat not to be missed! The food is good, but what really counts is the atmosphere and a view that can't be beat. Unlike the very expensive Jules Verne restaurant on level 2 of the Tower, this restaurant is very family-friendly and affordable. Menus and specials run for about €21 and €28. It's an unforgettable way to discover Paris and the Eiffel Tower.

Light Fare

BAKERY JEAN LUC POUJAURAN, *20, Rue Jean Nicot, 75007 Paris; Metro: La Tour Maubeuge or Invalides or RER: Pont de l'Alma; Open Tues-Sat, 8am-8pm. Closed in August.*

This bakery offers delicious breads and assorted sandwiches and pastries. It is a good place to pick up a picnic that you can enjoy in the Champs de Mars Park, looking up at the Eiffel Tower.

Invalides

HÔTEL DE TURENNE**, *20, Avenue de Tourville, 75007 Paris; Metro: Ecole Militaire, Invalides, or La Tour Maubeuge; Tel. 01 47 05 99 92; Fax 01 45 56 06 04; Email: hôtel.turenne.paris7@wanadoo.fr; Rates: €77-84 (double); €102 (triple). Extra bed: €9.50. Continental breakfast: €6.50.*

This hotel offers a friendly welcome in a cozy atmosphere. The rooms are small, but they are quite pleasant – some even have a view of the Eiffel Tower. The owners are happy to accommodate families, adding a bed to one of their larger rooms, or offering adjoining rooms with a common door. The hotel is located between the Eiffel Tower (and its large Champs de Mars park) and the Invalides and Rodin Museum. There are plenty of metros and buses to take you all over the city.

HÔTEL LE PAVILLON**, *54, Rue Saint Dominique, 75007 Paris; Metro: Latour Maubeuge or Invalides; Tel. 01 45 51 42 87; Fax; 01 45 51 32 79; Email: PatrickPavillon@aol.com. Rates: €95 (double); €140 (family triple or quad). Continental breakfast: €6.*

This pleasant little hotel is tucked away in a courtyard off the main road. It is situated in a nice residential neighborhood between the Eiffel Tower and Invalides. The welcome is very friendly and homey. The rates are quite reasonable. In warm weather you can have breakfast in the hotel's little garden. The rooms are not luxurious, but they are comfortable and tastefully decorated. Two of them are large enough for a family of four.

RESTAURANT: LES JARDINS DE VARENNE CAFÉ, *in the Rodin Museum, 77, Rue de Varenne, 75007 Paris; Metro: Varenne; Closed Mondays and from January through March.*

This is a lovely place to have lunch, even if you are not planning to visit the Rodin Museum. You can enjoy the gardens, filled with famous sculptures by Rodin, for €1 per adult (kids are free). The café proposes a large assortment of salads and sandwiches (€6-7). There is also a daily hot plate special. For dessert there is a nice assortment of tarts and ice cream. When you are done with your food, the kids can frolic among the sculptures.

Les Halles

HÔTEL VICTOIRES OPÉRA**, *56, Rue Montorgueil, 75002 Paris; Metro: Etienne Marcel; Tel. 01 42 36 41 08; Fax 01 45 08 08 79; Email: hôtel@VictoiresOpéra.com; http://www.paris-hotel-opera.com/; Rates: €192-350 (doubles); €335 (suite). Buffet breakfast: €12.*

Amid the charm of the Rue Montorgueil market street is this discreet, luxury hotel. You are in the center of the city, near Les Halles, the Marais, and the designer stores of the Place des Victoires. The rooms were recently remodeled and include marble bathrooms and air-conditioning. There are triple rooms, or you can book two adjacent doubles with a communicating door.

HÔTEL: NOVOTEL PARIS LES HALLES*, *8, Place Marguerite de Navarre, 75001; Metro: Châtelet (exit Place Sainte Opportune) or Les Halles (exit Forum des Halles, Porte Berger); Tel. 01 42 21 31 31; Fax 01 40 26 05 79; Email: H0785@accor-hôtels.com; Rates: €232-264 (queen bed+sofa bed; €345-396 (2-room suite with 2 twins/double). Children under 16 can share their parent's room for free. Buffet breakfast: €16 for adults, free for kids under 16.*

This hotel is modern and bright, and located smack dab in the center of Paris. It is very family-friendly, and there is even a special play space for little tikes on the ground floor. All the rooms are air-conditioned. Some are specially equipped for people with disabilities. The ones on the forum side have lovely views of the Forum des Halles and Eglise Saint Eustache. The family suites offer two, spacious rooms. The location is very central and convenient, with a big park, pedestrian streets, and a large indoor public pool in the Forum des Halles.

RESTAURANT: AU TONNEAU DES HALLES, *28, Rue Montorgueil, 75001 Paris. Metro: Les Halles. Tel. 01 42 33 36 19. Open non-stop 7am-11pm. Closed Sun.*

This restaurant is an old Les Halles institution. It was around in the days when the wholesale food workers in Les Halles would stop in for an onion soup, piece of wild boar, and glass of Beaujolais wine. You can still get good, traditional French food here. Count on €20-25 for a meal. In the summer you can eat on the terrace situated along the lively pedestrian street market of the Rue Montorgueil.

RESTAURANT: CHEZ CLOVIS, *33, Rue Berger (corner Rue des Prouvaires), 75001 Paris. Metro: Les Halles (west of the Forum des Halles); Tel. 01 42 33 97 07; Open for lunch and dinner. Closed Sunday.*

Another Les Halles institution, this restaurant serves good, traditional French food at reasonable prices. There are traces of the former Les Halles meat markets in the old photographs on the walls. You can also get a feel for them in some of the dishes such as andouillette sausages, beef stew, pheasant terrine, and salad with warm chicken livers. There is also lighter fare with choices of soups and salads. The lunch menu is €14. Dinner runs around €30-40.

RESTAURANT: LE PAQUEBOT EN LA BOTELLA, *14, Rue Sauval, 75001; Metro: Les Halles; Tel. 01 42 21 19 00. Closed Sun-Mon.*

This restaurant is decorated to look like an ocean liner. It is also very family-friendly. There is a "petit salon" just for kids - a corner with books and drawing supplies. The chef will prepare a simple macaroni or rice dish for fussy eaters. He'll even let them see the kitchen if it's not too busy. For the rest of us, there are tapas, paellas, and other Spanish foods, each made from fresh ingredients that change with the seasons. Lunch menus run €16-28. For €25-27, you can get a dinner featuring assorted tapas or tapas and paella.

Light Fare

NILS', *36, Rue Montorgueil, 75001 Paris; Metro: Les Halles or Etienne Marcel; Open daily for lunch and dinner.*

You can eat in or buy take-out food in this pleasant Scandinavian restaurant. Located in the jolly, Rue Montorgueil market street, Nils' offers interesting sandwiches, salads, meatballs, and hotdogs. It's good kid food — and not bad for adults. The price is right, too. A sandwich, drink, and dessert will only set you back about €7. Kids can get a meatball sandwich, dessert muffin, and drink for only €3.50.

BAKERY: STÖHRER, *51, Rue Montorgueil, 75002 Paris; Metro: Etienne Marcel or Les Halles. Open daily 7:30 am-8:30 pm. Closed last two weeks in August.*

The original Mr. Stöhrer was a royal baker who came from Austria to accompany Queen Marie Antoinette in the late 1700s. His pastries were a huge hit, and the shop continues to faithfully produce the same quality that was fit for a queen. You can also get nice sandwiches, quiches, and salads. But the main reason to bring your family here is to follow Marie Antoinette's advice, "Let them eat cake"!

Louvre

HÔTEL MOLIÈRE***, *21, Rue Molière, 75001 Paris; Metro: Pyramides or Palais Royal; Tel. 01 42 96 22 01; Fax 01 42 60 48 68; Email: moliere@worldnet.fr; www.hotels-exclusive.com/hotels/molierel; Rates: €155-275 (double); €190 (triple); €275 (4-person suite). Extra bed: €16. Buffet breakfast or continental room service breakfast: €12.*

This pretty hotel is located in a side street between the Palais Royal gardens and Avenue de l'Opéra. It is named for one of France's greatest playwrights, who died on stage at the nearby *Comédie Française* after a performance of his show, The Imaginary Invalid. The hotel's rooms are all air-conditioned, comfortable, and tastefully decorated. The 2-room suite can comfortably sleep four people. The staff is friendly and helpful. The location is very central and convenient to many of the major sights of Paris. You are just a block from the Palais Royal gardens where little ones can unwind.

HÔTEL LONDRES SAINT-HONORÉ**, *13, Rue Saint Roch, 75001 Paris; Tel. 01 42 60 15 62; Fax 01 42 60 16 00; Email: hôtel.londres.st.honoré@gofornet.com; Metro: Pyramides or Tuileries. Rates: €90-107 (double); €118 (triple); €130 (quadruple). Continental breakfast: €6.50.*

This hotel offers very friendly service, in a central location, at a good price. It's near the Tuileries Gardens, Louvre, and Palais Royal Gardens. The rooms are small, but have modern bathrooms, TVs, a hair dryer, and a minibar. Some of them are air-conditioned.

RESTAURANT: TOUPARY, *5th floor and rooftop terrace, Samaritaine Department Store 2, Quai du Louvre, 75001 Paris; Metro: Pont Neuf; Tel. 01 40 41 29 29; Lunch: Noon-3pm; Tea Room: 3:30pm-6pm; Dinner: 7:30pm-11:30pm. Closed Sunday.*

This restaurant is famous for its wonderful views of the city. You are right on the Seine, overlooking the Pont Neuf, with Nôtre Dame Cathedral to your left and the Eiffel Tower on your right. It's pretty spectacular. What's more, the food is excellent. The lunch menus are quite affordable at €12, €17, and €25 including a glass of wine. Dinner a la carte will run you about €40.

If you are not up for a restaurant meal, you can also enjoy breakfast or lunch in the Samaritaine's café called Les Sands. It is also on the 5th floor, with fine views of the city. Here you can order simple meals, such as salads and sandwiches.

UNIVERSAL RESTAURANT – FOOD COURT, *Located in the underground shopping section of the Louvre complex; 99, rue de Rivoli, 75001 Paris; Metro: Louvre Rivoli or Palais Royal.*

This food court offers a choice of take-out stands from all over the world. American children feel right at home here, and adults appreciate the fact that there is something for everyone. This is where one of our teenage friends decided to start his comparison test of American and French soft drinks. Evidently, a French Coca Cola doesn't taste the same as an American one. Test it out for yourself.

Light Fare

CAFÉ DENON, *On the outdoor terrace of the Denon Wing of the Louvre Museum, Level 1 (around the corner from Géricault's Raft of the Medusa). Metro: Louvre Rivoli or Palais Royal. Open for lunch and tea, 10am-5pm.*

This café offers light sandwiches, hotdogs, and salads. The food is okay, but the main attraction is the location. If the weather is nice, you can sit outside on the terrace, where you can peer through giant statues down onto the Louvre's glass pyramid. The Café Richelieu in the opposite wing of the museum also offers light lunch, tea, and great views.

CAFÉ VÉRY – DAME TARTINE, *in the Tuileries Gardens, on the N. side of the central alley. Metro: Tuileries. Open daily, noon-11:30 pm.*

This place is one of our favorites, especially after a morning of exploring the Louvre. You can sit at the terrace, under the chestnut trees in the Tuileries Gardens. There is also indoor seating if the weather is wet or cold. Children can run and play while you wait for your food. Although you are in the heart of a popular tourist area, you get good food at a good price, without being rushed to make room for the next customers. There are nice salads and open-faced sandwiches. You can also get interesting hot dishes featuring chicken and polenta, or sausage and potatoes. There is a kid's menu for €9.

CAFÉ: CHÂLET DE DIANE, *in the Tuileries Gardens, along the S. side of the central alley. Metro: Tuileries. Open daily, 7:30am-10:30 pm.*

This is another great spot to grab a light meal in the middle of the Tuileries Gardens. There are nice salads, traditional onion soup, and usually a daily hot-plate special. Children can run and play while you relax and admire the grace of the statues from your seat under the chestnut trees.

CAFÉ RENARD, in the Tuileries Gardens, S. side of the central alley. Metro: Tuileries.

Yet another great place to stop for a meal in the Tuileries Gardens. This one has a slightly larger selection of hot foods than some of the others. The kids' menu offers a choice of hotdog, chicken, ham, or Croque Monsieur hot sandwich with a great big Magnum ice cream for dessert.

CAFÉ DE LA COMÉDIE, *157, Rue Saint Honoré, 75001 Paris (across from Comédie Française Theater and Palais Royal garden entrance); Metro: Palais Royal.*

We like this café for its great location between the Louvre and Palais Royal. It is on a little square, Place Colette, across a funny modern entrance to the Palais Royal metro station. There is the usual café assortment of salads, sandwiches, omelets, hotdogs, pizza, quiche, steak with fries, and more. What's surprising is the freshness of the ingredients and quality of the desserts. When you're fed and rested you can check out the nice bookstore next door; go across the street to the Palais Royal gardens; head up the Avenue de l'Opéra to tour the Opera House; explore the Louvre; or hop into the metro for a ride to the Champs Elysées.

LA FERME, *55, Rue Saint Roch, 75001 Paris; Metro: Pyramides; Closed Sunday.*

This gourmet take-out place features fresh, organic foods. You pick up a basket and choose from a selection of sandwiches, salads, quiches, yogurt, fruit, fresh-squeezed juices, and more. Prices range from €2-5 per item. You can eat there, or enjoy a picnic in the Tuileries or Palais Royal gardens.

TEAROOM: ANGELINA'S, *226, Rue de Rivoli, 75001 Paris; Metro: Tuileries.*

This is one of Paris' most classic tearooms, where generations of children have been rewarded for good behavior with a thick cup of hot chocolate and fabulous pastries. The original owners were Austrian, so there is plenty of whipped cream on everything. The décor is Paris circa 1900. You can also order a light salad or sandwich. Just make sure you save room for dessert. Note that the lines to get in can become long, but it's worth the wait.

TEAROOM: MUSCADE, *36, Rue Montpensier, in the Palais Royal gardens. Open daily, noon-11pm.*

This is a great spot to enjoy an afternoon tea or hot chocolate with a pastry.

TEAROOM: JEAN PAUL HÉVIN, *231, Rue Saint Honoré. 75001 Paris. Metro: Tuileries.*

This tearoom offers delicious pastries, unforgettable chocolates, and excellent ice cream.

ICE CREAM: DAMMANN'S, *in the Tuileries Gardens, right by the Arch du Carrousel. Metro: Louvre or Palais Royal. Open daily, April-November.*

Chances are you would stop at this ice cream stand anyway if you were looking for a snack in the Tuileries or coming out of the Louvre, since it's right by the Arch du Carrousel. What a pleasant surprise then to discover that you are about to enjoy some of the best ice cream and sorbets in the city. You can choose from tangy fruits such as mango, kiwi, and melon. There are creamy choices such as Tiramisu and my personal favorite, Bulgarian yogurt. Yum!

Marais

HÔTEL DU 7ième ART**, *20, Rue Saint Paul, 75004 Paris; Metro: Saint Paul or Sully Morland; Tel. 01 44 54 85 00; Fax 01 42 77 69 10; Email: hôtel7art@wanadoo.fr; Rates: €75-95 (double); €120-130 (triple and quadruple). Extra bed: €20. Continental breakfast: €7.*

This is a fun hotel, and one of the few family-friendly establishments we could find in the Marais. The owners are very welcoming to their younger guests. The entire place is decorated with old movie posters and paraphernalia (the 7th art = cinema). The top floor room under the rafters is large enough to accommodate up to 4 people. There are also double rooms that can be connected with communicating doors. Guests can use the hotel's laundry room: a real plus! There is a large breakfast room that also serves tea and snacks in the afternoon. The hotel is located in the heart of the Marais. It's a real find, but book your rooms early, because they fill up quickly.

HÔTEL DE LA PLACE DES VOSGES**, *12, Rue de Birague, 75004 Paris; Metro: St. Paul or Bastille. Tel. 01 42 72 60 46; Fax 01 42 72 02 64. Rates: €120-202 (double); €140 (family room). Baby beds available.*

This hotel is right near the lovely Place des Vosges. In the 1600s the building was a stable. You can still see wooden beams and old stone walls. Today it offers nice clean rooms at a reasonable price, with touches of charm, and a pretty lobby.

RESTAURANT: MARC ANNIBAL DE COCONNAS, *2 bis, Place des Vôsges, 75004; Tel. 01 42 78 58 16; Open for lunch and dinner. Closed Mondays.*

The €28 menu here is quite reasonable considering the locale (literally under the arcades of the Place des Vôsges) and the excellent quality of the food. It features appetizers such as salmon tartar; warm goat cheese on salad; and tomatoes with pesto and mozzarella. The main course offerings include such things as grilled Gambas, leg of lamb, and lobster. Dessert includes such choices as fresh pastry with strawberries, roasted figs, or raspberry crumble. When the weather is nice you can eat outside, where you can watch over the gardens of the Place des Vôsges. The park's playground is just across the street. You may want to while away the time between courses by telling your kids the story of the *Hunchback of Nôtre Dame.* The author, Victor Hugo, lived just a few doors down at #6, Place des Vôsges.

RESTAURANT CARUSO, *3, Rue de Turenne, 75004 Paris; Metro: Saint Paul or Filles du Calvaire; Tel. 01 48 87 47 74. Open daily for lunch and dinner.*

This Italian restaurant is a favorite among the neighborhood locals. It is a little bit fancy, but the waiters are very friendly. Kids like the nice selection of pizzas, fresh pasta, and risotto dishes (€10-12). Adults can enjoy antipasti, and exotic dishes such as pasta cooked in black, squid ink. Daily specials are about €12. The lunch menu is €16.50. There are copious, three-course menus at €30 and €39.

Light Fare

RESTAURANT: DAME TARTINE, *2, Rue Brisemiche (across from the Stravinsky Fountain by the Pompidou Center), 75004 Paris; Metro: Hôtel de Ville or Rambuteau.*

This restaurant offers nice salads and interesting sandwiches. The prices are very reasonable considering the location. You are on a pedestrian square, next to the Pompidou Center and across from the delightful Stravinsky Fountain. It's a great spot to keep kids entertained. The fountain will keep your children amused for quite a while. To your left is the Saint Merri Church with its wonderful gargoyles, just ready to spit water towards you if it rains. There are no cars. There is a €9 kid's menu offering a Croque Monsieur (hot ham and cheese sandwich), ham, or hotdog, with salad or mashed potatoes, dessert and a drink. Sandwiches, salads, and hot plates range between €8-15, and there are menus for €10 and €15.

RESTAURANT/TEAROOM: LE LOIR DANS LA THÉIÈRE, *3, Rue des Rosiers, 75004 Paris; 01 42 72 90 61; Open daily.*

This place is famous for its cushy chairs, light fare, and weekend brunches. You can choose from a selection of salads, pasta dishes, quiches, and omelets. There also are yummy cakes and pastries. It's friendly, affordable and offers a calm haven in the bustling center of the Marais neighborhood.

DELI AND BAKERY: SACHA FINKELSZTAJN, *27, Rue des Rosiers, 75004 Paris; Metro: Saint Paul or Pont Marie; Closed Tuesday.*

This store has been in the Finkelsztajn family for three generations. It was originally just a bakery, but over the years they have added more and more deli items, too. You can stay for a bite or buy take out food. We always seem to end up here for dessert or a snack. There are plenty of delicious treats featuring apples and raisins. You can also try different types of cheesecakes. They are not like the typical New York variety we generally see in the US, but are well worth tasting.

DELI: JO GOLDENBERG, *7, Rue des Rosiers, 75004 Paris; Metro: Saint Paul. Open daily, 9:30am-past midnight.*

This classic kosher deli is a Paris institution. It serves up sandwiches, lox, dips, spreads, and other standard deli fare.

MI-VA-MI, *23, Rue des Rosiers, 75004 Paris; Metro: Saint Paul or Pont Marie. Closed Sat.*

In the 1950s and 1960s there was an influx of Jewish immigrants to Paris from North Africa. As a result, you can get excellent Middle-Eastern food in this traditionally Jewish neighborhood. This shop offers delicious falafel and pita sandwiches. You can sit inside at the few tables or order take-out. Platters range in price from €8-12.

DELI: BAGEL STORE, *31, Rue de Turenne, 75003 Paris; Tel. 01 44 78 06 05, Metro: Saint Paul or Chemin Vert.*

This kosher deli offers plenty of bagels, salads, and deli offerings. You can have a soup, sandwich, and dessert for €8; or have a sandwich, dessert, and coffee for the same price. For €10 you can get a combination falafel plate or cold meat platter. You can eat on one of the funny tables. They are made of glass cases with assorted things inside to delight your little ones. Or order take out and head for the lovely Place des Vôsges, a block away, where you will find plenty of benches, a playground, and big sandbox.

JADIS ET GOURMANDE, *39, Rue des Archives, 75004, Metro: Rambuteau.*

This shop is filled with chocolates that not only taste wonderful but also look beautiful. There are chocolate pianos, chocolate coins, and chocolate letters that you can pick to spell out the names of your loved ones. There are also creatively attractive gift boxes that are bound to be a hit with folks back home.

Bastille

RESTAURANT: BRASSERIE BOFINGER, *5 and 7 Rue de la Bastille, 75004 Paris; Metro: Bastille; Tel. 01 42 72 87 82; Fax 01 42 72 97 68; Open daily, 12pm-3pm, 6:30pm-1am (non-stop on weekends).*

This is a beautiful restaurant, a Paris classic, and a fun place to take kids who can enjoy a fancy meal. As with several other classic Parisian bistrots, this one is now managed by the Flo Restaurant chain. The food is no longer as spectacular as it once was but it is good and reliable. Make sure you show your children the beautiful Tiffany style skylight in one of the dining rooms. Upstairs there are paintings by Hansi, a famous Alsatian artist, depicting scenes of village life in Alsace. There is a €21.50 menu for lunch, €31.50 menu for dinner. The kid's menu is €13.50.

If you or your children are not quite up for the full Bofinger experience, you might want to try the **Petit Bofinger Restaurant** across the street. This bîstrot offers a 1950s decor, and plenty of excellent food at slightly more moderate prices. The lunch menu is €16, dinner menu is €23.

RESTAURANT DE PÂTES LUSTUCRU, *3, Rue du Faubourg Saint Antoine, 75011 Paris; Metro: Bastille. Tel. 01 44 67 44 67. Open daily.*

How kid-friendly can you get? Here is a whole 2-story restaurant devoted to pasta. Lustucru is a popular brand of pasta in French supermarkets, and now they've branched out into the restaurant business. It clearly targets the family market with lots of high chairs and lamps that look like eggs. There are plenty of pasta offerings – you can even order chocolate or banana ravioli for dessert. For €10 you get a choice of appetizers and main course or main course and dessert. For €15 you get all three.

TEAROOM AND PASTRY SHOP: DALLOYAU, *5, Boulevard Beaumarchais, 75004 Paris, Metro: Bastille. Closed Mon, and August.*

Although you can get wonderful pastries all over Paris, this remains one of the city's best known addresses for fine pastry. Judge for yourself. The tearoom is upstairs.

ICE CREAM: RAIMO, *59-61, Boulevard de Reuilly, near the Jardin de Reuilly, 75012 Paris; Metro: Daumesnil.*

This is a great stop if you are strolling along the *Promenade Plantée.* There are over 50 flavors of ice cream and sorbet to choose from (and you thought Baskin Robbins was tough with 31). Some are very exotic, such as cinnamon, maple syrup, tea, or chestnut.

Bercy

CLUB MED WORLD, *39, Cour Saint Emilion, 75012 Paris; Metro: Cour Saint Emilion; Tel. 08 10 81 04 10; Sunday brunch from 12pm to 4pm.*

On Sundays, Club Med World offers a special family-friendly brunch. Adults pay €30, kids pay €17. The food is only average, but parents get to enjoy it while children run and play with friendly Club Med instructors. For an extra fee, kids can take a trapeze or rock-climbing class. When you are done, you can walk off your meal together in the lovely Bercy Park or browse through the kid-friendly shops of the Cour Saint Emilion.

PARTIE DE CAMPAGNE, *36, Cour Saint Emilion, 75012 Paris; Metro: Cour Saint Emilion. Open daily.*

This bakery features delicious sandwiches and quiches that you can enjoy in the nearby Parc de Bercy.

Champs Elysées

HÔTEL DU COLISÉE (Best Western)***, *6, Rue du Colisée, 75008 Paris; Metro: Franklin Roosevelt; Tel. 01 56 88 26 26; Fax 01 56 88 26 00; Email: info@bw-colisée.com;; Rates: €170-206 (double); €230 (triple) Extra bed: €30. Buffet breakfast: €13.*

This hotel is conveniently located near the Champs Elysées, Arc de Triomphe, Place de la Concorde, and Tuileries Gardens. The rooms are tastefully decorated and are all air-conditioned. They are all doubles, but you can ask for an extra bed, or two rooms next to each other. Some are reserved for non-smokers.

HÔTEL DU ROND POINT DES CHAMPS ELYSÉES***, *10, rue Ponthieu, 75008 Paris; Metro: Franklin Roosevelt; Tel. 01 53 89 14 14; Fax 01 45 63 99 75; Email: hôtelrondpointchampsElysées@wanadoo.fr; Rates: €140 (standard doubles); €210 (superior doubles). Extra bed: €40. Buffet breakfast: €15.*

This hotel is friendlier than most in this neighborhood. The rooms are bright, airy, and very pretty. The location is very convenient for visiting the Arc de Triomphe, Champs Elysées, luxury shops, Tuileries Gardens and Place de la Concorde.

RESTAURANT: SPICY, *8, Avenue Franklin Roosevelt, 75008 Paris, Metro: Franklin Roosevelt. Tel. 01 56 59 62 59.*

This is a good address for fresh and interesting fare. It is close to the Champs Elysées, but somewhat removed from the heavy tourist scene of the avenue. The décor is hip and modern. You get a nice assortment of appetizers and main courses, such as pasta with olive tapenade sauce, roasted chicken with chutney, or catch of the day with baby vegetables. The €32 menu includes appetizer, main course, dessert (chocolate muffins, for example), and coffee. There is a kid's menu for €12 and a Sunday brunch for €32 with family-friendly entertainment.

RESTAURANT: THE CHICAGO PIZZA FACTORY, *5, Rue de Berri, 75008 Paris; Metro: George V; Tel. 01 45 62 50 23; Fax 01 45 63 87 56.*

Okay, it's not very French, but this restaurant is a good alternative to the over-priced fast food joints along the Avenue des Champs Elysées. American kids will feel right at home with the decor and menu offerings. It's very kid-friendly and the price is right: €10 and €15 for a lunch menu, including beverage; €17 for dinner; and an €8.50 kid's menu. Large pizzas are €15. For Saturday and Sunday lunch there are clowns and other kid-friendly attractions.

RESTAURANT: FLAM'S, *16, Rue du Colisée, 75008; Tel. 01 45 62 84 82; Metro: Franklin Roosevelt.*

This restaurant is part of a chain that features Alsacian-style food. The main offering is Flammenkeuche - a sort of white pizza with bacon, cheese, and onions. There are also salads and sandwiches. The food is decent and prices very attractive.

BAKERY: PAUL, *51, Avenue Franklin Roosevelt (corner Rue de Pontheiu), 75008; Metro: Franklin Roosevelt. Open daily.*

This large, bright bakery is just off the Rond Point des Champs Elysées. It features very nice pizzas, quiches, fresh fruit juice, and other delicious snacks. It is a great place to stop if you want breakfast, a light meal, or a snack as an alternative to the fast food chains along the Avenue des Champs Elysées. If the weather is good, you can take your food and enjoy a picnic in the gardens between the Rond Point and Place de la Concorde.

Opéra/Grands Boulevards

HÔTEL CHOPIN**, *10, Boulevard Montmartre (in the Passage Jouffroy), 75009 Paris; Metro: Grands Boulevards; Tel. 01 47 70 58 10; Fax 01 42 47 00 70; Rates: €75-86 (double); €94-100 (triple). Extra bed: free. Buffet breakfast: €7.*

This hotel is utterly charming and located in a wonderful spot. You actually go into one of Paris' pretty 19th century shopping galleries to get to the hotel entrance. Called the Passage Jouffroy, it features wonderful shops and tearooms to delight you and your kids. The gallery also contains Paris' wax museum, the Musée Grévin. The hotel has lovely rooms, especially on the top floor. Some are surprisingly spacious considering the price and class of hotel. You get views over the rooftops and skylights of the Passage Jouffroy. It's an experience unique to Paris that you will neither regret nor forget. Book in advance, however, because the rooms fill up quickly.

TERRACE CAFÉ, GALÉRIES LAFAYETTE DEPARTMENT STORE, *Rooftop Terrace; 40, Boulevard Haussman, 75009 Paris; Metro: Chaussée d'Antin. Open May-Sept, Mon-Sat, for late breakfast, lunch, and afternoon snack.*

This café offers nice pizzas, salads, sandwiches, pasta, and other light fare. The food is pretty good, but what you really come here for is the view. What a panorama it is! You can see most of the city, including a close-up view of the Palais Garnier Opera House roof and straight shot of Sacré Coeur Basilica on top of Montmartre.

TOP FLOOR CAFÉTERIA, LE PRINTEMPS DEPARTMENT STORE, *64, Boulevard Haussman, 75009 Paris; Metro: Havre Caumartin. Open Mon-Sat.*

If it is the wrong time of year or if the weather is too bad to eat at the Terrace Café in the Galéries Lafayette, head on over to this cafeteria. There is a wide selection of hot and cold platters, including a big salad bar. The dining room has big windows overlooking the Paris Opera and rooftops of the city. It's not as spectacular as the Galéries Lafayette terrace, but it's a close second.

RESTAURANT: LA PETITE RIPAILLE, *6, Passage des Panoramas, 75002 Paris; Tel. 01 53 40 83 15; Metro: Grands-Boulevards; Closed Sunday and Monday.*

This restaurant, located in one of Paris' wonderful XIXth century shopping galleries, offers good French fare at very reasonable prices. There are nice quiches and savory tortes for €9. The €16 menu features an appetizer, main course, and glass of house wine.

Light Fare

BUFFET DE LA COMTESSE, *13, Rue Taitbout, 75009 Paris; Metro: Chaussée d'Antin or Richelieu Drouot; Tel. 01 44 83 03 03. Open Mon-Fri.*

The original Comtesse du Barry shops were known for their foie gras and fancy bon bons. Here, you can sample the gourmet treats and eat in. It's very refined: for example, foie gras on thin slices of toast accompanied with fine green beans and artichoke hearts. The desserts are pretty yummy, too.

And because the French see babies as gourmets-in-training, this place is also very kid-friendly. They actually provide high chairs. Platters range from €5-10.

TEAROOM: LE VALENTIN, *30-32, Passage Jouffroy, 75009 Paris; Metro: Grands Boulevards; Tel. 01 47 70 88 50. Open daily.*

This charming tearoom sells delicious pastries and light meals inside one of Paris' wonderful 19th century shopping galleries. There are salads and sandwiches, as well as a daily hot-plate special. Kids can chose between ham and grilled chicken with mashed potatoes as part of their special €8 menu.

A LA MÈRE DE FAMILLE, *35, Rue Du Faubourg Montmartre, 75009, Metro: Grands Boulevards, Open Tues-Sat, 8:30am-1:30pm, 3pm-7pm.*

This is one of Paris' oldest candy shops. It features not only mouth-watering chocolates, but also many candy specialties from all over France. Pick some up as gifts to bring back home – if you can resist eating them all up yourselves.

Trocadéro & Passy

HÔTEL PASSY EIFFEL***, *10, Rue de Passy, 75016 Paris; Metro: Passy; Tel. 01 45 25 55 66; Fax 01 42 88 89 88; Email: passyeiffel@wanadoo.fr; Website: http://www.passyeiffel.com/index-gb.htm Rates: €122 (single); €140-170 (double); €170 (triple); €220 (4-person suite). Extra bed or crib provided free of charge. Buffet breakfast: €11.*

This hotel offers a very warm welcome to families. There are several, lovely family-sized suites. When those are booked, they will offer to put families in 2 adjoining doubles (with communicating doors) for the price of a suite. All of the rooms have air-conditioning and some have a view of the Eiffel Tower. The hotel is located in the lively Rue de Passy, filled with fun shopping, nice cafés, and an open-air market. You are a stone's throw from the Trocadéro Museums, and within easy access to the Eiffel Tower, Ranelagh Gardens, and Musée Marmottan with its collection of Monet paintings.

RESTAURANT: BÎSTROT DES VIGNES, *1, Rue Jean de Boulogne (between Rue de Passy and Rue de l'Annonciation); Metro: Passy; Closed on Sundays and in August.*

This restaurant offers delicious, traditional French fare at reasonable prices. Appetizers include choices such as shrimp and grapefruit salad; poached egg with sorrel and smoked salmon; zucchini and eggplant casserole with goat cheese. Main courses feature grilled fish on a bed of fennel; rabbit in mustard sauce; roasted chicken and potatoes; pasta with pesto. Top it all off with a fruit sorbet, chocolate mousse, fresh fruit tart, or cooked pear with ice cream and chocolate sauce. The menus range from €15-24.

RESTAURANT IN THE MUSÉE D'ART MODERNE DE LA VILLE DE PARIS, *11, Avenue du Président Wilson, 75016 Paris; Metro: Iéna; Open 10am-6pm. Closed Mon.*

When the weather is nice, you can eat on the big terrace next to the museum with a splendid view of the Seine River. You can choose from an assortment of fresh salads, sandwiches, quiches, and cold meat plates.

RESTAURANT: COFFEE PARISIEN, *7, Rue Gustave Courbet, 75016 Paris; Tel. 01 45 53 17 17; Metro: Trocadéro; Open daily, noon-midnight.*

This is a French version of an American-style diner. The décor and menu look American, but there is also a French twist. You can get American staples, such as chicken wings, nachos, hot club sandwiches, and tuna salad. Then there's salmon tartar, avocado and grapefruit salad, and tarte tatin (French version of apple pie). It's a good Franco-American combination in a nice, relaxed atmosphere. Count on €8-14 for main courses.

RESTAURANT: GR5, *19, Rue Gustave Courbet, 75016 Paris; Tel. 01 47 27 09 84; Metro: Trocadéro; Open for lunch and dinner. Closed Sun.*

This restaurant is named for the series of marked hiking trails, called chemins grandes randonnées (GR), that you can find all across France. The GR5 trail crosses France from North to South. You'll find plenty of food here to meet the needs of hungry hikers and tourists. You can get grilled salmon, curried chicken, and even steak tartar. For cold days, there are Alpine specialties such as cheese fondue and tartiflette (melted cheese and potatoes). All this is served on jolly red-checkered tablecloths. Main courses range from €11-14.

LIGHT FARE: TARTE JULIE, *14, Rue de l'Annonciation, 75016 Paris; Metro: Passy.*

This little restaurant/take out place offers a wide array of yummy quiches (lorraine, zucchini, spinach, feta and basil, salmon, etc). There are also salads, gratinées, and fruit pies. A kid's menu proposes a quiche, drink, and ice cream for €6. Adults can have a slice of quiche, drink, and coffee for €5.50. Add a dessert, and it's €6.50. A combination salad, drink, and dessert will cost you €8.

Montmartre

TERRASS HÔTEL****, *12, Rue Joseph de Maîstre, 75018 Paris (Metro: Blanche or Abesses); Tel. 01 46 06 72 85; Fax 01 42 52 29 11; Email: reservation@terrass-hôtel.com; WWW.terrass-hôtel.com; Rates: €250-300 (double, kids under 12 sleep in parents room for free); €340 (junior suite).*

This lovely luxury hotel is located across the street from the Montmartre Cemetery. It is a little off the beaten path. However, because of that you get four-star amenities at a more affordable price. What's more, you get wonderful views of the city, thanks to the hotel's hillside location. Rooms are large and pretty, decorated with colorful Provencal fabrics. They are all air-conditioned. Two floors are reserved for non-smokers, and two rooms are specially equipped for people with disabilities. The roof garden restaurant, open from May to September, offers fine food and a great view. The two-room family suites offer charm, space, and large balconies with sweeping views.

The Terrass Hotel's restaurant offers a wide selection of fresh dishes at its daily buffet. There are also menus ranging in price from €20-30. The melon soup or gazpacho are lovely choices for a hot day. The chef will prepare special dishes or portions for children.

TIMHÔTEL MONTMARTRE***, *11, rue Rovignan and 11, Place Emile Godeau; Website: www.timhotel.com/hotels/us/montmartre.html. Rates: €120 (doubles); €170 (triple); €210 (suite for 4). Buffet breakfast: €8.50.*

This hotel is located in the heart of Montmartre, next door to the Bateau Lavoir where Picasso and many others lived as starving artists in the 1920s. It is on a lovely square, away from traffic. The rooms have recently been redone. Each floor is dedicated to a specific artist, such as Toulouse Lautrec or Renoir. There are great views, especially from the upper floors.

HÔTEL UTRILLO**, *7, Rue Aristide Bruant, 75018 Paris (Metro: Abbesses or Blanche); Tel. 01 42 58 13 44; Fax 01 42 23 93 88; Email: adel.utrillo@wanadoo.fr; Website: www.hotel-paris-utrillo.com/; Rates: €76-82 (double); €96 (triple); Extra bed: €12; Buffet Breakfast: €6.5.*

This cheerful hotel is comfortably nestled towards the bottom of the Montmartre hill. It was recently renovated, so everything is fresh. The rooms are tastefully decorated in bright colors to celebrate the hotel's name (Maurice Utrillo was a Montmartre painter) and artistic history of the neighborhood. There's a warm welcome and even a sauna if you want to sweat off your troubles.

RESTAURANT: RELAIS DE LA BUTTE, *Corner of Rue des Trois Frères and Rue Ravignan, on the Place Emile Godeau; 75018 Paris; Metro: Abbesses.*

This is a fun restaurant, especially in the summer when you can eat outside on the pretty terrace. It is just off a quiet square where children can run between courses. On the upper half of the square is the historic Bateau Lavoir building where Picasso, Modigliani, Juan Gris, and many other artists and poets lived for next to nothing. The original building was destroyed in a fire in 1970, but was rebuilt according to the original plans. It still houses starving artists. The restaurant serves up fresh salads, pasta dishes, daily specials, and Italian-style desserts at very reasonable prices. The daily menu runs about €13: main courses €10-12.

RESTAURANT: RESTO ZÈBRE, *38, rue Lepic, 75018 Paris; Metro: Blanche or Abbesses. Open Mon-Sat.*

This lively little place is tucked along the jolly Rue Lepic. It attracts lots of locals who come to enjoy a light salad, pasta dish, or daily specials such as grilled tuna and onglet de boeuf. Prices are very reasonable, ranging from €6-11 for main courses.

ICE CREAM: LA BUTTE GLACÉE. *14, Rue Norvins, 75018 Paris (near Place du Tertre); Metro: Abesses.*

A great place to stop for ice cream or sorbet, with all sorts of tantalizing fruit flavors.

Chartres

HÔTEL: LE GRAND MONARQUE (Best Western)***, *22, Place des Epars; 28005 Chartres; Tel. 02 37 18 15 15; Fax 02 37 36 34 18; Email: info@bw-grand-monarque.com; www.bw-grand-monarque.com; Rates: €115-138 (doubles, triples); €235 (suite, sleeps 4-5). Note: some of the adjacent double rooms can be linked together as a 2-room and 2-bath suite. Buffet breakfast: €12. Garage parking: €10.*

This Grand Monarch does its best to offer rooms and service fit for a king, yet remain family-friendly. It is a family-run hotel located in the center of town, less than a 10-minute walk from the cathedral. The rooms are spacious and decked out with wallpaper and fabrics that can best be described as royal. They vary in size and style. The attic rooms are high on charm, the ones overlooking the garden are nice and quiet. There are two restaurants in the hotel. The fancy one offers gourmet meals with menus ranging from €25-54. The chef is very willing to make special meals and portions for children. The less formal brasserie offers non-stop service and good, traditional French fare.

HÔTEL: LE BOEUF COURRONNÉ**, *15, Place Châtelet; Tel. 02 37 18 06 06. Room rates: €29-56. Triples and quadruples available.*

This is a nice little hotel, located within an easy 5 minute walk from the cathedral. The rooms are not large, but they are very pleasant. The hotel staff goes out of its way to be friendly to families, offering free cribs and high chairs. The hotel's restaurant serves traditional country dishes. The food is decent, but will not blow you away. You can eat on the outdoor terrace in nice weather. The kid's menu (€8.50) offers a choice of chicken or hamburger, with dessert and a drink. The adult menus range from €20-30.

RESTAURANT: LE PICHET, *19, Rue du Cheval Blanc, 1 block from the cathedral, and near the tourist office; Tel. 02 37 21 08 35; Open for lunch daily and dinner on Thur, Fri, and Sat.*

This restaurant is very popular, because it serves up good French fare at reasonable prices. There's onion soup, duck, and lamb. On Sundays there's the special stewed chicken. The kid's menu offers a hamburger or chicken nuggets, fries, and ice cream for €6. Salads and soups are €6, main courses are €10. For dessert you can indulge in brownies, chocolate mousse, apple pie, or other regional specialties.

RESTAURANT: BRASSERIE NÔTRE DAME, *36, rue des Changes, Chartres (in the old town, 1 block from the cathedral); Tel. 02 37 36 14 54; Open daily.*

Chartres has many restaurants that offer fine dining and gourmet menus. This one doesn't, but what it does have is an affordable menu and family-friendly atmosphere. There are lots of offerings to choose from including soups, salads, sandwiches, omelets, and full meals. The daily special runs €8.50. In our case this was a duck in orange sauce (*Canard à l'Orange*) with scalloped potatoes (*Gratin Dauphinois*). The menus range in price from €12-23 for several courses and dessert. The tables are crowded together, the scene is good-natured, and there's all sorts of interesting art on the walls.

Versailles

RESTAURANT AND CAFÉ: LA PETITE VENISE, *in the gardens of the Château de Versailles, near the Grand Canal, by the bike rental; Open daily, 9am-7pm. Breakfast, Lunch, and afternoons snacks.*

This restaurant/café offers a gracious welcome in a pretty setting. The outdoor terrace is quiet and lovely. The interior dining room features a very modern décor, contrasting with the fact that the building was originally part of the royal stables. You can still see the wooden hay racks along the walls. The restaurant offers a nice variety of lunch choices at reasonable prices. The *Grandes Assiettes* (big plates) feature open-faced sandwiches, with either goat cheese and nuts, smoked salmon, foie gras, or a selection of vegetables all served on delicious Poilâne bread for €11-15. The kid's menu offers a hard boiled egg or paté; followed by a choice of ham or hamburger with fries, and ice cream or chocolate mousse for €8.40. A grander menu offers a nice array of appetizers, entrees, and desserts for €22. There are also breakfast pastries and fancy ice-cream treats.

RESTAURANT: LA FLOTTILLE, *in the gardens of the Château de Versailles, on the Grand Canal. Open daily, 8am-8pm.*

This restaurant offers lots of good basic café food in a pretty setting, just across from the boat rental for the Grand Canal. You can get a grilled chicken and salad for €10, warm goat cheese salad for €9.50, and an assortment of salads, pizzas, crêpes, omelets, and sandwiches for €5-8. The kid's menu offers a choice of chicken nuggets or fish sticks, with fries, a drink, and a surprise for €8.50. For dinner you can opt for the €21 menu with plenty of choices for appetizers, main course, and dessert.

RESTAURANT LEBANON, *11, rue de Satory, Versailles (Side street, near the front entrance of the Palace); Open 11:45-2:15, 6:45-10 for lunch and dinner. Closed Sundays.*

This restaurant is located in a lively pedestrian street lined with ethnic restaurants from all over the world. We chose this one on a lark and were not disappointed. The owners, a Franco-Lebanese couple, couldn't be nicer. The food is really delicious, with a good assortment of middle-eastern appetizers, kabobs, and kéftès. Prices are very reasonable, including weekday lunch menus at €10.50-13.

Chantilly

RESTAURANT: CARROUSEL GOURMAND, *in the Musée Vivant du Cheval, Grandes Ecuries, Château de Chantilly. Tel. 03 44 57 19 77.. Open daily, except Tues, March-October. Only open on weekends during the winter.*

You can watch some of the horsemanship displays from this nice family-friendly restaurant in the Horse Museum. The €11 kid's menu offers a burger, scalloped potatoes, dessert, and a drink. The adult menus at €14 and €20 feature regional specialties such as duck in honey sauce or rabbit in cider.

Fontainebleau

RESTAURANT: LE CAVEAU DES DUCS, *24, Rue de Ferrare, Fontainebleau. Tel. 01 64 22 05 05.*

Sit among the arched stone walls and imagine yourself eating with Dukes. The building dates from the 17th century. The menu features traditional French food. Kids can order a hamburger with pasta from the special €10 kid's menu. Adults have a wide range of platters and menus (€20-40) to choose from.

TEAROOM: DÉLICE IMPÉRIAL, *1, Rue Grande, Fontainebleau. Tel. 01 64 22 20 70.*

We're sure that even Emperor Napoleon himself would qualify the wonderful pastries and ice creams here as imperial delights. You can also get a light meal and enjoy it on the terrace in nice weather.

Vaux le Vicomte

RESTAURANT: L'ECUREUIL, *in the Vaux le Vicomte Palace. Maincy. Open 11-6, until 11 for candlelight tours.*

This self-service restaurant and tearoom is named for Nicolas Fouquet's emblem, the squirrel. It is located in one of the wings of the palace, with a lovely terrace where you can eat in nice weather. The food is good and reasonably priced. There is a kid's menu for €4 and daily special for €7. The restaurant is usually open for lunch and tea, but it also serves dinner on the evenings of candle-lit tours.

Giverny

RESTAURANT: LES NYMPHÉAS, *Rue Claude Monet, on the square across from Monet's house, Giverny. Tel. 02 32 21 20 31. Open daily except Monday, 9:30am-6pm. Closed November-March.*

Why traipse all over town when you can find a perfectly handy, kid-friendly meal across the street from Monet's house. Although this restaurant gets busy and crowded during high tourist season, you still get a pleasant welcome and good food. The prices are reasonable with €10-15 platters and menus. The lunch offerings are light and varied, with plenty of salads, quiche, soup, pasta dishes, and hot plate specials.

Disneyland Paris

Note: As with many hotels in Paris, you may be able to obtain special discounts or better rates by visiting the Disneyland Paris site, or booking a hotel through a travel discount operator, such as Orbitz, Travelocity, or others.

DISNEYLAND HOTEL****, *Disney Village. Tel. 01 60 45 65 00. Rates: €400 and up for a family of four, including 2-day pass.; Breakfast: €15 for adults; €12 for children.*

A pink Victorian building houses this luxurious Disney hotel. The lobby, fireplace, and staircase are majestic. The rooms are spacious and designed for a family of four. Enjoy the indoor pool, exercise facilities, and breakfast with Mickey, Minnie and other Disney characters.

HOTEL NEW YORK****, *Disney Village. Tel. 01 60 45 73 00. Rates: €400 and up for a family of four, including 2-day pass (includes breakfast).*

This hotel is modeled after 1920s New York, complete with brown-stones and skyscrapers. There are indoor/outdoor swimming pools, tennis courts, a roller skating rink, workout rooms, and all the amenities of a 4-star hotel.

NEWPORT BAY CLUB HOTEL***, *Disney Village. Tel. 01 60 45 55 00; Rates: €350 and up for a family of four, with a 2-day pass (includes breakfast).*

You can admire the Disney Lake from a rocking chair on the big front porch of this New England style hotel. Enjoy the swimming pools, exercise facilities, gardens, and even some apartment style rooms of this hotel.

SEQUOIA LODGE***, *Disney Village. Tel. 01 60 45 51 00. Rates: €350 and up for a family of four, with a 2-day pass (includes breakfast).*

This lodge is nestled among a forest of Sequoia trees. There is an indoor pool with a water slide and Jacuzzi, and an outdoor pool in the summer. There are exercise facilities, kids games, kids activities, and a kids menu at the restaurant.

HOLIDAY INN AT DISNEYLAND RESORT***, *20, Avenue la Fosse des Pressoirs, Marne la Valee. Tel. (in US) 888/HOLIDAY; in France 01 64 63 37 37; www.ichotelsgroup.com/h/d/hi/1/en/hd/pardi. Rates: €100 (family room for 4); €134 (2-room suite for 4). Other options with breakfast or theme park entries also available.*

This hotel is located 10 minutes from the Disneyland Resorts via free shuttle bus. It offers family friendly rooms, including ones with a double bed and two bunks or 2-room suites with a queen size bed, two bunk beds, and circus-themed decor.

HOTEL CHEYENNE**, *Disney Village. Tel. 01 60 45 62 00. Rates: €300 and up for a family of four, with a 2-day pass (includes breakfast).*

This hotel comes straight out of a Wild West movie set, including the cowboy boot lamps and a saloon. The rooms are nicely arranged for families with a double bed and two bunk beds. There is a fort/playground for kids to explore and enjoy. Little ones can even go on pony rides. The restaurant serves BBQ style food.

HOTEL SANTA FE**, *Disney Village. Tel. 01 60 45 78 00. Rates: €250 and up, with a 2-day pass for a family of four.*

This is the least expensive of the hotels in the Disneyland Park. True to its name, this hotel's theme is New Mexico. The rooms are arranged in Pueblo-style villages. They feature two double beds. There is an imitation Anasazi village for children to play in and explore. The restaurant serves Tex-Mex food.

DAVY CROCKETT RANCH, *Disney Village. Tel. 01 60 45 69 00. Rates: €250 and up, with a 2-day pass for a 1-bedroom bungalow (includes take-out breakfast).*

This ranch offers lots of outdoor activities, including archery, tennis, horseback riding, roller blading, and bike rentals. You can park your RV or rent a 1-2 bedroom bungalow that sleeps 4-6 people. There's an outdoor picnic table and BBQ next to each bungalow. A little train takes you to the Disney Village and a tropical swimming pool.

Parc Astérix

HÔTEL DES TROIS HIBOUX***, *Parc Astérix, Plailly; Tel. 03 44 62 30 30. Rates: €190-250 (family room) with breakfast. There are special rates that include day passes to the Parc Astérix and are calculated according to the number of adults, kids 12-16, and kids 3-11. Kids under 3 are free. Prices go down if you stay more than one night.*

This hotel is designed for families visiting the Parc Astérix. The place feels like a big lodge, with lots of wooden paneling. The family size rooms feature a main room with double bed and fold out couch, plus a side room with bunk beds, and a modern bathroom.

RESTAURANT: ARCIMBOLDO, *in Parc Astérix, across from the big lake.*

This restaurant is decorated to look like four famous paintings by Arcimboldo that hang in the Louvre Museum. They represent the four seasons and are composed of faces made from fruits and vegetables of the seasons. Here you get traditional French fare like cassoulet and wild boar.

RESTAURANT: LA HALTE DES CHEVALIERS, *in Parc Asterix, outdoor eatery with tents.*

Here you can enjoy typical Gaul food, like roasted boar and venison.

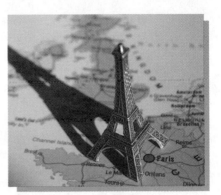

PART 2: PLANNING YOUR TRIP

Traveling with kids, especially very small children, can involve a lot of stuff. I used to pride myself on traveling with bags that were so compact I could carry them long distances and never had to check my luggage. That ended when we took our first-born son to Paris as a 7-month old. Suddenly we had a stroller, car seat, porta-crib, diaper bag, favorite teddy bear, toys, baby snacks, and full supply of pint-size clothes. Thankfully, as our boys got bigger, the amount of stuff they needed got smaller. They also started pulling their own roller-board suitcases. From ages 3-6 they used kid-size suitcases. Now if we have a trip lasting 1-2 weeks, we all use the size that can fit in the overhead compartment of a plane (12" X 20"). For a trip of 3 weeks or more, we use the next size up (16" X 24").

Parent Tip: Most children like to pack or help pack their own bags. It is exciting and empowering. Just make sure that you maintain supervision authority (and if needed, veto power). Once they are done, go through a checklist together to ensure they haven't forgotten anything important. Also check for hoards of unnecessary items, like the time one of our boys wanted to bring along his entire rock collection.

When packing, try to remember that less is better. No matter how many times you expect to find a porter or luggage cart, there will still be moments when you are the one who has to lift or carry your suitcases. You will have a hard time finding a cab if you have lots of gear, and big bags will take up a lot of space in your hotel or apartment room (generally small anyway by American standards).

If your trip includes airplane travel, be sure to bring enough toiletries, medicine, clothing (such as a fresh shirt and set of socks and underwear), and necessities in your carry-on luggage to last you an extra day. This will see you through if your plane or baggages are delayed. If you are traveling with a baby or small children pack several sets of clothes, a blanket, snacks, small toys, and a 2-day supply of diapers and wipes in your carry-on luggage to get through the flight and first day.

Note that other than special medications, most things you will need are readily available in Paris.

Parent Tip: Small toys and activities will help make the plane trip and down time more fun. Some suggestions:

• Teenie-beenies and other small stuffed animals
• Micro-machines, Polly Pocket, Legos, beads, and other small toys. Carry them in Ziploc bags.
• Small pads of paper, art supplies, stickers, activity books
• Travel versions of chess, checkers, or other games
• Books on tape or CD and favorite music with a walkman or CD player
• Lightweight, paperback books. You may want to use this trip as an opportunity to introduce your kids to classic chapter books, such a *Charlotte's Web*, *From the Mixed Up Files of Mrs. Basil E. Frankweiller*, Harry Potter, the Chronicles of Narnia, or *A Series of Unfortunate Events*.

Binoculars: Bring some for yourself and for your kids. They are very useful for looking at gargoyles and other faraway features.

Cameras: You will want pictures to remember your trip, so don't forget to bring along your camera or video recorder. Consider bringing cameras for your children, too. It's a great way to keep them engaged and looking at the sights around them.

There are wonderful, kid-friendly cameras on the market, including some for smaller children that you can hold with two hands. Disposable cameras are also a good option (you'll have no trouble finding these and extra film in Paris, if needed). Teenagers enjoy the instant gratification of Polaroid and digital cameras. There are also excellent books for kids introducing them to the rudiments of photography and how to do fun tricks. *Tricky Pix* by the Klutz Company includes both a book and a camera, with fun tips on how to make goofy pictures. Other useful books include: *Picture This: Fun Photography and Crafts (Kids Can Do It)* by Debra Friedman; *I Wanna Take Me a Picture: Teaching Photography and Writing to Children* by Wendy Ewald; *Cameras* (All About Series) by Chris Oxlade; *Absolute Beginner's Guide to Taking Great Photos* by Jim Miotke; and *Photography* (Make it Work! Science) by Andrew Haslam.

When the trip is over, encourage your children to create an album using their favorite photos, post cards, ticket stubs, and other flat souvenirs. It makes a great keepsake, especially if they add notes or comments in the margins.

Art supplies: It's amazing how something as simple as a pad of paper and box of colored pencils, markers, or crayons can help while away the hours on a plane ride or waiting for the next course in a restaurant. This is true even for our family, which is not particularly artistic. If your children are budding artists they will find ample inspiration in Paris. They may want to copy something they see in a museum. Or like many painters before them, they can try their hand at drawing the Eiffel Tower, a view from the Pont des Arts, a pony from a carrousel, flowers in Monet's garden at Giverny, the list is endless...

If your children balk at the sight of a blank piece of paper you may want to bring such items as coloring books, fun pads, activity books, mazes and puzzles, and MadLibs. You can also purchase nice examples of these in most of the major museum gift shops in Paris. They are useful for keeping growing minds busy anytime you want a breather or face a wait.

Travel diaries: Travel diaries are a great way for both parents and kids to record souvenirs and impressions of their trip. They don't need to be fancy, a small spiral notebook works well. You can also purchase special kids' diaries, travel diaries, or even kids' travel diaries at any major bookstore. The contents of any of these can take many forms. Some kids like to write each entry as a letter or postcard. Others like to respond to prompts: for example, "what I saw", "my favorite things", "my least favorite things", "something new I saw/did today", etc. Many children do best if they can combine writing with drawings, stickers, or souvenirs that they can paste into their diary. You may want to have them pick out a post card or two each day to insert in the journal and write about. Small children might want to just draw pictures or have you do the writing as they dictate their impressions.

We know one family that keeps a group travel journal in which each member writes a page at the end of the day. However, be aware that pre-teens and teens may not want to share their thoughts with anyone else. If so, encourage them to keep a secret journal, and respect their privacy. They'll be glad you did when they re-read it years later.

WHAT TO KNOW BEFORE YOU GO

Passports: Each member of your family must have a valid passport to enter France. No visa is necessary for stays of less than three months. If you need to obtain or renew a passport for any member of your family, do not put it off until the last minute! It can take as many as 90 days to process – even longer if you need to obtain a copy of your birth certificate or other required proofs of citizenship or identity. Passport application forms and instructions are available at your local Passport Agency Office, county courthouse, some post offices, and some travel agencies. They are also accessible online at: *http://travel.state.gov/*, or you can get them via mail by calling the National Passport Information Center: Tel. 900/225-5674.

Be aware that several new rules govern the issuance of children's passports. Make sure you read the special instructions for children's passports carefully, as rules change. As of January 2006, the following applied:

• As of July 2, 2001, any child under the age of 14 must have an application signed and presented by BOTH parents (or by one parent with a form and notarized signature from the other).

• Single parents or guardians must submit proof that a sole parent has custody or guardianship of that child.

• Even if you are renewing a child's passport and have the previous one with you, you also will be asked to present the child's birth certificate.

• Children's passport forms must be submitted in person at a designated post office or Passport Agency Office. Your child also must be present.

• Note that in some busy cities, you must call in advance for an appointment and may not get one for 2-3 weeks.

• Remember that adult passports are valid for 10 years, but children's passports are only valid for 5 years.

Climate: Although Paris is roughly on the same latitude as Fargo, North Dakota, the climate is much milder. Days are short in the winter, but gloriously long in the summer (in June the sun doesn't set until 10 pm). Winters are chilly, but temperatures do not dip much below freezing. The late fall and early spring can be quite rainy. Early fall and late spring are often sunny and pleasant. Summers are generally warm with occasional showers. Very hot weather is uncommon, which is lucky because it makes the city muggy and uncomfortable, and it raises pollution levels.

Customs & Fashion: French society tends be more formal than American. You will win major points by greeting people with a *Bonjour Monsieur* or *Bonjour Madame*, even if they are the only words of French you ever learn. If you do speak some rudiments of French, be sure to use the formal form "vous" rather than the informal "tu" with anyone other than close friends or children. If you are invited for dinner to someone's home, try not to arrive empty handed. A bouquet of flowers or box of chocolate is appropriate. If you know before you go that you will be visiting French people during your stay, you may want to bring something representing where you live. Examples could include a bottle of the local BBQ sauce, sports memorabilia from your local team, or a book of photographs featuring your hometown or state.

Clothing standards also tend to be a bit more formal in Paris. After all, it's one of the world's fashion capitals. As an adult you won't actually get kicked out of most places for wearing jeans, a t-shirt, and a baseball hat, but you will stand out (and do remember to remove your hat anytime you are indoors). Somehow, even when Parisians dress that way, they seem to look more put together. Maybe it's because they iron everything. If you want to blend in more, simply dress as people do for casual Fridays at work. Standards for children are pretty lenient, although you may want to avoid t-shirts with loud logos. If you want nice clothes for your kids, Paris is a great place to buy them. See below for a list of kids' clothing stores.

Regardless of the time of year you visit Paris, it is always a good idea to dress in layers. Even in the summer, the weather can switch from cool to warm and back again. Winters can be damp, and you will glad you packed that extra sweater or layer of fleece to ward off the cold. Be sure to bring a folding umbrella and rain gear for the kids.

Tipping: A 15% tip is usually included (*service compris*) with your bill in a restaurant or café. If the bill says *service non compris*, then you should leave a 15% tip. The customary tip for taxi rides is 10% as is the usual tip for hairdressers. A small tip of €0.50-1 is customary for washroom or cloakroom attendants. For hotel porters and room service €1.50 is the norm. A €1-2 tip is customary for tour guides and tour bus drivers.

Health insurance: Before you leave home, contact your health insurance company to see if it covers medical expenses abroad. If so, don't forget to bring along your membership card. If not, you may want to purchase supplemental health insurance for travelers.

The US Department of State maintains an extensive list of US-based companies that offer travel health insurance and emergency evacuation services at http://travel.state.gov/travel/tips/health/health_1185.html The website www.insuremytrip.com allows you to compare travel insurance plans. Another option for children and students ages 12 to 26 years; adults who are teachers or faculty members; and university students is coverage through the international student, youth, or teacher's ID available for $25. This card offers coverage for up to $2,000 in medical expenses and $5,000 in evacuation fees. It also offers many discounts to museums and other attractions. For more information visit www.isecard.com/index.html.

Safety: Paris is a relatively safe city, particularly compared to American ones. You can walk comfortably in nearly any neighborhood, especially the popular tourist and residential areas. As always, you do need to exercise common street sense and be careful of traffic.

Visitors to Paris do need to be mindful of pickpockets, however, particularly in crowded tourist areas or on public transportation. Stay alert as to the whereabouts of your wallet and valuables.

Our greatest fear as parents has always been of losing track of our children in unfamiliar places. Here are some tips to lesson the risk and anxiety of a lost child:

• If your children are old enough, have them learn the name of your hotel, hosts, or street and address where you are staying. Show them where it is on a map. Point out nearby landmarks. Pick up several of your hotel's business cards at the front desk and distribute one to each member of your group.

• If your children are small, secure a label to their clothes, such as the paper luggage labels you get at the airport. Include the child's name, your name, and your address and phone information in Paris. Make sure to show you kids what you are doing and explain why, with words such as, "If you are ever lost, this tag will show a grownup your name and where we are staying, so we can find you".

• When visiting a large museum or sight, be sure first to establish an easy-to-find meeting place in case you become separated. We learned this lesson one day when our older son got ahead of us in the Louvre (the world's largest museum) without a rendez-vous plan. When I caught up with him, I asked what he would have done if he had become lost. He answered with perfect 9-year old confidence, "I would have waited for you under the glass pyramid, of course." It was a great plan, except that the rest of us had not been clued in to it.

• Be sure to teach your children the age-old rule of staying in one place if they do get lost. You are more likely to find them if they are not a moving target. We also tell our kids to use the same advice we give at home. If you are lost, tell an official helper (like a police officer or museum guard) or look for another family with children and ask them to help.

• Don't forget to keep track of your adult companions, too. While my husband and I have yet to lose a child in a foreign place, we have lost track of each other. Be sure to have a meeting plan if you are off on separate missions, and throw in a back-up plan just in case.

• Equip everyone with a walky talky. Modern ones are lightweight, easy to use, and have a range of 2 miles or more. They come in sets of two, but you can buy more and set them all to the same frequency. Not only can you use them to keep track of each other, they are also handy when you need to stand in a long line. You can leave one adult in line, while the rest of the group looks at souvenirs, gets a snack, or runs around until it is nearly your turn.

BOOKS, VIDEOS, & WEBSITES ON PARIS
Fiction for younger children

Anatole over Paris, and other Anatole adventures by Eve Titus. Whittlesey House Weekly Reader Children's Book Club,1961. These stories describe the adventures of Anatole, a clever mouse who lives in Paris.

Eloise in Paris, by Kay Thompson, 1957, Six-year old Eloise, who normally lives at the Plaza Hotel in New York, visits Paris with her usual pluck and humor. Although the pictures were drawn in the 1950s, they still give an excellent view of Paris today.

Linnea in Monet's Garden, by Christina Bjork and Lena Anderson, Stockholm, Rabén and Sjögren Publishers, 1985. Young Linnea and her friend Mr. Bloom visit Monet's paintings in Paris and his house and gardens at Giverny. A lovely introduction to Impressionist art.

Madeleine, Madeleine and the Gypsies, Madeleine and the Bad Hat, and other Madeleine stories by Ludwig Bemelmans. The classic adventures of a little girl who lives in a boarding school located "in an old house in Paris". Lovely illustrations feature major city sights.

Metro Cat, by Marsha D. Arnold, Golden Books Pub. Co. Inc., 2001. Sophie is a pampered cat who accidentally finds herself in the subway one day where she discovers a new life of adventures.

The Red Balloon, (adapted from the movie) by Albert Lamorisse, New York, Doubleday & Company Inc, 1956. The adventures of a lonely boy and the balloon that brightens his life in the Belleville neighborhood of Paris.

Non-fiction for younger kids

Daily Life in Ancient and Modern Paris (Cities Through Time Series), by Sarah Hoban and Bob Moulder, Lerner Publications Company, 2000. This book brings together glimpses of Paris' history and everyday life.

The Inside-Outside Book of Paris, by Roxie Munro, E.P. Dutton, 1992. This books looks both inside and outside great Parisian sights, such as the Eiffel Tower and Pompidou Center, as well as more mundane places such as a pastry shop or booksellers along the Seine. An interesting and kid-friendly introduction to the city.

Let's Visit the Louvre Museum, by Claude Delafosse, Gallimard Jeunesse, (English edition, Moonlight Publishing, London, 1995. A handsome introduction to some of the greatest treasures of the Louvre Museum highlighted with transparent pages that let you see inside the glass pyramid or Egyptian mummy case.

Look What Came from France, Harvey Miles, New York, Franklin Watts, a division of Grolier Publishing, 1999. From scuba gear to April Fools' Day jokes, a nicely illustrated book outlining common products and customs that have come to us from France.

Monuments That Tell the Story of Paris, by Jean Daly, Editions Parigramme, Paris, 2001. A chronological introduction to some of the great monuments of Paris: from the Roman Arena and Baths, through Medieval and Renaissance splendors, to modern constructions such as the Pompidou Center, Grand Arche de la Défense, and La Villette Science Museum.

Paris (Cities of the World Series), by Conrad R. Stein, Children's Press, A Division of Grolier Publishing Co, Inc. New York, NY. 1996. This is an excellent introduction to the history and culture of Paris, described in broad strokes and illustrated with big, attractive photos.

Paris 1789: A Guide to Paris on the Eve of the Revolution, by Wright, Larousse Kingfisher Chambers, 1999. This book is written as a real travel guide to the Paris of 1789. It is a witty and clever introduction to Paris and the French Revolution.

This is Paris, by Miroslav Sasek, The Macmillan Company, 1959. With 1950s graphics and simple text, this remains one of the most delightful books on Paris for children. Look for it at your public library.

Books for Children About French Artists

Suzette and the Puppy: A Story About Mary Cassatt, by Joan Sweeny and Jennifer Heyd Wharton, Barron's Juveniles, 2000. This is a fictionalized tale about a little girl and a dog based on a painting by Mary Cassatt. It evokes life in Paris in the 1870s among the Impressionists.

Picasso and the Girl with a Ponytail: A Story About Pablo Picasso. By Laurence Anholt, Barron's Educational Series, Inc. 1998. Based on a true story of Picasso and a young girl named Sylvette whose profile and ponytale inspired many of his paintings.

Smart About Art Series, Grosset and Dunlap. This series features fictionalized stories about famous artists. Titles include:

Edgar Degas: Paintings that Dance by Maryann Cocca-Leffler; *Henri Matisse: Drawing with Scissors* by Jane O'Connor; *Claude Monet: Sunshine and Waterlilies* by True Kelley; *Pablo Picasso: Breaking All the Rules* by True Kelley; and *Vincent van Gogh: Sunflowers and Swirly Stars* by Joan Holub.

Katie Meets the Impressionists; *Katie and the Mona Lisa*; and *Katie and the Sunflowers,* by James Mayhew, Orchard Books. A little girl goes on adventures when she steps into famous paintings and gets to know some of the artists, their subjects, and styles.

Getting to Know the World's Greatest Artists Series by Mike Venezia, Grolier Publishing, Children's Press, New York. These books are wonderfully written for children with copies of the artists' works juxtaposed with those of their contemporaries. There are also funny cartoon illustrations by the author to help put each artist's story into a context that kids can understand. Some of the featured artists include: Mary Cassat, Paul Cezanne, Leonardo Da Vinci, Paul Gauguin, Henri Matisse, Claude Monet, Pablo

Picasso, Pierre Auguste Renoir, Henri de Toulouse-Lautrec, Vincent Van Gogh.

Fiction for preteens

The Adventures of Asterix the Gaul, and other Asterix comic books by Albert Uderzo and René Goscinny. These delightfully witty comic books feature the Gaul warrior Asterix and his pal Obelix living in 50 BC, who help their little Breton village resist the Roman occupation. Although they to not take place in Paris per se, they are a wonderful introduction to French history and culture.

A Chapel of Thieves, by Bruce Clements, Farrar Straus & Giroux (Juv), 2002. A teen boy adventure story set in 19th century Paris.

The Family Under the Bridge, by Natalie Savage Carlson, Harper Collins Children's Books, 1958. The story of a beggar and a poor family who meet as they live under a bridge in post-WWII Paris.

Mystery of the Metro (My Name Is Paris, Book 1), by Elizabeth Howard, Random House, 1987. This is a teen girl mystery adventure set in Paris at the turn of the 20th century.

Rosemary in Paris by Barbara Robertson, Hourglass Adventures #2, Winslow Press, 2001. A 10-year old girl's adventure at the 1889 Paris International Exhibition.

Books for teenagers

The DaVinci Code, by Dan Brown. This mystery/adventure story has become a best-seller and Hollywood movie. It involves great escapes from the Louvre and other Paris spots. True fans can go on entire DaVinci Code tours of Paris, but most teens will enjoy looking for clues from the book in the St. Sulpice Church and Louvre Museum.

The Hunchback of Nôtre Dame, by Victor Hugo. Set in Medieval Paris, this is the tale of the deformed hunchback Quasimodo, his love for the Gypsy girl, Esmeralda, and the public intolerance that leads them both to tragic fates.

An Immovable Feast, by Ernest Hemingway. This largely autobiographical account describes Hemingway's life in Paris as a starving young writer.

Is Paris Burning? by Larry Collins and Dominique Lapierre. A factual account of the Liberation of Paris during WWII, including how close Hitler came to destroying every major monument and bridge in the city.

The Man in the Iron Mask, by Alexandre Dumas. Set during the reign of King Louis XIV, a man is mysteriously imprisoned with his identity hidden behind an iron mask.

Les Miserables, by Victor Hugo. The saga of Jean Valjean, an escaped convict trying to make good but dogged by the relentless police agent, Javert.

His tale criss-crosses those of other characters forced into desperate situations by the trials of war, poverty, and revolution in 19th century Paris.

Père Goriot, by Honore de Balzac. This 19th century novel contrasts the lives of Pere Goriot whose love for his daughters leads to his ruin, with that of Rastignac, an upstart from the country bent on climbing the ladder of fortune and social ambition in Paris.

A Tale of Two Cities, by Charles Dickens. A Dickens classic set in Paris during the French Revolution.

The Three Musketeers, by Alexandre Dumas. This heroic adventures of Athos, Porthos, Aramis, and d'Artagnan, Royal Musketeers in the service of King Louis XIII.

The Bald Soprano, by Eugene Ionesco. A delightful example of French Modern Theater of the Absurd. It has played non-stop at the Théâtre de la Huchette in Paris since its first opening in the 1950s.

Videos

The Aristocats, A Walt Disney classic featuring a great jazz party among the rooftops of Paris.

Everafter, A charming version of the Cinderella story, set during the reign of France's king Francois 1st. Though it does not take place in Paris, it gives a nice glimpse of Renaissance France, including a Jeu de Paume match and Leonardo da Vinci, whose masterpieces such as the Mona Lisa still hang in the Louvre.

Madeleine, A delightful romp through Paris based on the books by Ludwig Bemelmans.

The Man in the Iron Mask, a French classic by Alexandre Dumas set during the reign of Louis XIV and filmed at the Vaux le Vicomte Palace outside of Paris.

The Red Balloon, A French classic about a lonely boy named Pascal whose life is brightened by a magical red balloon that follows him everywhere. It is set in the Belleville neighborhood of Paris during the 1950s.

Note: Avoid the Mary Kate and Ashley Olsen movie on Paris. They provide poor role models for making good travelers out of your kids.

Internet Sites & CD ROMs

France for Kids, from the Embassy of France, *www.info-france-usa.org/kids/*

Official Site of the Eiffel Tower, *www.tour-eiffel.fr/teiffel/uk/*

Webmuseum, Paris, *www.ibiblio.org/wm/*

Cluny Museum, kids page (in French), *www.culture.fr/cluny/intro.htm*

Louvre Museum (in French), with virtual visit, *www.louvre.fr/*

Musée d'Orsay, *http://www.musee-orsay.fr/ORSAY/orsaygb/HTML.NSF/By+Filename/mosimple+index?OpenDocument*

Versailles Palace, *www.chateauversailles.fr/*

French Government Tourist Office, *www.francetourism.com*

CD-ROM, Mobiclic, Discover France in All its Diversities, Presented by the Embassy of France, Milan-Presse Interactive.

CD-ROM, Rosetta Stone French Explorer, Fairfield Language Technologies

CD-ROM, Smart Start French Deluxe, Knowledge Adventure

CD-ROM, Kidspeak French, Ages 6 and Up, The Learning Company

FLYING TO PARIS

Generally speaking, you will save money on airfares if you book your tickets 4-6 months in advance, especially for travel during the high-seasons (June-August, December 15-January 5). However, discounts and charter tickets vary greatly from year to year, so there is no hard, fast rule. Keep your eye out for special fares advertised in the travel section of major newspapers. Remember to ask about reduced fares for children. If you have a trusted travel agent, this is a good place to start looking for bargain airfares. You can also let your fingers do the walking online. **Expedia** *(*www.expedia.com); **Travelocity** (www.travelocity.com); and **Orbitz** (www.orbitz.com) allow you to compare flights and rates on several major airlines. European airlines, such as **IcelandAir** (www.icelandair.com) and **Aer Lingus** (www.aerlingus.com) sometimes offer lower rates, though it may require more stops along the way.

If you go directly to different airline sites to book tickets, you will often get a lower rate than over the phone. You can also surf the web for travel consolidators with names such as cheaptickets.com or budgettravel.com that can easily save you 25% on flights and car rentals. Several car rental consolidators such as **AutoEurope**, Tel. 888/223-5555; www.autoeurope.com, and **Kemwel**, Tel. 877/820-0668; www.kemwel.com, also sell discounted flights.

Note that rules vary from airline to airline regarding children's discounts, how to seat babies, and regulations about traveling with young children. Check for specifics with your travel agent or directly with the airline.

Here are some tips for planning your plane trip:

• If you are flying to Paris directly from the US, try to book the overnight, trans-Atlantic flight as late in the evening as possible. The later you leave, the more likely you (and your kids) will get some sleep. The later you arrive in Paris, the more likely your body clock will be ready to face a new day.

• The return flight from France to the US is always a daytime trip. Be sure to bring plenty of snacks, (diapers, if needed), small toys, books, activities, and entertainment.

• Take advantage of stopovers and connections. Let kids stretch their legs, get some food, and watch other planes take off and land. If you are facing a long layover in an interesting city, consider extending it even more so that you can leave the airport and see some sights. We once took advantage of a long layover in Phoenix by renting a car and driving to a nearby state park where we hiked in the desert for a few hours. After a delicious Mexican meal on the way back to the airport, we were ready to face another long flight home.

Parent Tip: Waiting for meals on an airplane can be long and disappointing, especially for fussy eaters. What's more, many airlines have cut out onboard meals entirely on domestic flights. Our solution? Bring your own food. Pack a picnic or pick up some take-out food at the airport. This way you can eat what you like, when you want, and throw it away before you land. Be sure to bring beverages in a re-closable container. Some security checkpoints will not let you through with a drink in a paper cup.

Some of the major carriers offering flights from the US to Paris include:
• **Air France** – Tel. 800/237-2747; www.airfrance.com
• **American Airlines** – Tel. 800/433-7300; www.aa.com
• **British Airlines** (connections through London) – Tel. 800/247-9297; www.britishairways.com
• **Aer Lingus** (connections through Dublin) – Tel. 800/IRISHAIR; www.aerlingus.com
• **Continental Airlines** – Tel. 800/231-0856; www.continental.com
• **Delta Airlines** – Tel. 800/241-4141; www.delta.com
• **Icelandair** (connections through Keflavik, Iceland) – Tel. 800/223-5500; www.icelandair.com
• **Northwest Airlines** – Tel. 800/447-4747; www.nwa.com
• **United Airlines** – Tel. 800/241-6522; www.united.com
• **USAIR** – Tel. 800/622-1015; www.ual.com
• **Virgin Atlantic** (discount flights to London, transfer to train or European carrier) – Tel. 203/750-2000; www.virginatlantic.com

GETTING TO & FROM CHARLES DE GAULLE/ROISSY AIRPORT

The Charles de Gaulle/Roissy Airport is where all transatlantic flights arrive. It is located 30 kilometers (19 miles) northeast of Paris. It is well linked to the city via public transportation and taxis.

Taxi

This is the easiest option with suitcases and small children, and is not that much more expensive than public transportation if you are traveling as a family. If there are more than four of you, you may have to wait a bit for a minivan taxi, but it is very doable. Count on €40-50 for fare into the city, plus a charge for luggage and a tip.

Train

The Roissy-Rail Suburban B Line (RER B) connects the Charles de Gaulle Airport train station to the Gare du Nord train station and several other major subway stations in Paris, including Châtelet/Les Halles (a major subway hub), Saint Michel-Nôtre Dame; Luxembourg; Port Royal; Denfert Rochereau; and Cité Universitaire. From the airport you can follow the signs marked Paris par Train or take the free airport shuttle to the RER B Station. Trains run from 5 am to midnight approximately every 15 minutes (more often during rush hour). The fare varies depending on where you stop in the city. Count on €10-14 for adults. Kids ages 4-10 are half price. Kids under 4 are free.

This is the quickest mode of public transportation into the city, but it requires taking the airport shuttle and negotiating escalators at the train station. There are no elevators. It's fairly easy provided you are not loaded down with lots of luggage.

Roissy Bus

The Roissy Bus connects the Charles de Gaulle/Roissy terminals to the Place de l'Opéra in central Paris. Fare: €8.40.

Air France Bus

There are two Air France buses that will take you from the terminals into the city. One will take you to the Arc de Triomphe (Charles de Gaulle/ Etoile metro stop) then to the Porte Maillot metro.and stops. The other will take you to the Gare de Lyon and Gare Montparnasse train stations. Fare is €12 for adults and €6 for kids ages 2-11. Kids under 2 are free.

GETTING TO & FROM ORLY AIRPORT

The Orly Airport is located 18 kilometers (11 miles) south of the city. It is also well served by public transportation and taxis.

Taxi

This is the easiest option with suitcases and small children, although you may have to wait for a minivan taxi if you are traveling with more than 4 people. Count on €30-35 for fare into the city, plus a charge for luggage and a tip.

Train (option 1)

You can catch an airport shuttle bus to the Suburban C Line train station called Pont de Rungis. This train line connects Orly to several subway stops in the city including the Gare d'Austerlitz train station; St Michel Nôtre dame, Musée d'Orsay; Invalides, Pont de l'Alma; and Champ de Mars/Tour Eiffel. The fare varies depending which stop you go to in the city.

Count on €8-12 for adults. Kids ages 4-10 are half price. Kids under 4 are free.

Train (option 2)
You can catch a shuttle bus to the Suburban B line train station at Antony. This train will take you to numerous major subway stations in the city including Denfert Rochereau; Port Royal; Luxembourg; St Michel Nôtre dame; Châtelet Les Halles (a major subway hub); and the Gare du Nord train station. The fare varies depending which stop you go to in the city. Count on €8-12 for adults. Kids ages 4-10 are half price. Kids under 4 are free.

Orly Bus
The Orly Bus connects the Orly terminals to the Place Denfert Rochereau in Paris. Fare: €5.80.

Air France Bus
You can catch an Air France bus from the Orly terminals to the Invalides or the Montparnasse train station in Paris. Fare: €10.

ARRIVING BY TRAIN
If you are traveling to Paris by train you will arrive in one of Paris' six main train stations. Each of these stations is well connected to the rest of the city by subway and public buses.

Trains from northern France, England (via the Chunnel), Belgium, Luxembourg, Holland, and northern Europe arrive at the **Gare du Nord**.

The **Gare de l'Est** serves cities in eastern France, Germany, Switzerland, and Austria.

If you are arriving from southern France or Italy you will come into the **Gare de Lyon**.

The **Gare Montparnasse** serves Brittany and western France.

The **Gare d'Austerlitz** is where you will arrive from Spain and southwestern France.

If you are coming from Normandy or have taken a ferry across the English Channel you will arrive at the **Gare Saint Lazare**.

TOURIST OFFICES IN PARIS
• **Central Tourist Office**, 25 rue des Pyramides, 75001; Tel. 08 92 68 31 12 / 08 92 68 3000; website: www.parisinfo.com. Open Mon-Sat 10am-7pm; Sun and holidays 11-7. Gare du Nord Train station; 01 45 26 94 82; Open daily.

• **Gare de Lyon Train station**; Tel. 01 43 43 33 24; Open Mon-Sat.

• Eiffel Tower Tourist Office; Tel. 01 45 51 22 15; Open daily, May-Sept.

• Carrousel du Louvre Shopping Center Visitor Center; Tel. 01 44 50 19 98; Open daily except Tues.

GETTING AROUND PARIS

Paris is an easy city to navigate. Most hotels and major department stores offer free street maps. You can also obtain a free bus and subway map in any subway station.

Walking

Much of Paris' charm is best discovered on foot, so you will want to have comfortable walking shoes. This is an excellent way to explore the parks, shops, museums, markets, and cobbled streets of the city. When you need a rest, there is always a handy café or park bench where you can take a break. When our boys were little we relied on baby backpacks and sturdy but lightweight umbrella strollers to get around as a family. We found that these were best for negotiating narrow sidewalks, handling cobble-stoned streets, going into shops or museums, descending subway stairs, or climbing on and off of buses. As our children have grown older, they have become good walkers themselves, especially with the promise of an interesting activity and occasional bribe of ice cream or other treats.

Parent Tip: Many Parisians love dogs but hate cleaning up after them. Lately the city government, tired of paying millions of dollars a year to clean dog poop off city sidewalks, has imposed stiff fines for owners who don't pick up after their pets. It is now safer to take your eyes off the sidewalk and enjoy the sights of Paris, without living in constant fear of stepping into a dog's mess.

Public Transportation

When you need to cover more distance, you can use Paris' very reliable and user-friendly public transportation system, the RATP.

Subway tickets (*tickets de métro*) are good on all buses and subways within the city limit. You can purchase them in any subway station and in many *Tabac* stores. Individual tickets can also be purchased on a bus, but you will need exact change. You can buy tickets one at a time (€1.40), but it is easier and cheaper to buy a *carnet* of 10 tickets (€10.70). For children ages 6 to 10 you can purchase half-price *carnets*, called *demi-tarif* (€5.35). Children 5 and under ride for free.

There are also one-day or multi-day **passes** that are good on subways, public buses, the RER, the Montmartrobus and Montmartre Funiculaire. These can be purchased in any subway station. The *Mobilis* pass is good for unlimited travel for one day (Cost: €5). The *Paris Visite* pass allows unlimited travel for 1, 2, 3, or 5-days and includes free trips on the RER to Disneyland Paris or to the Paris Airports. It is easy and worthwhile if you will be taking numerous bus or subway trips each day. Rates for kids/adults are: €4.55/8.35 for a 1-day pass; €6.85/13.70 for a 2-day pass; €9.15/18.25 for a 3-day pass; and €13.70/26.65 for a 5-day pass.

If you are going to be staying in Paris more than a week and using public transportation, the best bargain for adults is the **Carte Orange** pass. A 1-week pass for unlimited travel costs €15.70 and a 1-month pass costs €51.50. You will need to supply a small ID photo when you apply for the card.

The public transit system also sells a card called **Musée et Monuments** for €18 per day. This card gives you free and priority access to 70 museums and monuments across the city. It may be an advantage for adults in your group. Children already benefit from reduced fares or free access to most of these sites.

Parent Tip: Looking for an original gift that really says Paris? Check out the Public Transit System (RATP)'s fun souvenir shop in the Châtelet/Les Halles metro station, near the Place Carée exit. Open Mon-Fri: 10:30 am-7:30 pm.

Métro

Paris has an extensive subway system called the *métro*. There are over 370 metro stations and 15 lines. Trains run daily from approximately 5:30 am to 1 am. The train lines are identified by the name of the last station at each end. An overhead sign on the train platform indicates which direction the train is heading. Transfers are also well indicated on orange and white overhead signs. The one downside to using the metro with small children is that it involves lots of stairs, which can be tricky with toddlers and strollers. On the other hand, older kids love riding the metro, especially if you let them figure out your route on the map.

RER

Some of the stations within the city will connect you to the suburban train system known as the RER or to the new **Meteor trains** which run automatically without a conductor. If you take the RER beyond the city limits, you will need to purchase a higher priced ticket from a station ticket agent or automatic machine. Hang on to your ticket for the whole ride. You may need it to exit the train station or be asked to present it during a random ticket control. Be aware that once the RER trains leave the city limits they don't necessarily stop at all the stations along the line. Check the lighted display board on the train platform. Make certain that the light next to the name of your destination is lit. If not, wait for another train.

Fun Facts about the Paris Metro

• The first Paris subway line was finished just in time for the Paris International Exhibition of 1900. It was designed by an engineer named Fulgence Bienvenüe, whose last name means, "Welcome"!

• The metro station entrances were designed by an architect named Hector Guimard in the *Art Nouveau* style that features swirling lines and plant-like forms. Many of these decorative entrances survive today.

• During World War I, the metro stations doubled as bomb shelters. With the outbreak of World War II in 1939, the metro ran day and night for 12 days in September to help ferry French troops and civilians in and out of the city. During the German Occupation of Paris, from June 1940 to August 1944, the German military converted some stations into airplane parts manufacturing factories. Jews were forced to ride in the last metro car, nicknamed the Synagogue.

• There are 11 dark, abandoned subway stations. The one called Saint Martin is used as a homeless shelter when the outside temperature drops below freezing. Some unused stations are rented out to film crews to shoot movies and advertisements.

Buses

Public buses are a great option, because they allow you to see more of the city. They are also easier than the metro to navigate with a stroller or small children because they don't involve stairs. Bus maps are available free of charge in any subway station. The bus stops are well marked by either a shelter with glass walls and a big bus map or a pole featuring a yellow and red bus symbol with the name of the stop. Many major streets and avenues have special lanes reserved for buses and taxis, so it is often faster to ride a bus than to try to drive through the city. You can ride on any bus within the city limits for one ticket, but if you transfer from one bus to another you will need to use a new ticket. You use the same tickets as for the metro and can purchase them in any metro station and many Tabac stores. Buses run Mon-Sat from 6:30 am to 8:30 pm. Special routes run until midnight and on Sundays and holidays. These are indicated at the stops. The *Noctambus* runs during the night.

Bâtobus

This is a fairly recent addition to Paris' public transportation options. It is a system of boats that crisscross the Seine River serving 7 stops between the Jardin des Plantes and the Eiffel Tower, including Hôtel de Ville, Nôtre

278 PARIS WITH KIDS

Dame, Saint Germain, Louvre, Musée d'Orsay, and Champs Elysées. The price of each ticket is calculated according to how far you want to go along the route. The first stop is €3.50 and each additional stop is an extra €2 per person. The Bâtobus is more expensive than other forms of public transportation, but it's fun. The best deal is a one-day or two-day pass that lets you come and go all day. A one-day pass is €10 for adults and €5.50 for kids. A two-day pass is €12.50 for adults and €6.50 for kids. The service runs approximately every 15-25 minutes from 10 am to 11 pm, April through October.

Open-Tour Bus

If you have never ridden on a double-decker bus, you may want to explore Paris on the light green *Open Tour* tourist buses. This is a service that is jointly run by the public transportation system and two private tour companies. There are three routes: Grand Tour; Bastille-Bercy; and Montmartre. You buy a pass for one route that is good for one or several days and can climb on and off the bus as much as you like. Buses run daily. The three routes go past major tourist sights and stop at clearly marked bus stops. Each rider gets a pair of headsets that you can plug in to each bus for a commentary in English or French. The lower deck is like a normal bus and the upper deck is open-air.

This is a great way to see major city sights in a short period of time. Kids love it. It is also a good option if you are jet-lagged and want to get a view of the city without having to expend a lot of energy – although you will have to spend some cash, because the tickets are pricey. You can buy your passes from the bus conductor or at Open Tour; 13, Rue Auber, 75009, Metro: Auber. Rates are: 1 day Adult Pass = €25, 2 day Adult pass = €28; Kids 4-11years = €12 for a 1 or 2 day pass; Kids under 4 are free.

Taking a Cab

Taxis are readily available at airports and train stations. There are also many taxi stands scattered throughout the city where you can generally find a cab quickly. It is difficult to hail a cab on the street, since they are generally full. However, they respond quickly to phone requests. You also can reserve a taxi in advance, especially if you need an early morning ride or a car that can fit more than 3 people. The front desk person at your hotel should be able to help. Here are some services you can call: Alpha-Taxi: Tel. 01 45 85 85 85. Taxi-Bleu: Tel. 01 49 36 10 10. Taxi-Etoile: Tel. 01 42 70 41 41. Taxi-G7: Tel. 01 47 39 47 39. The fare is displayed on a meter. Add a 15% tip.

Driving

Driving in Paris is not recommended since traffic is very congested and parking is both difficult and expensive. Having said this, we often end up in

Paris with a rental car to use for day trips and for traveling to other parts of France. One advantage of the traffic congestion is that it gives you time to figure out where you are and need to go. Fortunately, the streets and access to highways are generally well marked. Make sure to stay out of the bus/taxi lanes – generally the one furthest on the right.

Parking in Paris is a headache. Street parking is limited to two hours between 7 am and 7pm, and it's expensive. You will not find an American-style parking meter. Instead there are parking payment machines located along the street. Most of these no longer accept coins. Instead you must purchase a prepaid payment card from a Tabac store. As you insert your card, the clock on the parking payment machine will advance for up to 2 hours. When you've reached the time you need, push the green button. A printed ticket will appear that you must put on the dashboard of your car. Note: in most residential neighborhoods, parking is free on Saturday and Sunday, from 7 pm to 7 am, and during the month of August, but you should verify this on the parking machine. If you cannot feed the parking machine every two hours, you are better off putting your car in a parking garage. These are indicated by blue signs with a white letter "P." Most garages offer hourly, daily, and weekly rates.

If you get a parking ticket, you can buy a payment card at any Tabac store. Mail it in with the ticket.

Look for these Fun Cars in Paris

• The **SMART**: a little 2-seater designed by the people from SWATCH (the Smar Watch company). It fits into pint-size parking spots.
• The Renault **TWINGO**: a fun little 4-seater with rounded forms and a wacky dashboard.
• The Ford **KA**: another round little 4-seater that must have been named by Klingons.
• The Fiat **Multipla**: a sort of mini-minivan that seats six and looks like a frog.
• The Citroen **2CV**: An old classic, first sold in 1939. Although no longer manufactured, you still see old ones with their round shape and front windows that fold up.

Renting a Car

To drive in France you must be at least 18 years old and have a valid driver's license. If you want to rent a car, you will save money by reserving it in advance through an American consolidator or car rental company. Try:
• **AutoEurope**: Tel. 888/223-5555; www.autoeurope.com

- **Kemwel:** Tel. 877/820-0668; www.kemwel.com
- **Hertz:** Tel. 800/654-3001; www.hertz.com
- **Avis:** Tel. 800/331-1084; www.avis.com

Consider an Apartment

If you are staying in Paris for a week or more, you may want to consider renting an apartment. It is generally less expensive than a hotel for longer stays and offers you the freedom of having your own place. You may get more space with an apartment, are more likely to have a washing machine on site, and can make meals whenever you want. It's also a great way to experience Paris as a local.

Note: Most Parisian apartment buildings require that you punch in an access code to enter the lobby any time before 8am or after 8pm on weekdays, all day and night on weekends, and throughout the month of August. If you are staying in an apartment or visiting someone in an apartment, be sure to ask for the access code number.

You should be aware that French apartments are described according to the number of main rooms, rather than by the number of bedrooms. So a 2-room apartment (2-pieces) in Paris will have one bedroom and a living room – not two bedrooms.

These companies offer short-term rental properties in Paris:
- **A La Carte Paris Apartments**, 11, Rue d'Assas, 75006; Tel. 06 14 70 50 38; www.alacarte-paris-apartments.com
- **France Appartements**, 97-99 Avenue des Champs Elysées, 75008; Tel. 01 56 59 31 00; www.apartments-of-France.com
- **Paris Apartment Search**, 5 rue Villedo, 75001; Tel. 01 42 60 79 85; www.parisapartmentsearch.com
- **Paris Apartment Services**, 69, Rue d'Argout, 75002; Tel. 01 40 28 01 28; www.paris-appartements-services.fr

BASIC INFORMATION

Holidays & Business Hours

Most stores, museums, and public buildings are closed on holidays. Hospitals and police stations remain open, and there are always a few pharmacies on call. Holidays include:

January 1: New Year's Day

March or April (date varies): Easter and the Monday after Easter

May 1: Labor Day
May 8: Armistice Day (celebrating the end of World War II)
May (date varies): Ascension
May (date varies): Pentecost
July 14: Bastille Day (celebrating the French Revolution)
August 15: Assumption
November 1: All Saints' Day
November 11: Armistice Day (celebrating the end of World War I)
December 25: Christmas

Business hours vary. Most museums are open 9am-5pm (possibly later one night a week). National museums are closed on Tuesdays. City museums are closed on Mondays. Banks are generally open 9am-4pm, Monday-Friday. Some close for an hour at lunchtime. Post offices are open 8am-7pm, Monday-Friday, and Saturday 8am-12pm. Many food shops are open 9am-7pm, with a several hour break in the afternoon. Open-air markets are generally open 5am-1pm. Restaurants usually serve lunch between 12pm and 2pm, and dinner from 7pm-11pm. Many stores are closed on Sundays, including large department stores.

Parent Tip: You may want to change $100 into Euros before you leave home, especially if you are arriving in Paris by plane. This avoids the hassle of locating the airport ATM or exchange office and waiting in a long line when you are already dealing with jetlag, luggage, and tired children.

Money
Paris is well equipped with automatic teller machines that accept most American bank and credit cards (with a PIN). We have found that this is not only the most convenient way to get cash but also the one that offers the best exchange rate and lowest service charges. You can also change cash or travelers checks at an exchange office, most banks, and fancy hotels – but the fees and exchange rates are less advantageous. The Euro is the standard currency in France, Austria, Belgium, Finland, Germany, Greece, Holland, Ireland, Italy, Luxembourg, Portugal, and Spain. Its value as of press time is approximately equal to $1.20.

Credit cards, especially VISA, are widely accepted in France, everywhere from restaurants, hotels, and grocery stores to highway toll booths.

Note: Once in a while, credit cards or ATM machines just won't work. This is generally because the electronic lines connecting your transaction to the rest of the world are busy or down. You may have to try several ATMs or wait a few hours to obtain cash. If you VISA card is not approved when you are making a store purchase, ask the merchant to try again once or twice. Sometimes, the third try is a charm.

Electricity

My husband once absentmindedly plugged an American shaver directly into a French outlet. For a few brief moments it revved up to amazing speeds. Then the engine blew. Why? Electricity in France runs on 220 volts, compared to only 110 volts in the US. If you want to use American appliances in France safely you will need a converter and an adapter. These can be purchased at travel and major hardware stores in the U.S or in Paris at FNAC and Darty stores, or in the basement of the BHV department store.

Electricity is much more expensive in France than in the US. If you are a guest in someone's home, it is best to be mindful of this fact in your use of heating, hot water, lights, and electrical appliances. Note, too, that garbage disposals are non-existent in France. Toss food remains into the trash, not down the sink.

Parent Tip: Have laptop, will travel? Make sure to check your owner's manual to see if your computer can automatically adjust to 220 volts of power before you plug it in. Otherwise, use a converter.

TV Formats

French televisions are set to a different standard of lines per frame, called SECAM, than are American ones which function on the NTSC standard. As a result, you cannot use American-made videos in a French machine or vice versa. Similarly, DVDs are set to different standards across 6 world regions. The US and Canada are in region I, and France and the rest of Europe are in region II. If your disc is coded to a specific region, it will not play on a disc player manufactured in a different region. However some DVDs are not coded for any particular region and you can play them on any machine.

Laundry

While laundry can be just a menial chore at home, it can become a real challenge when traveling, especially with messy kids. We've encountered a variety of strategies for dealing with this issue:

• One family we know simply didn't do laundry during their 3-week trip to Europe. They packed cheap socks and underwear and just threw them away after each use. For the rest, they packed enough to wear for three weeks. This works, of course, but means that you will be carrying a lot of dirty clothes around.

• Our New York City friends were accustomed to taking their family's dirty clothes to the bulk laundry service at home. In Paris, they used the same method, dropping off bulk laundry at the local *"Pressing,"* which also does dry-cleaning.

• Then there is the old globetrotter method of rinsing out your clothes in the hotel sink. Many hotels frown on this, especially if you start stringing drippy clothes all over the room. However, they generally won't balk if you just rinse out a few items and dangle them carefully over the bathtub.

• Some hotels offer laundry and dry-cleaning services.

• One of the advantages of renting an apartment is that it is more likely to have a washing machine. However, few, if any will, have a dryer.

• The other solution is to take an hour out of your day and head to the local Laundromat (*Laverie*). Ask your hotel to recommend the nearest one. We suggest going first thing in the morning, when it is less crowded. You can always nibble on a breakfast pastry, plan out the day's activities, and write some post cards while you wait. Some Laundromats have detergent dispensers, or you can buy your own at the local supermarket, Monoprix or Prisunic, or corner grocer's. Increasingly, French Laundromats do not have coin-operated machines. Instead you go to a wall-mounted device, indicate which machine you want to use, and insert the money there.

Parent Tip: Many French front-load washing machines have a safety switch that prevents you from opening the door immediately after the wash cycle is completed. If you can't get the door open, just wait a minute or two for the lock to release automatically.

Health & Medical Tips

• Be sure to fill out the emergency contact information page in the passport of each family member.

• If you or any member of your family uses a prescription medication, bring enough to cover your trip. Ask your health care provider to give you a prescription with the generic name in case you need a refill.

• Know your child's weight in pounds and divide it by 2.2 to convert it to kilos. You may need to know this to find the proper dosage for French medications.

• Bring your own fever thermometer. French ones calculate temperature in Celsius not Fahrenheit.

• Stock your dop kit with fever-reducing medication (kid and adult varieties), a liquid antihistamine/decongestant such as Benadryl, anti-itch cream, antibiotic cream, Band-Aids, a fever thermometer, tablets for indigestion, Bandaids, and eye drops.

Emergency Contacts

• SOS Help English-Speaking hotline (open daily 3 pm-11 pm): Tel. 01 47 23 80 80

• US Embassy: Tel. 01 43 12 22 22

• Ambulance: Tel.15 or 01 43 78 26 26

• Police: Tel. 17

• Fire Department: Tel. 18

• Anti-Poison Center: Tel. 01 40 37 04 04

- Blood Transfusion Center: *Tel. 08 00 10 01 09*
- Burn Center: *Tel. 01 42 34 17 58*

Doctors & Dentists

The US Embassy in Paris maintains a list of doctors, medical specialists, and dentists who speak English. It is available on their web site at (www.amb-usa.fr/consul/acs/guide/default.htm) or at the Embassy's American Citizen Services, open Monday-Friday, located at 2, Rue Saint Florentin by the Place de la Concorde (Metro: Concorde). The Embassy phone number is: Tel. 01 43 12 22 22. For Emergencies during weekends and holidays, call that number and ask for the Embassy Duty Officer.

If you just want to find the nearest doctor, go to your neighborhood pharmacy. Each pharmacy maintains a list of local doctors, dentists, and specialists, including which ones who are open during holidays and weekends.

English-Speaking or Bilingual Hospitals

American Hospital of Paris (medical and dental care), 63, Boulevard Victor Hugo, between the Boulevard Victor Hugo, Rue Chauveau, Boulevard du Château, and Boulevard de la Saussaye in the western suburb of Neuilly. It is two blocks from the Seine (Metro: Pont de Levallois – a good 6 blocks away). Tel. 01 46 41 25 25.

Children's Hospital Emergency Care: Hopital Necker, 146-151, Rue de Sevres, in Paris at the intersection of the Rue de Sevres and the Boulevard Montparnasse, and Rue de Vaugirard (Metro: Duroc or Falguière). Tel. 01 44 49 40 00.

Hertford British Hospital, 3, Rue Barbis, between the Rue de Villiers, Rue Chaptal, and Rue Voltaire in the northwestern suburb of Levallois-Perret, (Metro: Anatole France). Tel. 01 46 39 22 22

Hopital Foch (many English-speaking staff members), 40, Rue Worth, 92150 (western suburb) Suresnes. Tel. 01 46 25 20 00

Late-night House Calls

S.O.S. Médecins provides after-hours house calls throughout the night. Tel. 01 47 07 77 77.

S.O.S. Dentistes will send a dentist to you in the middle of the night if it's urgent. Tel. 01 43 37 51 00.

Pharmacies

French pharmacists go through 6 years of specialized university training. They are well qualified to give advice about medications and will administer first aid. Pharmacists also maintain a list of local doctors, dentists, and other health care providers, including those that remain on call during weekends and holidays.

You can recognize a French pharmacy by its green cross symbol. English-speaking pharmacies in Paris include:

Anglo-American Pharmacy, 6, Rue de Castiglione, Metro: Tuileries, Tel. 01 42 60 72 96

British and American Pharmacy, 1, Rue Auber, Metro: Opéra, Tel. 01 47 42 49 40

British Pharmacy, 62, Avenue des Champs-Elysées, Metro:Franklin Roosevelt, Tel. 01 43 59 22 52

Anglo-American Pharmacy, 37, Avenue Marceau, Metro: George V or Alma Marceau, Tel. 01 47 20 57 37

Late-night or all-night pharmacies in Paris:

Pharma Presto. Provides 24-hour prescription delivery service. Tel. 01 42 42 42 50

Pharmacie des Halles. Open until midnight Monday-Saturday and until 10 pm on Sunday. 10, Boulevard de Sébastopol, Metro: Châtelet, Tel. 01 42 72 03 23

Dérhy/Pharmacie des Champs. Open 24 hours/day. 84, Avenue des Champs-Elysées, Metro: George V, Tel. 01 45 62 02 41

Matignon. Near the Champs Elysees, Open until 2 am, daily. 2, Rue Jean-Mermoz, Metro: Franklin Roosevelt, Tel. 01 43 59 86 55

Pharmacie Européenne de la Place de Clichy. Open 24 hours/day. 6, Place de Clichy, Metro: Place de Clichy, Tel. 01 48 74 65 18

Pharmacie de la Place de la Nation. Open until midnight, daily. 13, Place de la Nation, Metro: Nation, Tel. 01 43 73 24 03

Pharmacie d'Italie. Open until midnight daily. 61, Avenue d'Italie, Metro: Tolbiac, Tel. 01 44 24 19 72

Air Quality

Paris can become quite polluted due to the high volume of vehicle traffic, especially if the weather is hot and muggy. The AirParis phone service gives updated air quality information (in French) from 9 am to 5:30 pm daily. Tel. 01 44 59 47 64.

Public Restrooms

Always take advantage of rest rooms (toilettes) in public monuments, museums, department stores, cafés, and restaurants. They are generally clean and easy to find, although occasionally you will still stumble across an old squat-type hole-in-the-ground toilet. These are relics of a bygone era and pretty unappealing if you or your kids are not hardened globe trotters. Most large parks also have public rest rooms. Men's rooms may be labeled as

Messieurs, Hommes, or a picture of a man. Ladies' rooms may be labeled as Mesdames, Dames, or a picture of a woman. Some public toilets require a small payment to an attendant or in the door handle.

Paris also has a large supply of Sanisettes. These are pay toilets located in gray kiosks on sidewalks all over the city. They are convenient and self-cleaning. To use a Sanisette, first check to see if it is vacant (green dot), then insert the fee, and the door will open automatically. If there is an orange dot, it is occupied. If the dot is red, it is out of service (*hors service*). Once inside, you have 15 minutes before the door will automatically reopen. The flush and cleaning system will be triggered after you have left and let the door lock behind you. Note: Small children need to be accompanied by an adult.

Water Fountains

We have only ever found one American-style drinking fountain in Paris. It is in the Louvre Museum's Egyptian galleries by the red granite Sphinx statue from Tanis. Instead you will find plenty of outdoor fountains with clean, drinkable tap water. The most common and attractive of these are called *Fontaines Wallace* after the benefactor who installed them on Paris streets in the 1870s. They are dark green, and feature four female statues holding up a dome that is decorated with dolphins. A steady stream of water flows from under the dome. These are very handy for refilling water bottles as you explore the city.

Many public parks and squares feature another type of public water fountain that is dark green, squat, and sort of resembles a square fire hydrant. Some have a handle on the top that you rotate to get the water flowing. Others have a small spout with a button that you push to get water. There is one near the Arch du Carrousel in the Tuileries Gardens that draws long lines on hot days.

Do not drink from decorative fountains or from a park's garden hose. Their water comes from the Paris canals and is not clean. If you see a sign that says "eau non potable," do not drink the water. "Eau potable" means that it is safe to drink.

Many French people prefer the taste of bottled mineral water to tap water. There are at least 50 brands of mineral water available in France. The French drink an average of 100 liters of bottled water per person each year. That's twice as much as their annual wine consumption. Maybe it's the reason they outlive Americans.

Smoking

Smoking remains far more prevalent in Paris (and throughout Europe) than in the US. Restaurants are supposed to have a non-smoking section (*non-fumeurs*) available for customers and some are banning smoking altogether. However, this is not always the case in small, one-room restaurants or on outdoor terraces. Smoking is not allowed on public transportation nor at the airport. Some hotels have floors reserved for non-smokers.

Newspapers & Magazines

The *International Herald Tribune*, published in Paris, will keep you up to date on American news, sports, comics, and crossword puzzles. It is available, as are many other foreign papers, at most newsstands and newspaper shops (Magasins de Presse). There are numerous French daily papers. The most commonly read are *Le Monde*, highly respected and intellectual; *Le Figaro*, politically right-wing; and *Liberation*, politically left-wing.

You can find foreign editions of major American and English-language magazines at large newsstands, in *Magasins de Presse*, and in large English-language bookshops. The most popular French weeklies are the left-wing *Le Nouvel Observateur* and *L'Evenement du Jeudi*, the centrist *L'Express*, and right-wing *Le Point* or *Figaro Magazine*.

If you want information on the week's artistic, cinematic, and cultural happenings, pick up a *Pariscope* (which includes a short section in English) or *Officiel des Spectacles*. They come out each Wednesday.

English-language bookshops

WH Smith, 248, Rue de Rivoli, across from the Tuileries Gardens (Metro: Tuileries). Closed Sun. This is a big bookstore, with a large children's section upstairs.

Galigliani Bookseller, 224, rue de Rivoli, across from the Louvre (Metro: Palais Royal/ Musée du Louvre). Closed Sun. France's oldest English-language bookshop, this store offers an excellent selection of English-language books for both children and adults.

Librairie du Musée du Louvre, near the glass pyramid entrance of the Louvre. Open daily. You will find some books in English in both the children's and adult sections of this museum bookstore/gift shop.

Brentano's, 37, Avenue de l'Opéra (Metro: Opéra or Pyramides). Closed Sun. This store has been around for over 100 years. It offers a huge selection of English-language books on two floors. It also hosts a children's book club.

Librairie Cultaire-Mona Lisait, 17, bis Rue Pavée (Metro: St. Paul). Closed Sat. Although many of the books offered in this stores 3 floors are in French, there is a selection of English-language books in the back of the top floor. Many are at bargain prices.

The Red Wheelbarrow, 13, Rue Charles V (Metro: St. Paul). Closed Sun. This shop is small but filled with books in English.

Shakespeare and Company, 37, Rue de la Bucherie, across the river from Nôtre Dame Cathedral (Metro: St. Michel-Nôtre dame). Open daily. This famous hangout for English and American expatriate writers sells new and used books in English, and still retains its dusty charm and warm atmosphere. The kids' section is upstairs and discounted paperbacks are in racks and boxes outside.

Joseph Gibert, 26-30, Boulevard Saint Michel (Metro: Saint Michel). Closed Sun. Part of the 100+ year old Gibert bookstore chain, this shop offers new and used books in English both in the sidewalk racks and upstairs.

The Abbey Bookshop, 29, Rue de la Parcheminerie (Metro: Saint Michel or Cluny - La Sorbonne). Closed Sun. This store offers new and used English, Canadian, and American books.

Nouveau Quartier Latin, 78, Boulevard Saint Michel (Metro: Luxembourg). Closed Sun. This international bookshop offers books and videos in many languages, including English.

Tea And Tattered Pages, 24, Rue Mayet (Metro: Duroc). Open every afternoon. This shop offers both used books and a tearoom for a comfortable book browsing and buying experience.

San Francisco Book Co., 17, Rue Monsieur le Prince (Metro: Odeon). Open every afternoon. This store is chock full of bargain books in English, starting with the outdoor racks and continuing inside.

The Village Voice, 6, Rue Princesse (Metro: Mabillon). Closed Sun. This shop offers English language books, as well as poetry readings, book signings, and other presentations.

Bouquinistes along the Seine, especially on the Quai Montebello and Quai Saint Michel. (Metro: Saint Michel). Closed Mon. These are fun to browse and a great place to pick up small souvenirs. If you're lucky, you can find titles in English.

Telephones & Internet

Making a phone call in Paris can be somewhat confusing. All French phone numbers include 10 digits. The first two are the equivalent of an area code and must be dialed every time whether you are making a local call or phoning another region in France. The codes work as follows:

01: Paris and its suburbs
02: Northwestern France
03: Northeastern France
04: Southeastern France
05: Southwestern France
06: Cell phones
08: toll-free calls

If you are calling from Paris to another town in France: Dial the full ten-digit number. There is no special access code.

If you want to make an international call from France: Dial 00 + country code + area or town code + number.

Country codes are listed in phone booths and phone directories. The US and Canada are 1, except for Hawaii (1808) and Puerto Rico (1809). The UK is 44.

If you are trying to call France from the US: Dial 011 + 33 (Code for France) + drop the "0" and dial only the remaining 9 digits. For example to call the number 01 43 45 46 47 in Paris: Dial 011+33+1+43 45 46 47.

If you want to use a pay phone: Almost all the public phone booths in France now accept a *télécarte* rather than coins. These look like a credit card with a small memory chip on one end that slides into the pay phone. They can be purchased in increments of 50 or 120 units at any *Tabac* store, tourist office, post office, and even some newsstands. You can also buy phone cards similar to American ones, with a scratch-off code number that you dial from any telephone.

Many cafés have pay phones, generally next to the restrooms. Some accept coins, others require you to purchase a token from the cashier.

If you want to use a cell phone while you are in Paris: If your American cell phone functions on the GSM (Global System for Mobile communications) standard, you can contact your service provider and ask them to allow you access to international service. Count on spending $1-2/minute for local and long-distance calls. You can get cheaper service for calls within France by purchasing and installing a special phone chip, called a SIM card, available at large FNAC stores in Paris.

You can rent a cell phone to use in Europe from American companies such as Intouch USA (Tel. 703/222-7161, www.intouchusa.com); TravelCell (Tel. 877/CELL-PHONE, www.travelcell.com); Cellular Abroad (Tel. 800/287-3020; www.cellularabroad.com); Rent a Cellular (Tel. 877/902-7368; www.rent-a-cellular.com). Car rental companies such as Europecar (Tel. 888/223-5555; www.autoeurope.com) and Kemwel (Tel. 877/820-0668; www.kemwel.com) also rent cell phones you can use in France. Plan on spending $25-50/week for the phone rental, plus a shipping charge in some cases. Local and long-distance calls will run you $1-2/minute.

A cheaper option is to rent a cell phone in Paris from Call Phone, located at both Roissy/Charles de Gaulle and Orly Airports. There is also an office in the city at 2, Avenue de la Porte de Saint Cloud, 75016 Paris, Metro: St. Cloud (Tel. 01 40 71 72 54; www.callphone.com). The phone rental and delivery are free. Calls cost $0.80/minute for within France and $1.50/minute for international calls.

MINITEL: Launched in 1982, this little plastic box with its small screen and fold out keyboard was distributed for free by the national telephone company, France Telecom. One of the MINITEL's original purposes was to give phone customers access to an electronic telephone directory, ultimately replacing the use of phone books. However, the MINITEL's uses were quickly expanded. Today, customers can use it to access e-mail and the Internet, book plane or theater tickets, post wedding lists, and perform many other exchanges. Most hotels have a MINITEL, and they are also available for public use in French post offices. A few services are available for free, such as directory assistance, but most are subject to charges ranging from €0.6-1.50 per minute.

Internet Access: If you want to access the Internet or Email from your own laptop computer in Paris you will need several plug adapters: one for the electrical outlet (which takes round plugs rather than the flat American kind) and one for the phone jack (which is long and thin, instead of short and square). You may also need a converter if your computer cannot automatically switch from the 110 volt system in the US to the 220 volt system in France. You can buy converters and adapters in travel stores, electronics store, and large hardware stores in the US. In Paris, they are sold in the basement of the BHV Department Store (Metro: Hotel de Ville).

Another way to get online while in Paris is to drop into an Internet Café or Internet space in a museum. Note that they generally charge a per minute or per hour fee. Here are some addresses:

• **Cyberport Forum des Images**, in the Forum des Halles, Porte Sainte-Eustache, 75001 Paris; Metro : Châtelet-Les Halles; Tel. 01 44 76 63 44

• **Voyageur du Monde**, 53 Rue Sainte Anne, 75002 Paris, Metro: Pyramides; Tel. 01 42 86 16 00; www.vdm.com.fr

• **Le Shop Cybercafé**, 3 Rue d'Argout, 75002 Paris. Metro: Sentier; Email: shop@shop.imaginet.fr

• **Le Web Bar**, 32, Rue de Picardie, 75003 Paris, Metro: Filles du Calvaire; Tel. 01 42 72 66 55; www.webbar.fr/

• **Cyberia**, in the Pompidou Center, 75004 Paris, Metro: Rambuteau; E-mail: cyberia@easynet.fr

• **Cyber Café Latino**, 13 Rue de l'Ecole Polytechnique, 75005; Metro: Maubert-Mutualité; Tel. 01 40 51 86 94; www.cybercafelatino.com/

• **Café Orbital**, 13 rue de Medicis, 75006; Metro: Odeon; Tel. 01 43 25 76 77; www.cafeorbital.com

• **Cybermetropole**, in the Palais de la Découverte Museum, Avenue Franklin Roosevelt, 75008; Metro: Champs Elysées Clemenceau; Tel. 01 40 74 80 00

• **Espace AOL Vivendi**, 6-8, Rue de Tilsitt, 75008 Paris; Metro: Charles de Gaulle/ Etoile

• **Cyberzen Café**, 85, Rue Amelot, 75011 Paris; Metro: Chemin-Vert; Tel. 01 53 36 76 13

• **Apache Cybercafé**, 84, Rue du Faubourg Saint Antoine, 75012 Paris; Metro: Ledru Rollin; Tel. 01 53 46 60 10. Offers special kids' programs.

• **High Tech Café**, in the Tour Montparnasse Shopping Center, (Above C&A Department Store), 75014; Metro: Montparnasse; E-Mail: info@htc.fr
• **Planet Cybercafé**, 173, Rue de Vaugirard, 75015 Paris; Metro: Pasteur; Tel. 01 45 67 71 14
• **Travel Café**, 2 Rue d'Alleray, 75015 Paris; Metro: Vaugirard; www.abcvoyage.com/travelcafe.html

Post Offices

Post Offices are open Mon-Fri, 8am-7pm, and Sat, 8am-12pm. You can purchase stamps (timbres), buy shipping boxes and send packages (colis), and access the Minitel there. You can also purchase stamps in a Tabac store. As of February 2003, the cost of an ordinary stamp is €0.50. A letter to the US or Canada requires a stamp for €0.67. For toll-free information (in French) about postal services: Tel. 08 10 82 18 21.

You can also send packages through UPS. For toll-free information call: Tel. 08 00 87 78 77. There are two **UPS Express Shop** offices in Paris:
• 107, Rue Réaumur, 75002 Paris, Metro: Sentier
• 34, Boulevard Malesherbes, 75008 Paris, Metro: Saint Augustin or Madeleine

Religious Services

Most people in France consider themselves Catholic (81%) although many do not attend church. Muslims make up the second largest religious group (7%), followed by Protestants (1.6%), Jews (1.3%), Buddhists (0.7%), and members of the Orthodox church (0.3%).

Protestant services in English are held at the: American Cathedral, 23, Avenue George V, Metro: George V; American Church in Paris, 65, Quai d'Orsay, Metro: Invalides; Baptist Church of Paris, 48, Rue de Lille, 75007 Paris, Metro: Rue du Bac; Church of Jesus Christ of the Latter Day Saints, 64-66, Rue de Romainville, 75019 Paris, Metro: Telegraphe or Porte des Lilas; Saint John's Lutheran Church, 147, Rue de Grennelle, 75007 Paris, Metro: Varenne; Church of Scotland, 17, Rue Bayard, Metro: Franklin Roosevelt; St. Michael's Church of England, 5, Rue d'Aguesseau, Metro: Madeleine; St. George's Anglican Church, 7, Rue Auguste Vacquerie, Metro: Charles-de-Gaule/Etoile.

Most **Catholic** churches in Paris offer morning, midday, and evening services each day, with extras on Sundays (in French). The only time you will not be able to attend mass in Nôtre Dame Cathedral is on Christmas Eve (when it is reserved for parishioners and VIPs) and during State funerals. There are Catholic services in English at Saint Joseph's Church, 50, Avenue Hoche, 75008 Paris, Metro: Charles de Gaulle/Etoile.

There are numerous Jewish **synagogues** in Paris, including several in the Marais at 10 Rue Pavée; 15, Rue Nôtre Dame de Nazareth; and Rue de Turenne. Note that most Parisian synagogues are Orthodox. There is a reformed synagogue at 24, Rue Copernic, 75016, Metro: Victor Hugo. You can sometimes find Liberal services in English at Kehilat Gesher, 10, Rue de Pologne, in the western suburb of Saint Germain en Laye (Tel. 01 39 21 97 19).

Paris' main **mosque** is at 2, Place du Puits de l'Ermite, 75005 Paris, Metro: Place Monge.

There is a **Greek Orthodox Cathedral** at 7, Rue Georges Bizet, 75016, Metro: Alma Marceau.

The **Russian Orthodox Cathedral** is located at 12, Rue Daru, 75008 Paris, Metro: Courcelles.

The **Dharma Sah Buddist Center** is located at, 30 rue La Boétie, 75008 Paris, Metro: Miromesnil.

Time

Paris time is 1 hour ahead of London; 6 hours ahead of New York; 7 hours ahead of Chicago; 8 hours ahead of Denver; and 9 hours ahead of San Francisco.

Most schedules and timetables in France are written in military time, using a 24-hour clock. Thus 6 h is 6 am; 11 h is 11 am; 12 h is noon; 14 h is 2 pm; 20 h is 8pm; and 24 h is midnight.

Temperature Conversion Chart

°F	0	32	41	50	59	68	77
°C	-17	0	5	10	15	20	25

°F	86	98.6	100	104
°C	30	37	38	40

SHOPPING

Where to Buy Baby Products

Diapers: Known as *couches* (pronounced koosh), they are sold in large supermarkets, some small corner markets, in pharmacies, and at Monoprix and Prisunic stores.

Baby Bottles: You can find both glass and plastic baby bottles (*biberons*) at your local pharmacy. Plastic bottles and sippy cups are also sold at Monoprix or Prisunic stores and in some large supermarkets.

Baby Formula: Look for it in the baby food section of the supermarkets or at your local pharmacy.

Baby Food: Known as *petits pots*, you will find a wide range of baby food, including gourmet varieties, in grocery stores, supermarkets, and pharmacies.

Baby Sunscreen, Lotion, Shampoo, Powders, Teething Rings: These are sold in pharmacies and in Prisunic or Monoprix stores.

Strollers, Snuglis, Baby BackPack Carriers, etc: The best place to look for these are large department stores such as the Samaritaine, Galeries Lafayette, Printemps, and Au Bon Marché. Baby specialty stores, such as Natalys (see below) also carry these items.

Baby & Children's Clothing

Any Prisunic or Monoprix store: branches all over the city. These stores offer kids' clothing and gear for all ages at relatively low prices.

Du Pareil au Même: This is a great address for colorful kids' clothing from infancy to age 14. The prices are very reasonable and selection is good, even for boyswear. Branches located at 1, Rue Saint Denis, 75001, Metro: Châtelet; Forum des Halles, Level –2, 75001, Metro: Les Halles; 7, 14, and 34, Rue Saint Placide, 75006, Metro: Saint Placide; 168, Boulevard Saint Germain, 75006, Metro: St. Germain des Pres; 17, Rue Vavin, 75006, Metro: Vavin; 15, 17, and 23, Rue des Mathurins, 75008, Metro: Haver Caumartin; 120-122, Rue du Faubourg Saint Antoine, 75012, Metro: Ledru Rollin; 165, Rue du Chateau des Rentiers, 75013, Metro: Nationale.

Dipaki: Fun colorful clothes at reasonable prices for kids from infancy to age 8. Branches located at 20, Rue du Pont Neuf, 75001, Metro: Pont Neuf; 22, Rue Cler, 75007, Metro: Ecole Militaire; 18, Rue Vignon, 75009, Metro: Madeleine; 98, Rue d'Alésia, 75014, Metro: Alésia.

Jacadi: What the well-groomed, *bon chic bon genre*, Paris child is wearing. Excellent quality cotton and wool clothing. Don't miss the sales in early January and late July. Branches located at 9, Avenue de l'Opéra, 75001; 17, Boulevard Poissonière, 75002; 27, Rue Saint Antoine, 75004; 4, Avenue des Gobelins, 75005; 76, rue d'Assas - Angle 2, rue Vavin, 75006; 73, rue de Sèvres , 75006; 256 Boulevards Saint Germain, 75007; 17, Rue Tronchet, 75008; 54, Boulevard du Temple, 75011; 116, Rue d'Alésia, 75014; 331, Rue de Vaugirard, 75015; 114, Rue Lafontaine, 75016; and 60, Boulevard de Courçelles, 75017.

Natalys: Not as highbrow as Jacadi, but a charming assortment of baby clothes and equipment. Branches located at 74, Rue de Rivoli, 75001; Metro: Châtelet; 74, Rue de Seine, 75006, Metro: Odeon; 47, Rue de Sevres, 75007, Metro: Sevres Babylone; 109 Bis, Rue Saint Dominique, 75007, Metro: Ecole Militaire; 42, Rue Vignon, 75009, Metro: Havre Caumartin;

43, Avenue des Gobelins, 75013, Metro: Gobelins; and 5, Rue Guichard, 75016, Metro: Muette.

Petit Bateau: Good quality cotton clothing for babies and toddlers. Branches located at Forum Des Halles, 75001, Metro: Les Halles; and 323, Rue de Vaugirard, 75015, Metro: Convention.

Tartine et Chocolat: Cute clothes for children from infancy to age 10. Branches located at 24, Rue de la Paix, 75002, Metro: Opéra; 266, Boulevard Saint Germain, 75007, Metro: Solférino; 105, Rue du Faubourg Saint Honoré, 75008, Metro: Metro: Saint Phillipe du Roule; 22, Rue Boissy d'Anglas, 75008, Metro: Concorde; and 60, Avenue Paul Doumer, 75016, Metro: Muette.

Department Stores
If you're the least bit interested in shopping, you'll want to check out one or more of Paris' famous Grands Magasins (Department Stores). They are quite spectacular, which is not surprising since Paris invented the first department store. Launched in 1876 by a man named Aristide Boucicaut, it was called the Bon Marché (Good Bargain) and housed in a grand building designed by Gustave Eiffel (of Eiffel Tower fame).

Au Bon Marché, 24, rue de Sèvres (Metro: Sèvres-Babylone), Open Mon-Sat 9:30 am-7 pm. The world's first department store is still going strong. Don't miss the gourmet delis in the Grande Epicerie and nice children's sections in the basement.

Au Printemps, 64, boulevard Haussmann, Metro: Havre-Caumartin, RER: Auber or Haussmann-Saint Lazare. Open Mon-Sat. 9:30 am-7 pm (Thurs. until 10pm). Other branches of this store exist throughout Paris, but this one is by far the best. The main cafeteria offers terrific views of the back of the Opera.

Galeries Lafayette, 40, boulevard Haussmann, Metro: Chaussée d'Antin. Open Mon-Sat. 9:30 am-6:45 pm, Thurs until 9 pm. You will find other branches of this store in town, but this one is definitely the most spectacular. Don't miss the stained glass skylight. The rooftop café is a must stop in the summer for the great view. There is a big souvenir section, excellent toy section, and free fashion shows.

La Samaritaine, 19, rue de la Monnaie, Metro: Pont Neuf. Open Mon-Sat 9:30 am-7 pm, Thurs until 10 pm. The building is a beautiful example of Art Nouveau architecture. The top floor restaurant and rooftop café offer one of the best views in town.

Aux Trois Quartiers, 17, Boulevard de la Madeleine (Metro: Madeleine), Open Mon-Sat 9:30 am-7 pm. This store houses all kinds of interesting shops and eateries in its Art Deco style building.

BHV (Bazar de l'Hôtel de Ville), 52-64, rue de Rivoli (Metro: Hôtel de Ville), Open Mon-Sat 9:30 am-7 pm (Wed until 10 pm). This store features everything for the home from furniture to thumb tacks. You'll find converters and adapters for electrical appliances in the basement.

Toy Stores

There are wonderful toy sections in all the major department stores (see above). Other good addresses include:

Le Ciel est à Tout le Monde. Branches located in the Carrousel du Louvre shopping center, 75001, Metro: Palais Royal or Louvre; at 10, Rue Gay Lussac, 75005, near the Luxembourg Gardens, Metro: Luxembourg; and at 7, Avenue Trudaine, 75009, Metro: Anvers. This store has lots of nice wooden toys, models, kites, and sailboats that you can float on the pond.

La Ronde des Jouets, 86, Rue Monge, 75005, Metro: Place Monge. Another good address for good quality wooden toys, games, dolls, and activities.

Le Train Bleu, 55, Rue Saint Placide, 75006, Metro: Saint Placide. True to its name, this shop features lots of trains, as well as electric powered cars, planes, and other toys.

Si Tu Veux, branches at 10, Rue Vavin, 75006, Metro: Vavin or Nôtre Dame des Champs, and 68, Galerie Vivienne, 75001, Metro: Bourse. These are lovely stores with plenty to stimulate your child's imagination including costume and dress-up clothes.

L'Oiseau du Paradis, 211, Boulevard Saint Germain, 75007, Metro: Rue du Bac. A classic, classy toy store with lots of animals and things to play with.

Décembre en Mars, 65, Avenue de la Bourdonnais, 75007, Metro: Ecole Militaire. Lots of games, doll houses, and reproductions of old-fashioned toys.

Territoire, 30, Rue Boissy d'Anglas, 75008, Metro: Madeleine. This is a ritzy store in a ritzy neighborhood with dollhouses and wooden toys.

Au Nain Bleu, 406-410, Rue Saint Honoré, 75008, Metro: Concorde or Madeleine. This is the biggest toy store in Paris! What more can I say?

La Boite à Joujoux, 41, Passage Jouffroy, 75009, Metro: Grands Boulevards and La Boite a Doudou, 24, Passage Jouffroy. Both of these stores feature all sorts of toys, t-shirts, and collectables related to favorite cartoon figures such as Tintin, Asterix, and Betty Boop. They are worth a visit if for no other reason than it's a chance to check out Paris' wonderful shopping galleries and passages.

Pain d'Epices, 29, Passage Jouffroy, 75009, Metro: Grands Boulevards. This delightful shop, also located in one of Paris' lovely shopping passages, is filled with miniatures, ranging from soldiers and cartoon figures to everything you could want to outfit the dream dollhouse.

Jouet International du Monde, 28, Rue des Trois Bornes, 75011, Metro: Parmentier. Lots of fun toys from all over the world.

La Grande Recré, in the Galaxie Shopping Mall, 75013, Metro: Place d'Italie. A big toy store with a wide variety, including a large section for preschoolers.

Les Cousins d'Alice, 36, Rue Daguerre, 75014, Metro: Denfert Rochereau. This little shop is full of small, inexpensive treasures as well as books, games, and other toys.

Toys R Us, in the "Les 4 Temps" Shopping Center, La Défense; RER: Grande Arche de La Défense. Just like the ones at home.

Size Chart

Women's clothing

US	4-6	6-8	8-10	10-12	12-14	14-16	16-18
UK	8	10	12	14	16	18	20
France	36	38	40	42	44	46	48

Women's shoes

US	5	5 1/2	6	6 1/2	7	7 1/2	8
	8 1/2	9	9 1/2	10			
UK	3 1/2	4	4 1/2	5	5 1/2	6	6 1/2
	7	7 1/2	8	8 1/2			
France	35	35	36	37	38	38	39
	39	40	41	42			

Men's clothing

US/UK	34	35	36	37	38	39	40
		41	42				
France	44	46	48	49	51	52	54
		55	57				

Men's shoes

US	7	8	9	10	11	12	13
UK	6	7	8	9	10	11	12
France	40	41	42	43	44	46	47

Note: Children's clothing in France is labeled by age. So 6 mois = 6 months; 8 ans = 8 years.

PLAYGROUNDS & SPORTS

Paris is dotted with fine playgrounds from the smallest tot lot to large, elaborate ones. Here are some favorites:

The Tuileries garden has a small, but pleasant playground, located towards the middle of the gardens, closer to the Rue de Rivoli side, 75001.

In July-August and December-January, you can go to the Tuileries Fair and enjoy wild carnival rides and games. Metro: Tuileries. Entrance to the park is free.

The Jardin des Enfants aux Halles is a garden/playground that is exclusively reserved for children. It features tunnels, secret dens, rope swings, and pools of plastic balls. There are also organized games, led by friendly counselors. Although games are conducted in French, the rules are pretty universal. Our boys had no trouble joining in. Located in the Les Halles Gardens, at 105, Rue Rambuteau, 75001, Metro: Les Halles. Hours vary during the week and during the year. Call for a schedule (Tel. 01 45 08 07 18) or check the sign on the gate. There is a small entrance fee for a well-supervised, one-hour session.

The Jardin des Plantes has a small playground near the labyrinth and a lovely merry-go-round that features endangered and extinct animals. It is located near the Rue Geoffroy Saint Hilaire, and Rue Cuvier sides of the garden. Metro: Jussieu or Place Monge, 75005. Entrance is free.

The Arènes de Lutèce park has a nice playground, plus room to play soccer and other ball games in the old Roman arena. Located off the Rue Monge, Rue des Arènes, and Rue de Navarre, 75005. Metro: Place Monge or Jussieu. Entrance is free.

Luxembourg Gardens: These gardens feature a magnificent playground, along with a wooden merry-go-round, puppet show, and wonderful old-fashioned double swings. They are located on the western side of the park, towards the Rue d'Assas, 75006. Metro: Nôtre Dame des Champs. There is a small fee to enter the playground.

The Parc Floral in the Bois de Vincennes features beautiful playgrounds for children of different ages. There are also fun rides and a delightful mini-golf that features the major monuments of Paris. There are concerts, plays, and a small museum. Located between Avenue des Minimes and Rue de la Pyramide in the Bois. Metro: Château de Vincennes. There is a small fee to enter the park. Rides and minigolf are extra.

The Parc André Citroen has several small playgrounds and lots of wide open spaces. In the summer, don't miss the dancing fountains. They come right out of the pavement at irregular intervals. Kids love trying to run through them in warm weather. This is also where you can ride in a (tethered) hot air balloon above the rooftops of Paris. Located between Quai Andre Citroen and Rue Balard, 75015. Metro: Lourmel. Entrance is free.

The smaller Parc Georges Brassens has several playgrounds, including one for kids with disabilities. There is a fun climbing wall, and in the summer you can rent remote-control boats on the pond. Located in the Rue des Morillons, 75014, Metro: Convention. Entrance is free.

The Jardin d'Acclimatation in the Bois de Boulogne has wonderful playgrounds divided by age group and skill level. There are also carnival rides and games. The playgrounds are located on the western side of the Jardin d'Acclimatation. Metro: Les Sablons or take the little train from the Porte Maillot metro station. There is a small fee to enter the park. Rides are extra. The **Parc de Belleville** has a big climbing castle with several reallylong slides built right into the hillside. Located on the Rue des Courrones and Rue Julien Lacroix side of the park, 75019. Metro: Couronnes. Entrance is free.

The **Parc de la Villette** has terrific playgrounds. Attractions include a giant dragon slide, numerous moon bounces for different ages, foot-powered windmills, and other fun stuff. Located near the Cité des Sciences (Science Museum), 75019, Metro: Porte de la Villette. Entrance is free.

Bicycling

This is a great way to enjoy some of Paris' major sights as a family. There are more than 150 kilometers of bicycle paths and lanes within the city. You can also bicycle in the Tuileries Gardens, by the Seine River, along the Saint Martin Canal, and under the Eiffel Tower free from motorized traffic. If you are in Paris on a Sunday, or any day between July 15 and August 15, you can ride on the expressways along the Seine, which are closed to motorized vehicles.

Here are some good addresses for bike tours and rentals. If you need a kid-sized bike or kid carrier, it's a good idea to reserve in advance:

• **Fat Tire's Bike Tours and Rentals**. Store located at 24, Rue Edgar Faure, Metro: Dupleix (3 blocks south and west of the Eiffel Tower), Tel. 01 56 58 10 54. 24, Rue Edgar Faure, Metro: Dupleix (3 blocks south and west of the Eiffel Tower), Email: info@FatTireBikeToursParis.com Website: http://www.fattirebiketoursparis.com/bikes/about-fat-tire/index.shtml

This company organizes bike tours with English-speaking guides. Kids are welcome. Tours last 3-4 hours with plenty of breaks for photos, food, and rest. The groups leave at 11am and 3:30 pm (May-Aug) and 11am (Sept) from under the Eiffle Tower on the south side (look for the company's flag). Note: they also offer Segway tours of the city. Check out details on the Website.

• **Roue Libre-Tours and Rentals**. This group, run by the public transit system, organizes free 2-hour bike tours every last Saturday of the month. Groups meet at 9 am for hot drinks and pastries at the **Maison Roue Libre**, 95, bis Rue Rambuteau in Les Halles, Metro: Les Halles. The tour leaves at 10 am. Open daily. Tel. 01 53 46 43 77. You can also rent bikes and gear for adults and kids through Roue Libre every weekend, Mar- Oct, 9am-7pm at designated metro stations, including: Porte d'Auteuil; Château de Vincennes; Place Denfert Rochereau; Jaures-Stalingrad; Nationale; and Châtelet (exit Place du Châtelet on Avenue Victoria).

If you are in Paris in late July, don't miss the last leg of the **Tour de France**. This is one of the most famous bicycle races in the world. It takes place in July, lasting 3 weeks. The final stage of the race is traditionally in Paris, with the finish line on the Champs Elysées. The exact route through the city is published in one of the local papers on the morning of the race. If you want to avoid the crowds on the Champs Elysées, you can watch the riders from any other spot along the route.

Fun Fact

You can recognize **Tour de Fance** bike teams and champions by their jerseys. The racer with the fastest overall time gets to wear a special yellow jersey. The rider with the fastest times in the mountain legs of the race gets to wear a white jersey with red polka-dots. The one with the most points overall (awarded for time, sportsmanship, leadership, and such) gets to wear a special green jersey. See if you can pick them out.

For bike trips outside the city, consider some of these ideas:

Château de Versailles. Bike rentals for kids and adults available by the Grand Canal. There are plenty of trails.

Fontainebleau. Bikes are available at the train station and tourist office. Take the bike trails through the woods or cycle over to the Château.

Vernon/Monet's house in Giverny. Rent bikes in the cafés across from the train station in Vernon. Take the Rue d'Albufera and cross the bridge over the Seine River. At the traffic circle don't follow the sign to Giverny. Take the first right and first left to the bike path. You can ride all the way to Giverny (5 kilometers of flat terrain) safe from cars.

Many train stations across France rent bicycles. Ask for the free "Guide du Train et du Vélo" in any station.

Some **suburban RER stations** have "Stations Services Vélo" (bike service stations) where you can park your bike, get it fixed, or buy bike equipment like helmets or rain gear.

Bowling

This sport is surprisingly popular. In fact, it is easier to find a bowling alley in downtown Paris than in many American cities. There are more than 25 of them in the Paris region. Here are some favorites:

Bowling Mouffetard. Located in the heart of the Latin Quarter, in a passageway off the charming old market street of the Rue Mouffetard

between 73, Rue Mouffetard and 13, Rue Gracieuse. 75005, Metro: Place
Monge. There are only 8 lanes, but there are also video games and billiards.

Bowling Montparnasse. Located by the Montparnasse Train Station
and next to the Meridien Hotel at 27, Rue du Commandant René Mouchotte,
75014. Metro: Monparnasse-Bienvenue. Open daily 10am-2am, later on
weekends. Glow-in-the-dark bowling offered on weekend nights, as well as
billiards and video games.

Bowling de Paris. Located in the Jardin d'Acclimatation of the Bois
de Boulogne along the Avenue Mahatma Gandhi. Metro: Sablons. Open
daily, 9am-3am, later on weekend nights. This center also offers pool,
billiards, and video games. Glow-in-the-dark bowling is offered on weekend
nights. Note: You will have to pay the fee to get into the Jardin d'Acclimatation.

Bowling Foch. In a chic part of town, just west of the Arc de Triomphe
and across from 8, Avenue Foch, 75008. Metro: Charles de Gaulle-Etoile.

Bowling Front de Seine. Located west of the Eiffel Tower in the
modern towers on the Seine at 11, Rue Gaston de Caillavet, off the Quai de
Grenelle, 75015. Metro: Charles Michel.

Rock-climbing
This is a very popular sport in France. You'll see mini-climbing walls
on playgrounds and in schoolyards. For climbing information and gear go
to:

Au Vieux Campeur, 48, Rue des Ecoles, 75005, Metro: Maubert
Mutualité. This is the easiest place to try a climbing wall in Paris (the private
and city-run facilities require a membership). The store will provide the
shoes and let you try the wall. They also sell excellent guidebooks about rock-
climbing near Paris and around France.

If you want to climb real rocks, you will need to go to Fountainbleau,
65 kilometers southeast of Paris. You can contact the Association des Amis
de la Forêt de Fontainebleau (Tel. 01 64 23 46 45). They can give you
information about trails, gear, and how to join a group outing. The
Fontainebleau Tourist Office, located across from the entrance to the
Château de Fontainebleau, sells books with maps of the forest and trails to
climbing rocks.

Roller blading
If you like to roller blade, you'll feel right at home in Paris where it's
hugely popular. There are plenty of car-free paths through the Luxembourg
Gardens, Metro: Nôtre Dame des Champs or Luxembourg; Parc Monceau,
Metro: Monceau; Jardin des Tuileries, Metro: Tuileries; on the Champs de
Mars, Metro: Bir Hakeim or Ecole Militaire; in the Bois de Vincennes,
Metro: Chateau de Vincennes, or Porte Doree or Bois de Boulogne, Metro:
Porte d'Auteil or Sablons; and along the Promenade Plantée, Metro:

Daumesnil, Gare de Lyon, or Bastille. On Sundays, you can also ride along the parkways next to the Seine where they are closed to motorized vehicles.

Stunt riders gather at the Trocadéro Gardens, Metro: Trocadéro; on the Champs de Mars near the Eiffel Tower, Metro: Champs de Mars; on the esplanade at La Défense, Metro: Esplanade de la Défense, and in front of Nôtre Dame Cathedral, Metro: Cité or Saint Michel.

You can join a group outing with:

Rollers et Coquillages. Groups meet every Sunday at 2:30 pm at 37, Boulevard Bourdon, 75012, Metro: Bastille. Ask about special outings for kids and families.

Roller Squad Institute organizes outings for beginners on Saturdays at 3 pm starting from Les Invalides, Metro: Invalides. For information: Tel. 01 56 61 99 61. Open Mon-Fri, 10am-1pm, 2pm-6pm.

Friday Night Fever. Every Friday night around 10 pm (weather permitting) thousands of experienced roller bladers get together at the Place d'Italie for a giant group ride. It includes police escorts, first aid workers, and emergency health crews if needed. The tour covers about 20 kilometers through the city. The line of rollers can be as long as 1-2 kilometers. If you and your teenage kids are experienced roller-bladers, this may be fun to do. Otherwise, it's better just to watch from the sidelines.

You can rent roller blades and pads from:

• Go Sport, in the Forum des Halles shopping center, 75001, Metro: Les Halles

• Bike and Roller, 6, Rue Saint Julien le Pauvre, 75005, across the Seine from Nôtre dame, Metro: Saint Michel-Nôtre Dame or Maubert Mutualité, Tel. 01 44-07-35-89. Also located at 137, Rue Saint Dominique, 75007, Metro: Pont de l'Alma, Tel. 01 44 18 30 39

• Au Vieux Campeur, 48, Rue des Ecoles, 75005, Metro: Maubert Mutualité, Saint Michel, or Cluny, Tel. 01 53 10 48 48

• Roller Pro Shop, 18, Rue des Ecoles, 75005, Metro: Cluny, Tel. 01 43 25 67 61

• Nomades, 37, Boulevard Bourdon, 75012, Metro: Bastille, Tel. 01 44 54 07 44

• Vertical Line, 60 bis, Avenue Raymond Poincaré, 75016, Metro: Trocadéro or Victor Hugo, Tel. 01 47 27 21 21

Skateboarding

Favorite spots for skateboarding include the:

• Champs de Mars, near the southeast side of the Eiffel Tower, Metro: Bir Hakeim or Champs de Mars-Tour Eiffel;

• Trocadéro Gardens, Metro: Trocadéro;

• Esplanade in front of the Montparnasse train station, Metro: Montparnasse;

• Esplanade at La Défense, Metro: Esplanade de la Défense.

There are indoor ramps at the **Centre Sportif Suzanne Lenglen**, 2, Rue Louis Armand, 75015, Metro: Balard; and at the **Centre Sportif Boutroux**, 1, Avenue Boutroux, 75013, Metro: Porte d'Ivry.

For more information, contact the **Skateboard Club de Paris**, Tel. 01 40 60 77 18.

Soccer

The Paris men's soccer team, **Paris-Saint Germain (PSG)**, plays at the Parc des Princes, located at 24, Rue du Commandant Guilbaud, 75016, Metro: Porte de St. Cloud. For information on game schedules, to buy Paris soccer souvenirs, or to obtain tickets for soccer matches go to:

• **Boutique PSG**, 27, Avenue des Champs Elysees, 75008, Metro: Franklin Roosevelt, Open Sun-Thurs, 10am-11pm, Fri-Sat, 10am-midnight. Tel. 01 56 69 22 22.

• **Boutique PSG**, 91, Rue de Rivoli, Metro: Louvre-Rivoli, Open Mon, Wed-Sat, 10am-7pm, Tel. 01 42 60 22 14.

If you would like to kick your own soccer ball around, just remember that the grass is off limits in many French parks. However, there are large grassy stretches where you can play at the Champs de Mars, Metro: Ecole Militaire; Bois de Boulogne, Metro: Porte d'Auteuil, Porte Maillot, or Sablons; or Bois de Vincennes, Metro: Porte Dorée. You can also kick around a soccer ball in the Arènes de Lutéce, Metro: Place Monge.

Swimming

Paris has plenty of public swimming pools. Hours of operation vary. Most public pools are open early in the morning and in the afternoon. They tend to be open longer on weekends and during the summer holidays. Most pools are accessible to people with disabilities. Pools generally provide a basket for your clothes that you check into a cloakroom or put in a locker.

Some indoor pools require that everyone wear a swimcap. Caps and men's/boy's suits are often available for sale at the pool's ticket office or in vending machines near the entrance.

Parent Tip: Dress codes at French pools are different than in the US. Boys and men must wear racing style suits, not boxers. Women, on the other hand, may wear 1-piece or 2-piece suits and may even go topless at outdoor pools in the summer. Increasingly indoor pools are also requiring bathing caps – weather you have hair or not. Some will let you purchase these at the entrance.

Water Parks & Indoor Pools
• **Aquaboulevard**. Kids love this waterpark.. It has both indoor and outdoor pools, water slides, fountains, wave pools, hot tubs, a beach, palm trees, and fun for every age. There are also squash courts, food courts, and other sports facilities. 4, Rue Louis Armand,75015. Metro: Balard or Porte de Versailles.

For Indoor Pools:
• **Piscine des Halles -Suzanne-Berlioux**. In Les Halles. Palm trees and cactii. Porte Sainte Eustache, 10, Place de la Rotonde, Level 3; 75001. Metro: Les Halles.
• **Piscine Saint Mérri**. Behind the Pompidou Center in the Marais. Outdoor terrace. 16, Rue Renard, 75004. Metro: Hôtel de Ville.
• **Piscine Saint-Germain**. Under the Saint Germain covered market. 12, Rue Lobineau, 75006. Metro: Mabillon or Odéon
• **Piscine Jean Taris**. Near the Rue Mouffetard and Pantheon. 16, Rue Thouin, 75005. Metro: Place Monge.
• **Piscine Pontoise**. Art-deco style architecture. Evening swimming with lights and music. Diving boards and a lap pool with a current. 19, Rue Pontoise, 75005. Metro: Maubert-Mutualité.
• **Piscine Château Landon**. The oldest in Paris. 31, Rue Château Landon, 75010. Metro: Louis Blanc-Stalingrad
• **Piscine de Reuilly**. Grassy areas for sunbathing in the summer. Just off the Promenade Plantée. 13, Rue Hénard, 75012. Metro: Montgallet
• **Piscine Armand Massard**. Under the Tour Montparnasse. 66, Boulevard du Montparnasse, 75014. Metro: Montparnasse
• **Piscine Emile-Antoine**. Windows offer a close-up view of the Eiffel Tower. 9, rue Jean-Rey, 75015. Metro: Bir Hakeim.
• **Piscine Blomet**. Art-deco style with a beautiful stairway. 17, Rue Blomet, 75015. Métro : Volontaires or Sèvres-Lecourbe.

For Outdoor Pools/Pools with Retractable Roofs:
• **Piscine de la Butte aux Cailles**. Charming, old-fashioned, art-deco style. Fed by a natural underground spring. High and low diving boards. 5, Place Paul Verlaine, 75013. Metro: Place d'Italie
• **Piscine de l'Hôtel Nikko**. A pretty hotel pool open to the public. 61, Quai de Grenelle, 75015. Métro: Javel or Bir Hakeim.
• **Piscine Keller**. Retractable roof in warm weather. 14, Rue de l'Ingénieur Robert Keller, 75015. Métro: Charles Michels.
• **Piscine d'Auteuil**. In the Bois de Boulogne, near the horse racing track of Auteuil. 1, Rue des Lacs de Passy, 75016. Metro: Ranelagh.
• **Piscine Henry de Montherland**. Large windows, outdoor terraces, and diving boards. 32, Boulevard Lannes, 75016. Metro: Rue de la Pompe

Tennis

If you want to watch the pros, try to catch the French Open Tournament. It takes place in May at the red-clay courts of the Roland-Garros stadium. The stadium is located in the Bois de Boulogne, 2, Avenue Gordon Bennett, 75016, Metro: Porte d'Auteuil. The final matches are exciting, but if you get tickets for earlier rounds you'll get to see more of the players. Tickets are available by Tel. 01 47 43 48 00 or www.frenchopen.org.

The Paris Open Tennis Championship takes place in November at the Bercy Sports Stadium, Palais Omnisport de Bercy, 75012, Metro: Bercy. It features some of the world's top men's tennis players. For schedules and ticket information you can check the website at: www.atptour.com/en.

You can play tennis at these locations, but may need to reserve in advance:

• Luxembourg Gardens, on the western side of the park. The sign up sheet is in a kiosk near the courts. Tel. 01 43 25 79 18.

• La Falguière Sports Center, in the Bois de Vincennes, on the Route de la Pyramide, Metro: Chateau de Vincennes. Tel. 01 43 74 40 93.

• Henry de Montherland Sports Center in the Bois de Boulogne, at 30-32, Boulevard Lannes, 75016. Metro: Porte Dauphine. Tel. 01 45 03 03 64.

• Fonds des Princes, 61, Avenue de la Porte d'Auteuil, 75016. Metro: Porte D'Auteuil. Tel. 01 46 51 82 80).

• Quai de Saint-Exupéry has courts that are handicap accessible. 75016. Metro: Porte de Saint Cloud. Tel. 01 45 20 62 59.

• Stade Elisabeth, 7-15, Avenue Paul Appell, 75014. Metro: Porte d'Orleans. Tel. 01 45 40 55 88.

BON APPETIT!

In France, cooking is an art, and dining is a labor of love. Enjoying good food and companionship are a national pastime – and everyone is welcome to join! Kids, and even dogs, can enjoy a meal in the fanciest of restaurants.

One of the biggest challenges you'll face is choosing among the huge variety of food styles and traditions in Paris. Even if you just stick to French food, you'll face a vast array of regional choices and influences. Remember, this is a country that has more types of cheese than there are days in a year. Broadly speaking, French cooking can be divided into the gourmet "haute cuisine" handed down from royal recipes and practiced in fine restaurants to the everyday-style home cooking that is the joy of many a neighborhood bîstrot.

There are many regional styles. For example Normandy and northern France specialize in dishes featuring creamy sauces, richer butter, apples, and cider. Brittany is famous for fresh seafood, crêpes, and buttery cookies. In

Burgundy you find hearty beef stews cooked in red wine. Around Lyon you get sausages and quenelles (a fish or chicken based dumpling). The eastern region of Alsace features sauerkraut with sausages, onion pies, and a form of white pizza with cream, bacon, and onions called a Flammenkeuche. The Dordogne region is famous for black truffles, foie gras, cassoulet (a white bean and meat casserole), and foods cooked in goose or duck fat. Foods from Provence and southwestern France tend to show a Mediterranean influence with lots of olive oil, garlic, tomatoes, sweet peppers, and herbs such as thyme, basil, and rosemary.

Parent Tip: To help keep children distracted between courses in a restaurant, make sure to bring along some entertainment. Drawing supplies work well, as do activity books, small decks of cards, miniature games, small toys, postcards, journals, and story books.

We have included a list of restaurants in this guide that combine good food with a family-friendly atmosphere. Here are some common food terms to help you navigate the menus:

Petit Déjeuner - breakfast
Café – coffee (generally served as a small espresso cup in a café or larger cup if you are ordering breakfast in a hotel); café noir – black coffee; café au lait – coffee with milk
Grand café – big cup; café double – double shot
Thé – tea
Sucre – sugar
Chocolat chaud – hot chocolate
Lait – milk
Pain – bread
Croissant – buttery, flaky, crescent-shaped roll
Confiture – jam
Beurre – butter
Miel – honey
Oeuf à la coque – soft boiled egg
Oeufs brouillées – scrambled eggs (rarely offered)
Oeuf au plat – fried egg
Oeuf dûr – hard boiled egg

Déjeuner - lunch
Croque Monsieur – toasted sandwich with melted cheese and ham
Croque Madame – toasted sandwich with melted cheese, ham, and a fried egg on top
Glaçon – ice cube
Champignon – mushroom
Cornichon – pickle

Feuilleté – puff pastry dough generally filled with meat, fish, or vegetable stuffing

Frites – French fries

Fromage – cheese

Jambon – ham

Pâtes – pasta

Potage – soup

Legumes - vegetables

Ail – garlic

Aubergine – eggplant

Carottes – carrots; carottes rappées – grated carrot salad

Celerie remoulade – grated celery root salad

Chou – cabbage

Choucroute – sauerkraut

Choufleur – cauliflower

Citrouille – pumpkin

Courgette – zucchini Courge – squash

Fenouil – fennel

Haricot vert – green bean; Haricot blanc – white bean

Mais – corn

Oignon – onion

Petit pois – peas

Poireau – leek

Poischiche – chickpea

Pomme de terre – potato

Tomate – tomato

Cacauète – peanut

Fruits - fruits

Abricot – apricot

Banane – banana

Cassis – black currant

Cerise – cherry

Citron – lemon; citron vert – lime

Fraise – strawberry; fraise des bois – wild strawberry

Framboise – raspberry

Groseille – red currant

Melon – cantaloupe

Myrtille – blueberry

Orange – orange

Pêche – peach

Poire – pear
Pomme – apple

Poissons - fish
Anguille – eel
Bar – sea bass
Bouillabaisse – fish stew
Brochet – pike
Cabillaud – cod
Coquilles Saint Jacques – scallops
Crevettes – shrimp
Homard – lobster
Huitres – oysters
Lotte – monkfish
Maquereau – mackerel
Merlan – whiting
Moules – mussels
Raie – skate or sting ray
Rouget – red mullet
Saumon – salmon
Thon – tuna
Truite – trout

Viande - meat
Agneau – lamb
Biftek haché or steak haché – hamburger (generally not served with a
bun)
Boeuf – beef
Caille – quail
Canard – duck
Cassoulet – meat and white bean casserole
Contrefilet or filet – loin steak
Côte de boeuf – T-bone steak
Côtelettes – chops
Dinde – turkey; dindonneau – young turkey
Foie – liver
Gigôt d'agneau – leg of lamb
Jambon – ham
Langue – tongue
Lapin – rabbit
Lièvre – hare
Oie – goose
Perdrix – partridge

Pintade – Guinea fowl
Porc – pork
Poulet – chicken
Saucisse – sausage; Saucisse de Toulouse – hot dog
Saucisson – salami
Steak tartare – raw ground beef, topped with raw egg
Veau – veal
Bleu – nearly raw
Saignant – very rare
À point – medium rare
Bien cuit – medium

Dessert
Crème Chantilly – whipped cream
Crème Fraiche – cream
Fromage blanc – thick creamy, yogurt-like dessert
Gâteau – cake
Glaçes – ice cream
Orange givrée or citron givrée – frozen orange or lemon filled with orange or lemon ice
Patisseries – pastries
Petit four – mini pastry
Petit gâteau – cookie
Tarte – pie; Tarte Tatin – upside-down apple pie
Vienneroiseries – breakfast pastries
Yaourt – yogurt

Parent Tip: Do you have a child who functions primarily on peanut butter? It's not as common in France as in the US, but searching for it can provide an excuse for a fun treasure hunt through Parisian grocery stores. Peanut butter can be called either *Beurre de Cacaouète* or *Pâte d'Arachide*. It may come in a jar or a can. It might be located with the jams and jellies, by the peanuts and other nuts, or in the foreign food section. Occasionally you will have more luck in a small ethnic grocery shop than at the local supermarket.

WHAT'S THE WORD?
Parlez-vous Français?
No one expects you to speak fluent French. In fact, increasingly, you'll find that Parisians want to show off their knowledge of English to you. However, you will score major points in France if you just try to learn a few key expressions:

Bonjour Madame – Hello Ma'am
Bonjour Monsieur – Hello Sir
Bonjour Mademoiselle – Hello Miss
S'il Vous Plait – Please
Merci – Thank you
Au-Revoir – Goodbye
Pardon – Excuse me

That's it. The rest is merely icing on the cake.

If you want to be adventurous, here are some more handy words and expressions:

Oui – yes
Non – no
Parlez-vous Anglais? – Do you speak English
Je ne parle pas Français – I do not speak French
Je ne comprends pas – I don't understand
Pourquoi? – Why?
Combien? – How much?
L'addition, s'il vous plait – The (restaurant) bill, please
La note, s'il vous plait – The (hotel) bill, please.
Où est? – Where is?
Où sont les toilettes? – Where are the restrooms?
Qui? – Who?
Qui est la? – Who is there?
Quand? – When?
Qu'est ce que c'est? – What is that?
Quelle heure est il? – What time is it?
Quel etage? – Which floor?
Comment? – How? or What?
Comment allez vous? – How are you?
Avez-vous? – Do you have?
Pouvez-vous? – Could you?
Lequel or Laquelle? – Which?
Donnez-moi – Give me
Je voudrai – I would like
Ca – That
Celui ci – This one
Celui là – That one

Un or *Une* – one
Deux – two
Trois – three
Quatre – four

Cinq – five
Six – six
Sept – seven
Huit – eight
Neuf – nine
Dix – ten
Onze – eleven
Douze – twelve
Treize – thirteen
Quatorze – fourteen
Quinze – fifteen
Seize – sixteen
Dix-sept – seventeen
Dix-huit – eighteen
Dix-neuf – nineteen
Vingt – twenty
Trente – thirty
Quarente – forty
Cinquante – fifty
Soixante – sixty
Soixante-dix – seventy
Quatrevingt – eighty
Quatrevingt-dix – ninety
Cent – 100
Mille – 1,000

Premier – first
Second or *Deuxième* – second
Troisième – third
Quatrième – fourth
Cinquième – fifth
Sixième – sixth
Septième – seventh
Huitième – eighth
Neuvième – ninth
Dixième – tenth

INDEX

Things Change!
Phone numbers, prices, addresses, quality of service – all change. If you come across any new information, we'd appreciate hearing from you. No item is too small! Drop us an e-mail at jopenroad@aol.com, visit us at www.openroadguides.com, or write us at:

Paris with Kids
Open Road Publishing
P.O. Box 284
Cold Spring Harbor, NY 11724

TRAVEL NOTES

About the Author

Valerie Gwinner visited Paris as a child and lived there as a young adult. However, it was only when she returned with her own children that she discovered how kid-friendly Paris could be. When she is not immersed in travel projects, Ms. Gwinner writes about public health issues. She lives in Washington DC with her husband Britt, and two sons, Jeremy and Addison.

Open Road Travel Guides

Open Road Publishing has guide books to exciting, fun destinations on four continents. As veteran travelers, our goal is to bring you the best travel guides available anywhere!

No small task, but here's what we offer:

• All Open Road travel guides are written by authors with a distinct, opinionated point of view – not some sterile committee or team of writers. Our authors are experts in the areas covered and are polished writers.

• Our guides are geared to people who want to make their own travel choices. We'll show you how to discover the real destination – not just see some place from a tour bus window.

• We're strong on the basics, but we also provide terrific choices for those looking to get off the beaten path and experience the country or city – not just see it or pass through it.

• We give you the best, but we also tell you about the worst and what to avoid. Nobody should waste their time and money on their hard-earned vacation because of bad or inadequate travel advice.

• Our guides assume nothing. We tell you everything you need to know to have the trip of a lifetime – presented in a fun, literate, no-nonsense style.

• And, above all, we welcome your input, ideas, and suggestions to help us put out the best travel guides possible.